DON'T LOOK BACK

SATCHEL PAIGE

IN THE

SHADOWS

OF BASEBALL

Mark Ribowsky

Simon & Schuster

NEW YORK   LONDON   TORONTO   SYDNEY   TOKYO   SINGAPORE

SIMON & SCHUSTER
Rockfeller Center
1230 Avenue of the Americas
New York, New York 10020

Designed by Levavi & Levavi
Manufactured in the United States of America

10 9 8 7 6 5 4 3 2 1

Library of Congress Cataloging-in-Publication Data

Ribowsky, Mark.
Don't look back : Satchel Paige in the shadows of baseball / Mark Ribowsky
p.   cm.
Includes index.

1. Paige, Leroy 1906–   . 2. Baseball players—United States—Biography.
3. Baseball—United States—History. I. Title.
GV865.P3R53   1994
796.357′092—dc20   93-38802
[B]   CIP

ISBN 0-671-77674-6

Photo Credits
Alabama State Department of Health: 1; Bettmann Archives: 25; Carnegie Library
of Pittsburgh: 16; Craig Davidson: 4; The Kansas City Star: 27; Metro Goldwyn
Mayer/United Artists: 28, 29; Museum of Modern Art/Film Still Archive: 24;
National Baseball Library and Archive, Cooperstown, N.Y.: 6, 7, 17, 18, 26, 31,
32; H. V. Pat Riley: 21; James Riley: 3, 9, 10, 15; Jackie Robinson Foundation:
19;State Historical Society of North Dakota: 5; George Strock, Life Magazine: 11,
12; University of Chicago/Joseph Regenstein Library: 2, 8, 13, 14; Wide World
Photos: 20, 30

For my wife Sondra,
who has made each day
better than the one before.

Acknowledgments

Because the story of Satchel Paige lay buried under many layers of time and neglect, I am deeply indebted to the noble cult of Negro league historians within the ranks of SABR, the Society for American Baseball Research. These prescient annalists knew well before the rest of us that the Negro leagues were quite more than a sports footnote, that these motley leagues were no less than an American Atlantis, a lost subcontinent doomed by forces they could neither control nor understand. For many thankless years, these good people of SABR have pulled, bit by bit, the remnants of this American argosy from the ocean bottom. But for them, a true factual history of Satchel Paige and the doomed glory of his times would not have been possible.

Of this blessedly obsessed legion, my special gratitude goes to Jim Riley, a human Negro league encyclopedia who graciously and liberally opened his vast archives to me and who tirelessly plowed through reams of clippings and documents to ensure that the pages of this book would be accurate; thanks to him, they are compelling as well. Jim's peerless expertise and his wise counsel provided clear paths on which to tread through miles of obscure history.

To three other foot soldiers in the ranks of the SABR-men—Dick Clark, Phil Dixon, and Larry Lester—I extend my heartiest and most heartfelt gratitude.

Perhaps the most remarkable aspect of researching this book was not merely locating two men who ran with Satchel Paige down the ungiving streets of Mobile, Alabama—but finding that they retain vivid and insightful memories of those bygone days, and who can relate them as though decades-old events happened only days ago. My deepest thanks go to Wilbur Hines and Ed Otis for peeling back the years, and in so doing making it palpable that the cru-cible of Mobile had influenced Paige's life for years to come, long after he had left the city.

The Satchel Paige story is a saga of transition, from one era to another, one geographic area to another, one culture to another. I am fortunate indeed to have been able to enlist the aid of some of the few surviving Negro league players of the Roaring Twenties to carve out Paige's nascent baseball career with the Birmingham Black Barons and the Pittsburgh Crawfords. These men are them-selves legendary in the realm of colored baseball—Jimmie Crutch-field, Ted "Double Duty" Radcliffe, and Saul Davis. Vital personal information about Paige's later years with the Kansas City Mon-archs and with the Satchel Paige All-Stars was furnished by Byron "Mex" Johnson, Connie Johnson, Hall of Famer Buck Leonard, Buck O'Neil, and Gene Benson. I am thrilled to have spent privi-leged hours in the company of these men, who by any standards are true greats of the game.

I am thankful as well to Dick Powell and James Hendrix for some invaluable detail about Satch's near-ignored but pivotal time with the Nashville Elite Giants and the Baltimore Black Sox. To Dave Kemp and Todd Strand of the North Dakota Historical Society for filling in large gaps in Paige's rolling-stone excursions through the Midwest and the Dakotas. And to Steve Gromek and Gene Bearden for their honest, hard-eyed recollections of Satch's years with the Cleveland Indians.

Additional thanks to Bill Guilfoile, Bill Dean, and Bob Browning at the Baseball Hall of Fame in Cooperstown, New York, Steven Gietschier of *The Sporting News,* Craig Davidson, Sam Lacy, Terry Geeskin, Crystal King, Rob Ruck, Lloyd Johnson, and Rodolfo Fernández.

And to Satchel Paige, whom I now feel I know the way few men ever did when he was walking the earth, thanks for being you.

Contents

Introduction

In a life that stretched to seventy-five very full years—or, as some would have it seventy-seven years, or eighty-two years, or something approaching Methuselah's 969 years—Satchel Paige saw presidents deposed, houses of Congress voted out of office, and political parties rise and fall. He also saw a little baseball. While generations of Americans looked everywhere to find an agenda for a more perfect union, Satchel Paige knew what the problem was all along.

"Bases on balls," Paige once intoned, "is the curse of the nation."

Perhaps America's greatest existentialist philosopher, Leroy "Satchel" Paige may not have always known when the game began but he always knew the score. He could see more looking down from the pitcher's mound than most of his contemporaries could see through a Galilean telescope. Having taken his instructions from many ages of man and nearly every age of baseball, he knew long before anyone else how much baseball was quilted into the fabric of America, and thus how much of life began on Opening Day—though for him there *were* no Opening Days because his season never ended. As a result, Satchel Paige was a wise man and a tranquil man. He was so wise and so tranquil that no one realized how much pain was torturing him inside.

In truth, Satchel Paige came and then left this century as a walking, throwing paean to pain, or, more accurately, to the redemptive powers of agony and burden. In fact, if Satchel Paige hadn't existed, someone in art or literature almost surely would have invented him. Such characters are always needed to guide and provoke us. And Satchel Paige did that. He even counseled us: "Don't look back, something might be gaining on you," went his most famous peroration. If he had said or done nothing else in his long lifetime, that declaration alone would put him right up there with the great Zen masters.

Philosopher, wit, fabulist, icon, moral lesson—he was all of these, and for nearly four decades an effective pitcher as well. He was a man skilled both in baseball and product management; while pitching baseballs, Satchel Paige was also pitching himself, for a good long time trumpeting himself as "The Man Guaranteed to Strike Out the First Nine Men." Sometimes he even did it; other times he would, as promised, whiff the first three men on nine pitches—and if he didn't, well, spend a few more bucks and come to the game tomorrow, 'cause he'd do it then for sure.

Back when baseball was run like a plantation, Babe Ruth owned the mansion and Satchel Paige the back forty. Stuck in the dark orchard of beggarman's baseball, atop mounds in the Negro leagues, in the Caribbean, in Mexico; barnstorming from Manitoba to Mazatlán and Alaska to Argentina—anywhere that nine men could engage nine men for profit, if not fun—Leroy Paige may well have been the greatest pitcher who ever caressed the seams of a hardball; at the least, he must have been the most perfect pitching specimen ever created, since no one else has ever found a way to throw as hard and as straight and as long as he did. In a span of time that cannot be adequately recorded, only recalled in bits, pieces, and fancies, it seems that wherever Satchel Paige went, something important happened in the evolution of baseball.

Paige reached his high-water mark—not as myth but as one hell of a pitcher—during the most unsure years for America. Pitching from 1931 to 1937 for the Pittsburgh Crawfords, Paige helped make the "Craws" the Negro National League's answer to the '27 Yankees—as well as to the Frank Nitti gang, as their owner was also the numbers king of Pittsburgh, who paid off his players with money squeezed out of indigent blacks on the Hill. Then, when Paige made his way boatward to the Caribbean, a brave new world opened with the whitecaps; because of his lead, no fewer than nine Pittsburgh Crawfords followed him to the Dominican Republic in 1937—to play for a team owned by another charmer, the brutal dictator Rafael Trujillo—and in so doing debilitated the scuzzy franchise in Pittsburgh.

Like the hero of the great white Yankees, the mighty manchild Babe Ruth, Paige was not without vices or temptations; like King Solomon, he loved many strange women, sometimes too many at once. When Satch went off to play in Puerto Rico in 1941, he came home with a woman he introduced as his wife—which overlooked the pertinent detail that he already had a wife in Pittsburgh. His subsequent divorce from the first wife became the Case of the Two Mrs. Paiges.

Paige's career, with its dual sense of loss and celebration, came to its peak in 1948. That year, at (circa) age forty-two and with felicitous irony, he became the oldest rookie in baseball history as well as a significant residual footnote to Jackie Robinson: the seventh black to make the big leagues, he was the first black pitcher in the American League. He would claim a pair of other nifty distinctions: first black to pitch in the World Series, first to pitch in an All-Star Game.

For years, Paige staked his claim by trying to quantify his legend. If Babe Ruth had his certifiable numbers, his 714 home runs and 2,211 RBIs, Satch would see to it that he had his own numbers, and *big* numbers. And so, retroactively, he filled in a catalogue that was beyond the reach of historians and most eyewitnesses to verify. With no shame, he reckoned that he pitched somewhere on the order of 2,500 games—and won around 2,000. There were some hundred no-hitters, said Satch, and if he counted up all the teams he had played for the number would hover near 250. And where even the best and most durable pitchers started in the area of fifty games a season, he had once taken the ball in hand 153 times in one season.

Still, no matter how many fact-finding expeditions are made into the archaeology of baseball, and no matter how many box scores are found to debunk some of his claims, his longevity will always overshadow the little white lies. Paige's is one sports story in which both statistics and lies are immaterial. Consider the tale that Satchel Paige once told about coming into a game in relief with men on first and third. Having sneaked a ball onto the field in his pocket, the story goes, Satch went into his windup and without breaking form threw one ball to first, the other to third—so smoothly neither umpires nor the other team even knew it. Result? Said Satch: "I picked off both runners, and my motion was so good the batter fanned. That made three outs."

Only fools would search for truth in that. In a far more public, scrutinized landscape on the light side of the moon, Babe Ruth claimed to have "called his shot." Though never verified, the story persists and hardens to this day, a tribute to the grand scale of the man. Well, Satchel Paige moved with just as grand a scale, and so we grant him his little conceits.

Besides, as with Babe Ruth, the verifiable record itself oversizes the man. And there *is* a verifiable record, contrary to the fact that Negro league record-keeping was always the object of great scorn in the white world. (In 1940, the *Saturday Evening Post* told the story that, during one colored game, a rabbit ran out on the field, stopping the game. When the rabbit disappeared, the tale went, the game resumed—"until it was discovered that nobody remembered the score!" Such absurd slurs were sadly typical.) Even in this shadow world of baseball, meticulous records and box scores were compiled in the weekly Negro newspapers out of Chicago, Pittsburgh, and Baltimore. And while the veracity of these records is surely open to question, we learn from them how surprisingly stable a good many black teams were. Despite tremendous hardships, the Negro leagues played set schedules. They kept their buses rolling through the East, the South, and the Midwest, lodged their players in hotels and rooming houses, rented stadiums, printed and sold tickets, even traveled with portable lights a decade before the first big league night game. Above all, the men of the Negro leagues played serious ball.

From these grail-like pages we also learn a few things about Satchel Paige that had not surfaced in previously published biographies: that among those many teams he played for was the fabled Chicago American Giants, in 1927; that he took his first throws for the *other* cornerstone Negro team, the Kansas City Monarchs, not in 1940 but in 1935.

The recorded details of the 1933 season alone tell of the holy terror that Satchel Paige must have been at his peak. That year, he was 31-and-4 for the Crawfords, winning twenty-one games in a row and hurling sixty-two straight shutout innings. The next season, on July 4, 1934, he pitched a no-hitter against the Homestead Grays, one of three recorded no-hit games in his career (for the *non-*recorded ones, pick a number, any number; you may just be right).

The great moments of truth for Satchel Paige and those black-balled to a life in "blackball" were not, however, the feral competitions of the Negro leagues. Rather, they were posted during the postseason "all-star" tilts between black and white teams. In these generally overlooked games, some of the most vital baseball history was made—as well as some of the best money available for playing the sport back then. It was in these contests as well that Satchel Paige—whose éclat can be measured by his ability to assemble his own all-star teams for these engagements—pitched some of his greatest games. In 1934, he beat Dizzy Dean 1–0 in thirteen heavenly innings; in 1946, he beat Bob Feller while striking out sixteen. Such moments no doubt helped draw baseball's two worlds closer to the same orbit—and Satchel Paige closer to the big leagues, no matter his age.

Satch would pitch ably, even brilliantly for the Cleveland Indians, in later work for the St. Louis Browns, and then for the Miami Marlins of the International League—and that he could still get out big league hitters one year before his sixtieth birthday, in a three-inning stint with the Kansas City Athletics of Charles O. Finley in 1965, is the kind of Paigeism that makes fable no more astounding than plain fact.

Quite apart from those who insist that Satchel Paige could throw a fastball that would somehow vanish in midflight, hard-eyed major leaguers also happened to witness Paige in his heyday. Paige, said Bob Feller, "was the best pitcher I ever saw." Dizzy Dean agreed to the point, and their plaudits were significant since neither man was the most liberal thinker on the planet. For Diz, it was an especially large breach of etiquette for a man born in 1902 in Lucas, Arkansas, to say of a black man from Mobile, Alabama: "I know who's the best pitcher I ever see and it's old Satchel Paige. . . . My fast ball looks like a change of pace alongside that little bullet old Satchel shoots up to the plate"—although in Dean's case, this praise may have been delivered with a certain sense of safe condescension, one that was common in an era when white men with major league jobs knew they faced no true threat from even the most gifted of black men.

• • •

Satchel Paige, a contemporary of Duke Ellington, Paul Robeson, Marian Anderson, Josephine Baker, John Coltrane, Gordon Parks, and the "other" Satch—Louis Armstrong—was part of a black generation (several generations, actually) that refused to be defeated by racism and engendered their own idioms in spite of it. Along with him, other men nurtured in deprivation assumed identitie like Cool Papa, Boojum, Black Bottom, Ashes, and Skindown, an followed the great Negro urban migration of the 1930s and 194 coming to the big city cheek by jowl with rural, Deep South bl men named Muddy Waters, Howlin' Wolf, and Lightnin' Hop Negro leaguers, ignored by whites but cherished by blacks, the cream of an isolated "high tone" society, interspersed movie stars, musicians, ward heelers, speakeasy owners, and bers runners. The presence of a Satchel Paige in a bar could keep the joint lit up all night.

In a strong sense, there were two major conflicting ids within the Negro leagues, those personified by Satchel Paige and Josh Gibson—perhaps the most perfect *hitter* in creation. Though for several years they formed the battery of the Pittsburgh Crawfords, the two of them were miles apart in composition. Gibson, a baby-faced brute of a man, had none of Satch's bemused detachment about the hard world around him, and his insecurities tortured him literally to death in 1947 at age thirty-five, his end certainly hastened by years of alcohol and drug abuse. His death was a poignant if barely noticed reminder of the lost souls left behind in the year of Jackie Robinson's great leap forward; Josh Gibson, in his imploded agony, is baseball's Charlie Parker.

Satchel Paige, on the other hand, endured as baseball's Miles Davis, whose demons only made his trumpet—and his attitude— all the stronger over the course of a full life. In traversing an era of history that sought to systematically reduce him, Paige went where he went with only two companions: his valet and his attitude. He simply would not be reduced. He would not lord it over any other black man, no fussin' or whinin', but there'd be no bus rides for Satch; he'd ride on his own wheels, thank you very much, and he'd stay in the hotels of *his* choice, not the choice of Jim Crow. Better, then, that Satch wouldn't be getting close to anyone in his travels; 'f you aren't going to hang around for long, don't make any bud- es you'll be missing.

` Satchel Paige's world, too, nothing could disturb his rever-
 'or living without strain. Shuddering at the notion of physical
     he once said that all he had to do to get his arm in shape
        ake hands with the catcher. Even his most famous pitch
           nsouciance—the "Hesitation Pitch," which with its mad-
             'tancy to leave his hand made the eventual fastball all
               ing.

                ithout creating anything close to personal warmth,
                  'stry made more money and more leverage for
                    'n. Even those Negro leaguers envious of him, or
                      did not diss him. In Satchel Paige there is an
                        ' common men. When, in 1965, an elderly
                          nley's Athletics only to sit in the bullpen in
                            'ic consumption, many in a more racially
                              the Stepin Fetchit image that Paige him-

self had cultivated for decades and had not thought to alter even
in the same year that the Civil Rights Act was passed; to Satch, it
ʀas just another gig, another riff, another paycheck, another ego
ᵇ. And when he came out to pitch in his only game, he hurled
ᵉ shutout innings—but that, too, was by habit.

ᵑ so, history has a hard, often cruel glare, and great men are
 great as they seem to be. Paige surely knew this when he
ᵇligatory autobiography in 1962. This work was precious
ᵑg, as easy to digest as farina, more monkeyshine than
ᵈ yet with an odd, dissonant anger about being
 was the essential Satchel Paige—making history
ᵒwn terms, being funny by rote, yet producing the
ᵃt Satch himself wasn't really laughing. The les-
ᵉver learned was that honesty could have been
ᵉast better for it than bitterness.

ᶦth Paige is that many of those who played
ʷorn to romanticize him in the name of
ᵉntly, other published histories of Paige
ᵑot only of hard detail, subtle nuance,
ᶠ a long view of where he fits into the
ᶦed him along in its windsails.

ᵉ for the common man, but as a
ᵈ his frailties. If he was loath to
ᵈ be under the same obliga-
ᵗtand the compulsions that
 pitching mounds. To take
 bigamy suggests nothing
 of women, and games
ᶜh he was an expert—
ᵉs in his soul, there
 ffering something
ᶦity would proba-
ᵉ of adultery.

 book can be
Davis. Jazz
ᵉ "tracing

ᵉn so-
ᵖoint
ᵉ trac-
ᵑing

from something. The latter something, while it ate at him, never
did gain on him when he was alive. Now, we can look back for him
and see what it was at last. In doing so, we can see that for a hundred different reasons, the story line begins in Mobile.

1

Mannish Boy in Mobile

[H]e was in the chair again in front of the now bright and swirling fire, enveloped in the quilt like a cocoon, completely now in that unmistakable odor of Negroes . . . not the odor of a race nor even of poverty but perhaps of a condition: an acceptance, a passive acceptance by them themselves of an idea that being Negroes they were not supposed to have facilities to wash properly or even to wash bathe often even without the facilities to do it with; that in fact it was little to be preferred that they did not.

—William Faulkner,
Intruder in the Dust

Ain't no man can avoid being born average, but there ain't no man got to be common.

—Satchel Paige

On a bright, sunny summer day in 1913, President Woodrow Wilson came to Mobile, Alabama, to deliver an important address. The bold new president and his men had chosen Mobile for this speech for manifold reasons; a vital American Gulfport city burgeoning by the day, Mobile not only was a marker of twentieth-century Southern modernism but a gateway to the southern half of the hemisphere.

After his arrival, Wilson's Model-T motorcade wound from the

Louisville and Nashville Railroad depot, past the mannered lawns and alabaster houses of Spring Hill Avenue and Dauphin Street to the northeast, and into the center of town. Then, mounting the steps of the stately old Lyric Theatre, Wilson spoke to the ideal of a peaceful hemisphere by invoking American pluralism.

"The United States will never again seek one additional foot of territory by conquest," said the president. "[We] must regard it as one of the duties of friendship to see that from no quarter are material interests made superior to human liberty and national opportunity.

"This is not America because it is rich. This is America because it has set up for a great population opportunities of material gain for all."

On that summer day in Mobile, a young Leroy Paige was also thinking in terms of material interests, but he probably took no cues from Woodrow Wilson, even if he knew who Woodrow Wilson was. In the territory of Mobile that the president had *not* seen on the way in from the L&N station, in the suffocating slums of the South Bay, opportunity wasn't the stuff of polemics but rather the nature of the beast.

Of this Mobile, Satchel Paige once said, "I was no different than any other kid, only in Mobile I was a nigger kid. I went around with the back of my shirt torn, a pair of dirty diapers or raggedy pieces of trousers covering me. Shoes? They was somewhere else."

As a "nigger kid," Leroy Paige couldn't share in anyone's avowal of the American Dream: not in 1913, and certainly not in Mobile. In the Mobile that nobody important noticed or seemed to care about, human liberty was an abstraction without concept or meaning. Then, and for decades hence, the Negro race—"nigger" would be the operative nomenclature long into the future—existed not as a second class, but as no class at all. This was a form of racism most simple and most ordinary and therefore most terrible.

Up until 1902, with nothing seemingly amiss, dogs and farm animals received a better accounting than did humans of color, who were neither part of the city's census nor registered in the city directory. Then, when such notice was finally made, Negroes were branded in the directories with asterisks, or with a "c," for colored. Since almost no blacks in Mobile were born in hospitals, public health records could not corroborate details. What passed for an official record was not unlike the recorded caprices of Ellis Island immigration officers who would summarily tell arriving Europeans what their names were and how old they were, based on guesswork. If the Mobile chronicler wasn't a public health officer, it was likely to be the matriarch of the black household—who herself could only rely on memory for pertinent dates; often, they didn't really know when their children had been born, nor for that matter when *they* had been.

One of the thousands of such matriarchs was an inscrutable woman named Lula Coleman Paige. Married to a sometimes gardener who impregnated her frequently and then generously allowed her to feed and clothe their many children almost all on her own, Lula got through her hard life by erecting her own realities; her wit fast and rapier-like, her sense of irony overripe, she once claimed that she was the daughter of slaves and born in 1861. By elementary math, which may have been beyond her, this would have meant that Lula Paige—who birthed twelve children, the last one in 1920—was approximately *sixty* years old the last time she carried to term.

What is known about her seventh child and third son, Leroy Robert, is where he was born. The site of his birth can today be traced to what is now a narrow, weed-strewn alleyway between two genteel wood A-frame houses near the corner of a winding, birch-shaded lane called Alba Street. Once, before late-arriving civilization transformed it into a habitable area, this street lay hard within the dank and rotting slums of Mobile's South Bay. Though Satchel Paige always recalled his first address as 3 Franklin Street, it was called Bascombe Street at the time, and it was at 3 Bascombe where Leroy Robert Paige was born, brought into the world by a midwife in the back room of a tumbledown, four-room shanty he easily described as a "shotgun shack."

But *when* did this event occur? The myriad answers to that question, of course, would become one of the greatest sports enigmas of all time and play a huge part in bringing a sense of myth and mystery to Paige's life. The problem of verification was not alone of Satch's making; the far more tragic obstacle lay in Mobile's nonchalant institutional racism.

When Bill Veeck signed Paige to the Cleveland Indians in 1948, Veeck did as much to obfuscate the age issue—an issue he stoked constantly as a public relations gimmick—as Satch ever did himself. For aid and comfort in this, he could count on the succor, witting or unwitting or perhaps both, of Lula Coleman Paige.

"After a great deal of difficulty," Veeck wrote in his autobiography, "I was able to reach Mrs. Paige at her local general store in Mobile, which had the only phone in the neighborhood. I found out quickly enough the source of Satch's humor.

" 'I can't rightly recall whether Leroy was firstborn,' she said, 'or my fifteenth.' Having had her joke, she told me she really couldn't remember what year he had been born, but that she could guarantee he wasn't her oldest."

Another time, Lula confided to a sportswriter that her son was in fact three years older than he was thought to be; a few years later, she had another epiphany—he was, she said, *two* years older. This she knew because she had written down the year of his birth in her Bible, and it said, right there, plain as day, 1904.

When Paige committed his memoirs to print in 1962, though, he wasn't ready to go with that version. "Seems like Mom's Bible would know," he wrote, "but she ain't never shown me the Bible. Anyway, she was in her nineties when she told the reporter that and sometimes she tended to forget things."

But never let it be said that Satchel Paige didn't learn from his mama. "Mother always told me," he once related, "if you tell a lie, always rehearse it. If it don't sound good to you, it won't sound good to nobody else." And a decade and a half later, when Lula was gone, he was ready and well rehearsed in the fable told by Lula— only he expanded Lula's homily to include thirteen Bibles . . . and thirteen *goats*. He had, he admitted, never actually *seen* the apocryphal Bible—but that was the fault of one of those goats, which he insisted had mistaken the book for cabbage leaves and eaten it. He did know one thing, though: "That goat," he said with piquant irony, "lived to be twenty-seven."

Satchel, his droopy, basset hound eyelids and diffident gaze aiding in the delivery of one-liners, surely was wise enough to parlay the age thing into profitable marketing by the time he got to the big leagues. Indeed, almost everyone he knew was made into a bit player in the act. Wilbur Hines, who grew up with Paige and provided him with the Satchel sobriquet, has always thought he stood closest to the truth. "He was born in September," said Hines emphatically, "like around the twelfth. Satch was two years older than me and I was born in 1907. So I'd make it September 12, 1905.

"When he got famous and they was tryin' to find out his age, he told me, he came back to Mobile and he told me, 'Don't tell nobody my real age.' That kept him more famous and he wanted to keep that mystery goin'."

Then there was Bill Veeck. "Satch," Veeck insisted, "always [told me] his birthday [was] September 18."

Actually, what Satch himself always did was to keep everyone in the dark and the farce going strong—no doubt getting off on how many legs he could pull. Accordingly, some people walked the earth firmly believing that they were protecting the biggest secret since Charles Foster Kane and Rosebud. In reality, these were the people to whom Paige might dispense the biggest whoppers. Mobile native Ted "Double Duty" Radcliffe, who played in the Negro leagues for thirty-six years, takes great umbrage at anyone doubting *his* Satchel Paige revelation. With a harsh finality to his voice, Radcliffe swore that "Satchel and I were born on the same day—July 7—but he was born in 1900, I was born in 1902. He said otherwise, but he was a damn liar!

"Listen, I go way back with him, I knew him when I was twelve years old, that's when I met him, around 1912, 1913. The black teams from Birmingham and Pensacola would come through Mobile and we'd get together the best players to play 'em. We went up to Selma, to Montgomery, for those games. And we also played on the Mobile Dodgers. We played on them with Billy Williams's father, Hank Aaron's father, we played with everybody."

Actually, this is nowhere near the case. Paige did indeed play with Radcliffe on a host of black sandlot teams around Mobile—but it was much later than Radcliffe makes it, not in the mid-1910s but in the mid-1920s. The teenaged Satch had still not undergone the biggest conversion of his life, which occurred after he was sent to reform school in 1918. If Paige had been eighteen years old in 1918, he wouldn't have gone to reform school. He would have gone to jail.

●　●　●

One of the supplemental problems in discerning Satchel Paige's age was that his anatomy never provided any clues. Even in pubescence he defied natural growth. With his massive, pinewood hands, his hatrack of a body with its absurdly gangly arms and legs seemingly working at odds with each other, only his wide, bulbous nose kept pace with his vertical expansion; and with his boniness stretching his flesh snakeskin-tight, not an ounce of baby fat would survive past infanthood. His face was shaped like a grain of brown rice but with skin as pristine and smooth as obsidian; he was forever caught between ages—a mannish boy, in the Muddy Waters phrase. Always, there would be those who believed him to be either much older or much younger than he was.

Another complicating factor was his surname. In February of 1954, Ralph Chandler, the publisher of the *Mobile Press-Register*, obtained from the Mobile County Health Department a copy of a birth certificate in the name of one Leroy *Page*. It was dated July 7, 1906. For eight years, Satchel Paige would not countenance this document, and barely allude to it. And Bill Veeck, who had emerged as Satch's "godfather" with the Indians, and given him renewed big league life with the St. Louis Browns in the early 1950s—and would again with the minor league Miami Marlins in the mid-1950s—tried to besmirch it, in order to push his own PR designs for Paige as a literally ageless legend in knickers.

The fact was, Veeck had come by this same discrepancy in Paige's family tree years before. Veeck's showy "investigation" into Satch's age had included hiring a private detective to comb through Mobile's crude directories. That there had never been an entry for a Leroy *Paige* led Veeck to a very different, very circuitous conclusion, one better suited to his purposes.

"The Mobile records did not go back any farther than mid-1900," Veeck said in his autobiography, "and while there was no record of Satch himself, one of his younger brothers was in the 1901 list. . . . Since the names of all of Satch's brothers and sisters had been spelled correctly . . . [the detective] felt confident that we could scratch that [1906] date. This could only mean, then, that Satch could not possibly have been born later than the early part of 1900. . . . Assuming that a man has a sentimental attachment to his actual birthday, Satch could not have been born any later than September 18, 1899."

Nobody knew how disingenuous Bill Veeck was except those who double-checked his research. For all of his plaints about seeking the truth, Veeck took a secret to his grave in 1985: in truth, nowhere in those pernicious city directories can *any* member of that humongous family be found under the name *Paige*—not until 1926, when two of Satch's brothers, John Jr. and Clarence, adopted the new surname. At the same time, his father, John Sr., is to be found in the listings almost *every* year from 1902 until the year he died, 1926—as John *Page*. Rather than "all of Satch's brothers and sisters" being noted, in reality none of them made it into any directory until that inclusion of John Jr. and Clarence. Moreover, their mother, Lula herself, was listed as Lula *Page* all the way up until 1932. And Satch's older brother Wilson did not come around to the new spelling until *1942.*

The riddle persisted until 1962, when Satch himself finally cleared up a few things. Adopting the 1906 birth certificate for the record—though he maintained that he wouldn't bet his cars and wristwatch on it—he said, "Now I know it's made out to a Leroy Page, but my folks started out spelling their name 'Page' and later stuck in the 'i' to make themselves sound more high-tone."

Unfortunately, that explanation was still less than the whole truth. As will be seen, *Page* versus *Paige* may have been a reflection of the bad blood between John Page and his sons—his entire family, in fact. Clearly, Paige wanted no part in explaining such a thing; indeed, if he got his jollies implying that he had known all along what his date of birth was, and was simply running a game on American sports, his motivation may not have been mirth but pain. It could not have been much fun at all to embrace a birthdate dug up for him, not when it only called back to mind family divisions and the neglect of an entire city.

•   •   •

To experience what life in Mobile must have been like for Satchel Paige, one need only find an old woman named Palestine. Not far from where she grew up, Palestine Paige Caldwell lives in a home where the world has forgotten to turn. Her surroundings, a ramshackle four-room wood bungalow on Selma Street, has peeling walls, mildewed ceilings, and a strong scent of the old house on Franklin where the Page children came of age. Now, save for her seriously ill sister Inez, Palestine is the last surviving member of that brood of five sons and seven daughters.

Stooped now, weary but with puckish eyes, Palestine Paige is in her seventies. On a recent afternoon, a rusted gold Volvo was parked in the dirt driveway outside her home, a broken window on the driver's side covered over by a wrinkled piece of oilcloth. Inside the house, two automobile tires were propped against a table beside which Palestine—a widow who still works as a domestic—sat in a print housecoat folding laundry. This drudgery eases for her only when she speaks of the brother she called Leroy. Her large eyes aglint, she offers a visitor the tantalizing nugget that Satch "was younger than what he told people he was," and that she possesses a copy of Leroy's *real* birth certificate somewhere around the house—a claim she repeats often on this day, but without ever finding the certificate.

This, like most else about him, is lost now, scattered to the winds that carried Satchel Paige out of Mobile for good.

For his part, Satch managed to remember most of his siblings in his later years. In his autobiography he got eleven of them right—in descending order, John Jr., Wilson, Julia, Ellen, Ruth, Emma Lee, Clarence, Inez, Palestine, Lula Jr.—but failed to note Eugene, Palestine's twin who died as an infant. While Paige spoke copiously throughout his life of his mother, his father was practically expunged. In his book, for example, it was what he *didn't* say about John Page that bled from old wounds:

"My Dad, John, was a gardener, but he liked to be called a landscaper. My Mom, Lula, was a washerwoman. She was the real boss of our house, not Dad. . . . My Dad died in that house of ours, when I was about eighteen, I guess, although I don't remember for sure.

"I only remember pieces and snatches about him. He wasn't hardly a part of my life. We didn't talk too much, but after I started playing baseball as a kid he used to ask me ever so often, 'You want to be a baseball player 'stead of a landscaper?' 'Yes,' I'd answer and he'd just nod his head like he was satisfied."

And that was it. John Page—whose periodic desertions from the family made him a vanishing act anyway—never made it past page fifteen. Paige made admirable efforts to understand the roots of Lula's servitude, because in her family she found and protected her one source of autonomous pride. That protection, he pointed out, could be harsh:

"I used to think she hit me because she didn't know how I felt, [that] she didn't know how it was when they told me I couldn't swim where the white folks did.

"Then I realized maybe she did. She must have been chased away from the white man's swimming places. She must have gotten run off from the white man's stores and stands for just looking hungry at a fish. She must have heard those men yelling, 'Get out of here, you no-good nigger.' She must have heard it. I guess she learned to live with it."

For John Page, he cut no slack. And, in the long tunnel of time, the lack of love or even sympathy for anything in John Page's world casts the enigma of *Page* versus *Paige* in an acrid light. If *Page* was John's only real property, his family's forsaking it may well have been more than an act of high-toning; it may have been an act of separation, especially given the timing of the change and that the idea came not from John himself or even Lula—nor from Leroy. It began with John Jr., the eldest and most direct descendant, who added the "i" in 1924. When John Sr. died two years later, John Jr. *returned* to his original name, as if in belated tribute, or maybe retroactive guilt. In 1930, however, he made the change for good.

Leroy Page, meanwhile, didn't fully commit to the new name until the early 1930s; in the interim he bounced fitfully from one spelling to the other, or else used *no* last name. The black weekly newspapers that would cover his early pitching exploits identified him, with Leroy's consent, by a number of one-word eponyms—"Satch" or "Satchel" or "Satchell," even a misprinted "Sackell." It was as if he too was struggling with the guilt of a clean break from the legacy of John Page. But once he cast his vote, the rest of the family united behind him. It was then that John Page ceased to exist for all eternity as the chief male figure of the family. By proxy, that role fell to the boy who had made it out of Mobile. Leroy "Satchel" Paige.

• • •

And yet, it was never certain that baseball would loom as his pathway out. Only the high ironies of fate would bring about that, not anything in Mobile, which offered young blacks not open fields but withering asphyxiation.

If the children of the slums could breathe at all, it happened at the beach, which ran along the southeast corner of Mobile. Here, out past the railroad yards on Tennessee Street and the U.S. government shipbuilding plant, Leroy Page could dangle his bare feet in the cool waters of Choctaw Pass, drop a fishing line in Mobile Bay, and escape the slow death of Mobile.

Lula Paige could appreciate this preoccupation. Though she had enrolled her boy in the W. H. Council School when he was six, he rarely came near it. The school's principal, W. H. Brazier, would constantly report Leroy's truancy to Lula, who would only sigh but not press Leroy on it too hard. At the start of his class-cutting, he once related, "Mom came looking for me," but in time "she got kind of used to it.

"Fact was, she didn't put real big store by book learning. It ended up so she didn't get nearly as mad when I missed school as she got when I didn't come home with any money for food from selling empty bottles I'd found in the alleys and trash bins."

Any such decrees were of course made by Lula, commensurate with the authority she had by bringing in most of the household money while her husband either slept or dropped from sight making the rounds at local bars. Working on her knees in white folks' homes had made Lula one tough nut, and the great sport of Leroy's life was seeing how far he could make her bend to his conceits.

Wilbur Hines, who lived next door to the Pages when they moved to the nearby junction of Maryland and Dearbourne streets, began to run the same gravel roads with Leroy. Hines, wiry now as then, with only bad feet and thick glasses as a toll for his eighty years, can still feel the growl of that old hunger. "Tell you why he didn't go to no school," Hines barked. "It's 'cause we had nothin' to go to school *with!* We had nothin' in our pockets. No bus carried us, we had to walk, and when we got there we had nothin' to eat. So, instead of goin' there, we'd go down to the beach and catch catfish. Heck, fillin' my stomach was more important than readin' a book."

The dual demands of hunger and family pushed Leroy Page and Wilbur Hines to options beyond the returning of pop bottles. Their detours around the Council School frequently took them down the wide footpath of Government Street, which divided north and south Mobile, and to the waterside Louisville and Nashville Railroad station. This busy depot offered consolation to Leroy in a number of ways. In a broad sense, these tracks were like the Mississippi River of Mark Twain. To look at well-to-do folks with their duotone leather shoes and bulging valises was like standing at the mouth of a new world; and the money in their pockets was available to the quick and the strong. Leroy never left the old station without a profit. Floating about the platform, he would outhustle kids just like him who had the same idea, and plead with the business guys to let him carry their luggage to the nearby hotels along Commerce Street. For a nice long haul, he could make a dime, which was not bad coin.

Leroy was impatient for bigger kill, though, his sights set on those big bulging satchels. Willie Hines could see the temptation, and was there when Leroy could no longer contain himself. "One day he decided to run off with one of those bags," Hines said. "The man gave him the bag and he broke and ran with it. The fella caught him and slapped him, hard in the face, and took it back."

Hines rumbled with laughter. "That's when I named him Satchel, right on that day. All those years he said he got the name 'cause he carried satchels. Hell no—it's 'cause he *stole* 'em!

"And, fact is, he didn't *like* the name. I would say, 'Hey, Mr.

Satchel,' and he'd get mad, because he'd gotten caught stealin'
and he was embarrassed. Then he'd sneak up on me and hit me in
the head with a brick."

In light of its genesis, the nickname was an appropriate one.
Clearly, by age ten, Leroy Page was a polished thief. "He'd steal bicycles in a minute," confirmed Hines. "He'd ride 'em about. He'd
take a bike, ride where he wanted to go, and leave it for the kid to
find it when he got through with it."

Another of Leroy's running buddies was Ed Otis, whose son
Amos was one of many later-generation Mobilians to play in the big
leagues. Otis recalled walking down the street one day when Leroy
Paige streaked by him. "He had done something and the law was
after him. I think he stole a bicycle, and I come up Broad Street
and he was runnin'. He yelled to me, 'They after me,' and he just
ran outta sight."

Though moving too fast then to slow up for baseball games,
Leroy nonetheless did spend some time at some of Mobile's ball
fields—but only long enough to make spending money by mowing
grass or sweeping up the grandstand. By game time, his presence
was not welcome. One such ball yard was Eureka Gardens, a fair-
grounds near the Council School in which the Southern Association's Mobile Bears played. Willie Hines recalled it for its "big old
dancin' pavilion" and the fact that "Eureka was for whites."

The closest thing to a horsehide ball held in Leroy Page's long
fingers would be similarly shaped rocks. In his huge hands, he
could find useful applications for those rocks—even make a statement with them.

"His hands were so big," said Hines, "even then he could hold
two bricks in one hand. We'd go out in the woods and shoot at
birds and while I had a BB gun, he only had them rocks. But he'd
hit a bird flyin' in the air—bang, right in the head, and it'd fall out
the sky. He threw real straight, on a line. Nobody could throw like
that. And because he could, he'd go down to the gravel pit and
pick out rocks that fit his hand. He'd put 'em across his shoulder,
in a bag, and he'd be like Robin Hood. He'd pick out the right
rocks to fight with or hunt with."

As Paige once recalled, even though he was yet to discover the
fine art of pitching, "That's when I found out I had control. It was a
natural gift, one that let me put a baseball just about where I
wanted it about anytime I wanted to. I could hit about anything
with one of those rocks . . . chickens, flying birds. Most people

need shotguns to do what I did with those rocks."

Ed Otis assented, "People think he was lyin', but I witnessed this myself. Satchel killed butterflies with clamshells. He could throw, always he could throw."

That could be beneficial on the street. On this tough turf, there were frequent gang fights to be won. Long before Satchel Paige ever played against Double Duty Radcliffe, in fact, he had to fight him. "See, Double Duty—he wasn't no Double Duty then, just Ted Radcliffe—came from the northside, up around Brooklyn Park," Otis explained. "He was runnin' with the northside boys, and when we'd go over there, followin' the band in a parade or somethin' like that, we'd run into them northside boys and go on fightin' till someone stepped in and broke it up. It was like gangs today, it was vicious, but we didn't have no guns, only rocks."

In these encounters, Satch, the scourge of chickens and butter-flies, was a prized asset of the southside boys. "We could win them kind of battles," chuckled Wilbur Hines. "We had Satchel with us and they'd have to get out of the way 'cause he'd hit the side of your head every time. He knowed he could throw straight, and he'd get 'em."

A fortunate thing, too, since by nature Satch was far better suited to long-range running. Hines remembered that "if some-body'd jump him, he'd buck and run. He had those long legs and he'd run. But if you didn't watch yourself, he'd sneak up behind you and hit you in the head with a brick. Then he'd run again."

Still, Satch could pose as the guy to avoid, and this gave him alti-tude. Years and years later, he reflected in *Maybe I'll Pitch Forever* with profound eloquence on the core of his antisocial streak, one that never completely subsided.

"Maybe I got into all those fights," he surmised, "because I found out what it was like to be a Negro in Mobile. Even if you're only seven, eight, or nine, it eats at you when you know you got nothing and can't get a dollar. The blood gets angry. You want to go some-where, but you're just walking. You don't want to, but you got to walk.

"Those fights helped me forget what I didn't have. They made me a big man in the neighborhood instead of just some more trash."

They also further tested the tolerance of Lula Page, who tried mightily, albeit vainly, to keep her recalcitrant boy in line. It grieved her that while her other children had regular jobs, Leroy could not be tied down by any superior. That was fine up to a point; but if he got into trouble, Lula would take her exaction.

"She was strict on him, on me, on anybody," recalled Hines. "She'd whup us both if we was caught doin' anything."

If that was a deterrent to Satch, though, it was only temporary. He put a lot of faith in those elongated limbs. Using them to snatch and run, his petty larceny went unabated—but only until, at age twelve, he outwitted himself. He and Willie Hines were casing a jewelry store near the L&N depot when Satch grabbed some rings from atop a counter and made for the door. Willie saw only a blur, yet even Satch couldn't elude the store's guard, who chased him down Commerce Street and caught up to him.

"Satch had threw the stuff in his mouth," Hines can remember, "and the fella saw it and when he caught him, he hit Satch in the mouth and the rings flew out."

Taken to the police station to see her son, Lula could no longer raise her hand to him. All she could do was cry. Now, instead of standing against outside authority in cutting Leroy his freedom, she gave in. The police recommended that a kid with Leroy's reputation be sent to reform school. Lula Page shrugged and told them to take him away.

Now it was Leroy's turn to cry.

2

Ridin' on
the L&N

You can't say I really missed home. There wasn't a whole lot to
miss. And I must have been born to travel.

—Satchel Paige

On July 24, 1918, twelve-year-old Leroy Page was committed to
the Industrial School for Negro Children in Mt. Meigs, Alabama,
twelve miles outside of the state capital of Montgomery. (Those
looking for confirmation of Satch's age through Mt. Meigs records
will be frustrated; all such records were routinely destroyed eight
years after the release of each child.) The bus ride that took him
there from Mobile gave Leroy his first breath of air outside the
acrid South Bay, and the clear roads and open sky en route to Mt.
Meigs were, as Satch recalled it many moons hence, "like a dream."
Had he been left to the condemnation of Mobile, he knew, "I'd of
ended up as a big bum, a crook. That's what happened to a lot of
those other kids."

But that reality would not become clear until after Leory Page
was broken and then regimented into a functional being. That
transition would take five and a half years, though the only calen-
dar Leroy knew was the color of the sky, one day at a time. Wilbur
Hines, who managed to evade the law only a short while longer
than Leroy did, was busted for taking money from a cash register
and sent to Mt. Meigs the following year. He recalled the im-
mutable daily routine with a dead intonation:

"Five A.M., line up, eat breakfast, go to class, then go out there in dem fields. They had squads you went out in. You'd cut the timber, pick potatoes, pick cotton. This was sunrise to sundown. That was the only time you knew. Then at night they'd lock you in."

Willie soon thought that if he didn't get away, he'd die in the place. And yet for Leroy, Mt. Meigs was an object lesson and Mobile a metaphorical one. Back home, a fire in 1921 would raze forty blocks in the South Bay, destroying other natives' dreams by the dozen. Meanwhile, up in Meigs, Satchel Page was building muscle and character. Out in the fields, a full stomach could be bought with a hard day's labor, which wasn't a bad deal. His hosanna, many years later, went like this: "When you grow up as poor as me, a place like Mount Meigs can be mighty warm and good." And if there was discomfort, there was also an assuring familiarity. "There were double beds in the dorm and two kids slept in a bed," he mused, "just like we did at home."

And there was, for the first time in earnest, the potentials of baseball.

As Satch told it, he needed to make no great stride to the ball field at Mt. Meigs. Though he had played the game very sparingly—as sparing as his presence at the Council School, which was the only place he could play—in his autobiography he bragged on himself as "just about the best school pitcher they ever saw around there. There weren't too many up in the high schools who could throw as hard and sure as I did. And when those kids my age came up to the plate and I threw my trouble ball, they just wet their pants and cried."

To evaluate that, it is necessary to know that on the same page he called Willie Hines "the coach of the Council School team."

Hines cackled at the reference. "I never played or coached baseball, not one day in my whole life! And Satch, he wasn't around there long enough to be playin'. He was too busy shopliftin'."

The Mount practically forced Satch onto the field—though not yet to the mound. Sunday was rest day, but with his overheated pituitary gland, Satch couldn't keep his body still. He sang in the church choir in the morning, did woodworking before lunch, and put on a mitt by afternoon. As usual, Willie Hines was not far behind.

"Satch played, but he was on first base," Hines noted, "and I was playin' in the band, playin' the alto saxophone. The band would go everywhere they played ball on them Sundays. We had a sportin' goods fella out of Montgomery, and he used to come down and take the ball team all over, to other reform schools. The governor came in once to see 'em play."

Now *that* was altitude. Satchel Page, only months removed from the alleys and trash bins of Mobile, was being applauded by the suits of Montgomery. Perfectly content as a so-so first baseman, Satch heard Willie Hines make the suggestion that changed his life.

"We had a pitcher, and they kept on hittin' this guy, and so I told 'em, I said, 'Satchel could pitch better than that fella, put him in there.' So they put him in and he threw so hard he hit two of them fellas right off, and nobody else would get up to the plate and they called it a forfeit."

This was Satchel Page at age thirteen. Already he stood six foot three, and at 140 pounds he looked like four rubber bands glued together. "There was a lot to me," he recalled of those days, "but it was all up and down." He also, as Willie Hines remembered it, "wasn't that good a pitcher." Not yet. That would happen gradually, and with the forbearance of the Mount's coach, Edward Byrd, whose simple but valuable instruction made Leroy Page whole.

At Byrd's insistence, Satch began to kick his front foot high into the air—"so it looked like I blocked out the sky," he once said—and to release the ball at the last possible moment—"when my hand was right in the batter's face." He was taught to study the batter's knees—"just like a bullfighter; a bullfighter can tell what a bull is going to do by watching his knees. When [a hitter] swings and I see his knees move, I can tell just what his weaknesses are. Then I just put the ball where I know he can't hit it."

A natural, Satch never had to learn much more than that. He had not a clue about how to throw a curve nor would he for many years. All he knew was he could throw hard—*hard*—and as accurately into the glove of his catcher at the Mount, John Knox, as he had when the target was a seagull at Choctaw Pass.

The paradox now for Leroy Page was that, once he'd be out of Mt. Meigs, these skills seemed sure to be immaterial in Mobile. Thus, while he could later say that he had traded five years of freedom to learn how to pitch, Satch faced freedom with no small dread. Willie Hines, on the other hand, was ready after three years of the place to do something radical to get away. Out in the field as always, he was able to wander from his squad and hide in some tall grass, and when the guard strayed he got up and tore through the northern Alabama grottos. He didn't know where he was going, nor how dumb an idea it was. He knew only one thing—"I knew I wasn't goin' back."

Somehow, he wound up in New Orleans—"They couldn't get to me in another state"—and eventually went to sea as a merchant marine before returning to Mobile a few years later. By then, Satch would be out of Mt. Meigs and back home too—though his family were now practically strangers to him. Willie Hines could see that estrangement coming back the Mount. The worst day for both of them wasn't when they worked the hardest or were locked in the tightest; it was the first Sunday of the month—visitor's day. On those days, Leroy and Willie would bury themselves in baseball and the band, to forget that their families had once again not come to see them.

"I don't think," Hines said, "that Satchel ever got that out of his head."

•   •   •

Released just before Christmas of 1923, a leaner and now harder Satch came home to find a slightly different Mobile. On one of his first days back, while looking for work, he meandered by Eureka Gardens and, to his amazement, saw black guys from the neighborhood playing ball there.

Baseball was beginning to catch the fancies of the young men trapped in the Deep South, as elsewhere. When Babe Ruth took a big league barnstorming team through the region in 1924, many of Satch's old buddies, if not Satch himself, vied for places far beyond the outfield fences when Ruth came through Mobile. One, a young man named Herb Aaron, climbed a pine tree overlooking the park and watched the Babe smack one into a boxcar sitting on some railroad tracks beyond the right field wall. Nearly a half century later, Herb Aaron's son, Henry, raised in the Mobile sandlots, would break Ruth's career home run record.

A colored team, the Mobile Tigers, played their games at Eureka Gardens. And one of their best players happened to be Satch's older brother Wilson, who was a pitcher and catcher. Wilson, whose own big feet had earned him the nickname of "Paddlefoot," turned out to be Satchel Page's entrée to a new stratum. When Willie Hines got back to Mobile, Satch—whose sobriquet had been expanded to a companion "Satchelfoot"—was in his second season with the Tigers and was doing no boasting. "I'd come over and watch him," Hines said, "and he didn't want to pitch. He'd rather play first base.

He said Wilson was a better pitcher than him. And there was another fella, Chester Arnold. Satch said Chester pitched better than him too."

Still, the heat of competition around Mobile drew him in quickly. This is when those games Ted Radcliffe remembers made up many of their days. Ed Otis also remembered these and other games as high-stakes turf wars. "Satchel and my brother Amos used to play in those things, too. They'd put up money and they'd play under the name of a bar in town. The bar would put up money for them. So this would be good money, each guy would be in for like nine or ten dollars. And the northside boys would put up the same money and they'd play for it."

It was possible for Ted Radcliffe to catch Satch one day, then have to hit against him the next. And yet Otis recalled no wondrous exploits, nor any legend beginning to form around the head of Satchel Page. "He didn't do much around here," Otis put it. "Radcliffe can tell you, nobody was a star. But he was a good pitcher."

Even Satch dropped a hint as to the reality underneath the bluster. As his main motivation was money, and his pitching would have to take him to it, Satch had to go show biz from the get-go. It wasn't for the love of the game that he prospered, it was for survival. As he admitted, "The only way I knew how to get something better was with pitching. That meant I had to get a professional ballclub interested in me."

That was when Satchel Page first thought to get funky. Pitching for a semipro club called the Down the Bay Boys, he got into a jam in the ninth inning of a 1–0 game, and he stomped around kicking dirt, which riled up the fans. Hearing a swell of booing, he would recall that "somebody was going to have to pay for that." Satch called in his outfielders and had them squat in the infield as he went on pitching. With the fans and now his team howling, Satch worked out of trouble. Alienating almost everyone on the field, he made a name for himself.

He also made adjustments in his *personal* style. Sending up black nonchalance by exaggeration, he slowed his walk to a long-legged amble, striking a pose that could be hilarious until he let his fastball fly. "For an eighteen-year-old kid," he said, "the cheers I got were mighty pleasing. I got plenty of laughs, too."

•   •   •

The first pro team to take note of the small local cult of Satchel Page was the Chattanooga Black Lookouts of the Negro Southern League. In 1926, this league was a kind of minor Negro league, a notch below the big-city franchises of the Midwestern-based Negro National League and the Eastern Colored League, which operated out of the Northeast corridor. Composed of teams in Chattanooga, Memphis, New Orleans, Birmingham, Montgomery, Atlanta, and Albany, Georgia, the NSL was actually a relatively stable venture in a sea of here-today-gone-tomorrow colored teams. And, providentially for Satch, the player-manager of the Chattanooga Black Lookouts was a guy he knew from the Mobile slums, Alex Herman, who knew all about the turf wars north and south of Government Street.

Herman liked to scout those games, and on one trip he signed Julius Andrews to the Black Lookouts. He wanted to sign Paddlefoot Page, but Wilson—just months after John Page's death—acceded to Lula's will and stayed home, tempering baseball with the good, solid work of gravedigging. So Alex Herman took an interest in Satchelfoot Page. The deal for Satch was fifty dollars a month, but because Herman didn't know the kid was eighteen, he had to get written permission from Lula to take her son across the state line just in case he was legally too young. It was not easy.

"You're just a boy," Lula protested, disregarding her son's age. "You'll probably even play on Sunday!"

For Lula, the issue was drawn like a line in the Mobile mud. It was the sanctity of the neighborhood she stalked versus the profligate ways of the big city. Church and dignified work versus city temptation, city women, and the pagan gods of money. But, in the end, Lula too had a price, and when Herman promised that he would send her a stipend extracted from Satch's salary, she swallowed hard and sent her boy into the wicked wind.

Now Leroy Page could ride the L&N tracks, and in a parlor car. When he arrived with Herman and Julius Andrews in Chattanooga, though, the only time he threw the ball was to loosen some spending cash from human pigeons, prompting bets by swearing he could throw ten straight balls over a handkerchief or knock down ten bottles on a wall. He could win enough for a good night out on the town, but he was outwitting few people during actual ballgames. According to Satch, "I was their meal ticket" from the outset with the Black Lookouts. If so, the meals in Chattanooga were mighty cheap.

Page—going now under the name only of "Satchel"—pitched sparsely; toward the end of the '26 season, during an 8–5 loss to the Memphis Red Sox on August 29, Herman stuck him into the game in *right field*, batting him ninth, *behind* the pitcher. Earlier, on June 22, Herman had given him a pitching start during a four-game road series with the Albany Giants; hardly ready for stardom, Satch gave up thirteen runs as the pitching-short Black Lookouts were swept and run out of Albany.

Both the '26 season and much of the '27 season were a prologue, a time when Satchel Page could learn by careful inspection and imitation. Traversing the South he hadn't known existed, he appraised himself by how much he could absorb from other, wiser people. Indeed, these people were so knocked out by his raw talent and his good humor that they wanted a part in his rising. One, Bill "Plunk" Drake, a briny headhunter of a pitcher who was then with Memphis, advised Satch never to accept less money than he thought he was worth—and during one Chattanooga-Memphis game, Drake taught the impressionable young man the Hesitation Pitch that Satch would make famous. "I called it a 'delayed' pitch," Drake once recalled. "Stride and hold a second, *then* throw. I'd been doing that since 1914."

Alex Herman, though, was not fond of anyone messing with his precocious flamethrower. Satch himself came to Alex with the smart idea of learning to throw a curve. Herman nixed the idea, snapping at him, "You wanna ruin that arm of yours?"—which is normally what pitching coaches tell guys who *don't* throw off-speed. But Satch had the kind of arm that defied conventional wisdom and salary structures. Alex was nursing him along, and he desperately wanted to keep him. And so, turning an eye to the future, he mortgaged Satch's arm by making a remarkable concession to Satch's vanity. Midway through the '26 season, he upped the skinny kid's salary to a hundred a month. When Satch disappeared with his bounty, bought new duds, and went on a two-day drunk, Alex was frantic. Satch then showed up, penniless, and came to Alex with a cheeky request.

"Mistah Alex," he said, "how's about a loan?"

Herman was steamed, but was compelled to give him a token advance—all of two dollars. Now, however, Alex wouldn't let him out of his sight; when Satch made for the bars and bawdyhouses downtown, the manager was right there with him. Though Satch lived in a boarding house for two dollars a month, the beds where he normally slept were all over town. And Alex probably put in more time outside the cathouses, waiting for Satch to reappear, than he did at the ballpark.

Finally, Satch had enough of this nannying. Late in the season, during a road trip to New Orleans—a town offering a much bigger playground than Satch ever imagined, allowing him access to observe the supercool style of Jelly Roll Morton and "Satchmo" Armstrong at the honkytonks on Bourbon Street—the Black Pelicans' manager offered him eighty-five dollars a month. As this was less than he was making with the Black Lookouts, Satch hesitated, until the Pelicans anted up an inducement—a white jalopy, a bucket of bolts to be sure but, as Satch's first wheels, a treasure. Now he casually informed Alex Herman that, contract or not, "I ain't goin' back wid you" to Chattanooga.

Herman again fumed, but he could hardly raise a moral issue. Players jumping contracts was a common occurrence in Negro ball, regularly induced by avaricious club owners. Bouncing like a pinball from one offer to another, a player could go over the top several times a year. Wholesale player raids became epidemic in the 1920s; clubs would show up on the field expecting one team and find they'd have to face two or three added ringers. In one year, a Negro league World Series game would be forfeited because of just such hijinx—yet rather than clamping down once and for all on the problem, owners became so addicted to the practice that they sought to *profit* from their own jumpers by "renting out" certain players through "gentlemen's agreements" with other owners, for x number of games; when those games were done, the players would promptly be returned to their original team.

Small wonder that Satchel Page could treat his own defection so lightly that, looking back years and years later, he would giggle about Alex Herman and the Black Lookouts, "Those guys still are probably waiting for me to pitch that last week of ball."

All Alex could do was to try and talk him back. And, whether it was loyalty or caprice, after a winter of small-time barnstorming around the Deep South, Satch did begin the '27 season again in a Chattanooga uniform. In fact, Satch had his pick of several teams that spring.

Amazingly, Satch was already able to parlay his reputation, his promise of future splendor, and his desperado scent into a "name" that made him a gotta-have commodity around blackball. Hip to the way he could pull strings at least as well as he could fire fastballs, he found it of no small amusement that he had led several Negro National League teams to believe that he would play for them that spring, including the St. Louis Stars and two clubs that had moved up from the NSL that year, the Memphis Red Sox and the Birmingham Black Barons. Under no illusions that they could sign him—and none had any intentions of breaking the bank to land him—all these teams were at least willing to preserve a roster spot for him in case they could.

In effect, Satch set up a minor auction for his services, and the prestige of the NNL placed a distinct second to simple mercantilism for him, which is why he came back to Chattanooga: Alex Herman kicked in a slick Model-A roadster and a raise, a bump up to $200 a month.

After throwing a few games for the Black Lookouts, however, Satchel drove that roadster right out of Chattanooga again. This time the road took him down to Birmingham, the Black Barons having gotten around to offering $275 a month. Although it was Satch who had taken the Lookouts for a ride, the caste system of Negro ball stipulated that if a Southern League player signed with an NNL team, the former club had to be compensated; thus, the Lookouts could claim that the deal went down officially as a "sale." This saved Alex Herman some face, but not the hurt and embarrassment of being abandoned by Satchel Paige without a word of notice.

Not that Satch gave a second thought to Alex's pain. With his pocket heavier and his new wheels under his feet, he blew town in the same way he did Mobile, without looking back.

3

Today Will Be Yesterday Tomorrow

There were giants in the earth in those days . . . mighty men which were of old, men of renown.

—Genesis 6:4

There was this white team, a minor league club. Pretty soon those guys over there started hearing about Ol' Satch. . . . "We made a bet you couldn't throw as good as all of them say," one of them told me. He offered me a dollar to show them. . . . We went down on the field and one of them grabbed a bat and another a glove to catch me.

"No need for you to tote that wood up there," I yelled at him. "It's just weight. You ain't gonna need it, 'cause I'm gonna throw you nothin' but my trouble ball." I threw. Them little muscles all around me tingled. They knew what we were doing. The first guy up there swung and missed three fast ones. Another tried it. He just caused a breeze.

"We could use you," one of them finally told me. "If you were only white. . . . "

That was the first time I heard it.

—Satchel Paige,
Maybe I'll Pitch Forever

Black ballplayers began making small but symbolically important inroads into the American sporting culture in the decade following the Civil War, but such steps were not taken lightly. The players would learn that lesson hard. Because while the Emancipation Proclamation was explicit about bona fide rights, the notion that sports and games were inherently for the well-bred leisure classes was held very strongly.

The first baseball league in America, the amateur National Association of Base Ball Players, was established in 1867 with over one hundred teams in the northern United States. Fearing that blacks would apply, the NABBP elders specifically precluded "the admission of any club which may be composed of one or more colored persons." Four years later, when the first professional league, the National Association of Professional Ball Players, came to be, this rule was unwritten but clearly practiced.

Not to be co-opted, blacks formed their own teams, the earliest of which played out of Philadelphia with feisty names such as the Excelsiors and the Uniques. Some white semipro teams also included blacks, and the first known black pro—ironically born in Cooperstown, New York, the cradle of baseball civilization—was a second baseman named John "Bud" Fowler, who played with a team in New Castle, Pennsylvania, in 1872.

Fowler's meandering career was covered extensively in *Sporting Life* magazine—which classified him as "the noted colored player" or "the crack colored player"—as was the career of another black itinerant player, catcher Moses Fleetwood Walker. An honor student at Oberlin College, "Fleet" Walker and his brother, Welday Wilberforce Walker, starred on the school team before going out into the baseball wilds in 1883.

Unlike Bud Fowler, Fleet Walker, playing with the Toledo club of the major league American Association—and thus the first black big leaguer—had games in the South, where he endured lynch threats and constant verbal abuse; when he suffered a broken rib, he was released, presumably "for his own good." Fleet, and Welday for a time, then bounced around in the sticks with Fowler and newer black players like pitchers George Stovey and Frank Grant. Ultimately, they all found jobs in another minor league loop, the International League.

But now trouble was fermenting. In 1887 Adrian "Cap" Anson, manager and captain of the National League's Chicago White Stockings and a future Hall of Famer, began threatening not to play exhibition games against International League teams with blacks. The closest that Anson allowed a black man to the field was as a team mascot, and the one who performed that role for the

White Stockings was a singer-dancer named Clarence Duval—whom Anson openly called a "little darky," a "chocolate-covered coon," and a "no-account nigger."

Anson succeeded in axing an exhibition game in Chicago against George Stovey's Newark team in July 1887. Two months later, the National League's St. Louis Browns took the cue from Anson and refused to play a scheduled exhibition game against the all-black Cuban Giants—leaving a crowd of 7,000 people sitting in the stands. The ultimatum not to play came from the Browns' players rather than management.

"We, the . . . St. Louis Base Ball Club," the players wrote in a statement given to the team's owner on the eve of the game, "do not agree to play against negroes tomorrow. We will cheerfully play against white people at any time, and think, by refusing to play, we are only doing what is right."

By the end of the season, the trend begun by Cap Anson had become unwritten major league policy, and the International League was backtracking as well. Fearing an exodus of whites "on account of the colored element," as *Sporting Life* put it, the IL officially barred "[any] more contracts with colored men." Thus did professional baseball formally embargo people of color—not just blacks, but by implication Latins, American Indians, et al.—from the American Pastime. Promptly, Bud Fowler was released by the Binghamton team, Stovey by Newark; others, like Frank Grant and Bob Higgins, were close behind.

Fleet Walker, as a holdover, did manage to hang around the International League a few years longer, but as the other blacks fell out, he left baseball in 1889 in despair—to become, in later years, an editor and author, his baseball experience contributing to books and articles in which he pleaded the case for the Back to Africa movement for blacks. In America, wrote Fleet Walker, blacks could expect "nothing but failure and disappointment."

In rungs beneath the big league level, blacks still competed. Negro teams began to crop up in white leagues such as the Iron and Oil League of upstate New York, which featured the Acme Colored Giants. In the Middle States League, the Cuban Giants—a name that would endure long into the future—was actually a black team, with George Stovey and nineteen-year-old second baseman Sol White, the latter beginning a career that would endure almost as long as the team did. White hit .358 in 1889, and that same year Frank Grant, in his new home, the Eastern Interstate League, hit

.325 for Harrisburg—and, going against the grain of the times, the integrated Harrisburg club issued an ultimatum: they'd play with Grant or not at all.

These leagues came and went, and when they broke up, blacks—facing more and more hostility up North and prohibitive Jim Crow laws down South—found the island of blackball to be their only salvation, though colored teams were scarce indeed; one, the Page Fence Giants of Adrian, Michigan, was created by Bud Fowler in 1895 and starred Sol White. This was a prototypical colored team, parading through towns on bicycles to sell tickets and clowning on the field during games.

At the turn of the century, history records there were five colored teams, two playing out of New York, two out of Chicago—and one, the Red Stockings of Norfolk, Virginia. Sol White formed another, the Philadelphia Giants, in 1902, touching off a blackball boom in that city; four years later there were nine teams there, all named "Giants," which begat a proliferation of teams in other big cities, especially in Chicago, where the Leland Giants became dominant. On a smaller scale, one even sprung up in Topeka, Kansas.

This was the start of the golden era of blackball, yet what all these teams, many of which were top-notch operations, had in common was white ownership. Indeed, the genesis of the Cuban Giants is instructive. Originally a team of black porters formed to entertain patrons at a Long Island resort hotel, they were acquired in 1885 by a white man, John Lang. Lang named them the "Cubans" in order to avoid the stigma of their color and to get games on the road. The players were even told to speak pidgin Spanish rather than their native English, to perpetuate the con.

Not that Latin men were acceptable to the big leagues, especially dark-skinned Latins, but they didn't seem to offend American ethnocentrism as much as blacks did; ironically, it was through the example of this team that *real* Cubans began to trickle onto other teams named Cubans, as well as onto black teams—a process that opened Cuba and eventually all of Latin America for black and white ballplayers to play in the winter. In addition, two Cubans, Rafael Almeida and Armando Marsans, who played on the Midwestern Cuban Stars, were signed to major league contracts with the Cincinnati Reds in 1911; Marsans played eight major league seasons, Almeida three. Others, like Cristobal Torriente, José Méndez, and the great Hall of Famer Martin Dihigo had storied Negro league careers.

That Negro baseball bore the implicit sanction of the white base-ball culture could even be seen in what became the premier black franchise of its day, and arguably of all time: the Chicago American Giants. This imprimatur, to be sure, was well earned, having been pushed to its glory by a black man whose vision came to be em-braced by all in blackball as a kind of Delphic oracle. This was An-drew "Rube" Foster, whose legend already preceded him by 1920. Indeed, the course of Rube Foster's life could be seen as a parable of the black game, its accomplishments, its quixotic dreams, and its ultimate miscarriages.

Born in Calvert, Texas, in 1879, this son of a church elder saw his epiphany even as the big leagues were dimming out on people like Fleet Walker and Frank Grant. Riding the freight cars as a gypsy ballplayer, Foster found games where he could across the South, and got to pitch in exhibition games against Connie Mack's Philadelphia Athletics; in one of those, in 1902, Foster was said to have defeated the A's ace, Rube Waddell, earning him the nick-name of "Rube-beater," which then became simply "Rube."

Though never allowed to pitch in the big leagues, Foster was kept on a sort of loose retainer by both Mack and the Giants' griz-zled manager John McGraw—to teach their pitchers, including McGraw's Christy Mathewson, the art of the screwball. A hot com-modity in blackball, Foster reportedly won fifty-one games one year for the Cuban Giants, and also took the Cuban X Giants into the first organized Negro World Series—a challenge round with the Philadelphia Giants in 1903. Pitching four of the seven games and hitting cleanup, the big, strapping Foster won all four and his team took the series five games to two.

In Negro league fashion, Rube then took his best players—in-cluding Grant "Home Run" Johnson and outfielder Jap Payne—and jumped to the team they had just beaten, giving the Philadelphia Giants' player-manager, Sol White, a near-unbeatable hand. Molding players and tactics in his style—run-run, always take the extra base, keep the other guys' heads spinning—he developed teams that were the envy of big league managers, who were now studying his bold, unorthodox methods, such as throwing a curve on a 3-and-2 count and having runners go from first to third on a bunt.

The self-educated Foster, in fact, became something of an un-derground authority on the game, publishing baseball guides that were widely read. With the bases loaded, he wrote, pitchers could turn the tables on hitters by "appearing jolly and unconcerned. I have smiled often with the bases full with two strikes and three balls on the batter. This seems to unnerve them." And by "wasting a few [pitches], the hitter would be unnerved. . . . You will win by drawing him into hitting at a wide one," such as one of those 3-and-2 curves. To ensure that his "rabbits" could run, he contoured the first base line to hug the bunts they dropped down and keep them in fair ground.

With a growing sense of megalomania, Foster fed his ambition by again bundling up some of his best players, including Big Bill Gatewood, Pete Booker, and Pete Hill, and heading for the Chicago market, to play for the Leland Giants in 1906. With Foster as the club's player-manager, the Lelands, playing against both black clubs and white clubs, won the city's semipro crown, and Foster won accolades from the big league Cubs' manager, Frank Chance, as "the most finished product I've ever seen in the pitcher's box." Three years later, the Lelands played Chance's Cubs in an exhibition series and lost three very close games.

Now Foster, seeing more oracles, turned to bigger game: ownership. But because he didn't have enough capital, he had no choice but to turn to a white money angel to realize his dream. This was John Schorling, who owned a thriving tavern but, more important, was the son-in-law of Charlie Comiskey, the owner of the Chicago White Sox. Schorling thus came with some very helpful perks and contacts.

Buying out Frank Leland to take control of the club, Foster and Schorling changed the team's name to the American Giants, and with the acquiescence of Charlie Comiskey moved them into the old White Sox park on 39th Street, which was just four blocks from the Chisox's new home. With this added credibility, and direct ownership of the grandstand (Comiskey still retained title to the grounds), Foster went about consolidating black professionalism, and his own power.

In effect, Foster was carving a sultanate out of his sub-big-league authority in Chicago. Keeping his teams strong in the field, he raided the New York Lincoln Giants, signing their best players—pitchers Smokey Joe Williams and Dick "Cannonball" Redding, outfielder Oscar Charleston, catchers Bruce Petaway and Louis Santop, and future Hall of Famer John Henry Lloyd, the last a reed-thin line-drive machine who was billed as "the black Honus Wagner."

By paying these elite players a top-drawer $1,000 per month, Foster kept the team's core intact and winning, and often outdrew the White Sox down the street when their games coincided, prompting Charlie Comiskey to order his son-in-law and Foster to play at home only when the Chisox were out of town.

But by the late 1910s no big league big shot could push Foster around. Not only did he not accept Comiskey's dictum, but White Sox and Cubs players continued to participate under assumed names in citywide tournaments sponsored by Foster. Foster had money—he was charging a premium fifty cents for a box seat, which included all the ice water the spectator could drink—and he had dominion; *all* Negro or semipro games in Chicago were booked by Foster, who exacted a ten percent cut in return. Further, white clubs, like the Logan Squares and the Duffy Florals, kicked back a percentage of their receipts of all their games to the big man, whose influence in the Windy City wasn't far beneath Al Capone's.

Whether Foster was running a racket or not was an issue he considered secondary to what came to be his burning ambition—to cover in ebony the kind of power the white baseball promoters exercised in the East. There, the black/semipro circuit was firmly in the grip of such men, though some teams featured blacks as fronts. And, in what was essentially a role model for Foster, a tight web of promoters dished out the permits for games, with the requisite agent's fees.

The most powerful promoter of all was Nat Strong, who controlled the New York turf as well as the New York Black Yankees, the black Brooklyn Royal Giants, and Dexter Park in Queens, where most area games were played. Foster and Strong were in fact a great deal alike; if their methods were at time heavy-handed, in no way were they crooked, and their efforts to see Negro baseball succeed undeniable. But Foster loathed Nat Strong, seemingly on the assumption that if Negro baseball was to be exploited for the good of its perpetuation, that exploitation belonged implicitly to staunch black men like Rube Foster. Indeed, becoming progressively more race-militant, Foster (whose business accommodation with the white John Schorling nonetheless continued unabated) began promulgating Magna Carta–like edicts for all of blackball, to the effect that the black game should "do something about the loyalty of the black Race" and "keep Colored baseball free from the control of whites."

And yet Foster's parallelism with Nat Strong was underscored by the alliance Foster would ultimately set up with Strong, though on Foster's end it was a case of dealing with the devil for the benefit of blackball. This happened after Foster sought to consolidate blackball under one roof—which he wanted to be his own. Petitioning other successful black teams outside of Strong's purview, he convinced the owners of seven teams—the Kansas City Monarchs, Chicago Giants, Cuban Stars, Detroit Stars, Dayton Marcos, St. Louis Stars, Indianapolis ABCs—to each pay a $500 entrance fee to join with the American Giants in establishing the Negro National League, which would commence play on April 1, 1921.

This was not the first time an all-Negro league had been attempted, and the example of the precedents was hardly a good omen. As far back as 1887, the League of Colored Base Ball Clubs formed, only to fold after one *week*; its successor, the Independent Professional League of Base Ball Clubs—actually an integrated league, with black teams and white teams—was able to make it through its first and last season, in 1906.

But, in Rube Foster, the Negro National League had something its ancestors lacked: it had a messiah figure, a black overlord with style, money, and a first-class operation. (Foster took his team about the country in a Pullman railroad car, no small symbolism for blacks who otherwise were only porters on the Pullmans.) He had a zealot's drive to succeed—and as nothing less than as an equal to the two major leagues, with an eye toward eventually becoming a major league. It was nearly a coronation when Foster was named the NNL's president and secretary.

At the same time, Foster didn't intend the league to be the private duchy of the American Giants; seeking a healthy balance between teams, he shared some of his club's wealth by sending useful players to other teams, including Oscar Charleston to Indianapolis. He also saw to it that the Detroit Stars' owner, Tenny Blount, would have the same booking privileges in the Motor City that Foster enjoyed in Chicago. Still, Foster did appropriate a five percent cut of all NNL games, to cover operating expenses; and no one could keep the American Giants from winning the first three league titles.

Against all odds, the NNL turned a profit at the start—even though only Foster among the owners owned even a piece of his ballpark and the others had to pay, on top of Foster's cut, exorbitant fees to lease theirs from white minor league teams (and two, the Cuban Stars and Chicago Giants, played all of their games on the road). Several teams folded, others shifted cities, fly-by-night ones came on board—yet, in 1923, the NNL drew over 400,000 fans and reaped some $200,000 in gate receipts.

The NNL's early success, in fact, was an ironic cause of its ensuing problems. Other Negro leagues formed in hopes of striking the same mother lode: the Negro Southern League first, then in 1923 the Eastern Colored League—with Foster's role played by Nat Strong, who owned one ECL team and booked games for five of the six others, at a higher cut than Foster's.

Loathing Strong, Foster took strong exception to the ECL's ownership; although Foster himself shared ownership with a white man, Rube counted only one NNL owner as white—the Kansas City Monarchs' J. L. Wilkinson, who was considered a sort-of "brother" by dint of his commitment to his league—while the ECL counted just two non-Caucasian owners, Ed Bolden of the Hilldale club of Darby, Pennsylvania, and Alex Pompez of the New York Cuban Stars. To label the ECL "black," Foster sniffed, "is like calling a streetcar a steamship."

Yet by 1924 Foster had contracted with Nat Strong to co-exist in an uneasy alliance. This was the only solution to keep Foster from contracting to *murder* Strong, whose teams had been raiding the NNL's. The Indianapolis team, hit the hardest, lost ten players at once, including Oscar Charleston, and Rube himself was relieved of his best pitcher, Dave Brown. Though Foster's instinct was to fight fire with bigger fire, and though he was an accomplished raider of other teams from way back, he knew that internal cannibalization would wreck any dream of organized black leagues. And so he took a nonaggression pledge with Strong, scheduled games between the two leagues, and arranged for a Negro World Series beginning in 1924—won that year not by the American Giants but by J. L. Wilkinson's Kansas City Monarchs, in a best-of-nine series against the Hilldales.

Still making money and paying pricey salaries—the league's total payroll was around $100,000, its expenses around $160,000 more—Foster was turning a profit leaguewide. His own team was bringing in about $85,000 a game, more than many major league clubs. But too many teams were stretching talent and profit too thin, and by mid-decade fan interest began to wane as the white game flourished, wallowing in a Roaring Twenties bacchanal objectified by easy money and Babe Ruth.

Foster was a shriveling messiah. Torturing himself with his obsessions, he began acting crazily in 1926, the year the American Giants won the first of two straight Negro World Series—the last two played in the 1920s. Varying reports had Foster running around on the street chasing imaginary fly balls and ranting to himself. When he nearly smashed all the furniture in his home, his wife summoned the white coats and had him confined to an insane asylum in Kankakee, Illinois, where he died four years later, in 1930, at age fifty-one.

Foster's funeral accorded him the kind of requiem saved for Chicago VIPs like, well, Al Capone. As his body lay in state for three days, thousands filed past his casket, which was closed at roughly the time that American Giants games ended, and with "Rock of Ages" playing on a loudspeaker. The *Chicago Defender*, the town's highly respected black newspaper, eulogized him as a "martyr to the game" and "the most commanding figure baseball had ever known."

In fact, Rube Foster had died a failure; by the time he made his final out, his league, a steamship run aground without him, had ceased operations, accomplishing none of Foster's goals. Moreover, with this stern disciplinarian gone, the very decorum of blackball seemed to change, and the *Defender* cited numerous cases of player rowdyism, including fistfights with fans and with one another. If Foster was a martyr, few could now identify the cause.

If Foster left a legacy, it was in the men for whom he had been an Aristotle, and his dugout a Lyceum. Through him came those who would influence future generations of blackball. Those who would become powerful managers alone included Dave Malarcher, Dizzy Dismukes, Willie Wells, Vic Harris, Biz Mackey, Oscar Charleston, Candy Jim Taylor, and Newt Joseph.

Among whites, Foster's passing certainly went unnoticed—though, plainly, and due to him, it was getting harder for the white baseball establishment to avoid cohabitation with black players completely. The money that Foster had taken in was noticed, and the novelty of black-white competition provided a neat little sideshow for big leaguers on their winter sabbaticals.

Indeed, by now there was a historical context to the tentative gestures of amity made by the white game through the years, such as when Ty Cobb—an unabashed racist—had agreed to play against blacks when the Detroit Tigers barnstormed in Cuba in 1910, and when John McGraw had had Rube Foster teach Christy Mathewson the screwball.

Even before that, in 1901, when McGraw was managing the Baltimore Orioles (not the same team that carries that name today, but the team that moved to New York in 1903 and became the Yankees), he tried to sneak a black player through the big league parapets, putting a second baseman named Charlie Grant on his roster. Grant, who had been playing for a Negro team in Chicago, was the son of a black horse trainer in Cincinnati who coincidentally had features that could be mistaken for an American Indian; McGraw speciously—and pushing the color barrier even by doing this—listed him under the name of "Tokohama." Grant, who went along with the con, was slated to start his first big league game when Charlie Comiskey got wind of the truth and made much noise about it.

If McGraw insisted on keeping Grant, Comiskey said, "I will get a Chinaman . . . and put him on third [for the White Sox]." Ultimately, McGraw sent Charlie Grant back to Chicago, without playing a game in the big leagues.

Most of the country, however, knew little about any of this. Some of names in the blackball world rang a bell, but since the press rarely touched on the rumor that was blackball, there was no impetus for McGraw and his generation of ballplayers and managers to lend urgency to any such gestures. White players were free, for now, to play exhibitions against black teams, to cash in on the novelty, and also feel free to jake it when they did, safe in the knowledge that there weren't enough good black players to seriously challenge big league sovereignty. Not even Rube Foster could have staked the claim that more than a select few of them should have merited big league consideration or a true comparison with their big league counterparts.

As an allegory, the burnout of the first sustaining Negro league and all of its high pretensions was explicit: blackball, as it stood in the late 1920s, was separate, it was unequal, and it had little force to empower anyone in its ranks beyond very local and isolated fame. That, more than anything else, may have driven Rube Foster mad, for it was a lesson so painfully learned.

Latter-day revisionists have combed over the eye-popping but poorly verified statistics of the Negro league greats and overromanticized, even sanctified, men who lived not to engender a legend but only for the next game they could get. Some historians, reading the world into numbers that meant little in the context of the Negro game, and interracial exhibitions that meant even less, have blithely claimed superiority for these men, who never would

have made such claims for themselves—a Cool Papa Bell over a
Tris Speaker, a John Henry Lloyd over a Lou Gehrig, a Smokey Joe
Williams over a Lefty Grove. Comparisons of this sort are always
difficult, and essentially useless, even within the big leagues. Considering the weak overall talent of blackball, and the who-cares attitude of the often mediocre big leaguers who played against
blackball's best in exhibitions for some spare change, they are
sheer fantasy.

This is not to say that those who kept on truckin' in the shadows
don't deserve their romantic due; they certainly worked hard
enough for it. It is not even to say, definitively, that Cool Papa Bell
wasn't better than Tris Speaker, or Smokey Joe Williams not better
than Lefty Grove. It's only to say that, if the talents of the early
blackballers were known at all to people wired into the baseball
universe, so was the truth that it would take far more ignitable
names to invest blackball with the credibility to defy white men's
traditions and habits.

One such name, though, was on the way.

•   •   •

In the late spring of 1927, the last meaningful year of the Negro
National League, Satchel Paige was a growing cult figure and very
much on the mind of Rube Foster's protégé Big Bill Gatewood.
Gatewood, who had gone from Foster's American Giants to be-
come pitcher-manager for the black Albany Giants the year before,
was given the same job by the Birmingham Black Barons when the
Barons moved up from the Southern League to the NNL in 1927.
Now Gatewood was stockpiling the club with strong arms.

Already on his staff were two of the best around, Sam Streeter
and Harry Salmon, old pros who were mirror images of each other:
Streeter a squat southpaw junkballer whose out pitch was a spitball; Salmon a Satch look- and pitch-a-like, a toothpick with an
atomic fastball and whiplash sidearm delivery that made right-
handed hitters stand on jellylegs.

Satchel Paige was the last piece of the puzzle for Big Bill, who
went with the Barons' owner, a white man named Joe Rush, to
Chattanooga to sign him out from under Alex Herman's nose.

Unlike Herman and his proprietary approach, Gatewood encouraged Satch to learn from his baseball elders. Clearly, there was
much work to be done with him, though with all this attention being given him, Satch believed he needed no instruction. Watching

him go about his own way on the practice field, Gatewood—a large and generally mild-mannered man—lost all patience.

"Watch what you're doing!" Big Bill would scream at him. "You can't come all the way up with your foot like that. You can't hold nobody on first base like that!"

Growing testy under the blistering criticism by the old pro, Satch would turn a deaf ear. When Gatewood showed him the proper way to hold a man on or throw a curve, Satch would look right through him and say, "I don't do it that way."

Gatewood was particularly concerned that, given how slowly Satch got his long body into fielding position after the pitch, teams would bunt on him all day long and tire him out scrambling after all those dribblers. As it was, he was throwing so many pitches in the early games that he was losing steam in one or two innings. And those pitches were making people run for cover all over the park. In one game against Chicago, the American Giants out-fielder Jelly Gardner recalled Satch's repertoire like this: "One time [it came] at you, one time behind you, the next time at your feet. . . . I saw him the first day he pitched. You had to be an acrobat to hit against him."

Or catch him. The Black Barons' catchers, Nish Williams and Spoony Palm, stepped into Satch's line of fire—horsehide and verbal—when they tried to call the pitches for him.

"There ain't no need for signs," Satch rebuked them. "All you gotta do is show me a glove and hold it still. I'll hit it."

But he did that roughly as often as high tide, and his frustration only made him more perilous to people's health. On June 27 he started against the powerful St. Louis Stars of Cool Papa Bell and Willie Wells in the third of a four-game series in St. Louis. The Stars had already beaten Streeter and Gatewood in their bandbox ballpark, and because the Stars were crowding the plate on him, Satch was in a foul mood from the start. In the bottom of the second inning with the score tied 1–1, whether it was wildness or purpose or both, he drilled the first three Stars hitters—the last, catcher Mitch Murray, in the small of the back with a *real* trouble ball.

Cut to his knees by the pitch, Murray got up and—still holding his bat—rushed the mound, chasing Satch all the way to second base, where Murray then hurled the bat at Satch's head. It whistled past his ear, whereupon Satch picked up the lumber and began chasing Murray with it. That touched off a huge and frightening melee among teams and fans, which wasn't broken up until St. Louis police in riot gear descended on the field. At that point, the home plate umpire, John Donaldson, ejected both Murray and Satch. Enraged that Satch could get the thumb even though Murray began the fight, Bill Gatewood pulled his team off the field and forfeited the game.

Afterward, Murray continued the fight verbally, saying that Satch threw a "bean ball" meant to intentionally injure St. Louis players—a point that the Stars made in the fourth game when they brought in a player to catch. His name was "Blood" Smith, and he was there to prevent a replay.

Thus did Satchel Paige first make headlines, though it was pseudonymously—NEAR RIOT AT ST. LOUIS WHEN DONALDSON REMOVES PITCHER, blared the *Chicago Defender* head, referring to the mysterious man known only as "Satchell" in the game story and box score, making it apparent that Satch's cult status had not yet reached the black press. And though Satch would confirm this bizarre and noteworthy event in his autobiography, he played down the wildness angle. Rather than being nervous, he insisted, he had been in control of things the whole time.

"I hit a few batters that day, but I meant to," he wrote. "Why, I haven't hit more than two batters in my entire life except when I wanted to." Besides, he added, "I'd thrown my letup so I wouldn't kill [anybody]."

In fact, Satch could write that with twenty-twenty hindsight, given that over the balance of his career he never did indulge in indecencies like headhunting, nor even the spitball, a common and legal option in blackball. Not that he was a saint, but his ego deemed these artifices unacceptable and irrelevant—"I don't call that baseball when I got to cave in your ribs to get you out," he once averred.

But if Satch resisted aping Sam Streeter's oozy spitter, the round little pitcher did keep on Satch to correct his host of structural flaws. When Satch wound up, Sam would repeat, "Watch the batter, watch the batter," to keep the kid's eye on the plate, and to keep his body from listing to the side, which threw him off balance. And from Harry Salmon, Satch acquired little tricks. With a man on first, Satch would twitch his shoulders ever so slightly, freezing the runner for a crucial split second, just before striding off the rubber. In other words, he was now starting to use his brain in conjunction with his arm.

Still, his progress was slow, and Gatewood used him mainly in relief until he grew more comfortable and his control improved. With the Black Barons—who finished fifth in the first half of the split NNL season—making a strong move to the top and vying for the second-half title, Satch's improvement marked the drive, though he was always capable of wild excess. Starting against the Kansas City Monarchs on August 14, he took the hill after the Barons had lost the first game of a twin bill, and though he was rocked for four early runs, he turned in six and two thirds innings—striking out nine and walking six, a somewhat typical Page outing. A week later, he relieved Streeter midway through an 8–1 loss to St. Louis, striking out four in three innings.

It was in late August that Satch really came of age. Starting against the prolific American Giants in Chicago, he nearly self-destructed, giving up three runs in the first inning. He then settled in and held the Giants scoreless through seven, whiffing four and walking just one. The Barons came back to tie it, only to see Streeter and Robert Poindexter lose it in relief in the bottom of the ninth.

But the Barons now stormed to the second-half title on their final homestand, cleaning up on the lowly Memphis Red Sox and Cuban Stars. Satch racked up two shutouts against Memphis, a 10-strikeout, 2–0 beauty (also going 2-for-3 with the bat in that one), and a 10–0 laugher.

In the five-game Cubans series, played September 11–15, Satch won the second game, a 5–0, four-hit complete game. Then, in the first game of a doubleheader that closed the season—and with the Barons needing to win both ends—Big Bill Gatewood brought him in to relieve Harry Salmon in the first game. Down 5–4, Satch held the line over the last three innings and the Barons rallied to win 6–5. Now, with the season on the line, Gatewood started him in the nightcap, and he won 7–2, yielding six hits in a game called by darkness after seven innings.

Suddenly, Satchel Page was a *pitcher*, getting guys out with a tightly controlled fastball that he had refined to two main varieties—his "Bee Ball," thrown with the fingers on the smooth of the ball, which rode as straight as a clothesline; and his "Jump Ball," with the fingers across the seams, which began straight but with its backspin would explode into the catcher's mitt as though on a tailwind, rising half a foot. Either one, it seemed, he could spot on any border of the plate. Most always, Satch found a safety zone in the area of the batter's knees.

He was, by the end of the regular season, a strange hybrid: the number three starter, but also the stopper out of the bullpen. And yet, Gatewood got nervous about using him in the NNL playoff with the first-half-champion American Giants. Going for experience from his proven veterans, fresh in Gatewood's mind was an earlier game against Memphis. When Satch was called in to relieve Streeter in a 4–4 game, Red Sox left fielder Bill Pryor led off the thirteenth inning and smashed a home run so long and far it looked like the ball might leave the state.

If the old Negro league stats are to be believed, Satch finished at 8-and-3, with eighty strikeouts and nineteen walks in ninety-three innings, and—with no differentiation between earned and unearned in the stat-keeping of the day—gave up slightly more than three runs per game. He had as many shutouts, three, as did Salmon and Streeter (each of whom won a reported fourteen games) combined. But in the playoff against Chicago beginning on September 19 at Birmingham's Rickwood Field, the American Giants routed Salmon and Streeter twice each while handling the Barons' two .400 hitters, Red Parnell and Nish Williams, to sweep the series four straight and go on to beat the ECL Bacharach Giants of Atlantic City in the Negro World Series for the second year in succession.

Satchel Page, in his idleness, could only help turn a 5–4, eighth-inning lead in Game Two into a 10–5 defeat as the Giants mopped up on him for six runs in the inning. Bill Gatewood could only ponder the meaning of Game Four—when Satch went in for a battered Streeter in the first inning and surrendered only two runs the rest of the way with seven strikeouts and no walks in the 6–2 clinching loss. But for Gatewood, it was too late. In his big rush for a title, he had guessed wrong. The next year, Sam Streeter would jump to the Homestead Grays, and Harry Salmon become a .500 pitcher. The Black Barons fell out of contention, and after the '28 season, Bill Gatewood was gone from the game.

•   •   •

Satchel Page, meanwhile, would stick around Birmingham and gain fame as the "new" Bullet Joe Rogan, after the lean and durable Kansas City Monarchs fireballer to whom Page bore an uncanny resemblance, both facially and in pitching style. Satch would go 23-and-15 the next two seasons, with 184 strikeouts in 196 innings in 1929, both league highs—and the strikeout mark a Negro league record that would never be matched at least in the known statistics. He fanned seventeen in a game against the Detroit Stars, also an apparent Negro league record that would last only until he broke it himself six years later.

Against his grain, Satch had gotten close to a newer teammate, catcher Bill Perkins, whom he would insist be his catcher most every time he pitched. According to Satch, Perkins "handled a pitcher like nobody's business," and while Perkins did have a cannon for an arm, what Satch liked most about him was that Perkins had no problem with Satch calling his own game; unlike with Nish Williams and Spoony Palm, Satch was the boss on the mound. If Perkins had a gripe with not calling the game, he never did show it. Catching a man like Satch gave Perkins a certain amplitude, and because owners later would entice Satch to jump to their teams by going and getting Perkins first, Bill earned a very nice living in Negro ball for nearly two decades.

This approach did much for Satch's ever-growing ego, but did little for his main flaw—those annoying bunts trickling free up the baselines. To Satch, they were not unlike a Chinese water torture, and his opponents delighted in nickel-and-diming him to distraction. Willie Powell, who won twice for the American Giants in that '27 NNL playoff, couldn't get over how mulish Satch was about not adjusting. The book on Satch, Powell said, was to "bunt and run, bunt and run, bunt and run. That's how you beat him." Powell also liked to twit Satch about his one-speed pitching.

"Satch, you better learn how to throw a curveball," he'd yell across the diamond.

"Ain't no one can hit my fastball," was Satch's defense.

"You're right," Powell said. "But someday they will."

• • •

By the end of the '29 season, Satch was a star, and was comfortable enough to forge a new identity based on his separation from John Page. Negro teams that hoped to be covered in the two major national black weeklies, the *Chicago Defender* and the *Pittsburgh Courier*, were instructed to send in box scores and game stories; periodically, as per Satch's orders, throughout 1928 and 1929 the name of "Satchel Paige" began to creep into these pages, though the several other forms of the name would continue to show up for years.

On July 20, 1929, when the *Defender* wrote up Satch's watershed game—his seventeen-strikeout, 5–1 victory over the Detroit

Stars—the lead paragraph read: "The Dixie pastimers garnered the laurels . . . behind the effective hurling of 'Satchel' Paige, [who] was in rare form, limiting the bludgeons of the Detroiters to two bingles and setting 17 down via the strikeout route. The elongated one issued one free ticket."

On August 11 of that year came news in the *Defender* of the "pitching duel between Satchel Paige and Chet Brewer, elongated [Kansas City] Monarch hurler, with the latter having the edge in pitching and fielding support," though "Paige settled to his task and chopped the Monarchs down to a point where they could not pile up the score." Satch, in fact, struck out nine, but fell to Brewer 4–3.

This wonderfully stilted period prose was like vespers to blacks who depended on these two newspapers for news of the black culture not available anywhere else. Young black men could read them and dream. Verdell Mathis, a Negro league pitcher of the 1940s, recalled that reportage/romance language as his introduction to baseball in Crawfordsville, Arkansas. Realizing the raw power of the highfalutin name of Satchel Paige, the new Black Barons' owner, R. T. Jackson—who dreaded that Satch would exercise his new earning leverage by jumping his team—tried to co-opt that possibility by jamming in on Satch's mercenary side in the tried and true Negro league way: Jackson offered his ace to any interested team for a game or two to draw a decent crowd, with both Jackson and Satch taking a cut. As Satch recalled this arrangement—one tailor-made for Negro ball—the Barons "would rent me to another city so I could pick up a piece of change and get [Jackson] some." The other team would get the leftovers, which could be no more than spare change.

Satch obviously had no moral objections, since the bread was good, but this underside of Negro ball could have its dangers. In one very semipro game in Albany, Georgia, Satch was called out for missing a base while running out a hit and got into a nasty argument with the umpire—who also happened to be the white sheriff of the town and who threatened to haul Satch's skinny butt in if he didn't calm down. Satch, unmollified, picked up one of his enormous feet and pleaded, "How could I miss the base with feet *this* big?" However, as Satch well knew, the sheriff—who was getting a cut as well—wasn't about to make good on his threat. Indeed, it may have been the only time in the history of Jim Crow that a white sheriff ever needed a black man to be on the premises.

But now Satch was getting tired of this small-time stuff. His

name was something of a public relations machine, and he was
working overtime to raise awareness of himself. Stories—rehearsed in the Lula Page tradition—were making the rounds
about Leroy Page and the satchels he toted (but not stole) at the
old L&N depot; about his background; about the terrible and
folksy pitches that screamed from his hand, now broadened to include the "Bat Dodger" and the "Hurry-Up Ball" and the "Midnight Creeper" and the "Four-Day Rider" and the "Nothin' Ball."

And so this growing media creature turned to bigger game after
the '29 season, game that stalked the earth many worlds from Mobile. The first stop on his safari was the arid loam of baseball-
crazed Cuba.

4

"Mister Satchel"

If you think the world is crazy it may be you that's crazy.

—Old proverb, cited in the
Pittsburgh Courier, June 21, 1930

Importing black players to Cuba was the work of a promoter named Abel Linares, who had removed the teeth from a typically petty big league effort to consolidate segregation. Linares had been around ever since American League teams barnstormed in Cuba starting in 1908, his biggest rush coming one year after the 1910 tour by Ty Cobb's Tigers. Then the world-champion Philadelphia Athletics of Connie Mack came to the island and had to sweat hard in splitting six games against a team of Cubans and American blacks.

That was also the last tour by a big league club, as the aptly named AL commissioner, Ban Johnson, prohibited league teams from "going to Cuba to be beaten by colored teams." That high display of dignity, which would serve as the model for Kenesaw Mountain Landis's overall ban on big league team competition with Negroes a decade and a half later, threatened to undo Linares's big-money operation.

But Linares had done his homework by studying the Negro game and how it "adopted" Cubans—at least as a nickname—to gain acceptance. In order to extend the concept, Linares sent Martin Dihigo—a man who could play every position equally well—to the Cuban Stars and the New York Cubans, teams that employed real Cubans, and Dihigo became a Negro Hall of Famer who every winter returned to play in Cuba for Linares's Santa Clara team.

That route was followed by slugger Cristobal Torriente, who played for four Negro league teams.

Linares's biggest coup was in getting around the Ban Johnson edict by enticing individual players to keep on playing in Cuba in the winter. In 1920, he paid Babe Ruth an astounding $1,000 a game to play with John McGraw's New York Giants on a tour of the island, though the Babe was not happy at seeing all those black faces in the other lineup. Even Cristobal Torriente offended him, noting that the Cuban was "as black as a ton and a half of coal in a dark cellar."

Then Linares decided to go after Satchel Paige, for a bargain-basement $100 a game—still huge coin for Satch, who for the first time could lodge in a nonsegregated hotel. Yet, playing with Dihigo's Santa Clara team, he too found the competition stiff—although his biggest disappointment came not on the field but in his hotel.

Walking into the lobby early on, he loudly said, "Let's get someone to mix up a snort!" That's when he found out that the betting action among Cuban fans was so virulent that the ballplayers were precluded from drinking, so as to remain upright for games. Satch and Sam Streeter, who had come to Cuba with him, had to make do with bribing the bartenders and smuggling vodka bottles up to their room.

Homesick for open carousing, hating the food, chafing at the constant inspection, and baffled by the language—"Speak English, boys," he would plead with his teammates, "I is with you"—Satch's stay on the island lasted for eleven doleful games. He generated six wins, five losses, and unlimited hostility by the *aficionados*. Costing a lot of them a lot of bets, he got himself in deeper *guano* when the mayor of one hamlet called him in and asked him, in Spanish, if he had intentionally lost one particular game. Satch, not understanding a word, vacantly nodded and smiled, figuring the guy was fawning all over him.

As Satch would recall the scene, "He almost jumped over his desk and one of the guys standing around watching us had to hold him down. They got me out of there quick. . . . Knowing how the mayor felt, those boys got me out of town fast."

For his sanity and his health, he then left the country. With his $1,100, he caught a steamship out of Havana, the whole Cuba thing a good lesson to him.

"I found out those boys in the islands like you real good—if you can throw that ball," he recalled. Though Cuba would remain a choice winter ball outlet, Satch would never go back.

•   •   •

Satchel Paige considered himself a star now, neck deep in the selective world of his own reality. That was when a reality he didn't need intruded on him and his world. As usual, it had to do with Mobile.

Satch had only fleetingly returned to his hometown since he went away with Alex Herman. While he had sporadically sent money home to Lula, not once did he reach out for his immediate family. Instead, whatever idle months he had were spent in the closest thing he had to a real home base—at his grandmother's tumbledown house just outside of Birmingham. It was she who had given permission for Satch to play there when Bill Gatewood had come to sign him.

This exile could be partially explained by a migrant life lived out of a suitcase. Then, in 1928, Satch found a much more convincing reason to stay away from Mobile. Finally bracing himself for a trip back home, he believed for all the world that this homecoming would be a deliriously satisfying event, Caesar come home from the Gallic Wars. But, like Caesar, he was betrayed on his own streets.

Satch, playing the part to the extreme, did not foresee his ides, nor the seamy ironies that could put men like him in his place. He drove home in his shiny red roadster, looking as fly as a man in a blue suit, straw hat, and spats could look. *Too* fly. Tooling down the highway, he was in clear sight of the Alabama State Highway Patrol—who took one look at him and believed he just had to be a miscreant sitting atop stolen wheels. As his name was meaningless to them, they took him in and held him in the Mobile county jail. He was not released until the following day.

"They took his car and his rings," recalled Palestine Paige Caldwell. "They figured he must've stolen everything. They thought he was crazy when he told 'em he was a ballplayer, just laughed at him. My Lord, he had to call someone up in Chicago, at the *Defender*, to vouch for him, before they'd give everything back and let my brother go."

Go he did. Satch's old buddy, Wilbur Hines, answered the phone that day and heard Satch pleading to find some way to get him out of the can. Wilbur suggested calling the *Defender*. When Satch was sprung, Hines recalled a man "so bitter" about his treatment in his own hometown that "he stayed away for years after that."

Eleven years, to be exact. During that time, if the thought arose that he was a long way from home, Satchel Paige taught himself not to care.

•   •   •

Tottering since the mid-1920s, black baseball was in trouble after the coming of the Great Depression. The once haughty Negro National League felt the ax on its neck right away, not that it was unexpected. Though still technically extant, and still technically in competition with the equally terminal Eastern Colored League (which disbanded after 1928, resurfaced as the Negro American League the following year, then folded for good in 1932), no Negro World Series had been played since 1927, and the NNL was as close to dead as was its former leader, Rube Foster.

Foster's dreams of a racially pure blackball had taken its cruelest blow in 1926, when the American Giants were sold to white businessman Robert Cole. At the same time, Foster's once Godfather-like control of the Midwest had been encroached upon by the latest behind-the-scenes force in blackball—and not one in the Foster but rather the Nat Strong mold. This was Abe Saperstein, an enterprising young promoter who saw black athletics as a novelty.

Saperstein had the same desire as Foster and Nat Strong to see blackball thrive, but not as an analogue of the white game; rather, by turning up the contrast between black and white, by moving the races further toward polar ends, Saperstein saw blacks in sports much as Hollywood and Broadway producers saw blacks in show biz—basically as funny and outrageous people, bestial but benign.

Saperstein's entire mien could be determined from his major property, the Harlem Globetrotters. Created in 1926, not in Harlem but in Chicago, they were a minstrel show in the guise of a basketball team; while magnificent athletes, their attraction was that they were not permitted to be merely athletes but rather most whites' conception of Negroes. Some were pop-eyed and loud, some sleepy-eyed and shuffling, and each had a specified talent, be it dribbling between his legs or holding the ball aloft in a massive hand. Only then, after displaying their wares, could they shoot the ball, which was expected to go into the hoop every time, much the way the players were metaphorically jumping through hoops. For years, as Saperstein took his team trotting literally around the globe, this was the only way much of the world would be introduced to African-Americans.

Saperstein did none of this out of malice, only mainstream entertainment values. Indeed, J. L. Wilkinson, the white man who owned the Kansas City Monarchs and who was considered a great friend of blackball, was also a great friend of Abe Saperstein's, and his mentor. Wilkinson, who originated the "Globetrotter" concept with a baseball/vaudeville team called the All Nations in 1912 (they didn't travel to all nations, but employed blacks, whites, Cubans, American Indians, Mexicans, Asians, and even a woman, who was called "Carrie Nation"), used his own gain in influence to book the Globetrotters around the Midwest. This helped Saperstein gain a foothold in and eventually capture the Chicago territory.

By the late 1920s, Saperstein had also gained an ownership interest in several colored baseball teams, and some name ballplayers, such as Goose Tatum, Piper Davis, and the Monarchs' Ted Strong, played on the Globetrotters during the winter; in time, Saperstein also instituted a Globetrotter baseball team, as well as teams he named the Zulus and the Ethiopian Clowns. The Zulus would play in grass skirts, the Clowns in red noses and, appropriately, *whiteface.*

For black teams stripped of the credibility of a league, the stripping of their dignity was the price to pay if it meant a team could survive as a barnstorming unit. Once, many teams had split into two squads, one for league games and another just to tour. Now it was hard enough to keep one team going. This was a death knell to many Southern Negro teams, since by Jim Crow laws there could be no competition with or against whites. Satchel Paige had taken the Birmingham Black Barons to their apogee, but that merely meant he had overrun the team's ability to keep paying him. At four bits a ticket, Satch could still pack Rickwood Field against any team, but now there weren't enough teams that could stay in business.

The American South as a whole was going dark, not to be taken off Tobacco Road until the postwar economic boom; for blacks, it would never again be resurrected as a self-sufficient sports combine. The black baseball action, which had been drifting northward for some time, now gave the urban clubs leverage to keep their heads slightly above water—and every one of them craved Satchel Paige.

The '30 season was the last year that a full schedule was played in the Negro National League. In 1931, the NNL would go from eight teams to six. In 1932, it would be gone. In Birmingham, meanwhile, R. T. Jackson continued his shuffleboarding with Satch. In the early spring Jackson leased him to a Northern team, the Baltimore Black Sox of the soon-to-be-defunct American Negro League.

Satch's attachment to this team was so tenuous that in recalling it he got nearly every fact about his stay there wrong—placing it *after* the '30 season, when he said he was sold to the Black Sox not by the Black Barons but by the Memphis Elite Giants, for whom he would play briefly in 1931. In fact, Satch maintained that he didn't actually play *in* Baltimore at all, or anywhere near it, but rather out on the road on a Black Sox barnstorming gig with a big league all-star team he said was led by Babe Ruth—a team that never existed.

But if Satch had trouble remembering the details of Baltimore, it may have been that he didn't care to remember. When he got there, he found himself an outsider, his name not the grabber he thought it would be in the Northeast. The Black Sox, who had won the ANL title the year before, were a solid and set team led by the bowlegged third baseman Jud "Boojum" Wilson. On a roster of mostly Northern blacks, Satch was a different cat—not only an outsider but kind of a hick, with an attitude to boot. And he was not alone. Similarly off-put was another jumper from the NNL, Alabama-born slugger Mule Suttles.

The Black Sox had reason for their arrogance. Together with Nat Strong's Lincoln Giants of New York, they played the first Negro game in Yankee Stadium. With the club owned by a white man—a saloon owner named George Rossiter—many players got a vicarious high hanging around Rossiter's tavern in the neighborhood where Babe Ruth was born. Satch, meanwhile, headed right for the other side of Baltimore, downtown, to the grimy and overheated environs of the Woodside Hotel.

Dick Powell, who decades later would own a Negro league team in Baltimore, was born in the shadow of the Woodside. As a young man back then, his own tastes drew him to the heaving excitement around the place. "There was the Woodside and the Smith," he said, "and virtually all the big-time show people as well as the black ballplayers who came into town to play the Black Sox stayed in them. Florence Mills used to stay at the Smith, and Count Basie used to rehearse in the basement of the Woodside.

"This was the area in which the lively girls were, let's say, the ladies of the evening. And Satch, he would come around and he'd be shootin' the bull with everyone. He'd have his Cadillac with a canoe on top of it, 'cause he liked to go hunt and fish. He'd stand in front of the hotel and he'd keep you laughin' for hours. Satch was a likable fella, a damn good what people like to call a raconteur—what we called a damn good liar!"

Always, these parts of town would be Satch's womb. Happy there, he was miserable at the ballpark. Chastened by the idea that he was a regional star not ready for prime time in Baltimore, Philly, and New York, he counted the days until he was ready to jump. What bugged him most, according to Dick Powell, who saw many Black Sox games, was his status—set in cement by player-manager Frank Warfield—as the club's number two pitcher.

"The star of the team was [pitcher] Lamon Yokeley," Powell recalled, "and Satch didn't do as well as perhaps he could have, because at that time they played two games when they played; it was customary to play a doubleheader. And he would go second. Yokeley went first.

"I saw him pitch, and the people liked his style. He'd get that leg way up in the air. But Yokeley overshadowed him and that perhaps more than anything prompted him to want to leave. I think even as a young fella he had that type of ego where he wanted to be the star of the show. So I don't think Satch stayed there three months. He got lonely and wasn't happy."

If some Black Sox players cold-shouldered him, relations between the players in general hardly made for camaraderie. The previous winter, two Sox infielders, shortstop Dick Lundy and third baseman Oliver Marcelle, had also played in Cuba and got into a huge fight during a poker game—which ended when Lundy, obviously a man with a hearty appetite, *bit off Marcelle's nose.* George Rossiter was also anguishing. Losing money in gushes, he would sell the team in 1932 to a man Dick Powell called a "cheapskate." By 1935, it folded.

Satch didn't wait for the team to crumble. He pitched the nightcap of doubleheaders on April 23 and May 5, beating the Chicago Cubans and the Hilldale club of Darby, Pennsylvania. On June 13, he blanked the Hilldales 14–0, a four-hit, eight-strikeout gem. On June 19 he fell to the Lincoln Giants 7–5. Then, without a word, he and Mule Suttles were gone, Suttles back to the St. Louis Stars, Satch back to Birmingham.

The abrogation of the Baltimore deal cost R. T. Jackson, but not for long. While he looked to expedite another shuffle, Satch conducted business as usual. On July 15, Satch beat Detroit with a 2–1 four-hitter. A week later, he threw a monster game against St. Louis, a 4–0 four-hitter in which not one Stars player reached second base.

Even decades later, that game always seemed to have happened only yesterday in the mind of an elderly Jimmie Crutchfield, who shortly before his death at age eighty could still clearly see Satch pumping all those fastballs by the Stars' big hitters. Another reason Crutchfield remembered that game so well is that it was the first one he played in his sixteen-year Negro league career. "My first game," he said, shaking his head in wonderment over sixty years later at the kindly fates that put him in the field behind Satchel Paige on that day. Just eighteen, Crutchfield, a wee blasting cap of a man, was in center field against St. Louis.

"They were the powerhouse team of the league . . . Cool Papa, Mule, Willie Wells," he said, "and Satch shut 'em out. Threw that fastball right by 'em, *whoom, whoom, whoom.* And I got three hits that day off Ted Trent, I won the game with a home run. Hit it between Cool Papa and the right fielder, and they said it had to be hit pretty hard and I had to be pretty fast to get a ball past Cool Papa Bell and then beat his throw in. I *was* pretty fast. I could move."

Crutchfield had never met Satch until that day. Yet he felt he knew him, through Big Bill Gatewood, who had settled in Crutch's hometown of Moberly, Missouri. When he ran into the old Black Barons manager, "all he would talk about was Satchel, Satchel, Satchel. Satch was the man. In fact, I didn't even know his full name and nobody called him Leroy. He was 'Mister Satchel.' "

Satch followed up his gem against St. Louis by beating the American Giants 5–4 on August 4. Six days later he tamed St. Louis again by an 8–6 score, following that with a 6–5 nod over the American Giants before being raked over by Detroit 7–2 on August 27— a game that had the *Chicago Defender* punning in its lead of the game story that "Leroy (Satchel) Paige proved a mere brief case."

Weeks before, on August 9, the *Defender* carried an item that had Satch "signaling his intention to return to Baltimore"—which, given that very strained union, must have given both Satch and George Rossiter a good laugh. In truth, R. T. Jackson had now found further mercenary use for his top banana—not in Baltimore but in Chicago, with the storied American Giants.

While the Giants were making a belated run at the second-half NNL title, the club had a more pressing need for Satch than their pursuits in the anemic league they had begat. They were about to

play a home-and-home series against the Houston Black Buf-
faloes—a very good and highly publicized team out of the Texas-
Oklahoma League—and these games would be the Giants' biggest
draws of the year. More than up to the task, Satch beat the Buf-
faloes and his old Black Baron teammate Lefty Pipkin with a 4–3,
nine-strikeout game on September 12, though in the September
29 game in Houston he was yanked out of a game the American Giants eventually lost 3–2.

Returning to Birmingham, Satch looked up and saw that there
were practically no Black Barons anymore, the Depression cashing
them in along with most of the Negro leagues that year. R. T. Jackson was about to sell off the club, and fairly typical of the instability
of the era was the plight of another Black Baron, pitcher Sug Cornelius, who came home to Birmingham after the following season
and found his money was looted by the new owners. "And I've
never been able to catch up with those guys," said Cornelius many
years later.

•   •   •

The winter of 1930–31 was a critical interlude in the history of
Negro ball. To take stock of the game at that time was to see a slow
death of the noble cause begun with Fleet Walker and the Cuban
Giants. With organized leagues moribund, the players felt no different than usual having to nightcrawl on wheezing buses, pass the
hat at ballparks, even sleep on the concrete grandstand between
games. These were men who rarely if ever were cut in on the real
money of blackball anyway, and were by now numbed to all of the
degradations. A hundred or so years later, one longtime Negro
league player, Ted Page, looked back with the alloy of pride and
pain that only he and his brethren could possibly understand.

"We'd ride all night, but that doesn't really explain the problems we had," Page said. "We'd ride all night. So what? A lot of people ride all night. But you can't gather the problems we had, how
tough it was. But to us it wasn't tough. It was part of our life."

Some were even idealistic in the face of despair. "When you're
doing something that you love to do, there's nothing lousy about
it," waxed Jimmie Crutchfield. "And to me, I thought it was the
first step toward going to the top of the world."

The difference now was that in the trickle-up economics of the
Depression, even the owners of these teams, black and white, were
feeling the pinch. And with white money leaving the game, it was
obvious that if Negro ball was to be saved, blacks were going to

have to do it themselves or perish trying—the very concept that Rube Foster had perished trying to effect.

But the trouble with reordering priorities was magnified by the schisms within the evolving black culture. A new generation of blacks—more Northern, more educated, more sensitive to their image vis-à-vis whites—approached the game with a self-conscious sense of presence. Rubbing off them, young black journalists were coursing through the newsrooms of the *Defender* and the *Courier*, some of them open activists and some among them who believed that Negro ball could and should go its own way, with no need for sympathy and largesse from the Man.

While this heightened black nationalism never made it into the dugout, many voices within the game were becoming fed up with the lingering elements of early Negro ball that to them weren't Gas House Gang as much as Nut House Gang, not fitting for a race of man. In 1927, the *Defender* ran a stern column rebuking unruly fans and accusing the players of inciting them with bush league histrionics. "Games are delayed by unnecessary squabbles on decisions," the editorial complained. "The whole team of the [American] Giants is getting the fans sore because of the storm and the fuss. . . . Proper police protection for the umpires . . . would soon stop the trouble."

Indeed, the unkempt nature of the black game, once thought to be so charmingly ingenuous, was now a matter of embarrassment. The *Defender* even got on the hometown American Giants' management for "the condition of the women's toilet," calling for it to be "cleaned up, enlarged and a woman attendant put there." And the dugouts, the paper noted, often looked more like a crowded boxcar, crawling with freeloading buddies of the players: "People who pay for their admission are just about tired of seeing the bench cluttered up with every Tom, Dick and Harry. . . . Looks real bad. Get rid of the extras. Half the time the home club can't find seats on the bench."

The etiquette of Negro ball was, in this view, as important as the games. Drinking, gambling, and swearing were sins. On blistering hot days, even shirtless fans would be upbraided—"men naked to the waist have no place at our baseball games." Pointedly, the black papers' society pages were now like an Easter Parade of fashionable dandies seen at the ballpark, as well as celebrities such as Lena Horne in attendance. The message was clear: blackball *was* black society.

Not that the ballplayers considered themselves society nabobs, yet neither did they consider themselves tragic figures. Never in their slogging from one hellhole to another did they bemoan what they were missing. The white envy was for owners, the notion of baseball as a symbol of political worthiness for the newspaper pundits. Vassals in much the same manner as the white ballplayers, there was a solidarity of a kind with the big leaguers. As well, seemingly *comforted* at times by the distance between their two orbits, there was even room in the great void for some bravura posturing.

"I never heard a Negro ballplayer in those days talk about playing in the major leagues," Dave Malarcher, Rube Foster's successor as manager of the American Giants, once insisted. "Because we always played them at the end of the season, on all-star teams, and we always beat 'em." Actually, the Negro leaguers won a good many of those games, maybe most, but they were nonetheless entitled to the "we won 'em all" fib—they needed that little fib.

And yet, as the 1930s began to unfold in a gray shroud, they needed something else. The black papers were replete with industrial league, post office league, and Sunday school league games; with the scores of lingering semipro associations. Erstwhile big league Negro leaguers challenged one another to an unofficial "World Series" by the week. The New York Black Yankees were outfitted with old surplus New York Yankees uniforms—proving that blacks could put their pants on the same as the greatest whites, or at least put on the same *pants.*

But what blackball lacked was a grand design to pull together all of the loose and tattered ends of this important netherworld. As it stood in 1931, the impetus for that design was going to have to come, for better and worse, from one more black Napoleon.

5

Feast of the Nimrods

In their religion they are so uneven,
That each man goes his own byway to heaven.

—Daniel Defoe,
The True-Born Englishman

In the spring of 1931, Satchel Paige's quandary was that no team in Negro ball could easily afford him. One owner who thought he could was Tom Wilson of the Nashville Elite Giants, a team that had been kicking around for years in the Negro Southern League and was now moving into the comatose Negro National League.

Wilson's money seemed Depression-proof. A black businessman who had come to Nashville from Atlanta in the 1920s, his largest profit came from the numbers racket in Nashville that burgeoned as a quick-fix solution to hopelessness—mostly among the black jobless who could least withstand the infinite odds against hitting the number. Not the least bit troubled by this moral incongruity, the jumbo-sized Wilson lived it up on his profits. Even in his fifties he was a hound from the get-go, hoarding women by the gross, and this situation did not change when he began living a common-law marriage with an eighteen-year-old schoolgirl.

But while Wilson was doing all he could to keep the Elite Giants (in Negro ball parlance, teams with this nickname pronounced the word "E-LIGHT") afloat, all the racket money in black America wasn't sufficient to stem the death of so many other black clubs in the South. Just after the season began, Wilson had scant alternative but to move the team, and it wound up in Cleveland, as the Cleveland Cubs. Giving it a go here, Wilson peeled dollar bills from his bankroll and signed a number of useful players late of the (temporarily) defunct Birmingham Black Barons, not incidentally trying to keep Satch content by the addition of ex-teammates Nish Williams, Lefty Pipkin, and Satch's main man, Bill Perkins. But no matter the name and the roster, Wilson's ship went down by season's end. Awash in red ink, he would move back to Nashville and return to the NSL for that league's final season in 1932.

Yet, once again, with his fine-tuned ability to keep the cruel Fates at bay, Satch wouldn't be there for the final breaths of the Giants, though he did turn in a few mostly forgettable starts for the Cubs. In one, a game the Cubs managed to win despite him on May 24, the *Defender* noted that the Chicago American Giants "sent Satchel Paige to the showers with a five run attack in the fourth inning." On June 13 he was again doused in a 5–2 loss to the Louisville White Sox. Even pitching well was no guarantee—that was made evident by two almost identical 1–0 losses to the Detroit Stars. In the latter, Satch and Willie Powell matched zeroes all game, but Satch cracked first, giving up a long homer to Turkey Stearns.

All in all, Nashville/Cleveland/Nashville was a very bumpy ride, and for Satch it was a painful education of the heart. For the first time in his life, he met a woman whom he actually wanted to stay with once the sun came up. Unfortunately, the woman was Tom Wilson's Lolita-like live-in. Tall, striking, and naive, Bertha Wilson may have had a schoolgirl's crush on a famous ballplayer, and Satch may have merely seen an opening into something good. But, in time, it grew to much more for both. For several years after Satch left Tom Wilson, he kept a residence in Nashville, gearing his winter meanderings to run through the city, if only for a day or two.

If Tom Wilson knew anything of this, he either didn't let on or didn't care; and if he did he would have at least known what kept Bertha mollified during his own philandering. As for Bertha, she apparently grew to believe that Satch needed her.

Throughout the next few years, wherever his travels took him, he would gather up the nerve to confront his inner yearnings and try to express them in letters sent regularly to her. Though Satch had only crude grammatical and writing skills, these epistles came dripping with such emotion that Bertha would tie them in neat bundles and preserve them. Much later, long after Tom Wilson's death, a *Nashville Tennessean* writer, Richard Schweid, came to ask Bertha about Negro ball in old Nashville. Schweid was startled when Bertha, then in her seventies, digressed and with much sentimentality spoke of the cherished private times she shared with Satch. She even mentioned those heavily emotional missives, though she would not reveal the exact contents of them, nor that of the relationship. To do that, it was apparent, would have been to soil what for her was sacred.

Clearly, Bertha Wilson saw a very different Satchel Paige than did almost all others. Serving him tea and drinking in his attention, she could sense Satch's vulnerable side, see and feel his pain. He was a needy man, far more so than he would ever let on himself, and when Bertha saw him in this light it was hard for her to keep her hands off him; indeed, it was only through such eyes that Bertha could have described a man of Satchel Paige's looks as "a handsome man" and "a good looker," as she did to Schweid. The only possible explanation for that was that love surely does blind.

It did not, however, bind. Instead of solidifying Satch's place in Nashville, this strange love affair may have driven him away from yet another town. Not that Satch had a problem with the morality of bedding a married woman—very early on, that had ceased to be a problem. Rather, he may have simply felt things getting too complicated in this weird triangle, or maybe it was that it was tying him down at a time when he should be spreading himself among other lucky ladies across the land. In any case, there was just too much of him to give it up to one woman—yet—and especially to one married woman. Besides, amoral as he was, if he was sneaking around behind Tom Wilson's back, he might have had a hard time looking the old man in the eye. Who needed that kind of pressure?

Providentially, one avenue of egress promised to—if not solve— at least distance this sticky wicket. It ran to Pittsburgh and to people who managed to make Tom Wilson look saintly.

● ● ●

Blackball's primal innocence ended along that same avenue. Whereas the biggest deceit of the early days was that black men masqueraded as Cubans, encountering Negro ball in Pittsburgh in the early 1930s was more like entering the gates of the Black Babylon. This was a realm that almost everyone in baseball—black and white—knew would have to fall someday, crushed under its own ungainly weight. But those same people also recognized that, for now, what happened there was yet another compact with the devil that had to be made.

Satchel Paige would not only step into the epicenter of all that was proud and profane about Negro ball, he would be a major player in the drama. His entrance came in late June of 1931 when, languishing in Cleveland, he received an offer from the Crawford Colored Giants, an independent club owned by the indomitable William A. "Gus" Greenlee. Already loved, feared, and never ignored, Greenlee was a man of many nicknames, each befitting his mythic dimensions, but the one appellation he always longed for he would never obtain—that of a man of legitimacy.

Gus Greenlee's offer to Satch was for $250 a month, the return for which would be no less enormous than Colonel Ruppert's for buying Babe Ruth from the Boston Red Sox for small change. For Gus Greenlee it would be his best chance at validation; to his credit, he realized this as soon as he discovered the credibilizing powers of Negro baseball. While he was one of the most powerful underworld figures in Pittsburgh, Greenlee was wise enough to feel the political/cultural rumble of people like Satchel Paige.

Greenlee had put in years learning the lengths of power attainable in the ghetto. Though only just into his thirties, he had small, tired eyes embedded in dunes of larded flesh; yet they could snap into gear, tearing through what they saw, constantly sizing up all before him as friend or foe. Plainly, those eyes had seen too much, and his body bore the effects of a disdain for tomorrow. Six foot three and wide as a Frigidaire, Greenlee almost always had a big Havana cigar stuck in his mouth. Physically imposing, even frightening when he wanted to be, Gus preferred to come off as no more than a big lug. Because of a gap between his front teeth, when he smiled he seemed to take on a goofy approachability, and he often found that a laugh could get more out of people than a scowl.

But Gus considered himself above the gutter, by blood as much as by disposition. His mother was the daughter of a white man in Marion, North Carolina, and with his red hair and caramel skin Gus assumed that he was not at all a commoner of his race—"Big Red," some called him, to his delight. Gus not only had great skin, he had great bloodlines. Two of his brothers became doctors, another a lawyer, and Gus himself reckoned he could have gone down any glorious path had he not dropped out of college and decided to rough it—hopping a boxcar to Pittsburgh, he shined shoes, was a fireman, and drove a cab. Gus loved the action; when he went to war he fought at St. Mihiel and got his leg shot up, but he was no less active when he got back stateside.

"Gasoline Gus" was the nickname then, won through hard labor bootlegging booze around Pittsburgh and Homestead in his cab. Like Satchel Paige, Gasoline Gus was attracted to the inseam of these rough towns, cushioned by whores, gambling, booze, and fops with ice on every finger. When he had enough dough he opened a speakeasy called the Paramount Club on Wylie Avenue on the "Hill." Here, Greenlee imported big bands and drew an interracial crowd, but when white women were seen consorting with black men, the city closed the place down. That only told Gus he needed political clout, and he got it when he chose the right side during Pittsburgh's crusades, its bloody gang wars in the late 1920s.

As a minor underworld lackey, Gus's choice was between the invasion of Lucky Luciano's Chicago mob looking to gain control of the town's business and the local crowd of pimps and gamblers connected to Pittsburgh's crooked politicians. Big Gus and his henchman, Woogie Harris, stood with the homeboys, even hijacking beer trucks headed for Chicago. When the Chicago boys eventually were beaten and headed home, Gus was suddenly assured that he could open *two* clubs on Wylie, the Sunset Cafe and the Crawford Grille, with a big piece of the gambling and numbers action under his roofs as a reward for his loyalty. Gus now had important friends, mainly ward healers who determined who got what and how much. As long as Gus paid his protection money, he and Woogie were safe to carve into the city's $2 million a year numbers business.

Indeed, so intertwined were politics and the underworld in the fabric of inner-city Pittsburgh that mayors and councilmen and even state senators came and went without a thought that by sharing in pimping and common racketeering they were doing anything remiss. Allegheny County Senator James Coyne, in fact, *owned* one betting parlor—which sat across the street from a police station. By the 1930s, one of Coyne's closest goodfellas was Art Rooney, the owner of the NFL Pittsburgh Steelers—and a ward chairman who was said to run the numbers racket on the north-side. Another was Gasoline Gus Greenlee.

From Art Rooney's example Gus Greenlee learned about the power of largesse and of sport. With his refined tastes, Gus hated the notion of gang wars, and he was relieved that things could go down on the Hill with such quiescence. Not that a little muscle wasn't needed once in a while to protect one's turf. Like musk, pungent stories always trailed Greenlee about enemies seen one day and not again thereafter. Gus often told these stories himself, for effect, and found that they were a preventive strike. By 1931, they were calling Gus "Mr. Big," which Gus took to mean big-hearted.

Gus never turned his back on the good people of the Hill, at least those who aggrandized him. If they were in debt to him, he had a moral debt to them. Big as an office building anyway, Gus appropriately made himself into a bank. When the Steel City Bank went under, taking from blacks on the Hill their meager savings, Gus and Woogie loaned money by the thousands, never with any collateral. Seeing the *Pittsburgh Courier* on the edge of bankruptcy, and knowing how vital it was to the black identity, Gus's bankroll saved it.

As it was, nearly everyone who was anyone in town would come to see Gus, his three-story Crawford Grille truly the Café Américain of Pittsburgh, an oasis of amorality in the neutral zone between black and white hustling. Like the Woodside and the Smith hotels in Baltimore, the Grille was the magnet for the hip and the wormy. They would come to hear Duke Ellington, lay bets, pay homage to Big Gus, get snockered, and forget all about what sunrise meant outside on the Hill. Gus's whole life was a blinder; when some game-hunting buddies returned after a safari, Gus feted them with a "Feast of the Nimrods," the dinner being bear meat. Outside, on the famished Hill, they made do with the aroma of bear chops wafting from the VIP Room.

● ● ●

Negro ball brought Gus Greenlee some of his biggest bear, yet his original interests in the sport stemmed from ulterior motives. Greenlee had had a small hand in keeping small-time baseball solvent in the 1920s, and he warmed to the possibilities of the game. When one sandlot team sponsored by the Crawford Bath House needed money to keep playing, Gus made sure they had it. Given life, the Crawford Colored Giants—whom everyone called the Crawfords—became a proving gound for young black ballplayers in the Pittsburgh ghetto, including a burly teenager who worked in the steel mills, Josh Gibson. A small sensation, the Craws were by the end of the decade crimping the attention paid to the crosstown Homestead Grays, one of the most successful Negro league teams.

Gus Greenlee, of course, knew all about the Grays and its owner, the estimable Cumberland Posey, and admired him greatly as a black mover. But Posey would soon get so under his skin that Gus would obsess about beating Posey at his own game. This occurred after the Crawfords, again in fiscal crisis, petitioned Big Daddy Gus in 1930. This time, Gus bought the team outright—mainly so he could emblazon their uniform shirts with the name of Jim Coyne during Coyne's campaign for county commissioner. When Gus then familiarized himself with the team, he learned of the head-lock that Cum Posey had on the sport, not only in Pittsburgh but throughout Negro ball.

Indeed, Rube Foster seemed like a mole mouse next to the im-possibly vain and ruthless Posey. *No one* made Posey flinch, and if Greenlee got off on profiting from his race without identifying with it, Posey was born to do it. His father was a captain of industry in Pittsburgh, possibly the city's wealthiest black man, and his son's life read like an Ivy League résumé. His entry eased by his hazel complexion and straight hair, Cum Posey was an athlete and scholar at Holy Ghost College (now Duquesne University) and Penn State, then a magnificent semipro basketball player and coach, then a magnificent outfielder, captain, and manager with the Grays in the 1910s and 1920s—"the outstanding athlete of the Negro race," he was called by the *Pittsburgh Courier*, of which his father was once president; and given the evolving snobbery of many Northern-generation blacks, the title fit him.

When Posey bought the Grays in the early 1920s, he made the team his fiefdom. He also made it damn near unbeatable. Beating the bushes, the Grays took on all comers, including an American League all-star team promoted by Connie Mack's son. For that se-ries, Posey did what he usually did when he wanted good players—in the Negro ball tradition, he stole them from other teams. Luring the great outfielder–first baseman Oscar Charleston to jump the Hilldale club, Posey later collected Cool Papa Bell, Judy Johnson, Willie Foster (Rube's younger brother), and the venera-ble pitcher Smokey Joe Williams. With them, the Grays became the top team in black sports, running off winning streaks that reached upward past thirty and forty a year against everyone from the Kansas City Monarchs to the Carnegie Elks Club.

Too busy victimizing other black teams, except for a brief time

in the American Negro League in 1929 Posey would not join any of
their rinky-dink circuits. He viewed blackball as de Gaulle did
France—Cum Posey *was* blackball. As with Foster in Chicago, he
came to dominate the entire black sports scene in Pittsburgh.
Posey booked games for his and other clubs, taking a cut of the
gate. He pushed the Grays in his own *Courier* column. He struck an
arrangement with the Pittsburgh Pirates to use Forbes Field for
Grays games.

Posey was so entrenched in power and *hauteur* that not even Gus
Greenlee fazed him. While Gus figured the two of them could be
brothers under the skin, allied in promoting baseball for the common good in Pittsburgh, Posey reeled at the thought. To him,
Greenlee was the antithesis of the black Renaissance Man, a viper,
a slug, all that was wrong with the race—and something less than a
baseball man, since Gus's primary concern with the Craws was to
route his numbers money into a legit cover. While Posey showed
his independence from whites by acting as white as he could,
Greenlee showed his by getting down with the homeys whose
money he was living off of.

And yet, while they were opposites on the surface, they were in
fact very much alike. From polar ends, each one closed in on whatever germ of power was open to him, blind to his hypocrisies.
While Gus's were evident, Posey's meticulously cultivated bluenose
image—he allowed no swearing and no gambling in his domain,
not even card games in the locker room—was compromised by the
adulterous debauchery he practiced in the cities the Grays visited.

Perhaps because they knew how alike they were, each hated the
other for what he was. At first, they got on amicably. With the
Craws emerging as a competing but kindred attraction, Gus even
convinced Posey of the mutual benefit this could engender. At
Gus's urging, the two teams finally played each other, in the summer of 1930. The natural rivalry drew over 20,000 black fans to
Forbes Field, all but a few of whom figured—and laid bets—that
the Craws would be easy meat for the Grays of Josh Gibson and
Cool Papa Bell. Yet the Craws shocked the Hill by making the game
uncomfortably close for Cum Posey in a 2–0 loss.

Now Gus began to obsess. He immediately turned the Crawfords
into a full-blown for-profit operation, charging admission at its
Bedford Avenue home, Ammon Field. Next, he began construc-
tion on a new stadium down the block—Greenlee Field—to be
owned and operated by the team. Then he booked a schedule for

1931 against the same kind of eclectic opponents that made Posey so rich, and purchased two seven-passenger Lincoln Town Cars to ferry the players about. Finally, he went shopping, wheedling the defections of some quality Negro league talent. Greenlee, who had learned enough about baseball by now, did this with a purpose. Several of the new Crawfords—Jimmie Crutchfield, Sam Streeter, Bill Perkins—had a common thread: they had all played and been tight with the man Gus really craved. That was Satchel Paige.

The problem, as Gus would find out all too well, was that Satchel Paige was about as easy to pin down as a speck of dust. Greenlee's messengers, assigned to stalk Satch out in the hinterlands, learned that he wouldn't show up at the park until just before the game began and he was gone from the park and out into the hazy landscape before they could intercept him.

Greenlee had to open the '31 season without his big intended weapon, and the Craws lost their second meeting with the Grays 9–0. But Gus eventually did get his man, out in Cleveland. Satch signed for $250 a month and made it to Pittsburgh in time for the third clash with the Grays, on August 6, though the Craws' manager, Bobby Williams, started the team's veteran pitcher Harry Kincannon in the game.

There were fewer people at Forbes Field for this one, the novelty and the Craws' threat having faded. But, surprisingly, the Craws surged to a lead, scoring three in each of the first two innings off of Ted Radcliffe, who had jumped to the Grays that season. The Craws led 6–2, then added two more in the fourth. But then the Grays awakened and scored five in their half of the fourth, cutting the lead to 8–7 and chasing Kincannon. In relief now came Satchel Paige in his Steel City debut.

In recalling the arrival of this moment in his autobiography, Satch wove this tale: "As soon as Gus heard I was in [town], he came busting over. '[The Grays are] the best there is, Satch. You beat them and you're number one.' I just nodded. . . . I went out to warm up. This was Pittsburgh's first look at me, but I didn't feel very nervous. I was young and I could throw like nobody else.

"When I kicked up my foot and threw that first one, the crowd screamed. . . . I kept kicking that foot up in the sky, twisting like a pretzel, pausing, and throwing."

He also said, "I beat the Grays without any trouble and struck out sixteen to boot," and while he actually had six strikeouts in his five innings, the exaggeration could be excused; walking not one good bread and Los Angeles—where most of the games would be played—offered a good gig at a time when all players could use one. The growing cosmopolitan terrain of southern California had cultivated a nice little hornets' nest of competition and heavy betting action overseen by Joe Pirrone, the West Coast equivalent of Abel Linares, Nat Strong, and Abe Saperstein. Pirrone had for years been staging a schedule of composite teams, with big leaguers sprinkled among minor league, semipro, and even high school players in a six-team league running through the fall and early winter. Several years before he had opened up the CWL to blacks—but not to integration; the blacks had to stay separate but equal.

In fact, they were more than equal this time, and if Pirrone didn't realize this when he made the schedule, he did to his consternation once the season began. Pirrone liked to collect most of the better white players for his own team, but few quality big leaguers came out and nearly all the ones who did—Babe Herman, Wally Berger, Fred Haney, Alex Gaston—dropped out along the way once Tom Wilson's team began to dominate.

Thus, the league was lean meat for the cream of Negro ball. In Satch's first game, on October 24, he beat the Pirrone All-Stars 8–1, allowing five hits and fanning eleven while hardly breathing hard. Saving his high heat for the most viable big leaguer, he struck out Babe Herman all four times he came to bat. Wilson's Giants didn't lose a game in taking the first-half title; then, beginning the second half, Satch effortlessly ran the ball past the water-thin Pirrones, picking up a 3–0 three-hit win and striking out fifteen. Such was the blacks' domination that no playoff game was held; the conclusion was foregone.

The rancid irony of these games, played before large crowds that included movie stars such as George Raft and Talullah Bankhead, was that they did nothing to eradicate the deadly burlesquing of blacks among Hollywood types; locked into a denial pathology of their own, liberal movie-makers would revere the New Deal of Franklin Delano Roosevelt and go on depicting the black nation as an Aunt Jemima–hood. They too betrayed men like Satchel Paige.

Satch himself was ambivalent about facing sclerotic big leaguers who took these exhibitions with a yawning indifference. On the one hand, his ego was fed by mowing them down one after another—and by the fact that, against them, *he* was the show. He would recall, fairly bursting, that Sam Agnew, an old-timer who batter, Satch's performance was, in the prose of the *Courier,* "masterful and sensational." And when the Craws rallied for three in the sixth against Chippy Britt, he was credited with the win in the 11–7 game. All the while, remembered the Craws' center fielder Harold Tinker, the Grays "hardly hit a foul ball off Satchel. . . . He was throwin' nothing but aspirin tablets."

For longtime Crawford players, who had lived in the long Gray shadow, the victory meant they could now die happy. But for Gus Greenlee, it was just the beginning. Cum Posey was preparing to start his own circuit in 1932, the East-West League, and Gus at once petitioned for membership. But instead of Gus's hoped-for alliance with the Grays, the crustaceous Posey imposed conditions that amounted to extortion—*Posey* would decide who would play for the Crawfords, when they played, and who they played. And Cum's brother Seward would have to be the Craws' *manager.*

By these terms, Posey meant to affront Greenlee and drive away the menace he represented. And while it did drive off Gus, who dropped his petition and played the Craws as an independent, he did not go away meekly. Now the battle was joined—for the good of Pittsburgh and for all of black baseball. With Satchel Paige in hand—at least for the moment—Gus Greenlee stoutly believed he already had won the opening salvo.

• • •

Satch continued to give Greenlee needed exposure in the black media. Where once the Crawfords rarely made the pages of even the hometown *Courier,* whenever he took the mound the game was instant news. On August 20, for example, a five-paragraph story covered the Craws-Hilldales game in Darby—a 3–1 Hilldales victory in which "Phil Cockrell outpitched Satchell Paige . . . in a real pitchers' battle," a two-run triple by Rap Dixon doing in Satch.

But bigger publicity awaited Satch after the season. In September, word came in the *Defender* that Tom Wilson was assembling a Negro all-star team to play in the California Winter League, under the name of the Philadelphia Giants. Wilson, needing bankable names, had selected Willie Wells, Cool Papa Bell, Turkey Stearns, Biz Mackey, and his old confrere Satchel Paige, whom he called "the man who can throw a baseball harder than any other pitcher in the country."

Whether Satch felt he owed one to Wilson, or wanted to further expand his baseball borders, the fact was that Wilson was waving had once caught Walter "Big Train" Johnson with the Washington Senators, told him after one of the coast games, "When I was playing, I never saw so many fastballs as you threw."

Little wonder that, during one game, he was moved to do the old riff of calling in the outfield and pitching without them—with a one-run lead. His catcher, the Lincoln Giants' Larry Brown, couldn't believe it.

"Satch," Brown scolded him, "you the biggest fool I ever saw! Long as I been playin' I never saw nobody do that with a one-run lead!"

No matter to Satch. In many ways this was his first big league audition, and for those who had not observed his performances, he later recalled it by injecting the presence of no less than Babe Ruth and Hack Wilson—neither of whom had been within a thousand miles of L.A. at the time. The Babe, he conceded, hadn't hit against him in California. But he claimed Hack had, only to—natch—go down swinging.

But one thing Satch did get right was the plaintive truth contained within another of his whoppers—that he had struck out twenty-two in one of the Pirrone games.

"I never counted those twenty-two as my one-game record," he explained, "even though I hit twenty-two in other games, lots of times. But . . . I don't count exhibition games. I know some of the boys aren't in shape when I whiff them in those games."

The corollary of that was not lost on him. It would be a good long while before those games would do anything good for Satchel Paige.

•   •   •

When the winter league season was concluded, Satch went back east with Tom Wilson, who put him up at his house. This afforded Satch convenience in continuing his secret-or-not liaison with Bertha Wilson. At the same time, another woman occupied his thoughts. This was Janet Howard, a waitress at Gus Greenlee's Crawford Grille. Having blown almost every cent he had looking to buy love in small rooms in the pit of the night, his moments with Bertha Wilson and Janet Howard were unique. With Janet they were particularly so, in that while she was only nineteen she had the kind of attitude that could go jab for jab with Satch's. She was cool, sometimes icy, with a shyness that seemed to be calculated to ensnare men. But while she gave him all the right signals, she never pushed herself on him, which was maddening to him. Janet was not one for the short term; she was long run all the way. But Satch decided to keep her at arm's length, possibly while he tried to sort out things with Bertha Wilson. Bertha, however, seemed to hold *him* off. She was, after all, Tom Wilson's property, and they would in time legally marry.

If this was how love worked, Satch could not have been thrilled with the prospects. Still, nobody would be allowed to see his vulnerabilities. Comforting himself with silly chauvinist brio, he would write years after of Janet Howard's emergence that she "was all big eyes for me. I could tell that. And I just figured those big eyes was because I was such a fine-looking man. . . . What I didn't know was those eyes were trying to look at all of me at once, trying to spot a weak point so Janet could hook me."

Then, with the disclaimer out of the way, he came as close to unburdening his impregnable soul as he ever would.

"I'd learned you got to be mighty careful of love," he said. "Up to meeting Janet, I'd been wounded so many times by love I had to learn something. I'd learned to be careful."

6

Abode of
the Gods

The gods were of human proportion: they were created out of
the human spirit.

—Henry Miller,
The Colossus of Maroussi

Josh and I were such big guns on that [1932] club that Gus
Greenlee started advertising us instead of the Crawfords. He
sent out a bunch of posters saying, "Josh Gibson and Satchel
Paige, greatest battery in baseball—Josh Gibson guaranteed
to hit two home runs and Satchel Paige guaranteed to strike
out the first nine men."
  [But] even though he advertised both Josh and me, Gus
knew I was pulling the big crowds.
  When I was out there, there'd be a park full watching. But
when Josh was there and somebody else was pitching, there'd
be only about half or two-thirds as many.

—Satchel Paige,
Maybe I'll Pitch Forever

The battle royale of blackball began in the winter of 1931–32.
By then, Gus Greenlee had decided that if Cum Posey would not
play ball with him, Gus would just have to own the ball. After all, if
anyone in Pittsburgh had that right, it would have to be Big Red.
  Gus geared everything toward making the '32 season into Posey's

Armageddon; a man with no small thirst for revenge, Big Gus went right for Posey's jugular vein—Josh Gibson. Already owning Satchel Paige's contract, Greenlee probably had damp dreams starring Satch throwing bee balls into the mitt of the new behemoth of Negro ball. And the wonder of it was that all it would take to make the ready-to-open Greenlee Field the site of this jubilation was money, which was a mere bag of shells for Gus.

To get Josh now would, furthermore, *really* turn the knife inside Posey's intestines. Just turned twenty-one, Gibson was coming off a season in which his massive home runs were the talk of blackball. Talk had still not died down about the two meteorites he'd hit a week apart late in the '30 season—one at Forbes Field, one at Yankee Stadium; at around 450 feet each they may have been the longest balls ever hit in those meccas of baseball. The next year, in the Grays' 200-plus games, he was said to have hit seventy-five homers and bat over .600.

A six-foot-two, 220-pound mound of bituminous, Gibson's power seemed to emanate from the tension coiled within that immense body, but he was actually more like Henry Aaron than Babe Ruth. While his gammon-thick arms held his forty-ounce bat in a vise grip, it was his wrists that triggered his swing. Gibson was a canny man at the plate; rarely trying to pull an outside pitch, his swing was economical, a quick, savage slash that sent line drives screaming to all fields. And if he got under the ball even a little, he could lift it far into the clouds, frequently with one hand on a half swing.

An absolutely petrifying sight, especially for third basemen in the direct line of his swing, his bestial reputation never brought Gibson much security or self-worth—actually just the opposite; his ineffable talent proved a source of constant confusion and angst. For all his strength, Gibson was dogged by a feeling of powerlessness ever since his teenage wife died during childbirth in 1930. Every moon shot he hit made him wonder if he'd ever be able to hit another.

Negro leaguers hadn't yet learned that they could limit Gibson by playing with his head. He seemed simply too awesome to fool with. As such, Gibson was yin to Satchel Paige's yang—Satch up on a hill, all arms and legs, on the verge of flight; Josh, a fortress dug in the dirt, pulling the exploding ball from the sky. The madcap prince and the brooding warrior, they were compatible icons, and Gus Greenlee needed both of them.

For Gus, it was an easy heist—another $250 a month, another

mega-star in the bank. The fact that Cum Posey couldn't, or wouldn't, ante up the $100 a month more that would have matched Greenlee's offer was an implicit sign of trouble for Posey, one of many that would arise in 1932. Seeing how easy it was to pry away Gibson, Greenlee immediately robbed the Grays of Oscar Charleston, who became the Crawfords' player-manager, and Ted Radcliffe.

Moving hard on the PR front, Greenlee began the season by making the April 30 opening of Greenlee Field—the first completely black-owned stadium in the country, grounds and grandstands included—a saturnalia of self-adulation. Gus invited the mayor, the entire city council, and all the county commissioners. Gus himself was brought onto the field before the packed house of over 4,000 in a red convertible surrounded by a marching band. When *Courier* editor Robert Vann dedicated the stadium he led a standing ovation for Gus, who ambled to the mound in his all-white silk suit, tie, and shoes, and threw out the first pitch.

Satch then took the ball against the New York Black Yankees and made it a rumor, shutting them down through the eighth. But his counterpart, Jesse "Mountain" Hubbard, who was said to have regularly carried sandpaper in his back pocket to scuff the ball, matched him inning for inning. Then, in the top of the ninth, the Yanks' Ted Page—exploiting Satch's old bugaboo—beat out a bunt. Trying to make something happen against Paige, Page stole second and went to third after kicking the ball away from shortstop Chester Williams. Clint Thomas then bounced a high chopper just over Satch's upraised glove, and when he beat Williams's throw to first, Page came home with the game's first run. In the home ninth, Hubbard faced Josh Gibson with two outs and Josh crushed one to dead center that Thomas caught against the fence.

Satch would get even, and then some, beating the Black Yankees twice that season. The first time, on June 9 in Yankee Stadium, he struck out twelve in seven innings. But that paled beside the other game—Satchel Paige's first Negro league no-hitter, a 6–0 pearl on July 16 in Greenlee Field.

By then, Gus Greenlee was on top of the Hill, having done severe damage to a weakening Cumberland Posey—who had done damage to himself as well. Plagued by money woes from day one, Posey's East-West League went belly-up in June—a double blow for Posey, as he owned two clubs in the league, the other being the Detroit Wolves. Bucking the Depression, Posey resisted consolidating the Grays and Wolves, stubbornly holding on to the latter and squeezing the payroll all the more tighter. When the end came to the EWL, Gus Greenlee pounced, taking Cool Papa Bell, second baseman John Henry Russell, and pitcher Leroy Matlock from the Wolves. Greenlee, working the pocketbook with no end, had also sucked in another Gray, shortstop Jake Stephens, as well as Boojum Wilson from Baltimore, Jimmie Crutchfield from Indianapolis, Ted Page from New York, and Judy Johnson and Rap Dixon from the Hilldales.

With the Crawfords holding, for now, five future Hall of Famers, there could not have been much doubt who the true "Black Yankees" were now.

But with Gus Greenlee's spending going through the roof in his desire to show up Cum Posey, Gus was creating severe financial troubles for himself. He had sunk $100,000 into Greenlee Field, and would end up losing $50,000 in 1932; he never was able to show a profit. For now, though, he only saw Posey as the enemy— and the cagey Cum would save face when his Grays beat the Craws three out of four games in a challenge series in September, old Smokey Joe Williams beating Satch in the opener 13–10.

Still, it was Greenlee who was in position to dominate Negro ball. After a season in which the Craws took in more than $100,000 in paid admissions over 135 games (ninety-nine of them wins), the team also took five of seven games from a big league all-star team managed by Casey Stengel, then a Brooklyn Dodgers coach. In this series Satch finally did face a now-fading Hack Wilson, in a 10–2 victory highlighted by four hits by Josh Gibson and fifteen Paige strikeouts, though again the big league squad was jerry-built— while Satch had won twenty-three games in 1932, his opposite number was the New York Giants' Roy Parmelee, a man who was winless that season. In contests like these, it was almost too easy to pity the big leaguers. Almost.

•　•　•

At twenty-six, Satchel Paige was the single biggest name in Negro entertainment, on a par with Joe Louis and Satchmo Armstrong. As such, he was also a feeding trough for those around him. While Josh Gibson, who allegedly hit sixty-two homers in 1932, was getting more publicity in the black papers than he ever had, being yoked with Satch on Gus Greenlee's billboards let him dare to elevate his ego without having to fly it alone.

It was not a stretch for Satch to claim that he sold out ball-parks—big, major-league-sized ballparks—practically all by him-self; and in doing so he brought more and more white fans and white sportswriters to those parks. The Black Yankees, by example, rarely played in Yankee Stadium until Satch and his boys came through. After one such game in 1932, Damon Runyon, the great caricaturist of heroic small-timers, chose to lionize another Paige teammate—Ted Radcliffe, who caught Satch's 5–0 shutout in the first game of a doubleheader and then went out and pitched a 4–0 shutout in the nightcap. In his newspaper column the day after, Runyon wrote that it was worth the price of admission to see "Dou-ble Duty" Radcliffe pitch. He would remain Double Duty from then on, and it was a bankable monicker for him in the years to come.

Gus Greenlee, like R. T. Jackson before him, was also eager to capitalize on Satch's earning power. Over the whole of 1932, Satch pitched roughly once a week for the Craws, generally before the big crowds on Sundays; the rest of the week he was, in deals cut by Gus, pitching three-inning stints for semipro teams wherever the Craws were playing—taking with him Gus's placards with Josh Gib-son's name excised and patched to issue only the Satchel Paige nine-strikeout guarantee. Only because he was accompanied by one of Greenlee's lieutenants did he ever know where he was. But he did know the money was fabulous.

"If it hadn't been for Gus," he would recall, "I never could have kept all those offers to pitch straight. He was my agent, booking me around. . . . He was a sharp—a real one. He knew just how to book so I'd make plenty. . . . I pitched in about every town you can think of. And I was getting as much as five hundred a game for some of those jobs."

Not incidentally, only Satch and Gus were profiting much among the Crawfords, and the pampering of Satch became a touchy subject among the other players. While no one said a word out loud, the *Courier*—which, like the *Defender*, was a marvelously chaotic bulletin board of diverse, even contentious black opin-ion—ran an unsigned item after the season that had obviously been fed to it by players and owners. The item read:

> Satchel is a great pitcher, but he can't be used as an example of
> colored baseball players. Satchel was picked up by Gus Greenlee
> when all the other owners were disgusted with him. Gus exploited

Satchel throughout the United States and forgot all about such men as Gibson, Matlock, Bell, Oscar Charleston, Perkins, the men who made the Pittsburgh Crawfords.

For Satch and the others, the subject lingered beneath the awkward silence maintained by teammates who were not about to make an issue of it to his face. Most players knew Satch's importance to their own interests; with leagues folding and teams disappearing, a drawing card of a teammate meant continued employment. Few in 1932 would have questioned the role Satch laid out for himself in fierce self-defense decades later.

"I laughed at first," he said in his autobiography of the newspaper item. "Why, the only owners disgusted with me were the ones who couldn't make that big money because I wasn't pitching for them. . . .

"Before I started cutting loose around Pittsburgh in 1931, there was no big money for anybody in the Negro leagues. Guys were making only about a hundred twenty-five a month. Then they started getting nice, fat checks—and those checks were paid by the fans.

"I got the fans out and I opened up the major league parks to hold them.

"That's why they paid me more. Some guys didn't like it, but most of my teammates wouldn't say Gus Greenlee had forgotten them and was just taking care of me. Fact is, they were probably glad Gus was taking such good care of me so I wouldn't head someplace else.

"With me someplace else, the fans would be someplace else."

But the money gap, added to the old, simmering black culture clash, made Satch a natural lightning rod for a variety of discontentments. In fact, the geographical divisions between North and South were not resolved, and would not ever be for at least one Crawford of the day, the veteran shortstop Jake Stephens, who hailed from York, Pennsylvania, and reflected the Cum Posey sensibility.

Strenuously avoiding Paige for as long as they played together, Stephens believed Satch was stealing headlines from men who had been paying dues for far longer. Satch, Stephens sniffed many years later in a book entitled *Black Diamonds*, by John B. Holway, should have had to "carry bats and balls [for] fellows like Jud Wilson and Oscar Charleston."

He went on: "Satchel and . . . those southern boys lived a different life than we lived. We didn't even much associate with them off the ball field, because they were what you'd call clowns. They didn't dress the way we dressed, they didn't have the same mannerisms, the same speech.

"And you have this other problem with southern boys. They've never been used to making money. Give them a hundred and fifty a month, first thing you know they go all haywire, living on top of the world, walking in the restaurant with their baseball jackets on that say, 'Pittsburgh Crawfords.' The older fellows, we had neckties on when we went to dinner, I mean because that's how you're supposed to do. You're a gentleman, you're a big-timer."

Stephens's final verdict was that "Satchel Paige is the most overrated ballplayer ever God put breath into."

Such priggishness—and not just by Stephens, who was known as a chronic pop-off—was an inverted form of Tomming, and it surely damaged the unity Negro ball needed to stand tall with the big leagues. Blackball had a long way to go if its most heralded player—one who was putatively the hardest-throwing pitcher in the world—was a semipariah among his own.

Ironically, even Gus Greenlee—who had helped Satch become the capitalist tool many now abhorred—was having small but ominous friction with him. When Double Duty Radcliffe jumped the Crawfords after just one year to play full-time in the lucrative semipro fields of the Midwest, Satch spoke openly of going the same route. Gus, who couldn't see the hypocrisy of his anger about it, had to cut Satch in on more of the barnstorming profits to keep him. And this time, he took Satch's apparent lack of loyalty as a personal affront.

●   ●   ●

Heedless of Cum Posey's sad lesson with the East-West League, in 1933 Greenlee took his own shot at organizing a fully self-sufficient league, in the Greenlee style. This meant that, to be included, an owner could be just about anything as long as he accepted Gus Greenlee as president and godhead of the new Negro National League. Not by accident, among those who did were Greenlee bedfellows from way back—including Tom Wilson in Nashville, who more than qualified to be named vice president and treasurer, and the big numbers men in Harlem (Alex Pompez), South Philadelphia (Ed Bolden), and Newark (Abe Manley). Two old-line powers, the Chicago American Giants and Baltimore Black Sox, made it in as well, along with teams in Detroit and Columbus.

Cum Posey originally came in, chastened enough to lie down with dogs. "Regardless of opinions concerning the owners of the clubs," he wrote of the league in the *Courier*, "it is helping the Negro Race morally and financially." Posey's East-West League had been crippled by the agent's fees demanded by Eddie Gottlieb and Nat Strong, and while Greenlee was now grandstanding against Strong—denying his New York Bushwicks entrance—the admission of the Chicago and Philadelphia teams meant the implicit sanctioning of Abe Saperstein and Gottlieb, who were the exclusive bookers for those teams.

Such hypocrisy—especially by Posey, who had openly railed against all of these agents—was rampant in the new NNL, the root money of which wasn't only dirty but was in some cases nonexistent. But the biggest sham came after the season's first half when the owners met and voted to suspend the Grays until Posey returned two players he had taken from the Detroit team—such conduct being a violation of the league's *code of ethics*. Posey, amazed by this deceit, dropped his pretense; refusing to return the players, he pulled out of the NNL and went back to potluck, independent baseball.

These follies typified the dilemma facing Negro ball. While keeping the league in harness, Greenlee posed its biggest menace; in essence, black baseball now consorted openly with unsavory men, which afforded the big leagues a chance to pose in the white light of purity—even though the memory of the Chicago "Black Sox" scandal was still fresh. Now, moral uprightness was an implied rationale for separating the races on the ball field. Indeed, one need not look far to see improprieties in the black game. Greenlee, for example, had on the NNL payroll *Courier* sportswriter Rollo Wilson; doing Gus's dirty work, Wilson had recently savaged Cum Posey in print as "the mighty somnambulist of a vanished dream."

But even Cum Posey would eventually come around again to the inevitability of Gus Greenlee's tawdry new world order.

• • •

The inaugural NNL season, plagued by the same logistical problems experienced by every other Negro league—by the time the Craws had played twenty games, Baltimore had played just seven—did manage to one-up Cum Posey's EWL by completing a regular season schedule. And with blackball's two showcase teams—the Crawfords and the American Giants—in a tight battle for first place, the season was personified as a private war between blackball's two showcase pitchers: Satchel Paige and the American Giants' Willie Foster.

The *Courier*, going heavy on this angle, splashed both of their pictures on page one of the June 17 sports section, separated by a copy block reading: "Willie Foster, ace lefthander of Cole's Chicago American Giants, and Satchel Page [sic], slim speedball artist, who tosses from the right side of his person, are bitter rivals off the ball field. For several years each has fought desperately to down the other. Last season Page had the edge, but so far this season he has succumbed to Foster's bid for victory on a trio of occasions."

Satch, however, was getting saturation coverage all by himself. After he beat the American Giants 3–1 on June 6—whiffing fifteen and walking *none*—the *Courier* trumpeted:

> It was Satchell [sic] Paige's night of triumph. Colorful in his actions and a born showman, Satchell presided on the mound like a learned jurister on the bench. He fast and slow-balled his way to 15 strikeouts, fanning several of the best batters in Negro baseball. . . . "Satch" allowed but five hits, all of which were widely scattered. And the only thing which kept the elongated Alabama speed ball artist from scoring a shutout occurred when Perkins missed the last strike on [Alec] Radcliffe, first man up in the sixth inning, Rad going to first and scoring in that stanza.

So badly did the American Giants want to beat Satch and his store-bought team that they brought in Willie Foster for a very rare relief stint, to pitch in the seventh inning of that game. But this was a new, and better, Satch, comfortable enough now to start mixing in a few curves with his heat. The *Courier* scribe made mention of this following the 8–2 Satch win over Detroit on June 24: "Working in his most approved fashion," said the game story, Satch "proved a puzzle throughout. Mixing a fastball with a puzzling hook and baffling change of pace, he was never in any trouble."

Given the expectations, it was possible now to charge Satch with the misdemeanor of winning too easily. Wrote the *Courier* man: "The elongated southern lad, whose fastball ranks with any in organized baseball, loafed through the last three frames, yet the scorebook shows that he limited the Stars to five hits and struck out an even dozen men."

With the American Giants leading the league by one game, the first-half championship came down to a two-game series in Greenlee Field in mid-July. Here, Oscar Charleston was faced with the dilemma that would bedevil many of Paige's managers through the years. As no manager could ever be assured that Satch would interrupt his partying and show up on time for a game he was scheduled to pitch—for games he wasn't supposed to pitch, you could just as well send his uniform out to the cleaners—a fallback was always necessary. For Charleston, the first game of the series was too important to leave things hanging until game time. While he prevailed on Satch to get to the park with plenty of time to spare, Oscar named Satch's normal fallback man—Bertram Hunter—as the starter, hoping that Bert would come through against Willie Foster, setting up Satch for a climactic one-game championship.

Oscar's stategy seemed to be working like a charm when Hunter beat Foster 3–2 in the opener. But, with the flag on the line, now Satch ran down. He gave up three runs in the first inning, and after the Craws tied it, fell behind when Turkey Stearns singled and later scored on a ground out. A Josh Gibson error let another run in, and Sug Cornelius shut out the Craws over the last seven innings to get the win 5–3, quelling a late Pitt rally when Charleston was thrown out trying to stretch a double and Cornelius got Judy Johnson to hit into a game-ending double play.

· · ·

By mid-summer, the other center of fan interest in the NNL was the upcoming East-West Game. This event was the best idea Gus Greenlee ever had, though it was no more than a knockoff of the big league All-Star Game originated that July 6 in Comiskey Park. That game—a who's who of the baseball elite and featuring a Babe Ruth home run—begat an instant classic, and Greenlee and Tom Wilson correctly perceived that the real strength of Negro ball wasn't its amorphous leagues and team rivalries but its own transcendent players.

In these games black fans—and a good many white ones—would come out in numbers to see those magnificent bowlegged men with the legacy of their nicknames. In addition, the notion of blacks being able to vote, at will, in *any* election with relevance to them had a major subliminal impact of its own.

But the most indelible black ballplayer in the land was left out of that first game, as if reflecting many players' own biases and because he seemingly had not paid sufficient dues. The big vote-getters were instead old pros who had aged with dignity—Oscar

Charleston (who got the most votes, almost 60,000), Turkey Stearns, Willie Wells, Biz Mackey. With the unpleasantness of Satch's alleged money fixation having hit the papers as well, he was passed in the balloting by teammates George Britt and Sam Streeter; and though Satch, with almost 24,000 votes, had nosed out Bertram Hunter, Gus Greenlee—well aware of Satch's difficulties with alarm clocks and timetables—chose the proven Hunter to start in what was essentially a contest between the Crawfords and the American Giants.

Played in Comiskey Park on September 8 before 20,000 fans, the East-West Game was an immense success for Gus Greenlee (who took five percent of the gate); Abe Saperstein (who took five percent); the ubiquitous Willie Foster, who went all the way and beat Streeter; and Mule Suttles, who hit a home run in the 11–7 West win. But Foster and Suttles, like all the other players, made not a cent beyond expenses; there wasn't enough room in Gus Greenlee's foresight for that.

Satch, meanwhile, could hardly have missed Greenlee's stern message about staying loyal to the Craws—though he probably could not have cared less, especially when the players got stiffed. Indeed, uncharacteristically humble about the whole thing, he would shrug off the snub years later with the canard that "I was new around the league then and I guess that's why they didn't name me, even if I was one of the top hands around."

Neither did he harbor any grudges against Greenlee—he was far too self-absorbed for that—nor did he have any compunction about Gus's character. In that he was united with the rest of the Crawfords. To call Gus a racketeer had no meaning; he was an entrepreneur, a power broker, a sportsman, a man's man, who didn't have to suck up to any white man. Gus had brought them all into the belly of the whale, into the *power*.

Judy Johnson, for example, doubled as Greenlee's part-time chauffeur. When Gus's boys were taking his numbers cash in for deposit, Judy would be parked outside and would watch in awe as the bank would promptly close, to do Gus's business in secret. Ted Page tasted the power when Gus put him to work in the off-season as a lookout outside the Crawford Grille's gaming room—an unnecessary job since, if the cops planned a raid, Gus would be tipped off by an informer well in advance.

Satchel Paige, however, got closest to the power by getting the biggest cut of Gus's money. But he was not comfortable being "Gus's boy." As much as he liked Greenlee, he was nobody's boy, not when a boy had to look after himself. Thus, their relationship was always a little strained, particularly after Satch made those noises about jumping to the Midwest. That is precisely what he did during the summer of 1933; as threatened, he skipped off to the heartland to throw a couple of games with Ted Radcliffe for a semi-pro team in Wichita, although he quickly returned to Pittsburgh for the end of the NNL season. And while Satch took the high road about that first East-West Game, he never gave an inch in the future. If he was in Pittsburgh in the late summer, he'd be available to play in the game; if not, screw it, he had other, more profitable mackerel to fry.

By spiting Satch, Gus Greenlee had spited only himself and his league. The East-West Games were the best advertisement for the joys of Negro ball, and keeping Paige away wasn't so much a snub as a self-inflicted wound. The trouble was, Satch too could wound Gus and the league. It was a predicament that made Greenlee's big belly growl in anxiety.

7

"It's Paige and Goodbye Ballgame"

Satchell, elongated and a consummate showman, whose whip-corded right arm rifles a ball plateward with the speed of a bullet, has as fast a ball as any ever uncorked in big league baseball. Shades of "Lefty" Grove . . . Walter Johnson . . . and other stars of mound fame, come almost unbidden to one's mind as he marvels at the speed and cunning contained in those long arms of the boy who came to Pittsburgh via Alabama and Tennessee. He literally throws a ball past hitters in a pinch [and] he has developed a baffling rook, which he uses to further bewilder all opposition.

—Pittsburgh Courier,
July 1, 1933

The [American] Giants and some 3,000 fans who braved threatening weather . . . got a good look at Satchel (Stepin-fetchit) Paige, long, lean and angular slab ace of the Smoky City crew. And Mr. Paige was something to look at too.

—Baltimore Afro-American,
May 19, 1934

The second half of the 1933 Negro National League season ended in a deadlock between the Crawfords and the Nashville Elite Giants. A best-of-three playoff was arranged, to be played in Cleveland's League Park, with a doubleheader on the afternoon of

October 1. Gus Greenlee and Tom Wilson hoped to make a killing by bringing these climactic games to a major league amphitheater, but were hit by a dual blast of reality: the Depression and the irrelevance of Negro league championship games. The hefty stadium rental fee, and the Indians' cut, more than offset the pocket change Greenlee and Wilson made on the gate of 3,000, and yet the first game of the doubleheader was blackball at its pulsating best.

The *Courier* sent its city editor, William G. Nunn, to cover the games, and Nunn turned in twenty paragraphs on the Crawfords' tense sweep—which began with, in Nunn's verbiage, "Satchell the mighty . . . matching wits and his blinding speed against [Jim] Willis." Up 1–0 in the third, Satch gave up a game-tying single to Sam Bankhead, but seemed to have it in hand, working with a 4–2 lead in the ninth. But then Bankhead led off with a single, and with one out Willie Gisentaner—a pitcher—pinch-hit a perfect hit-and-run single to left on which Bankhead scored all the way from first. When Jim West then singled to center to tie it, Oscar Charleston yanked Satch and brought in Leroy Matlock to pitch to Candy Jim Taylor, one of the most famous player-managers in Negro ball.

Taylor hit Matlock's first pitch into the left field seats—foul by inches—then hit the next pitch for an inning-ending double play. Finally, in the twelfth, Cool Papa Bell lined a shot up the alley in left-center and burned rubber around the bases, digging for an inside-the-park gamer. As the throw came homeward, wrote Nunn, Cool Papa's "flying spikes marked 'finis' to as great a diamond struggle as we've ever seen."

The second game, made to seem gothically anticlimactic by a dusky fog rolling over the ballpark, had to be called after seven innings with the Craws ahead 3–1 behind Bertram Hunter. This should have set up a championship playoff with the first-half winners, the Chicago American Giants, but Gus Greenlee—having seen fan interest wane after the East-West Game and not eager to risk all against the potent Giants—unilaterally ended the season right there. Robert Cole was miffed, but could do nothing about it; he could do just as little two months later when Gus, deeming it important for history's sake, declared in the *Courier* that the 1933 champions of the NNL were the Pittsburgh Crawfords.

For Gus, this edict bore no grounds for challenge. He didn't invent his league to necessarily play through to a World Series; that mattered only in the big leagues. He did it to enumerate a champion for the record books, by rights as much as by technicalities. In the years to come, the NNL would play all the way through sporadically, but in the main the champion would be announced after the playing stopped and the shoddy men who ran the NNL began playing their own games. Indeed, these games—which weighed the political strength of certain clubs—were the real Negro World Series, and their knavery only played into the hands of the big league merchants who would scoff at even their legitimate efforts.

Still, Greenlee heard enough grumbling about his action that, as a sop to the notion of honesty, he named the first NNL commissioner, whose stated function was to arbitrate any and all disagreements. Gus's commitment to this high ideal was reflected in his choice: his *Courier* flack, Rollo Wilson.

And yet, with the first NNL season literally in the bank, Gus could be proud of himself. Cum Posey was—for now—disposed of. The NNL was shorn but still standing. And Satchel Paige, who went only 6-and-6 in 1933, would remain in Pittsburgh long enough in 1934 to make his bones once and for all.

●   ●   ●

If Satch felt any resentment from certain quarters of Negro ball, and he could hardly miss it given how he'd been slammed in that anonymous *Courier* item, he dealt with it in his usual fashion—he tuned it out.

"He was an odd guy," Jimmie Crutchfield said. "I never heard him knock another ballplayer. But it always seemed like he had a little problem with most guys. He was a one-nighter kind of guy. He didn't take to too many ballplayers as very close buddies. That's why I always appreciated the fact that he liked me for some reason, I guess because Bill Gatewood started me out, too, and Satch was always lookin' out for me the way Bill did with him.

"He was a good guy, always full of fun, kidding, joking. But he'd pitch on a Sunday and then we wouldn't see him until next Sunday. Very seldom did he travel with us; he'd just get there by himself.

"But, like I say, I was one of his favorite ballplayers. I remember he took me with him once—and he *never* took anybody with him. We drove from Pittsburgh to Philadelphia in his '28 Ford with one jack and no spare tire. He drove pretty fast, but that's how he lived; he always had to be movin' on. And the one thing I remember is that he never talked about his pitchin', never tried to tell a guy how to pitch. It was like he had to get away from that, too. He'd talk about his hittin'. He loved to hit. He didn't feel no pressure when he was hittin'."

That was the nature of Satchel Paige: a Jimmie Crutchfield could be allowed into his world, and be entertained to no end, but all the while Jimmie could sense a wall keeping him from the essential Satch—from *Leroy*, a man with a hurt inside that he could not address. So if Satch could cozy up to anyone, he used his gifts of amiability as a buffer, never really intending to bond on a deep level. In that way, the players were the same for him as the crowds—keep 'em laughing, send the circus through town, and then be gone, alone in the night.

Even on the field, he preferred to avoid the rituals of bonding. Crutchfield told of one game when Chester Williams, the chirpy shortstop, made Satch nuts with too much comradeship:

"Chester was a guy who'd get all worked up, and Satch would be firin' that ball and strikin' out guys and Williams'd get a little carried away. He'd be like chanting, 'Satch! Satch! Satch!,' tryin' to get him all pumped up. And, boy, this one time Satchel was mowin' 'em down, he's all busy pitchin' and he don't wanna hear all this chatter. So he just stopped, just sat down on the mound and yelled to Chester, 'You ugly so-and-so, cut out that stuff! I can't hear myself think!' "

The flip side of Satch's insularity was that, when human contact was transitory and disposable—crowds at a ballpark, crowds in a bar—he loved holding the center spot on stage. Perhaps that explains why he could be so casual about coming to the park. It wasn't just irresponsibility and recalcitrance that made him late; people on the outside, faceless and fawning, could have a narcotic effect on him. Being at the hub of a mob waiting for him to buy them drinks in exchange for a pat on the back, *that* was a high. Oh, when he'd awaken the next morning (or whenever), his head would be pounding and his pockets would be empty and he'd know he was a damn fool. But he also knew that if he could scrape up a few bucks, another night in another bar was waiting.

Gus Greenlee, worried about Satch's cycle of binging and splurging—though only for its monetary erosion, not its potential erosion of his health—told him after he straggled in after one long night, "Satch, you must know something, the way you spend money."

"I don't know anything," Satch said, with a sad laugh.

• • •

If the '33 season could be condensed into a pitched battle between Satch and Willie Foster, the '34 stanza of blackball would develop into a similar matchup of Satch and Stuart "Slim" Jones. A twenty-one-year-old lefthander, Jones came to the Philadelphia Stars with wicked stuff and a fondness for bars—which is to say that he struck many people as another Satchel Paige. At six foot six and 160 bony pounds, Jones *had* to pitch against Satch just to prove the two of them could be seen on the same field at the same time.

But if these two men had near identical skills, and if the pitching mound and the bar stool were each one's refuge, there was a critical difference between them. Satch, who went into bars as much for their impersonality as the booze, had an alarm bell inside his head that restored the order in there. Innately, whether by accident or common sense, Satchel Paige knew how to hold his booze and when to stop pouring it. Jones had no such inner brake.

When they first faced each other, on May 20, neither was at his best. Satch struck out eleven but gave up fifteen hits and lost to Jones 10–5. But from then on, both were all but untouchable. Leading up to the August 26 East-West Game, Jones had won sixteen of his next eighteen league starts, with one loss, one no-decision, and two more wins in relief. Satch, pitching less frequently due to his outside gigs, won eight of his next eleven league starts, with one loss, four NDs, and one more win in relief. Each had four shutouts in that time.

For Satch, the first real milestone of the season was the July 4 game with the Grays at a packed Greenlee Field. Pitching the first game of a doubleheader, he gave up a walk to Buck Leonard in the first inning—then got every other hitter, in order, except for one who reached on an error. Blowing the ball past eight of the first nine Grays, and past twelve of them over six innings, Satch ended the 4–0 game by scorching the last two dazed hitters for seventeen strikeouts in all, which set a Negro ball record and tied Dizzy Dean's then–big league standard. It was the first time Cum Posey's team had ever been no-hit.

Leonard, the Hall of Fame first baseman, was in his first year with the Grays then. He would play seventeen more and never see a man throw a ball like Satch did on that July 4. Astonished by the deadly, rising swoop of the ball, Leonard repeatedly asked the umpire to look at the ball, not knowing if it was of this earth. When the ump removed one ball from play, Satch cackled.

"You may as well thrown 'em all out," he bellowed, "'cause they're all gonna jump like that."

Recalled Leonard, in a mantra recited often in Negro ball, "You knew what he was gonna throw you. You just couldn't hit it. It came in down here, but it wound up up here."

Satch was rather pleased by this awesome game, though in his memoirs it came out—as usual—stirred and shaken with the detritus of other recollections.

"That [game] was on July 4," he recalled. "I remember because somebody kept shooting off firecrackers every time I got another batter out. Those fireworks still were popping when I ran out of the park, hopped into my car, and drove all night to Chicago. I got there just in time to beat [Ted] Trent and the Chicago American Giants one to nothing in twelve innings."

The wonder of this fabrication was that what actually happened next that day was a good enough story in itself. In what the *Courier* subheadlined "Paige Tries Iron Man Stunt," Satch came into the second game of the doubleheader in the seventh inning with the score tied 2–2 and the go-ahead run on base. As the *Courier* reported:

> The stands went wild when the elongated Satchell leisurely strolled across the field, proceeded to execute his quadruple windup, and then struck out [Neil] Robinson . . . then faced [Joe] Strong, his rival moundsman, and proceeded to "shoot the works" in an effort to strike out his opponent. A dramatic silence settled over the crowd, but in an instant it was broken with the crack of a bat and Strong had poled out a mighty double. It was the first hit the Grays had made off of Paige in ten innings during the day and the fireworks started. From then on Homestead reigned supreme.

With Satch again having been burned by a pitcher at the plate, the Craws lost 4–3. And if Satch chose understandably not to recall this failure, the *Courier* man made it clear that great hordes would—and, indeed, that the integrated crowd that had visited Greenlee Field on Independence Day were in themselves a story pertinent to the fortunes of Negro ball:

> Hundreds of fans were forced to miss the first part of the game because the ticket sellers exhausted their supply of dimes. . . . There were plenty of ofays at the games and lots of them brought their women. During one of the exciting moments of the first game the colored fans around an ofay couple got excited and started to doing things. The Nordic woman didn't seem to mind these antics at all,

but her escort held her as close to him as he could so that none of
the dark fans around them could touch the fair lady.

Satch and the Crawfords did meet up with the American Giants
days later in a four-game series in Chicago; Satch's 3–0 five-hitter
in the opener was apparently the game he had in mind years later,
though he beat not Ted Trent but Sug Cornelius as the Craws
broke up Sug's own no-hitter with three runs in the eleventh inning—with Satch singling in the last run himself.

The American Giants had already clinched the first-half NNL title, but the Craws swept the series, and Satch's shutout was his
third against Chicago in 1934. This was all too much for the
Chicago Defender, which in sorrowful admiration bemoaned, "When
the Craws left the city no one was sorry. Truth of it is we hope they
never come back here, and, if so, our plea to Greenlee is please,
please, leave Satchel Paige at home."

•   •   •

Gus Greenlee certainly would have been content if Satch had
stayed at home more often. But in early August, when Satch was
ready to fly again to the Midwest, Gus took preemptive measures
in concert with the Kansas City Monarchs—from whom Gus had
learned much that benefited him.

Unaligned with any league since the death of the first Negro National League, the Monarchs were really America's black team, a
popular attraction in the farm belt where blacks were scarce and
where the shared poverty line obscured any color lines. It was in
the emaciated heartland, where the Monarchs played most of their
games against white semipro clubs, that the future of baseball
could be seen every day in the summer.

This applied not only to the color of the game's future but to its
incandescence. Since 1930, the Monarchs had been playing night
baseball, utilizing a portable lighting system that was the rage of
Negro ball, as it allowed more fans to attend games. The Monarchs'
owner, J. Leslie Wilkinson—who had been the only white owner allowed by Rube Foster into the original Negro National League, os-
tensibly for his longtime commitment to the Negro game but not
incidentally for his hard-won booking control in the Plains states—
took the risk of his life banking on night ball. He mortgaged his
home and drained his savings to manufacture the $50,000 traveling
light show—a motor/generator contraption in which six light

banks were hauled around on trucks and could be either slapped atop a grandstand roof or propped on stilts. But despite the cost, and the unending din of the motor that sat in center field consuming fifteen gallons of gasoline an hour, J.L. made out like a bandit, not just saving his own team from Depression extinction but leasing out the lights, at a price, to other teams.

As much for the lights as the players—who included the great pitchers Bullet Joe Rogan and Chet Brewer—the Monarchs came to small towns on a bubble of anticipation. Booked now by co-owner Tom Baird, by the early 1930s they had played—often day *and* night, around 150 games a year—in eighteen states and in Canada and Mexico. The Monarchs' first game under the arcs in Chicago had drawn over 12,000 people, and the club's home field, Muehlenbach Stadium, was the most famous black park in the country—every reason why Gus Greenlee decided to spring for lights at Greenlee Field in 1933. Poor as these early lights were, it is doubtful Negro ball would have survived without them.

Though Greenlee would soon have problems with Wilkinson and Baird, they aided him now. Baird had been booking both the Monarchs and the House of David teams on their barnstorming routes, including the many games the two teams played against each other. And with the Monarchs' popularity running so high, Baird now booked both teams into the annual *Denver Post* baseball tournament in early August of 1934, marking the first entrance of a Negro team in the tournament.

Having gained this entrée, Tom Baird was not leaving anything to chance. This tournament—called the "Little World Series"—was very big league in the betting world, and Baird had no intention of losing his cut of the $7,500 first prize by allowing his teams to lose to minor league and semipro opposition in Denver. So Baird called Gus Greenlee and made a typical Negro ball deal: for the usual cut off the top, Gus loaned Baird Satchel Paige and his favorite caddy Bill Perkins—but not for use by the Monarchs. Needing to beef up the Monarchs' eventual challenger in the final round—and with integrated teams not permitted—Baird shunted Satch and Perkins to another of his teams in the tournament, the Colored House of David.

As this rather odd pairing of terms suggests, the House of David concept had traveled far from its origins in the business of barnstorming. Founded at Benton Harbor, Michigan, in 1903, the Hasidic sect named for the shepherd king of Israel were at the beginning simply traveling salesmen of faith, though they were surely the first religious order to use baseball as a missionary tool; the vision of men with beard and *pais* swinging from their heels and charging after hot grounders was as awesome as the one at Lourdes.

In later years, though, guided by the Barnum-like J. L. Wilkinson, the idea was less proselytizing than profitizing—playing ball in front of gambling, swearing heathens was enough of an act of faith as long as the team won. Indeed, toward that end many David teams haunted the land, using names more suited to a carnival freak show: the Original House of David, the Eastern House of David, the Bearded House of David, the Kansas City House of David, even the Mexican House of David. The Colored House of David that played in Denver carried some decidedly goyish names, such as Mullen, Holland, Cross, Blakeney—and Perkins and Paige.

Satch didn't care about religious matters, but the Davids' trademark beards were a revelation to him. As his face was rarely host to anything shaggier than some kiwi fuzz about the chin, he was concerned about appearing *gauche*, not by the color of his skin but by its nakedness. Doing all he could by growing a thin mustache, his team spirit so impressed his teammates that they presented him with a fake beard—a bright red one—which he wore for the championship game.

All of Satch's games in the tournament—three wins in five days—were near copies. With hitters squinting after the ball in the magnified candlelight, he almost couldn't help but whiff fourteen, and eighteen in two shutouts against the semipros. Then, on August 17, in the awaited main event, Merchants Park squeezed in 11,120—more than 6,000 over its usual capacity—for the Monarchs against the Colored Davids, with Chet Brewer facing Satchel Paige—these two black men fronting the greatest sporting attraction ever seen in Rocky Mountain country, the bosom of Aryan America. Not for nothing could the *Pittsburgh Courier* gush that this game was "a baseball battle of the century."

Satch, ever reverential, entered this epic with his henna whiskers glued in place, and he rolled right on. Tom Baird, beefing up his own team for the tournament, had leased the services of Turkey Stearns and Sam Bankhead to boost the attack, but despite Stearns's double and seven other hits, Satch held the Monarchs scoreless through seven innings. Then, leading 1–0, in true Samson form, Satch weakened when during one delivery the beard be-

came entangled with his arm, was ripped from his face, and fell to
the ground. Thoroughly disoriented, Satch allowed a hit, and then
an error tied it. But the Davids scored one in the bottom of the
eighth and Satch, sans beard, regrouped—striking out twelve in
all in the 2–1 win by the Davids.

In deliberating on the game even in his old age, he would recall
the cold fear he felt that day—which came not from facing the
Monarchs' lineup, he inisted, but from cluttering up his own face.
"It was the tamperin' with nature that rattled me," he said.

· · ·

This year, no amount of ill will from within could keep Satch
from his rightful place in the August 26 East-West All-Star game.
The fans got behind him in strength; his vote total in the newspaper polls was the highest of any East player, and 2,000 more than
the next highest, Slim Jones. Even so, because Gus Greenlee still
felt that he couldn't trust Satch to be there, Jones was named the
starter against Ted Trent, with Satch named a reserve.

Again, this contest was essentially the Crawfords (with Jones and
Newark shortstop Dick Lundy) against the American Giants; but
unlike the '33 game, this one was to be for the pitchers—with
Satch having no idea of the critical role he would play. Arriving at
Comiskey Park, he went to the bullpen with his normal diffidence
about games he didn't start. During the early innings he sat with
one long leg draped over a bench, dragging on cigarettes and carrying on with fans in the bleachers.

But this game would be his. It was scoreless in the sixth when
Harry Kincannon, who had replaced Jones, gave up a leadoff double to Willie Wells. Then, wrote the *Courier*'s sports editor Chester
I. Washington, "Pandemonium reigned in the West's cheering section. An instant later, a hush fell upon the crowd as the mighty
Satchell Paige, prize 'money' pitcher of the East, leisurely ambled
across the field toward the pitcher's box. It was a dramatic moment. Displaying his picturesque double windup and nonchalant
manner, Satchell started shooting 'em across the plate."

Describing the moment himself years and years later, Satch said,
"I'd been sunning myself out in the bullpen, but my manager
wanted me in there now. I headed for the mound and when I
passed first base I walked over toward the bench and tossed my
jacket in there. That's when I heared this guy in the stands.

" 'It's Paige. Good-bye ball game.'

"He didn't know how right he was.

"Three men came up against me and three men died while that runner stayed glued on second."

If anything, this time he *understated* the case. What he did was to strike out Alec Radcliffe and then get Turkey Stearns and Mule Suttles—a Murderer's Row, just the two of them—on soft fly balls. In the eighth, Cool Papa Bell led off with a single and stole second, and with two outs, when Boojum Wilson dribbled a grounder to second and beat the throw, Cool Papa flew all the way around to score. But that run, as Satch would say, "was as good as a dozen." Stifling the West over the last three frames, he yielded a one-out hit to Suttles in the ninth but got Red Parnell and Willie Wells to seal the win.

With typical Negro press abandon, Chester Washington called this East-West Game "the mightiest and most colorful drama of bats and balls in all diamond history." And in the afterglow, it became clear that this contest had moved blackball into a new stratum. As usual the black press covered the game to death, but this time the white press saw fit to give it some important play as well. The *Chicago Times* ran a breakthrough piece by sportswriter Marvin McCarthy entitled "Black Matty," comparing Satch to Christy Mathewson. Significantly, in McCarthy's take on blackball's showcase moment, only Satch was mentioned by name:

It's the last half of the sixth. The score is 0 to 0. At the end of the fifth the boys from the West showed signs of getting to the East's second pitcher. Each pitcher is scheduled to go three innings just like the National-American league all-star game. Well, the first western batter up in the sixth cracks out a clean two-bagger. There's a man on second and none out. Comes a halt, a brief conference and East's pitcher starts for the dugout.

Silence, then all eyes on the field and in the stands are drawn to the right field foul line. With measured tread an African giant crosses the line and heads for the pitcher's box. "It's Paige! It's Paige and goodbye ballgame," whisper the stands. And it is. He must stand 6 feet 6 inches in his sox. Gaunt as old Abe Lincoln. He walks with that slow Bert Williams shuffle. Maybe it takes him two minutes to cross the 50 yards to the box.

He stoops to toy with the rosin bag—picks up the old apple. He mounts the bag, faces third—turns a sorrowful but burning eye toward the plate, nods a nod that Hitler would give his eye for—turns his gaze back to the runner on second—raises two bony arms high toward heaven, lets them sink slowly to his chest. Seconds pass like hours.

The batter fidgets in his box. Suddenly that long right arm shoots back and forward like the piston on a Century engine doing 90. All you can see is something like a thin line of pipe smoke. There's an explosion like a gun shot in the catcher's glove. "Strike!" howls the dusky umpire. . . . Thereafter the great Satchel Paige had 'em striking out like a labor union leader. . . . The long, lean lanky [Paige] is truly the black Mathewson.

Given the fevered tone of coverage in the black press—in which "a hush" was always descending on the crowd at any given moment—McCarthy's imagery could just as easily have emanated from a black reporter's typewriter. What's more, Satch himself was rather fond of such hyperbole—and would lift McCarthy's "It's Paige and goodbye ballgame" as a signature phrase.

Still, at least one black chronicler of the day took umbrage at what he read into McCarthy's prose and his motives. This was Dan Burley, who was an early black Renaissance Man and an influential leader. A respected jazz pianist on the Chicago honky-tonk scene, Burley was also an at-large contributing writer for the Associated Negro Press. When Burley chose to cover black sports events, his musings carried much weight; black newspapers across the country often ripped his stories off the wire machine and ran them as is. In the 1940s, Burley would move east to become the theatrical editor of the *New York Amsterdam News*, during which time he would record, with Lionel Hampton, "Ridin' on the L&N," a song that was at least metaphorical to Satchel Paige.

Burley was so bent out of shape after reading Marvin McCarthy's apparent panegyric about Paige that he was moved to speculate on what nuance lay behind this homage. Wrote Burley, as picked up in the September 8, 1934, *Defender:* "White sports scribes are in a quandary as how to take the presentation of honest-to-goodness baseball as played in the [East-West] classic. Some writers see a chance [to] burlesque Negroes in the game. . . . Marvin McCarthy, in his burlesque conceptions of the game, got a jump on the rest of the white scribes. He was SURPRISED himself that Negroes could play that kind of baseball, but tried to cover it up with a narration a la Roy Cohen." (Burley's reference was to the author of popular detective novels of the era that featured stereotypical black characters with names like Florian Slappey and Epic Peters.)

Whether or not condescension was what McCarthy had in mind, and it is a hard call to make, it is true that Satch's growth in the public eye—black and white—seemed to have little to do with his wondrous pitching, per se. By now, he had taken on a near-mythic role in American pop culture, one that those in the black press were helping to create by their own hyperbole.

In the much larger context of mainstream culture—black and white—it was a given that blacks could only imitate whites, not be equal to them; and they would always be set apart from whites by their *funniness*. Accordingly, the black press that Dan Burley implicitly pardoned for its excesses was increasingly calling Satch not the black version of anyone in the white game but a new version of another black icon of the 1930s—movie actor Stepin Fetchit, whose real name was Lincoln Theodore Perry. In one such allusion, the *Defender* in 1934 made reference to "stringbean pitcher Satchel 'Stepinfetchit' Paige."

This pairing was an obvious match, and it was not even close to a slur, not in 1934. Just as Stepin Fetchit's lazy, feeble-minded movie roles were a matter of pride in the black community simply for the man's ability to act in the movies, so were Satchel Paige's droop-eyed, hurry-not moves a symbol of great self-glorification.

Consider too that Satchel Paige was the first black superstar introduced to a mainstream audience since Jack Johnson, the turn-of-the-century heavyweight champion whose carnal reign so frightened America that each of his opponents came to carry the label of "the Great White Hope." Satch was as vainglorious as Johnson, but he was far less conscious of race. For him and for millions of blacks, any ironies inherent in his mock clowning were for future generations to ponder; for them, the notion of being a "showman" was the highest order of flattery. If Satch had no idea about how to live with his fame as anything but a showman, neither did the press—black and white—have any idea about how to codify him as anything but, and really never would.

In the end, all that mattered to Satchel Paige in 1934 was that he was causing a serious fuss wherever he went. The nature of that fuss—and even sometimes the spelling of his name—he would leave to others.

•   •   •

It sometimes seemed that blackball was now running according to Satch's schedule. In early September of that 1934 season, the Philadelphia Stars and the Chicago American Giants were two games into the NNL championship playoff when Gus Greenlee—perfectly happy to steal the headlines—booked a four-team charity benefit doubleheader at Yankee Stadium. This type of attraction being where the big money was, the Stars and Giants interrupted their playoff and detoured to New York, where the American Giants would play the Black Yankees now owned by Bill "Bojangles" Robinson—another black cultural icon, though this great tap dancer was also fitted into the shuffling, lackey stereotype—in the first game, followed by the Stars and Crawfords.

In the overhyped world of Negro ball, where each week could bring the most recent "greatest game ever," this event—or, more accurately, the nightcap matchup of Satch and Slim Jones—would quickly replace the recent East-West Game in the pantheon for the black press—again with reason, as Satch and Slim had been heading toward a fateful confrontation all season long.

The Stars, who had been playing in front of a few thousand fans in the playoffs, looked up to find 30,000 people staring down at them from the three tiers of the House of Ruth, the biggest turnout for a Negro league game up to then. Thousands more couldn't get in because the Yankees management expected far fewer and had opened only a few ticket booths.

The pregame poop that brought in all of those people had made the game into a prizefight between men of destiny, with the promise of almost a spiritual rebirth inherent in the abrupt rising of Slim Jones. As the innings passed, Jones seemed to be perfectly cast; allowing no one to reach base, he led 1–0 going to the seventh.

For Satch, the Fates appeared to have something else in store. Having driven all night from Pittsburgh, he was exhausted by the time he reached the Bronx; he pulled over to the curb a few blocks from Yankee Stadium and slept until an hour before the game. Never fully awake, he later said, "I was a little tired and didn't do as good as usual." Still, he'd only given up one run, on a first-inning groundout by Boojum Wilson, when Oscar Charleston broke up Jones's perfect game in the seventh with a single. In the eighth, Judy Johnson doubled and scored on a hit by Leroy Morney to tie it.

Then, with a grainy darkness gathering in the last of the ninth, the Stars went for the kill. With one out Boojum singled and went to third on a throwing error. Biz Mackey walked, and with Satch clearly winded and the winning run ninety feet up the line, the Stars' old warhorse player-manager Webster McDonald pinch-hit.

But now the Fates were with Satch. With the musky sky shrouding his Trouble Ball, he mowed down McDonald and another pinch-hitter, Jesse Brooks—walking off with what is regarded as a Negro league record eighteen strikeouts.

With this gasp of redemption, the umpires called the game because of the dark, leaving the tie score as a rightful judgment on Paige and Jones. Satch, though, wouldn't hear of leaving it at that. Six years later, no less than the *Saturday Evening Post* would write of this celebrated game, its misinformation provided by Satch; picking up the story from his weary arrival in New York, it recounted the events this way:

> Instead of catching some sleep at a hotel, he drew up alongside the curb at 137th Street and Seventh Avenue—practically the social center of Harlem—and fell fast asleep, his radio blaring. Harlem tiptoed by, gazed awesomely at the Great Man healing his road-weary nerves. That afternoon, Satchel pitched one of the best games of his career, nosing out Slim Jones in the eleventh, 2–1. In the tenth, Satch grew careless, found himself with none out and two men on base, thanks to sly bunts. But he threw exactly nine balls thereafter, striking out the next three men—one of whom was Buck Leonard, the Lou Gehrig of Negro ball.
>
> Harlem still rings with the exploit. "Satchel wouldn't of let the game go so far," a witness told me, "but he didn't jes have enough sleep. He could'a gone to a hotel, but that car was bran'-new, and Satch he live with a new car like it was a bride."

Later still, when Satch covered it in his autobiography, he repeated this account. "I'd won another, two to one," he wrote. "But it'd taken eleven innings after two days without any sleep except that nap in my car."

Such were the mythological properties of the game that anyone could have a good time with it, either in a pandering or earnest manner. But even Jimmie Crutchfield, who played in it, would later recall the game as it wasn't.

"Slim Jones outpitched Satchel for nine innings and we went into the ninth tied one and one," he insisted. "Then they filled the bases with nobody out and y'know what happened? Satchel struck out the side!"

Even as it was, however, Negro ball canonized this tie game. A month later, when the same four teams played a sequel doubleheader in Yankee Stadium, Bojangles Robinson himself presented Satch and Slim travel bags in recognition of—naturally—"the greatest game ever played." Then Satch went out and laid waste to Act Two of Paige versus Jones, winning that game 3–1 with seven strikeouts, ending it with an emphatic one-two-three ninth.

Slim Jones won twenty-two games that season, including the NNL title-clinching game against Chicago, and lost three—besting Satch's 13-and-3 (31-and-4 in all games). Jones also beat Dizzy Dean in a game against big league players, as would Satch. But from the zenith of this high, Jones would fall hard, winning no more than four games in any of the next four seasons, his road to ruin strewn with liquor bottles. His alcoholism growing ever worse, he collapsed in a stupor on a bitter cold Philadelphia street during the winter of 1939 and froze to death at age twenty-five.

In the end, the legacy he and Satch shared was just a blip on the screen. For Slim Jones, the good life never went beyond that one incredible year of 1934. For Satchel Paige—who did the incredible fairly routinely—the road was just now stretching out before him.

8

Ain't Got
No Home

I was a wandering man . . . but Janet was against all that wandering. She wanted a man who ran a store or something and came home every night, a guy who'd never leave her and if he had to go somewhere he'd be the kind who'd take her with him. I wasn't that kind at all back in those days. . . . When I got those trips away from Pittsburgh, I wanted to go alone. I didn't want a wife tying me down in those towns I visited.

—Satchel Paige,
Maybe I'll Pitch Forever

Working his solo gigs in the Midwest the year before, Satch had made some important contacts, none more vital than Ted Radcliffe. Double Duty had become the latest Negro leaguer to prosper in the outlands, and his lucrative example pulled at Satch all during the 1934 season.

Black participation—and profit-taking—in this alabaster region dated all the way back to the seminal days of Negro ball. In the 1890s, Bud Fowler played on a Lincoln, Nebraska, team; another, Walter Ball, was on a Grand Forks, South Dakota, team. In the years thereafter, a team in Waseca, Minnesota, won a state tournament with three black players, and the Sioux Falls Canaries had integrated the National Baseball Congress tournament in Wichita with a black player named Jake Collins. There was even an all-black team of some note, the Algona (Iowa) Brownies.

In the teens, Plunk Drake—the man who taught Satch the Hesitation Pitch in Chattanooga—played with a white semipro team in

Brunswick, North Dakota, and for the black Tennessee Rats in Holden, Missouri, before joining J. L. Wilkinson's first barnstorming team, the clownish All Nations. One of his teammates on that club, pitcher John Donaldson, would become the paradigm of independent player-entrepreneurs. Promoting himself to any club that would hire him in between starts with the Kansas City Monarchs, in 1929 the Colored House of David was formed around Donaldson in Sioux City.

When Ted Radcliffe jumped the Crawfords to mine these fertile ball fields, the getting was so good that he would not return to the Negro leagues full-time until 1946. In 1934, the marquee value of Double Duty carried him to an integrated team in Jamestown, North Dakota, for which he became player-manager. That team, with freelancing Monarch Chet Brewer and veteran Negro leaguers Quincy Trouppe and Red Haley, barnstormed in the fall with an impressive big league all-star team featuring Jimmie Foxx, Jimmy Dykes, and Tommy Bridges, and beat them left and right all the way up the Dakotas and into Winnipeg.

A quiet integration was fomenting throughout the Dakotas, spurred by the frenzied betting action in state tournaments. In an easy-money fever, local businessmen were offering black stars up to double what they were paid by the gangsters of the Negro National League. As long as they kept to themselves, living in their segregated compounds, the players could be made to believe that they owned the town.

With all this as preamble, Satchel Paige found himself in the fall of 1934 with an offer from a semipro club in Bismarck, North Dakota, that was just now changing its own color line in order to enter the big time of small-time baseball. This move was the doing of the team's sponsor and manager, Neil Orr Churchill, an overweight forty-three-year-old automobile dealer with infinite ambitions. As a young man, Churchill was traveling through Bismarck when he became deathly ill with ptomaine poisoning; taking his recovery as a sign from above, he stayed in the city and became a car salesman, then opened one of the first Chrysler distributorships in the country, Corwin-Churchill Motors, in 1924. Fabulously successful, Churchill wanted greater visibility and sought it through his big dream—guiding a ball team to glory.

But while he got his team, which was simply called the Bismarcks, there was no glory until Churchill learned some vital lessons from the integrated Jamestown team of Ted Radcliffe. Now, in the manner of that club, Churchill opened his doors and his wallet to blacks. In keeping with his profession, Churchill was a big talker, but he also took the time to familiarize himself with the Negro league scene before he made his move. For a middleman, he turned to Abe Saperstein, who, along with the Monarchs' J. L. Wilkinson, was the controlling force in the Midwest and would use this in to establish a Colored House of David basketball team as a rollover opponent for his Harlem Globetrotters.

Broached by Saperstein on Churchill's behalf, Satch at first held off, as he had with Radcliffe's entreaties, thinking that he might have to don a coonskin instead of a baseball cap. "I wasn't exactly sure that North Dakota belonged to [Uncle] Sam," he later explained. What made him relent was Janet Howard, with whom he was now getting serious. She wanted him to go, and wanted to come along with him. As Satch recalled, "Janet says jump, so we jumped." Other factors were compelling, too. For his services—which would not be needed for long, since the Bismarcks' season was in its final month—Churchill would pay him $400 and give him a late model from off the Corwin-Churchill lot.

Gus Greenlee was almost relieved that Satch had waited until the very end of the NNL season to jump. It did Gus no harm, and he still had Satch committed to an upcoming postseason series between the Crawfords and a barnstorming team fronted by Dizzy Dean. Satch had to be wary about Bismarck, since in these Dakota outposts blacks were still alien beings in a lingering wilderness where descendants of Canadian-American fur trappers lived in uneasy peace with the Indian tribes their grandfathers had tried to slaughter. But, wary as he was, Satch did recognize that his stay in Bismarck would have some significance.

"I was going to be playing with some white boys," he stressed years later. "For the first time since I'd started throwing, I was going to have some of them on my side. It seemed real funny. It looked like they couldn't hold out against me all the way after all.

"I'd cracked another little chink in Jim Crow. But when I got to Bismarck I got a pretty cold shoulder. . . . Those mean folks didn't want any colored people around. They didn't want us living by them."

Trying desperately to walk a taut line between his customers and his new star, Churchill secured for Satch and Janet lodging—in an old railroad freight car in an area by the stockyards downtown, which boasted Bismarck's one black church. Janet in particular resented this incivility and—forgetting that she had encouraged him to come here—now turned her ire on Satch.

"If you didn't go running all over the country we wouldn't have to live like this," she told him snippily.

"You want to eat, don't you?" he replied, which only made her wonder about the cost of his fame and whether it was worth it to cash in on it in places like this. Already, in one year, he had gone from Kingfish Satch with no money to Boxcar Satch with money. What would he be next year?

For now, he had to live with Bismarck and Neil Churchill's Bismarcks. He went about it as he had back in Chattanooga, by turning heads with his frightening powers with a baseball. He did the old sideshow tricks, like knocking down a matchbox resting on a stick next to the plate with thirteen out of twenty pitches. The Bismarck catcher, told to warm up Satch, found that he could not even get a glove on the high-rising Long Tom.

And still, during his first start, a crisis developed when he had words with his outfielders, who had messed up on a number of fly balls. On the bench between innings, Satch got on them and one of them called him a "dirty nigger," and when the next inning began all three refused to take their positions behind him. This was surely an ironic twist—the old no-outfield riff now done in defiance of Satch. As he once recalled, "The fans loved it. They thought it was a stunt. I'd pulled plenty of stunts like that before, but this time it was serious business."

For long minutes the standoff went on, with Satch on the mound glaring at the outfielders in the dugout. Not even Neil Churchill could break it. It fell to Satch to do it in a most un-Satch way—by backing down. "When you show how big you are, you can be pretty nice to the little guy," he allowed. "I apologized and my outfielders did the same."

The entire incident made for a nice punch line and a feel-good aftermath in Paige's autobiography: "I decided from then on out I'd be the quiet guy, like I'd always been before. . . . After that game, I didn't have any troubles in Bismarck."

Actually, there would be plenty of trouble there for him, forcing him to seek comfort and friendship from about the only people in Bismarck who warmed to him away from the field—the Sioux Indians. They began calling him "Long Rifle," which Satch adopted as a nifty double entendre about his manhood. Fascinated by life on the reservation, thirsty for their firewater, and envious of their deadeye aim in the brush with a bow and arrow—the deer and squirrel rarely had anything to fear from Satch's use of a real long rifle—he may have even found the answer to perpetual youth. Or at least a good story about the topic for his catalogue of parables.

As Satch recalled a few years later in a *Collier's* magazine profile, "One day this Dorothy Deer invited me out in the hills to meet her papa who raised rattlesnakes in a deep pit in back of his hut. I looked at the snakes and said good-by. Before leavin', however, I ask the old man if he'd ever been bit, and he said lots of times, but he had an ointment that took out the harm. When he gave me a great big jug of it, I ask him if the ointment might be good for rubbin' my arm. He said he wouldn't advise it."

So of course he couldn't resist doing just that, to find out how this magic potion might juice up his weary arm. Daubing on this goo, he related with the Lord as his witness, his arm warmed, then tingled, then twitched. Mercy, it damn near revved up, separated from his shoulder, and took off for the next county without him.

"My mistake was I didn't dilute it," he recalled, wincing. "Man, it's a wonder my arm didn't fly outta the room."

But if the snake oil didn't really extend the life and already mystical torsion of the Long Rifle, he got just as much mileage out of it as a metaphor for the enigmatic abstractions of his life. "Since then," he said much later, "I always [kept] some in a jar and it kept my arm nice and young. It's real fine oil. . . . The formula is a secret. I promised those Indians I wouldn't tell it, but I'll put it in my will when I got no more need for it."

Though it was speculated that what he had in that jar was really olive oil, kerosene, or wolfbase and cherry stems, Satch merely called it "Deer Oil." In the Ballad of Satchel Paige, only the lonely, the disenfranchised, and the medicine men knew the best answers and the best secrets.

In his last game for Bismarck, snake oil turned snake eyes. Before that, Satch had shown Neil Churchill how easy the tables could turn in the Dakotas. The first time he faced Double Duty Radcliffe's illustrious Jamestown Red Sox, he threw a fifteen-strikeout shutout. But now, in their next meeting, he did himself in—again with irony biting his bravado in the butt.

Somehow managing to survive in the game, he led 15–14 when the Jamestown boys put a runner on with two out in the last of the ninth. Perspiring heavily, he absentmindedly began to mop his brow with both of his arms—a gesture that happened to be the signal he used to call in the outfielders in, that old routine having become a ritual of nearly every game on this gig.

This time, having no idea that his three new friends in the out-

field were squatting in the infield, he blissfully went into his
windup and watched in astonishment as a catchable pop fly
plopped into the vacated right field. Before anyone could get to
the ball, the batter circled the bases with a game-winning home
run.

With this acrid taste in his mouth, when Satch left the prairie, he
told Ted Radcliffe, it was not his intention to see the good people
of Bismarck again anytime soon.

•   •   •

A much more edifying assignment for him was to match fastballs
with Dizzy Dean. Indeed, Satch and Slim Jones had barely gotten
through with each other when each of them took their best shot at
the biggest name pitcher in the world.

Dean, who had won thirty regular-season games in 1934 and two
more in the St. Louis Cardinals' World Series victory, had agreed
to a two-month barnstorming schedule right after the Series. His
squad of "all-stars"—most of whom were really snot-nosed semi-
pros—would meet the Kansas City Monarchs in games played from
Oklahoma City down through Texas. They then would swing
through Philadelphia, D.C., the Alleghenies, and the coal dust
country of western Pennsylvania and eastern Ohio, playing a Negro all-star team drawn from the Crawfords and the Philadelphia
Stars. Then the Deans would end up as an entry in the California
Winter League.

While these games were ardently hyped, they provided no true
measure of the relative strength of Negro ball, and were immaterial vis-à-vis the color line; their real meaning was that yet another
white man—a white man from Arkansas, no less—wanted in when
Satchel Paige, Slim Jones, and Bullet Rogan shook their money-
makers. That he could cut himself in merely by calling a bunch of
moaxes the "Dizzy Dean All-Stars" did not ameliorate bigotry; it re-
inforced it and all its vulgarity. Dean once confided that he made
more on these tours than he had for winning the World Series, and
the real significance for blacks was that men like Satch and Joe Rogan were making up to $1,200 in games like these. Again, black
versus white could pay big dividends.

And so Dizzy Dean came to Philadelphia, where he lost to Slim
Jones in Shibe Park. And when he later matched up against Satch
in Cleveland, the colored boys laid it on him again, winning 4–1 as
Satch struck out thirteen. In another game, in Forbes Field, Satch

put out a fire by coming into the game in relief and striking out the side to preserve another Dean loss.

What must have discomfited Diz the most wasn't losing to the coloreds—the money was too good, his team too weak, the press coverage too skimpy for him to care. Rather, it was the brawl that erupted in that game at Forbes Field. With the two teams prodding, pushing, and taunting each other—but avoiding a fight that might be taken as racial warfare—Josh Gibson ambled over to Diz, placed his huge arms under Dean's armpits, removed him from the ground, and deposited him on his can some ten feet away. This would have never happened to him in Lucas, Arkansas, and as Dizzy Dean was propelled through Forbes Field at the speed of one of his pitches, the scent of change was riding in the air with him.

•   •   •

Comforted as he was by the solitary, endless outline of the road, Satch considered himself less of a Pittsburgh Crawford than ever. He was not happy that while he was wearing out tires and his body on his excursions to the boondocks, Gus Greenlee was in repose at the Crawford Grille waiting to split the fees earned by the Paige arm and name.

Not that Satch hadn't earned a certain éclat because of Gus's bookings. For one thing, there was the rush of being able to threaten to leave a full grandstand in the lurch unless the promoters put him up in the lodging of his choice. With Gus's name as an inducement, those local boys could pull strings at motels and lunch counters. In return, he would play "Satch," be the gooney bird, the coony superhero—but, always, it was gonna cost the locals. And if he felt like pitchin' just three innings and then taking a hike, well, they'd gotten Satch and were to be pleased with it.

Believing that he had earned his indemnity, he was itchy to cash in on his booming fame—alone, with no partners. The problem was that—aside from his power to quake men—Gus Greenlee could make one feel so nice. And Gus did that anew in late October of 1934, when Satch could no longer hold Janet at length and set their wedding date.

Janet, more emboldened by every day she kept Satch in her bed, had escalated her talk of marriage to the level where Satch had to give in or lose her—or so she said. And, by now, Satch was ready to fall. Having finally made the break from his delusions about Bertha Wilson, he figured that marriage to Janet would put that sad chapter to rest—though his ongoing letters to Bertha in Nashville belied his intentions. To his regret, he would soon learn the grief of marrying for the wrong reasons.

The wedding, on October 26, was held at the Crawford Grille. Gus Greenlee made it the biggest social event on the Hill since the Feast of the Nimrods, catering an eight-course dinner and an all-night party featuring three big bands and a tap-dance show by Bojangles Robinson, who was Satch's best man. Only after the vows, when the party was in full swing, did Satch discover that Gus's generosity had a catch to it.

Half in the bag, his ears ringing and his spats danced out, Satch was called to the head of the stage by big Gus, who had an announcement to make. Rather than the toast everyone expected, it was instead another of Gus's preemptive strikes.

"Satch won't be leaving us, don't worry about that," he bellowed, raising an issue he had heretofore kept between him and Satch. "I got a new contract here for him."

Sharp-minded as ever, Gus wasn't about to blow this kind of dough on Satch without getting him to finally stay put in Pittsburgh. In fact, even with Satch's eyes rolling about in separate directions, Gus insisted that he sit down with him right then and there and sign the new contract—for the same $250 a month he'd been receiving for a while. Feeling a pen placed in his hand, Satch scribbled an incontinent marker and stumbled back to the dance floor, not the slightest concerned with the contract—when was he ever concerned with a contract?

Instead, in what was a dire omen, he went back to scoping the women at the Grille, barely conscious of his new wife. Without thinking, and with words slurred, he even asked Bojangles where they were going to bounce later that night, just the two of them, the way they always did when Satch got to Harlem. But Janet, walking her new turf, reminded him that a honeymoon suite awaited them in a hotel on the Hill. No doubt feeling like she had him pinched by the ear, he was out the door. Looking back much later, he would recall that October 26 as truly the end of the party.

"I've been trying to forget that date for a long time now," he said. "I just don't like to think about that wedding anymore. We were just like a lot of folks. We made a mistake and it never should have started at all. We didn't find out different until it was too late."

He went on: "I felt like I would have if I had a three and two count on Josh Gibson and the bases was loaded. Knowing how he could hit, you don't want to let go of the ball, but you had to."

Gus paid for the honeymoon, too, in Los Angeles, though Satch saw as much of Dizzy Dean out there as he did Janet. Diz's team had made it to the coast, far behind in head-to-head play with the black opposition but fortified by a number of wintering big leaguers. But Diz still had no chance against Tom Wilson's reconstituted "Philadelphia Giants" all-star unit, which would again destroy all comers.

Satch, who had won eighteen of nineteen games in his California sojourns, met Diz again in what at the time was likely the most avidly promoted and hungrily attended game in Los Angeles history. A record 18,000 fans packed Wrigley Field that early November day, and if the in talk had it before that Satch was the equal of any big leaguer, this would be when the scuttlebutt expanded a bit—equal nothin'; the man was *better*. Because as solid as Dizzy Dean was against the cream of blackball, what Satch did against a lineup of capable big leaguers was extraordinary.

For thirteen innings these two gawky emus with fractured tongues took turns humiliating the hitters and gleefully ragging on each other. Before the game, Dean had told an interviewer that Satch "got a great fastball but no curve." The first time Diz came to bat, Satch yammered at him, "I hear you're goin' around tellin' people I ain't got a curve. Well, then, you tell me what this is." He then whiffed Diz—no big deal, to be sure—on three curves.

"How's that for a guy who ain't got a curve ball?" Satch gloated.

Diz, who had seen that Satch's blather was a benign kind of lip, laughed hard at the remark and at the comic potential of all these games. And while Satch too could enjoy the fact that he and Dizzy Dean seemed to be separated only by shades of pigment, that very difference gave the games an element of tragicomedy.

As Satch once said of his feelings and objectives when such meetings occurred, "They were saying Diz and me were about as alike as two tadpoles. We were both fast and slick. But Diz was in the majors and I was bouncing around the peanut circuit. If I was going to get the edge over him, I had to set him down in a little head-to-head baseball."

All gangly limbs, Satch and Diz could fuse every ounce of their being at the peak of their delivery, as if for one brief and perfect moment the movement of muscle and the snapping of joints made awful thunder. One of those who faced Satch on that day, the Boston Braves' Wally Berger—who had hit .298 that season—recalled that Paige and Dean "were about the same size and they both pitched with about the same speed—about ninety-five miles per hour."

And Berger was the one big leaguer who did well with Satch, getting the only hits off him that game, a double and a triple. The rest of the batting order came and went. Diz, in the meantime, was blowin' down the likes of Mule Suttles and Turkey Stearns and Cool Papa Bell and Willie Wells. By midgame, each pitcher treated any base hit with contempt.

On one of Berger's hits, he said, Satch "got one down a little too low and I hit it off the center field fence. As I was running, he followed me to second and yelled, 'How'd you hit that one?' "

The next three hitters were Dolph Camilli, Frank Demaree, and Gene Lillard—big leaguers all. Satch blew them away with dispatch—nine straight strikes. Satch and Diz looked as if they could go on like this forever, and when the Giants finally pushed across the winning run in thirteenth, the game ended with Diz having notched fifteen strikeouts, Satch seventeen.

As brimming with legend-making fodder as this duel and bravura performance was, it occurred far from the national media, both black and white. But Dizzy Dean, who was absolutely floored by Satch's ability, seemed to have had a pitching mound conversion from cracker to crooner for racial equity—and for Satchel Paige in particular—because of this game and series. A few years later, when Dean wrote a sports column in the *Chicago Tribune*, he repeated many of the same paeans that had no doubt stunned many of his old friends in Lucas, Arkansas. He wrote:

A bunch of fellows get in a barber session the other day and they start to arguefy about the best pitcher they ever see. Some says Lefty Grove and Lefty Gomez and Walter Johnson and old Pete Alexander and Dazzy Vance. And they mention Lonnie Warneke and Van Mungo and Carl Hubbell and Johnny Corriden tells us about Matty and he sure must of been great and some of the boys even say Old Diz is the best they ever see.

But I see them fellows but Matty and Johnson and I know who's the best pitcher I ever see and it's old Satchel Paige, that big lanky colored boy. Say, Old Diz is pretty fast . . . and you know my fast ball looks like a change of pace alongside that little bullet old Satchel shoots up to the plate. And I really know something about it because for four, five years I tour around at the end of the season with all all-star teams and I see plenty of Old Satch.

He sure is a pistol. It's too bad those colored boys don't play in
the big leagues because they sure got some great ball players. Anyway, that skinny old Satchel Paige with those long arms is my idea of
the pitcher with the greatest stuff I ever saw.

Putting aside the issue of Dean's sincerity in making these remarks—the man was, after all, a huckster and a baseball shaman,
and since overstatement was his trademark, at least some of what
he said was calculated for effect (such comments couldn't have
hurt in keeping the barnstorming coals hot)—the fact was that
such encomiums brought blacks no closer to big league consideration than the black barnstormers of Rube Foster's day.

Dan Burley, of course, dismissed as condescension such overboard endorsements even from well-intentioned white opinion-
makers, and if Burley himself went a little overboard in his
indictments—on the surface, the huzzahs of Dean and Marvin Mc-
Carthy seemed overgenerous to a fault—certainly it was time now
for less heat and more hard light to be trained on blackball and its
stars. In 1935, the shame of Dizzy Dean's benefaction was that it
only served to keep Satchel Paige in the distant mists of fantasy.

Still, Satch was eating up the acclaim, and it stoked him whenever he faced white teams. Continuing his rampage through the
California Winter League, he bested the Cubs' Larry French and
former Dodger Sloppy Thurston in games against Joe Pirrone's
team. Through January, he did not lose a single game in the CWL.

"To be sure," wrote the *Chicago Defender*'s James Newton in a February 1 story from Los Angeles, "the big fellow hasn't even come
close to being defeated while facing some of the best pitchers the
All-Stars have been able to borrow from the major leagues."

Riding the crest of a growing wave, Satch had another victim
dead in his sights. This one bore the imposing figure of Gus
Greenlee.

9

Upright
and Lowdown

Cheer the weary traveler
Along the heavenly way.

—Negro spiritual

In this, what may be called the "Dizzy Dean phase" of Satch's career, the best ballplayer not in the major leagues manifestly believed that he was too big for blackball—and he would make two
symbolic moves to prove it. First, even in the midst of the California Winter League season, he decided to turn his back on Tom
Wilson's so-called Philadelphia Giants, whom he had been steering
toward yet another league title.

His timing made the point with emphasis. In early March, during the last week of league competition, he jumped to a competing
team, the El Paso Mexicans, who were about to face the Giants in
Los Angeles's White Sox Park. Thus, on March 3, 1935, Satchel
Paige took the mound backed by people named Gonzáles, Lima,
Carillo, and Ocampo—to pitch *to* Cool Papa Bell et al. History
records this queer event as a misstep; though Satch struck out the
first four hitters, and eleven in all, he was cuffed for twelve hits—
three by catcher Larry Brown—and went down 7–2.

If by this seemingly gratuitous jump Satch was readying himself
to flee the Negro leagues, the Negro leaguers were ready to hold
open the door. Their disdain for him having ripened over the
years, Satch's association with Dizzy Dean now acted as a wedge between him and the other blacks. The alliance was no gain for them,

and solely benefited him. Many Negro leaguers, and especially those predisposed against Satch as a hick, pilloried him as very much the equal of Dizzy Dean—which was no compliment off the field.

Jake Stephens, Satch's teammate in 1932 and his most vocal critic, couldn't resist the comparison in damning Dean with the faintest of praise. Diz, he said, "was a hell of a pitcher. But he wasn't the kind of guy you'd want to introduce your sister to. Dean had a big mouth, like Satchel, ignorant. Didn't know right from wrong. Just a cotton picker, didn't have no education."

On all sides, then, the Dizzy Dean phase brought Satch little that was fruitful, except perhaps a new surge of nerve directed at Gus Greenlee. For months, Satch had been pissed off about Gus's wedding night squeeze play, and how Gus took advantage of him. Not that Gus hadn't done that kind of thing before—but at least Satch was conscious when it happened.

Now, when he returned from California—after winning seventeen of nineteen games—just as the Crawfords were about to open their spring training camp in Hot Springs, Arkansas, Satch pulled his own squeeze play. With unnatural virulence, he showed up at the Crawford Grille, slid into Greenlee's booth, and demanded more money. Gus, who was growing penurious in the wake of the club's financial losses, didn't budge; $250 a month, that was his limit. Years later, Satch would remember this frosty moment with the same hostility with which he walked into the Grille that day.

"Ol' Satch didn't get mad too many times back in those days, everything going so good," he wrote in his autobiography. "But I perked over right then and there.

"Gus wouldn't give in. All he said was something like 'don't forget the game we got coming up next week.'

"I was so mad I went home and started throwing clothes into a suitcase."

He was so enraged that he would have gone to the ends of the earth for a pitching job outside the Greenlee orbit. As it turned out, he nearly did just that: he went back to Bismarck.

He had little choice, really. Neil Churchill's terms were still on the table, $400 a month and another late model off the used-car lot, and knowing this had put the iron in Satch's veins in challenging Greenlee. The only downside was Bismarck, and Satch had no intention of taking a cranky Janet along to remind him of the deprivations of the town; still, knowing he'd be getting back to the bachelor lifestyle may well have eased his flight from Pittsburgh.

And so he took to the road again, walking out on his new two-year Crawford contract. When he did, it had to hurt Gus that Satch was the first man he'd known who could defy him with such indifference. Every gangster in the East feared him, but those were squirrely little men. That Satch paid him no heed ate at Gus on a human level; Gus always worried that Satch had scarcely more sense than a ten-year-old, and Satch's exodus was like a child running away from home. Gus still thought he could somehow discipline him into seeing the light; after all, Gus had his pride, his interests, and the guise of Negro National League integrity to think of, to say nothing of potential gate losses that would be severe with Satch's defection.

A show of force was necessary and Gus made one, if at first gingerly. On April 26, he planted an item in the *Pittsburgh Courier* that reported that Satch had been "assigned" to Ray L. Dean, who was Greenlee's Western promoter. "It is believed," the item said, "that the sensational right hander is being disciplined and will be required to perform for House of David. A clause prohibiting his appearance of service in games against league clubs has been inserted [in his contract]."

By this rebuke and the mention of the House of David, Greenlee was apparently attempting to shame him back by boxing Satch into the small time—but the real intent may have been to set the stage for something more serious. As Satch would recall of his post-jump ramifications around Negro ball, "Back in Pittsburgh Gus Greenlee must have really been burned up. . . . I started hearing he was after me for jumping out on that contract and going to Bismarck. He was trying to get the Negro leagues to ban me."

This could not have bothered Satch much. With the wealth of the backroad baseball universe open to him, he was elated at the chance to stick it to the NNL bandits. Said Satch: "Those Negro league owners were just spiting themselves, I figured. Everywhere I went those days I set attendance records.

"There was plenty of green floating in, and I was getting my share of it, but Gus and his pals weren't. They felt it, too, and don't let anybody tell you different."

He even told of an alleged offer that came about that spring, by a semipro team set to play an exhibition game against the Pittsburgh Pirates. The manager of that team, he said, tendered him $400 to pitch just that one game—which never took place, the tale went, because the Pirates' player-manager, future Hall of Famer Pie Traynor, refused to let his team stand in against Satch. As he quoted Traynor, "Paige is too good for my boys at this stage of the training. Why, he might go out there and strike out sixteen or seventeen. Can you imagine what that would do to their morale?"

Meanwhile, back in the NNL, team pictures of the Crawfords and the Grays ran on the front page of the *Courier* in early April. Noticeable by his absence was Satch. Yet Greenlee, his fellow racketeers, and much of the black press trusted that Satch would be home for the August 11 East-West Game. As late as mid-July, the *Chicago Defender* ran an overheated full-page advertisement for that showcase game of Negro ball that read "HERE IT IS FOLKS!! JUST WHAT YOU'VE BEEN WAITING FOR—THE 'TOPS' IN BASE-BALL. AMERICA'S GREATEST ALL-STAR COLORED PLAYERS IN ACTION. THE GAME OF GAMES. THE THRILL OF A LIFE-TIME!!" Among the ten stars listed in the ad was the absent Satchel Paige.

In another issue, the *Defender* splashed a two-page illustration of Satch under the heading FANS, MEET BASEBALL'S GREATEST FIGURE and the subhead "The East's Main Hope in the East-West Game."

But flattery got Gus Greenlee and the *Defender* nowhere. Hardly what Satch was waiting for, he stayed away from the game, a long way away.

•   •   •

In Satch's state of self-commitment, Bismarck suddenly had its seductions. To begin with, Neil Churchill had become a scale-model Gus Greenlee, or at least the Greenlee of a few years ago, aggrandizing Satch and willing to lay out huge coin to surround him with available black talent—which he did almost entirely at the expense of the great Jamestown team. The Bismarcks began the 1935 season with four Negro league veterans: Satch, his Crawford moundmate Barney Morris, catcher Quincy Trouppe, and infielder Red Haley. Midway through the summer, they were joined by two more colored stars, Double Duty Radcliffe and the marvelous Monarchs pitcher Hilton Smith.

If the '32 Crawfords were the Yankees of blackball, this unit was the Crawfords of prairieball; and yet for Satch the biggest kick about the whole thing was that Churchill got him out of the railroad yards and into a house trailer on the southside of town, one large enough for him to entertain some of the friendlier people of Bismarck—people who, to Satch's great delight, happened to be women who were young and white.

Ted Radcliffe, who came to town and bunked in the trailer with Satch, grinningly recalled that this aluminum funhouse had a "revolving door for the ladies." On most days, he said, "one would be goin' in as one was goin' out."

Very pleasantly distracted by this tap of good cheer in a town that defined the word prosaic, Satch often did not leave that trembling trailer for days at a time. It came as no shock to Radcliffe when Satch woke up one morning with an itchy discomfort that was later diagnosed as gonorrhea, prompting an unscheduled trip with Neil Churchill to Rochester, Minnesota, to the Mayo Clinic for penicillin treatment. Somehow, that episode didn't make it into Satch's memoirs.

Radcliffe maintained that Satch was so wrung out from his Dakota saturnalia that he was ineffective for much of the season: "He couldn't throw a ball across the street," Radcliffe said. "He couldn't pitch for a whole month. I told him, 'You can just roll it up there. They scared of yo' name, they ain't gonna hit it.' "

Double Duty made the claim that he had to step in for Satch as the Bismarcks' ace, even though Satch was continually billed as the starter everywhere the club went. Paige, said Radcliffe, would draw the crowd and start, only to ask out after four innings. Radcliffe said he would catch and then have to relieve the bone-weary Satch and close out the last five innings. For this, Radcliffe condemned his old hometown chum for years after as a first-class loafer. Satch, he pointed out, had failed to show up during one Bismarck road trip. "He went fishin' with some rich man and didn't show up till the next Sunday. And you couldn't fire him 'cause he'd quit. That's a bitch, ain't it?"

Radcliffe insisted that, then and for years later, "I can give him hell," for these alleged character flaws, " 'cause he and I were buddies." Even as Satch grew as a reputed icon of baseball liberation and was idealized by most of his contemporaries in the name of public solidarity, Radcliffe said he wouldn't cover up for him. "I used to tell people, 'He's bigger than the game, man. You can't find him and you can't fire him. What you gonna do with him?' "

Radcliffe concluded: "I don't care if he could throw the ball so hard you couldn't see it. If he couldn't take orders I wouldn't want him, would you?"

Yet, on this count of indictment, recorded history is much kinder to Satch than is Ted Radcliffe's memory, putting the motives of Radcliffe—a self-promoting man who for many years all but demanded his own inclusion into the Hall of Fame—in doubt.

For one thing, Satch not only did not miss many starts with the Bismarcks that season, he labored far beyond what would have been deemed appropriate. Neil Churchill wasn't just after prestige; he wanted to break the bank, and he simply would not have heard the cash register bells if Satchel Paige didn't take the mound almost every other game.

This was the season when Paige's arrival made the team big news in the pages of the *Bismarck Tribune*; while some of the coverage was spotty, a fairly comprehensive record of box scores and game stories tells of a routinely remarkable Satchel Paige season. Absent in that reportage is any reference to Ted Radcliffe catching Satch (the number two pitcher, Barney Morris, did so regularly), or his off-repeated claim that he would relieve Satch after four innings. But there are several references to Paige playing right field on the days he did not pitch.

By July 1, when Satch and Barney Morris beat the Colored House of David in both ends of a doubleheader—ending the Davids' thirty-three-game winning streak—Paige had already chalked up seventeen wins in the Bismarcks' fifty-some games to that point. If there was stiff competition, Satch was the man. When Charros de la Junta, the Mexican League champions, came to town in early July and shut out the Bismarcks in the first game of a doubleheader, Satch was called on to save face. According to the *Tribune*, he "completely handled the situation in the second game," striking out nine and giving up two hits in five innings before a Midwest storm wiped out the scoreless game. Ten days later, the teams met again and Satch rode two homers by the Bismarcks' big slugger, Moose Johnson, to a thirteen-strikeout, 8–1 win.

The Bismarcks' top priority was the season series against the depleted Jamestown Red Sox, and Satch set the tone with a 4–2 victory on July 7. Barney Morris then cleaned the Sox 8–1 in mid-July, and Double Duty Radcliffe, in his first start for Bismarck, dispatched them with a 2–0 one-hitter late in the month.

The money, though, was to be had on the long road during tournament season. First came the Canadian tournaments—and the Bismarcks were absolutely relentless, smashing Canadian teams across a dotted line of cities from Esterhazy to Russell to Langenburg to Virden to Portage la Prairie. In the final Canadian tournament, in

Manitoba, Satch threw a title-winning 5–2, fourteen-strikeout triumph over the fabulously named Devil's Lake Satans, a Cleveland
Indians farm club.

That earned the Bismarcks a half-page team photo in the *Tribune*
on August 9, under the heading CARRY BISMARCK'S HOPES IN
NATIONAL TOURNAMENT IN WICHITA. Satch and the team
warmed up for that, the National Baseball Congress championship, with a frightening twenty-two-hit, 21–6 win over the Twin
City Colored Giants—a game that was so surreal that when Satch
kept the fans awake by calling in his outfield *and* his infield in the
last inning, the *Tribune* man didn't quite know what to make of it
all and by playing it straight composed one of the classic double-
take paragraphs of all time:

"The game ended with only Bismarck's battery on the field,
lanky Satchel Paige in the box and Barney Morris behind the plate.
This unusual calling in of the fielders gave the visitors one more
home run and two more runs than they rightfully earned."

The Negro press, used to the Satch shtick, handled such news
with a tad more élan. On the way to Wichita, the Bismarcks played
a semipro unit in McPherson, Kansas. Satch was staked to a 14–0
lead, but his ears were ringing from a game-long stream of racial
invective from the grandstand. In the ninth inning he again had
the outfield and the infield go to the bench, whereupon he blew
away the McPhersons on nine pitches. For this, the *Baltimore Afro-
American* ran a huge picture of Satch, who, it said, had "entered
baseball's hall of fame . . . by calling in the infield and outfield of
his team . . . in their game with a white Kansas nine."

The Bismarcks arrived in Wichita with a twelve-game winning
streak and a season's record of sixty-six wins, fourteen losses, and
four ties. But even as manager of the tournament's top-seeded
team, Neil Churchill ran into immediate static in town. As with the
Kansas City Monarchs' experience in Denver the year before, the
entrance of black men in this whitebread tournament caught the
locals off guard. Not realizing the overall complexion of the team,
a hotel in Wichita had granted reservations for thirty people—but
when the half dozen blacks walked into the lobby with the team,
the desk clerk refused to give them rooms. As luck would have it,
Satch and Ted Radcliffe had been through these parts in the past
and knew where to find a black rooming house, to the great embarrassment of Neil Churchill.

Radcliffe laughed hard about this. "Churchill thought we were
mad. He didn't know we *preferred* to stay there. There were roomin'

houses all over the country where we stayed. That was our family. Since you couldn't bring white girls into them hotels, you *had* to have a room, man. We stayed in this place for three dollars a night and got two home-cooked meals. We didn't need no hotel."

More ominously, some of the competing teams were not eager to play the Negro leaguers. Not because they were black, per se, but because they were downright awesome on the field. As was his custom, Satch personalized the situation in recalling how "some of them managers was talking about keeping me out . . . because I was too good. A real big fight got going, with the fans wanting me to play and the managers saying I was really a major leaguer and they couldn't match me with any of their white boys."

This, of course, was one of the dirty secrets of the times—that many of these men put down in big league circles as too "intellectually inferior" to play on that level were in fact very big league. But this worked to their advantage only selectively. While it was perfectly fine for a Satchel Paige or a Double Duty Radcliffe to come through a hick town, rouse up a crowd, and beat the pants off the yokels, their rights to acquire big prize money in state tournaments was something else. In Wichita, the issue caused such a ruckus that, laughed Radcliffe, "They tried to cause a meetin' on us. . . . They said that Satchel and I were niggers—but we were *big league* niggers."

The Bismarcks did play, but they were told that they would not be invited back thereafter, which was a common fate of many black and integrated teams who dominated white teams in big tournaments—they got one chance at the prize and then it was adiós. The Bismarcks made most of their chance, against some choice opposition in a thirty-two-team field. In Wichita, they were a buzzsaw, tearing through teams with names straight from the pediment of Americana, among them the Wichita Watermen and the Denver Fuelers. Having beaten the Halliburton Cementers of Duncan, Oklahoma, in an earlier round, they faced them again in the title game.

Satch, coming into the game with three tournament wins and as "easily the outstanding pitcher in the tournament," according to the *Tribune*, allowed the Cementers nine hits but whiffed fourteen—ringing up a record sixty-six for the tournament. But it wasn't until he drove in two runs with a clutch single in the seventh inning, breaking a 1–1 tie, that the Bismarcks were home free with a 5–2 win.

At $1,000 per victory, Churchill's boys left Wichita $7,000 heavier, while back in Bismarck the *Tribune* went batty with the town's first national title of any kind. The news ran on the front page, in thick type, right under a headline about the state adopting a grain credit plan to aid victimized farmers.

Satch got his due with a caricature in the sports section, one that was indicative of the semifacetious bombast that the white press considered to be appropriate in exulting men like Satchel Paige. Depicted as a kind of simian creature with a mitt, a sequence of illustrations hailed him for "combining the speed of Jesse Owens with . . . the dynamite in a Joe Louis punch—That's Satchel Paige's Delivery!" Under a cartoon of him winding up, a caption read: "No, Elmer. Not an Ethiopian war dance. Just Satch winding up that steel spring in his right arm." Satch was pictured as saying, "Ah got live powah!!" About the only non–mock heroic part of the strip was a handbag with the legend: "Plenty of what it takes chucked away in that Satchel!"

Satch had indeed come to Bismarck because of filthy lucre. And he and his team more than doubled their take in Wichita on the season's final stop—the *Denver Post* tournament that Satch had made into his personal playground the year before. He would do much the same this time, and it seemed almost to be orchestrated by Satch that he would meet in the title game the same Colored House of David team with which he had *won* the thing last year— though the highlight of this tournament probably came a week before in a doubleheader between the Bismarcks and the Davids.

Satch, who had pitched the day before, wasn't scheduled to pitch on this Sunday but—as was often the case on days like these—he turned out to be the star of both games. In the opener, he came on in the seventh inning after Radcliffe had fallen behind 4–3. Double Duty then went behind the plate and caught Satch, who struck out seven hitters over the next three innings and drove home three runs with a bases-loaded double in the eighth, a screamer down the right field line that was the gamer in the 6–4 Bismarck victory.

Then, in a near replay, he came on in the seventh inning of the nightcap. The Bismarcks were trailing 2–1, and as the *Chicago Defender*'s game story reported, "When Satch was called in . . . the crowd rose to its feet and gave him a rousing cheer and called for a shutout [the rest of the game]. Paige did as they requested, holding the bewhiskered gents hitless . . . and striking out four. His teasing curves and smoking fast ball left the [Davids] swinging through the thin air."

His only real problem in the title game—a 2–0, eight-strikeout waltz—came not from the bats but the confounding beards of the Davids. Tampering with nature once again, Satch was cruising when a Trouble Ball got away from him in the seventh inning and played some *real* chin music as it hummed through the underbrush of the Davids' hitter. When the umpire ruled it a hit batsman, Satch—no doubt recalling how he'd been sabotaged by his own "beard" the year before—now raised an intriguing point of order.

"Empire," he argued, "if you will kindly observe here, you will see that these whiskers can't rightly be called no part of a man. They is air."

The umpire thought about this conundrum for long minutes before deciding to stick with his original call, though perhaps wishing that Solomon had been around to make the final judgment.

•   •   •

Now Satch faced another fork in the lonely road. The Bismarcks' season over, he again resolved that he had played his last game for the team—a reasoning that coincided with a tempest brewing in the town, one that had led him to load all of his belongings into his Caddy when the team set out for Wichita.

More and more, the goings-on in Satch's trailer had become public knowledge in Bismarck, and they far overrode the communal joy in a winning ball team. The town's white fathers, who cheered these black men on the field, were not about to contribute their daughters to these same men's private comforts. As Ted Radcliffe said, by summer's end Satch didn't know day to day whether he would hear the sound of cheering at the park or that of gunfire.

"It's amazing," Radcliffe insisted, "that we all got outta that place alive."

Neil Churchill, whose Chrysler dealership depended on the goodwill he could build in his town, was thankful that he could keep a lid on Satch's carrying on. Now, he wisely determined that he had gotten all that he needed from Satchel Paige. When Denver was conquered, Churchill settled up with Satch for a job well done. Forgetting about $970 Satch owed him in outstanding payments for yet another car from off the lot, he also gave him $500 out of his pocket—a mere cherry stuck on top of the $5,000 confection that Satch had dished up for himself in just those last two tournaments—

and wished him well. Satch, of course, knew the score. Nevermore would Bismarck or anywhere else in the Dakotas enter into his plans, though he figured he had taken that gig to the max anyway.

Neil Churchill never had another ride like the one he had in 1935. Ted Radcliffe and some of the other players remained, but the Bismarcks were a burnt-out bunch in '36, and soon after the team had new sponsorship and went into the Northern League as a white team. But Churchill did well for himself as a leader of men. In 1937 he opened a second Corwin-Churchill Motors in Fargo, and created a huge auto parts factory. In 1939, his name known in every household, Neil Orr Churchill was elected mayor of Bismarck, and served in office until 1946.

•   •   •

Satch, on the other hand, could not go home again, having put himself on the outs in the NNL. Not having acceded to Gus Greenlee's dictum to do a brief penance with the House of David, he had officially been banned from the league for the 1935 season. Among league people, the smug assumption was that his alternative had been a sterner punishment than the House of David; they believed he had been stuck in Purgatory in Bismarck.

But that was fine by him; Satch enjoyed being the top gate attraction in salt-and-pepper baseball—one step closer, after all, to white baseball—after the black powers cast him adrift. But then, people with power in the organized baseball world were firmly on his spit list now; all authority was the enemy. In his autobiography, Paige would be bitterly cynical about this period, when his achievements would be followed by a flux of unfounded rumors that he and other great black players were about to be given big league tryouts. Any such hints to that effect he dismissed out of hand as bamboozling—"Big talk," as he called it. "Those [big league] owners said some big-hearted things and then just shut up. They always like to talk but some of the worst medicine I ever swallowed came in some sweet-tasting candy."

Needing a team to play for in September of 1935, and with his big-time options limited, Satch now turned to the estimable John Leslie Wilkinson. Having played along the same prairie circuit as the Kansas City Monarchs and their many satellite teams, Satch considered himself a goombah of Wilkie's, and J.L. must have thought such an entreaty was heaven-sent. He was so elated by Satch's coming aboard that Wilkie risked suffering the indignation of the grand pasha of blackball in the East, Gus Greenlee, with whom he had been on distant but amiable terms. Landing a master showman like Satchel Paige was worth it.

J. L. Wilkinson was after all the progenitor of blackball as vaudeville act. Born in Perry, Iowa, in 1874 as the son of a college president, Wilkie was, like Cum Posey, a college man, attending Highland Park College in Des Moines. A pitcher on the school team, he played semipro ball under the name of Joe Green to avoid detection in this plebeian pursuit by his stuffy father.

Wilkinson was hopelessly bitten by the game, playing for peanuts in one-horse Iowa towns like Marshalltown and Creston. Playing for the Hopkins Brothers Sporting Goods team, when the club's manager absconded with the gate proceeds one day, Wilkie became manager, which fed his baseball ambitions further. The Hopkins team was an important incubator for Wilkie, as the brothers also sponsored a girls' baseball team—only instead of all girls, many players were actually men in drag, including J. L. Wilkinson.

This set the stage for Wilkie's own team, the All Nations. But, to Wilkie's credit, the All Nations, and later his Monarchs, sidestepped the Abe Saperstein style of bushball farce. None of Wilkie's men (or woman) of the All Nations wore clown white or grass skirts, nor did they screech and act out America's vision of an amusing race of subhumans. They considered the game to be sacred, if not the means necessary to get folks to buy tickets to see it.

The All Nations were based in Des Moines, but their success rested out in the hinterlands. They became a traveling road show, Wilkie's idea being to surround some excellent, multiracial players with fluff like a dance band to play before games, wrestlers to wrestle after games—and players such as the great Cuban pitcher José Méndez, the legendary lefty John Donaldson, and the man who would later teach Satchel Paige the Hesitation Pitch, Plunk Drake.

Another Wilkie trademark was the first-class accommodations he provided his team. The Nations, aping Rube Foster's American Giants, traveled in a $25,000 Pullman car, and Wilkie increased seating capacity by toting with the team portable bleachers. To save money, the players took their own tents with them and slept on the field they'd play on the next day.

The All Nations became a blackball power. In 1915 they beat Foster's American Giants two out of three games in Chicago, and *Sporting Life* claimed that they were "strong enough to give any major league club a nip and tuck battle." Only because World War I took many of its players, and the times worsened, did the club eventually disband.

But out of their ashes came Wilkie's jackpot attraction, the Monarchs, which he began in 1920 with remnants of the All Nations in the growing urban center of Kansas City. Gorging on power, forcing his way into the first Negro National League, Wilkie had his Monarchs in the first two Negro World Series. But barnstorming—always under the highly conjectural title of "World's Colored Champions"—was his real money game, and his lights and conjunctions with the House of David ensured his success after that league went under.

By signing Satch on a game-by-game basis in late September 1935, Wilkie may have offended Greenlee and the Eastern teams, but he put Satch in a Monarchs uniform in time for a huge series in early October between the two regional titans, the Monarchs and the American Giants, to be played in Chicago, Omaha, and Kansas City. If these games featured old Negro league worlds in collision—Rube Foster's spit and polish versus J. L. Wilkinson's see-what-sticks-to-the-wall eclecticism—more immediately it also reactivated the old rivalry between Satch and Willie Foster, who faced each other in the opening game on October 4 at Comiskey Park.

The *Defender* hyped and covered this game as maniacally as the Eastern black press had the Paige-Slim Jones showdown at Yankee Stadium the year before—SATCHEL PAIGE TO FACE GIANTS, WILL BE ON MOUND FOR KANSAS CITY HERE SUNDAY, squealed its headline days before. Over 7,500 fans turned out in forty-degree cold for this year's latest "greatest game ever." Moreover, while the rivalry carried over to the press corps in those cities, the *Defender* hinged all of its reportage around the string-bean expatriate, with just cause, even though Satch lost to Foster 7–1. Satch pitched five shutout innings and struck out eight before his arm stiffened in the cold and he had to come out with a 1–0 lead. Chet Brewer and Charles Beverly then let the game get away, yielding seven runs in the last two innings. But instead of praising the comeback, Dan Burley, whose coverage was carried in the *Defender*, came to praise Satchel Paige.

The ubiquitous Burley—who of course had ridiculed Marvin McCarthy's "Black Matty" piece—chose to apotheosize Satch now as a black Cassius, turning to Shakespeare and Julius Caesar for inspiration. Playing off Caesar's "Yond Cassius has a lean and hungry look" soliloquy, Burley delivered this parable:

[The loss] wasn't the fault of Lean and Hungry Mr. Paige. His "hungry" thoughts outsmarted the Giants at every turn when they sought to chase runs across the pan. His "lean" delivery was lean in truth insofar as base hits were concerned and was leaner in the granting of runs. . . .

Were it possible for old Julius the Roman conquerer to take form out of the ashes which were scattered to the four winds the day after Brutus laid him low, and were it possible for him to lamp the angular giant, winding his right arm up like King Jones used to wind up his left leg while doing the Charleston, he would have been forced to doff his iron headgear in abject respect to an abler giant who was master of his calling all the way. . . . They must have whispered to large Willie Foster . . . that there would be Balm in Gilead when the "Lean One" marched away.

Paige and Foster went at it again the following Sunday at Kansas City's Muehlenbach Stadium, and they jousted man for man over seven suffocating innings, each allowing three hits before the 0–0 game was called because of darkness.

Keeping on his Monarchs uniform, Satch returned with the club to Omaha for a game with a semipro team built around several Detroit Tigers fresh from their World Series victory, including Charlie Gehringer and Schoolboy Rowe. Before 5,000 people, Satch was matched against Tommy Bridges for three innings. He fanned five and gave up no hits as the Monarchs mauled Bridges for four runs in the first three innings on the way to an 8–2 win.

While Satch could thank J. L. Wilkinson for getting him some profitable action in spite of the NNL ban, it was Tom Wilson who influenced his foreseeable future. When the Monarchs were done for the season, Wilson invited him to again pitch for his traveling Philadelphia Giants contingent against Dizzy Dean's All-Stars on the Deans' latest Eastern barnstorming tour. In the opening game of a series between the teams in York, Pennsylvania, Satch had all he needed when Josh Gibson slammed one over the wall for three runs in the first inning, and beat Dean 3–0. Then he beat Diz again, 3–0 in Forbes Field, this time behind Boojum Wilson's homer.

Tom Wilson had every intention of keeping Satch in tow in the California Winter League, but bigger prey awaited Paige on the coast. Just after the new year, he got the chance to front his own team—the Satchel Paige All-Stars. That occurred at the behest of northern California promoter Johnny Burton, who needed a marketable team to face an all-star squad composed of big leaguers out of the Bay Area—including Ernie Lombardi, Augie Galan, Cookie Lavagetto, and Gus Suhr—and a certain minor leaguer from the Bay Area whom everyone in the hardball world was eager to see hit against top-shelf pitching.

This was to be Joseph Paul DiMaggio's last stop before joining the Yankees for his rookie season. In 1935, playing for the San Francisco team in the Pacific Coast League, DiMaggio had hit a mere .398 with 154 runs batted in. While his big league debut was still months away, DiMaggio may have faced baseball's best pitcher on February 7, 1936, in Oakland.

Satch's problem was that he would be facing this hardy group essentially by himself. With only one other Negro leaguer—New York Black Yankees catcher Ebel Brooks—on his team, the rest of the players came from black sandlots around Oakland. And yet this game ran along roughly the same lines as most all of his others. With more than 4,000 fans cramming the ballpark, he smoked the ball the entire game. He struck out Suhr, the cleanup hitter, three times and Lavagetto twice—twelve in all over nine innings, while allowing three hits. DiMaggio grounded out, flied out, and was nicked by a pitch.

Paige had one moment of weakness in the second inning when he gave up successive doubles to score a run, but he slammed the door shut thereafter and—batting sixth in the order—drove in the tying run with a ground single in the fourth. As Satch recalled the game, "The . . . innings rolled by and they hadn't gotten another hit off me. But we couldn't dent the plate. I'd done everything I could. I'd slid into first trying to beat out a hit. I'd busted into second to break up a double play. Why, those two slides were more slides than I'd had for the whole season.

"And when I wasn't batting or running, I was down at first trying to coach those plumbers playing with me."

He would forever swear that "some dumb umpire who didn't know safe from out" robbed him by calling him out at first base on a slow roller in the ninth with two gone and Ebel Brooks on third. "I was so mad," he said, "my stomach started crying and I had to belch to ease the miseries." When he went back out for the bottom of the tenth, the dusk had removed nearly all sight of the ball. He struck out two more, but Dick Bartell managed to single.

That brought up the precocious DiMaggio and Satch seared two quick strikes by him, though Bartell stole second on the first pitch and went to third when the fissionable fastball got by Ebel Brooks for a wild pitch. Now, with Joe D trying somehow to get wood on an invisible object, Satch pumped and another screamer came in. DiMaggio swung and topped the ball just to Satch's left—which *Satch* couldn't fully see. Sticking out his glove, he deflected it toward the second baseman, who, as Satch would recall, looked "half frozen. It looked like an hour before that sandlotter moved." Slow to grab it, the guy threw late to first, and the scratch hit scored the winning run.

"I just stood there on the mound awhile," Satch said of the play's aftermath. "Finally I moved off the mound and walked by those major leaguers. DiMaggio was there grinning to beat all. He was talking to his teammates. I didn't hear all he said, but I did hear him say something like, 'Now I know I can make it with the Yankees. I finally got a hit off Ol' Satch.' "

And, in fact, there was reason to believe that, even if this hit did not resemble a fountainhead, the mere act of beating Satch did carry heavy mythological weight among many white people. Some years later, a Yankee scout who had been at the game would recall that he had wired the big club a report that day which read DIMAGGIO ALL WE HOPED HE'D BE: HIT SATCH ONE FOR FOUR. Satch definitely made note of *that* in his memoirs.

Even then, this game seemed to presage the making of a big league career for Satch. On the day after, the black *Oakland Journal* ran sportswriter Eddie Murphy's game story, which hinted at big doings for Paige.

"The greatest baseball pitching attraction in the world is being passed up by scouts, club owners and managers only because the doors of organized ball are closed to him," wrote Murphy, "[but] there's a movement to have [Paige] appear here next Sunday as pitcher for the Minor League All-Stars, and oppose the Major Stars again." There was also renewed scuttlebutt about granting tryouts to certain Negro leaguers.

Having heard such persiflage before, Satch's response was acrid and dismissive—and, as usual, prophetic.

"I'm probably drawin' more money right now than any other pitcher in baseball," he told one writer. "What owner is goin' to pay that kind of money right now at my age? Even if I did jump, I don't think those white boys from the South'd stand it. They got ahold of somethin' bitter when they were little and they ain't been able to relax and smile at the world since then."

He went on: "This business of tryin' us out at the tail end of the season makes me laugh. If they wanted to try out colored ballplayers they'd take them to training camps, same as the white boys. . . . No sir, I'm not giving up any of my money just to make some owner look good-hearted."

To the surprise of absolutely no one, the "plan" to find Satchel Paige a place on a minor league team died aborning.

10

Mucho Calor

Baseball in Trujillo City is not commercial. Money makes no difference. Baseball is spiritual in every aspect, as indulged in by Latin races.

> —Dr. José Enrique Aybar,
> adjutant of President Rafael
> Trujillo, 1937

I had it fixed with Mr. Trujillo's polices. If we win, their whole army is gonna run out and escort us from the place. If we lose, there is nothin' to do but consider myself and my boys as passed over Jordan.

> —Satchel Paige

Much more pressing business to Satch than any big league fantasia was the resolution of his marriage. After his summer-long bender in North Dakota, he was again ready to settle in with Janet, who gave him no choice about it: either he came home to Pittsburgh or she was filing for divorce. For all his rueful alienation about the subject of love, the frightened boy in him cowered when confronted by rejection.

"I'd seen that coming," he recalled of her demand. "I should have just called it quits with Janet then, but I was still trying to hang on."

And so he came back to the Hill, to make an interim peace with Gus Greenlee—who happened to need Satch more than ever now. Running the NNL had become a terrible chore for Gus, something on the order of holding together a hornets' nest fallen from its tree. Even though his Crawfords had won the 1935 NNL title, Gus's losses on league expenses were several thousand dollars. Greenlee also had a costly new hobby, building a stable of champion black prizefighters; while one of his fighters, John Henry Lewis, won the light-heavyweight title in October 1935, Gus footed the costs of a dozen or so other fighters as well as a gym, trainers, and travel to and from bouts.

All told, with Satch's absence having cost the Craws at the gate, Gus's puddle of red ink deepened to over $10,000 even in that championship year. His relations with his fellow owners worsened by the day, with charges flung back and forth—accused of skimming way too much off the top of the East-West Game, Greenlee shot back that the other owners were stiffing the league of their dues. Striking a no more Mr. Nice Guy pose, he warned the other wiseguys that "up to now I have been a congenial fellow," but that now, to save his honor, "you'll see a fighting Greenlee equipped with everything needed to win."

With Tom Wilson having inveigled Satch some of the way back into the NNL fold, Gus scrambled to welcome back to Pittsburgh the biggest weapon in Negro ball. Indeed, when talk circulated about Satch getting a shot in white ball, Negro league club owners were not at all excited by what would be a foot in the big door; they were *aghast*, as such a development would rob their game of its most lucrative commodity. And if Gus Greenlee was distrustful of his fellow paladins in the NNL, he was adamant about the proprietary rights of his shaky league: if the big leagues were going to open up to anyone black, he believed, it should be lower-level guys at first, running interference for the novas who would come later—at a price.

If the Satchel Paiges and Josh Gibsons were held back, Gus and his brothers could retain an economic concession when the wall came down. Gus didn't only want Satch now; he had to have him, even if he had to retract his salary line and pay Satch a whopping $600 a month, by far the highest in Negro ball.

Satch, who felt he owed Greenlee nothing, took Gus's call and his offer as a temporary sop. Still leery of authority, no happier about having to take what he even now considered a slave wage from the plantation boss, Satch ridiculed Greenlee's capitulation while ignoring his own. "While that major league talk was going around, the Negro league owners decided to be nice to me again," he said years later, his sarcasm fairly oozing. "They wanted those fans I could pull . . . [and] that's what made Gus Greenlee get ahold of me."

There was also something in it for J. L. Wilkinson. To keep Satch away from the Monarchs, Greenlee extracted from Wilkie a promise not to re-sign Paige; in return, J.L. was assured that the NNL would recognize a competing league the following season, to be made up of Midwest teams and overseen by Wilkie in the manner Gus ran the Eastern clubs. That would be preparatory to renewing the Negro World Series, which had not been played since 1927.

Plainly, Satchel Paige was causing decisions to be made, designs to be shaped, and outlines to be drawn all over the face of baseball. Just as plainly, Satch couldn't have cared less about any of it. The man who was central to Negro league affairs was moved only by his own. Once it became evident that his reconciliation with Janet was doomed, he again began counting the days of his confinement in Pittsburgh—which, like the Nashville of Bertha Wilson, had become a symbol to him of love lost and never found. This happened once it was clear that a demeaned Janet would not let his Dakota days slide.

"She'd boiled all winter at my being gone," he once said, "and when I got back she couldn't wait to start nibbling at me about it. One thing led to another and soon we were just waiting to fall apart. It was all over, that feelings we once had."

Satch's habitual womanizing, which resumed shortly after his return, humiliated her—a reaction that he found wholly unreasonable. Steering wide of the subject of his adultery, the pages of his autobiography were streaked with a reflexive, self-exculpating misogyny when he discussed Janet Howard Paige.

"All she could think of was, 'You didn't have to go off and leave me,'" he wrote. "You can't convince a woman that argues like that. Fact is, you can't convince a woman about hardly anything. Once they put their minds on it, that's where their minds stay. . . .

"After that I didn't even try to smooth things out whenever the Crawfords went on the road. I just went. I was glad to get away."

The pitching mound, as ever, was his most comforting escape. Of his nine league starts in 1936—seven wins, two losses—three were shutouts. Still, it was unmistakable that Satch's commitment to the Craws was flagging. More and more, the great third baseman Judy Johnson noticed that Satch seemed to be on the field in body alone, and that only a personal challenge—and a swift kick in the butt—could fire up his concentration and consternation. In one game against Philadelphia, the Craws got out to a four-run lead behind a somnolent Satch. Barely paying attention, he gave up a run in the eighth, which scored on his fielding muff. Then Ted Page, the ex-Craw who knew Satch like a book, laid down a bunt and beat it out to load the bases with none out.

Judy Johnson had seen enough. He walked to the mound and purposefully played with Satch's head. The Stars, Judy told him, "were hoping you'd get in this spot—them people in Philly been sayin' you nothing but a big pop off." Now Satch got serious. He exploded third-strike fastballs by Roy Parnell and Dewey Creacy. But his old nemesis, Boojum Wilson, drove in two runs with a single. Now holding a one-run lead, Satch faced the dreaded Turkey Stearns in the game's climactic moment. Satch kicked high, reared back, and scorched one Trouble Ball after another. Turkey never had a chance; he went down on three swings.

"Now go back to Philadelphia and tell 'em about *that!*" a BB-eyed Satch screamed into the Philly dugout as he walked from the hill. In the ninth inning he blew away two more, for fifteen in all, though he had seemingly been there for only five of them. His leisurely exploits, in fact, crafted the lead paragraph in the *Courier* the next day: "Satchell Paige, sultan of the mound, eased his long frame and casually struck out 15 of the Stars' best batsmen in an exhibition that has not been seen for a long time."

Buck Leonard remembered another time, when Satch was inserted into a game against Homestead to play right field after all the other Crawford outfielders had been used. When a Grays hitter skied one to right, Leonard said, "We looked for Satchel to be standing under it—but he was on the sideline getting a light on a smoke from a fellow in the stands."

The Craws, who could often reflect Satch's breezy sensibilities, got off to a sluggish start in 1936, losing the first-half title to Tom Wilson's relocated Washington Elite Giants. Gus Greenlee was incensed when Satch took a leave in late May and went all the way to San Francisco to do promoter Johnny Burton another good turn, pitching against a minor league team, the St. Louis Blues, in what was to be a large promotion. However, the exhibition turned sour when the Blues kicked Satch's tail. He and his "Southern Pacific" team—a sorry collection of odds and ends from the Bay Area's black sandlots—went down 11–2, the victims of a Paige-like twenty-two strikeouts by the Blues pitchers.

This reversal in form did not sit well with the black press. Satch's

weak effort particularly disturbed the *Chicago Defender*, the paper
had expected the game to strike a blow for integration, and it ran a
harsh and even petulant review by writer E. L. Porter. Under the
headline SATCHEL A FLOP, Porter groused that the "miserable
showing of the highly touted Satchel Paige"—compounded by an
outrageous ticket price of seventy-five cents—had "left a bad taste
in the mouths of both white and Race fans."

A month later, Satch had made it back to the Craws and was
warming to the summer heat. On July 10 he blistered the Grays
with a 3–0 three-hitter, regaling 10,000 fans in Cleveland's League
Park with what the now pleased *Defender* called "several stunts to
amuse the crowd." With the temporary acquisition of the American Giants' ace Willie Foster—who formed with Satch a dream
lefty-righty mound combo—the Craws surged toward the second-
half title.

That crusade was interrupted by the August East-West Game, for
which the fan balloting gave Satch the highest vote total among the
Eastern pitchers—4,919—and second highest overall in the East to
Josh Gibson's 5,187. But, once again, Gus Greenlee was skittish
about Satch's attendance in Chicago, so the Craws' Leroy Matlock
was the East's starter and winner in a 10–2 rout before 30,000 fans.
Satch mopped up with three flawless innings.

As these all-star showcases were always the apogee of the blackball season, the NNL now turned not to arcane kingmaking—for
once, Greenlee would be content to set aside his ego and name *no*
champion for the season—but to further profiteering. Tom Wilson was all for that, as his Washington Elites were en route to a
last-place finish in the second half and were not eager to meet the
hot Craws in a playoff. Instead, in order to prevent Midwest semipro teams with leased blacks from winning scads of money in
those hinterland tournaments, Wilson arranged with Greenlee
and Cum Posey—whose Grays had reentered the NNL the year before—to pool their players and take the best ones on tour, first to
the lucrative *Denver Post* tournament.

Managed by Wilson, the Negro All-Stars—a monster team that
included Paige, Gibson, Cool Papa Bell, Leroy Matlock, Buck
Leonard, Felton Snow, Wild Bill Wright, and Sammy Hughes—
swept the Denver field in seven straight games to cop the $5,000
first prize. Gibson hit four home runs and Satch won his three
games by scores of 7–2, 12–1, and finally 7–0 with eighteen strikeouts in the title game against a cruelly overmatched semipro unit
from Borger, Texas.

That game was otherwise noteworthy for a novel defensive measure by the Borger team that was a baseball first, one born of cold fear. Not believing that any human could normally strike out so many and still have such pinpoint control, the Borgers had ordered plastic helmets to wear while they batted against Satch, for self-protection. In Denver, their hitters would not remove them even though one of the Negro stars, Jack Marshall, swore that Satch "never threw a ball higher than the belt line" that entire game.

If the Borgers had seen enough of the Tom Wilson All-Stars, so had the tournament promoters. As with the Bismarcks of a year ago, the Wilson team was politely told that they too would not be welcomed back to Denver anymore. The people at the Wichita tournament had the same idea; they didn't even let the Negro stars enter.

Next on the joint barnstorming agenda was a Midwest series in October with a big league contingent led by Rogers Hornsby—the aging "Rajah," having finished his Hall of Fame career, was now player-manager of the St. Louis Browns—and this is where Satchel Paige met the future, the real future. While Hornsby was along purely for marquee value—Satch struck him out almost every time he batted—the key to the Hornsby team for Satch was the seventeen-year-old pitching wunderkind of the Cleveland Indians, Bob Feller.

Playing in the tall grass of Iowa, the land that had spawned Feller, Paige mowed down bona fide hitters like Jimmie Foxx and a youthful Johnny Mize with such ease that the big leaguers decided to cancel the last five games of the two-week tour. But in Bob Feller there would be the scent of unfinished business. Feller had just completed half a season with the Indians, going 5-and-3 and striking out 76 hitters in 62 innings. But because the Tribe had taken Feller from a Western League team that owned his rights, Feller didn't know where he'd be playing the next season. While the baseball commissioner, Judge Landis, deliberated on Feller's fate—which would be to let the Indians keep him, in return for a $7,500 payment to the other team—the incredibly talented kid barnstormed in the corn fields against this great colored team.

In Des Moines, he engaged Satch in a flame-throwing contest neither man would forget. Over the first three burning innings, Feller struck out eight and Satch seven; each gave up but one hit. The black team pulled out a late win, but what endured was the memory of Paige and Feller and the high heat they made in the corn fields that day. In time, the two of them would enter into a business relationship that, unlike the Paige–Dizzy Dean duels, would make racial trammels move like ten-pins.

For now, though, they moved on, in quite different directions. Satch passed up the Negro Stars' tour of Mexico and the California Winter League season so that he could give it one last try with Janet. But in the spring of 1937, that break would be nearly complete. By then, Satch would be miles and miles from Pittsburgh— literally and figuratively.

•   •   •

Satch had by now reconciled his itchy sense of independence from the NNL. With the Dakotas and the prairie out of the question for him—J. L. Wilkinson's Monarchs were in league with Gus Greenlee in keeping away from him—the Craws were the only game in town for him. Satch at least had the satisfaction of knowing he had bled Greenlee a little by his light-footed maneuvers.

But now the center of gravity would again shift on him. After his latest Denver triumph, offers arrived almost daily from another hemisphere of small-time ball, the bleached islands of the Caribbean. Satch had always elbowed them aside as profferers of mere key money. Discoursing later on the economic realities relevant to him up to that time, he accurately noted that "I was the one guy the Negro league teams would pay for, no matter what."

But now there were other realities, some too handsome to ignore. Down in the Caribbean, men with generals' stars on their khaki uniforms were discovering the power of baseball as a political tool. In Cuba, in Haiti, in the Dominican Republic, in Panama and Mexico, ballplayers were becoming the last link to dying freedoms. Thus, every aspiring politician cum dictator could have himself a power bloc in the countryside by assembling a team—a *winning* team—in his name. To do that, lynx-eyed generals had to hoard the best players available in the land, in *any* land.

In the spring of 1937, Satch was Job One among the Caribbean recruiters—and they, along with Gus Greenlee, were scared half to death when Satch went to spring training in Hot Springs, Arkansas, and damn near became a casualty of his excesses. Driving his Cadillac too fast, as usual, he collided with another car on April 2 and suffered leg, arm, and shoulder bruises. Though these were minor injuries, for a time wild stories spread that it was more serious— SAY SATCHELL PAIGE HURT IN CAR WRECK, was the feverish headline in the *Afro-American*, and the *Courier*, taking a snipe at his lifestyle reported that "Manager Oscar Charleston and the staff of the [Crawfords] admitted they were . . . worried [about] the elongated playboy of the league."

But then, on April 15, a healthy Satch joined the Craws on a swing through New Orleans. That was when he found out that he and many of his teammates had been targeted by the islanders. New Orleans was crawling with tawny men in Panama hats and white suits looking to beat one another to the cream of the Crawfords. These emissaries of various tropical *presidentes* and their wannabes came bearing gifts in the form of folding money, and Gus Greenlee knew exactly what they wanted. "Haitian pirates!" he bleated one day when he saw two of their number in attendance at a Crawfords workout. Using some influence with the local authorities, Gus had the city police come and arrest and detain them, his grounds being a "conspiracy" to steal contracted players—though by this instant creation of law almost every Negro league owner could have been thrown in the slammer.

When it was ascertained that the two interlopers were Dominicans, and when they explained what they were prepared to offer Negro leaguers to play in their eight-week season, players were suddenly looking for *them*. Not so Satch, who played it coy and smart by acting uninterested. Not knowing who had offered Satch what, when the Dominicans finally were able to catch up with him—and by now Gus Greenlee was pushing hard to have them deported by the State Department—the offer was enough to make even Satch move fast.

The Dominican point man was Dr. José Enrique Aybar, dean of the University of Santo Domingo and deputy of the Dominican Republic's national congress. More critically for Dr. Aybar's immediate future, he was also director of Los Dragones, the team that played out of Santo Domingo—although that capital city had been renamed Ciudad Trujillo by the *presidente* of this banana republic, Rafael Leónidas Trujillo.

Trujillo had come to power in 1930 via the usual means for a man of his cut-throat instincts: fear, intimidation, and taking control of the once-American-financed National Guard. Having nationalized all of the country's sugar and rum businesses in spite of their American investors, Trujillo enforced his rule with a secret police, press censorship, midnight executions, and—not unlike Gus Greenlee—by trying to cloak and soften his crudeness with the opiate of baseball. In the 1930s he invited the Cincinnati Reds to the country and they had a successful tour. Now, in administering his city's ball team, he and José Aybar sought a lock on the competition by going after the best American ballplayers available, as well as the best available Cuban and Puerto Rican players. They did this while prohibiting the top Dominican players from playing outside the country.

Trujillo's baseball interest was particularly urgent in the spring of 1937. A political challenge was rising in the port city of San Pedro de Macorís—a place where, not incidentally, a ballteam named Las Estrellas Orientales were using the same methods to draw American blacks under the sponsorship of a politician Trujillo despised. With national elections coming up, Trujillo knew that all the secret police and firing squads in the republic would be useless to him if that politician's team beat Ciudad Trujillo on the ball fields of this impoverished island; indeed, about the only thing that could topple Trujillo from power was a political movement fueled by the zeal of the country's voracious baseball fans.

This is where Satchel Paige entered the arena of international politics, the case made for him when José Aybar unlocked a large suitcase and emptied onto Satch's hotel room bed so many bills of large denomination—$30,000 in sum—that Satch must have heard the Ave Maria. Upon regaining his breath and his eyesight after staring into this divine miracle, he was altogether ready to talk turkey with José Enrique Aybar. He agreed to jump to Los Dragones, and the $30,000 was deposited in a bank account in Satch's name. Then, as the agent for Rafael Trujillo, he was to convince other great Crawford players to breach their contracts and play with Los Dragones; dealing with them on his own, he could divvy up the money any way he chose fit, keeping as much as he wanted for himself.

Admirably, Satch went about the task without caprice; wanting nothing that was misbegotten, not looking to take any more than what he would deserve for doing the job asked of him, he dutifully brought eight more Negro leaguers over to Los Dragones, leaving him much leeway to enrich himself while still doing well by the others. Satch's take dovetailed perfectly with what had been the biggest offer for his services up to then: in 1934, the owners of the Brooklyn Eagles, Abraham and Effa Manley, had wanted to purchase him for $5,000—and were turned down flat by Gus Greenlee. Now, for eight weeks of work in the tropics, he would collect

$6,000, the others getting $3,000 each. As he once explained this delirious arithmetic, "Ol' Satch was making good money, but thirty thousand was more than three thousand apiece, even if I didn't skim some off for managing the whole thing."

Having been given a license to skim, he would use it again in the future.

•   •   •

Gus Greenlee found out about the jumping on April 25, the day that Satch left for Ciudad Trujillo aboard the *generalísimo*'s private plane—taking with him, for now, one other Crawford, his main man, Bill Perkins. The following day, the *Courier* broke the mushrooming story with the headline SATCH AND PERKINS ON ISLAND; OTHERS MAY SIGN.

Growing more apoplectic by the hour, Greenlee now began scurrying around like a madman trying somehow to either blunt or cope with the raids. First he ran herd on the black press to denounce the defectors and to cast him in a heroic light. The black *Philadelphia Tribune* carried word on April 29 that "Gus Greenlee and his minions are hot on the trail of the Dominican Republic, which they say is stealing players from the rolls of the National Negro Association."

By now, Greenlee had learned the full extent of the Trujillo raids. Wheedled by Satch, no fewer than five important Crawfords had gone with him to Ciudad Trujillo—Cool Papa Bell, Leroy Matlock, Sam Bankhead, Harry Williams, and Herman Andrews—and a number of other Negro leaguers were on the verge of going to other Dominican clubs. Feeling the tremors within the Negro leagues, both Satch and Greenlee were of the same opinion that Satch later noted with a lofty sense of accomplishment: on the day that he went to the Dominican Republic, he believed, "I likely broke up the Negro leagues."

Gus told everyone he could that that would surely be the consequence of Paige's leap if the league did not head off the avalanche right away. Yet his first countermeasures only demonstrated the absurd hypocrisy of Gus Greenlee playing the aggrieved archangel, and of his and his league's moralizing against "player stealing." Greenlee went out and signed the great pitcher Chet Brewer away from the Kansas City Monarchs, and quickly added Satch's old Bismarck teammate Barney Morris. Gus even tried to make the point that these two players were a far better steal. Brewer and Morris, echoed the *Philadelphia Tribune,* "had seen their names spread across the newspaper pages for the past five years without developing 'temperaments' or stirring up strife among other players."

But just days later, Chet Brewer also ran—having accepted an offer from the Aguilas Cibaeñes team of Santiago.

Probably feeling cursed, Greenlee was really on the spot now. He had rammed through his own election as league president only weeks before with a pledge to rid the NNL of its white booking agents once and for all, and Gus now had to play hardball against not Nat Strong or Eddie Gottlieb but Satchel Paige. In the last few days of April, he conferred with his latest puppet commissioner, Ferdinand Q. Morton, and the president of the Negro American League, Robert Jackson. On May 1 he issued an ultimatum to Satch and all of the other jumpers: they were to return to their league teams by May 15 or be banned for one year and fined heavily. Furthermore, Greenlee announced that no league club would play in any ballpark where the outlaw players appeared after they came home. "When they return," he warned, "they will have nowhere to play."

While Greenlee also let drop word that the league had hired lawyers to take action against the players—"Indictments have already been issued," he said—the main target of his bile was obvious.

"When Satchel Paige jumped his Crawfords contract to play with the Santa Dominican [sic] club," wrote one of Greenlee's flacks in the *Courier,* "he proved again that he is about as undependable as a pair of second-hand suspenders. Satch, along with [his cojumpers] should be barred . . . until they learn to regard a contract as more than a mere scrap of paper."

•   •   •

As it turned out, Paige and Greenlee were wrong about the incipient death of the Negro leagues. Instead, only Gus would fall. When Satch led the Crawfords' mutiny, the minarets of Gus Greenlee's fortress began to sway—though in truth they had been listing for some time. Amid his fits of Macbeth-like rage and self-pity about the Trujillo raids, Greenlee overlooked the fact that eight weeks alone could not have crippled his dynasty.

'Twas Gus who inflicted the fatal damage.

By the spring of 1937, many of the players who were guileless cast members in the tragic comedy that was Gus Greenlee were more than ready to leave the stage. One of them, the brilliant Cool

Papa Bell, had been steaming for many months about Gus's short-shrifting him, and his methods in justifying it.

Bell told John Holway in *Voices from the Great Black Baseball Leagues* that, during the championship season of 1936, "I was hitting .500. Josh Gibson was hitting more than me, but when I started gaining on him, they [Crawford management] said, 'Don't you send out any statistics [to the newspapers] about what you're doing.' The secretary of the Crawfords wanted to tell the truth but they fined him. They didn't want to rate me over Josh or Satchel Paige, because I'd ask for more salary.

"I stole 175 bases that year, but they only gave me credit for 91. The last game I played I got five hits out of six [at-bats], stole five bases. But they didn't take the score book out there that day and I didn't get credit."

Even Josh—whose numbers Gus wanted padded—felt that Gus was stiffing him. As a bargaining ploy, Gibson had jumped the Craws for the last few weeks of the '36 season to his original team, Cum Posey's Homestead Grays. Standing firm on his rights, Greenlee listed Gibson on the Craws' '37 roster, but when Gus would not meet his salary demands, Josh went home and held out.

Gus then planted a nasty item in the *Courier*—penned by John L. Clark, a reporter who doubled as the NNL's secretary—that made the ludicrous case that Gibson was "not the kind of asset that more colorful and less capable players might be [because] he has not developed that 'it' which pulls cash customers through the turnstiles, although he has been publicized as much as Satchel Paige."

By this public flogging, Greenlee hoped to shame the insecure Gibson; but, as with Gus's earlier dress-down of Satch, it did him no good. With no choice, he reluctantly gave up on the Babe Ruth of blackball and arranged a pragmatic deal with Posey: Gibson and Judy Johnson to the Grays for catcher Pepper Bassett, third baseman Henry Spearman, and $2,500 in cash—the biggest player transaction in the history of Negro ball, the money figures second only to the Manleys' $5,000 earlier offer for Satch—although Gibson too detoured to Ciudad Trujillo, at Satch's urging.

Inevitably, losing Satchel Paige and Josh Gibson cost Gus Greenlee dearly. His once mighty reputation was fast eroding—or rather, eroding further, since he had been coming under heavy fire even before the entrance of Rafael Trujillo. During the '36 season, for example, an item in the white and widely read *New York Mirror* had blown open an issue that had triggered rumors for years around

Negro ball—that its inveterate gamblers might have been fixing their own ballgames. Citing not one source, sportswriter Dan Parker led his September 7 "Broadway Bugle" column:

> Gamblers got to several members of the Pittsburgh Crawfords, champions of the Negro National League, at Dexter Park last Wednesday night and made a clean-up, taking the short end of 9 to 6 odds against the [Brooklyn] Bushwicks. The Bushwicks won, 7–0. One description of the game read: "What angered Manager Oscar Charlestown [sic] was the awkwardness with which his club conducted itself." Awkwardness is hardly the word for such superb acting.

Sent reeling by this nonchalant accusation—and aware that this was the *last* thing Negro ball needed in coverage by the white press—Greenlee had John L. Clark fire off a telegram to Dan Parker, which read: KINDLY GIVE ME NAMES OF CRAWFORDS PLAYERS WHOM GAMBLERS DEALT WITH ON SEPTEMBER SECOND AT DEXTER PARK AS MENTIONED IN YOUR COLUMN TODAY. PRESUME YOU KNOW THE GAMBLERS.

Parker, in venomous contempt, wired back: IN REPLY TO YOUR TELEGRAM OF SEPTEMBER SEVENTH, I AM NOT IN THE DETECTIVE BUSINESS.

However, it was Parker who ultimately had to back down. Having had no reliable source material, Parker quickly retracted the smear when every member of the Crawfords signed affidavits denying any part in or knowledge of a fix. "Someone steered me wrong on that tip that gamblers fixed several members of the Pittsburgh Crawfords in a recent game with the Bushwicks here," he wrote in his column a week later, "and I hereby make amends to the Crawfords for casting suspicion on them, unjustly."

Still, as reckless and spurious as the Parker accusation proved to be, the PR damage remained, inviting further rumors about Negro ball being shady—a topic on which the big league owners were no doubt taking notes. And, to be sure, the climate seemed to be right for rogues and swindlers right about now. Greenlee's numbers business was bankrupting him; he had to pay off on an inordinate number of winning bets in 1936, and a new breed of city politicians was rising who could not abide him. With the danger of an arrest always a clear danger, and tax evasion charges a signed writ away, Gus was paying his lawyers far more than he was his players.

In a morass of debt, Gus could only take small solace from the fact that all of the league's gangsters seemed to be suffering from their own gambling losses. Among many of them, the big dream now was to move their ball teams from a gambling front to a legitimate business. Their paragon for this was Tom Wilson, who had divested himself of the rackets and concentrated all of his efforts into running his Elite Giants after the club's latest move, this time to Baltimore. But Gus Greenlee, with much of his team lifted out from under his jowls, could only stare deep into the abyss.

• • •

Satchel Paige, a man who had not known the territorial status of North Dakota, arrived in Ciudad Trujillo knowing only that the rum must be strong on the island if *el presidente* was paying him all these thousands of dollars to pitch here. His education improved vastly when he and Bill Perkins were met at the airport by barefoot soldiers with bandoleros wrapped around them and carrying rifles with long bayonets. Over the next eight weeks, battalions such as these would become the personal security force for Satch and his Crawford teammates—and the source of many of their nightmares.

The Cuban and Puerto Rican players on Los Dragones, who had lived in squalid conditions similar to those in the Dominican Republic and who had to fend for themselves in Ciudad Trujillo, thought the *americanos* had it *too* good. But that was the rub—the Americans understood neither the language nor the customs, nor the reality that they were being protected. All they knew was that uniformed men with bayonets would not allow them out of their sight. Wherever they were, the riflemen would stand watch, then usher them back to their home base, the Hotel Inglata, where they stood guard all night outside the doors.

Not that Rafael Trujillo didn't have another motive for such guardianship. As he had hoped, the only thing the players could really do with themselves was to play baseball, or to think about it. But when they got to the ballpark, more failures of communication caused acute paranoia: there, Trujillo's men would also ring the field during games, and at times they would fire their rifles to the skies and shout: "El Presidente doesn't lose!"

While this was a common ritual, and the fans loved it, it scared the hell out of the Americans. When the Dragones did lose, they absolutely believed they were going to be lined up and shot. Yet they lived on, despite the army's bullet-riddled pep talks.

Years later, Satch would say of Los Dragones, "I had one of the world's greatest black baseball clubs down there." One look at the roster confirms that. A true All Nations of brown-skinned men, in addition to the Negro leaguers Trujillo had imported arguably Puerto Rico's best player, Petrucho Cepeda (father of future big leaguer Orlando Cepeda); Cuba's legendary manager Lázaro Salazar; and heralded Dominicans Enrique Lantigua and Amable Sonlley Alvarado.

Still, Los Dragones did not run away with the pennant. Trying to keep pace with Trujillo's moves, all three Dominican League teams had fortified that summer. Following the Dragones' script, the Aguilas Cibaeñas of Santiago had imported Negro leaguers Chet Brewer, Pat Patterson, Showboat Thomas, Spoony Palm, Johnny Taylor, Clyde Spearman, and the Crawfords' Bertram Hunter and Thad Christopher—as well as Cuba's best player, pitcher Luis Tiant, Sr. The manager was the magnificent Cuban Martin Dihigo. Midway through the season, Chet Brewer beat Satch and Los Dragones with a no-hitter.

The team that Trujillo had mobilized to head off, the Estrellas Orientales of San Pedro de Macorís, got into the recruiting game late and could draw just two Negro leaguers—Spoon Carter and George Scales—but this was partly by choice; in the name of high nationalism, the Estrellas wanted to make the statement that it was the Dominican's team and kept its roster ethnically pure. Not incidentally, it also had the best of the Dominican players.

As Trujillo gnashed his teeth, the competition between the teams became a dogfight. All three of them jockeyed with one another the whole season. But Trujillo's hunt for Satchel Paige paid off. Only because Satch won a league-best eight of his ten games—and because Josh Gibson hit a league-high .453—did Los Dragones finally pull away. Los Dragones were also aided by some providential forfeitures in their favor ordered by Trujillo when antigovernment activity broke out in San Pedro de Macorís midway through the season. Ciudad Trujillo, with an 18-and-13 record, nosed out the Aguillas Cibaeñas by three and a half games and the Estrellas Orientales by four—capping the season with an unbearably tense seven-game championship playoff series.

If the Negro leaguers on the Dragones were to be believed, their very lives depended on winning that series. And of them all, the most terrified "survivor" had to be mild-mannered Cool Papa Bell, who would tremble when he would tell of the time the team had returned from a losing series during the season against San Pedro and were met in the hotel lobby by an army officer.

"Cool told me about it when he got home," recalled Jimmie Crutchfield, who went into hysterics as he retold the story. "Seems this general came up and said, 'Look, you play for the *presidente*. We don't lose.' And then he took his big .45 out and *boom boom*, he's shootin' at the walls right down there in the courtyard. And Cool Papa's cryin', '*I gotta get the hell outta here! How we gonna get away from here?*' "

Those kinds of stories made the rounds for years when the Negro leaguers spoke of the Dominican escapade. But one of the Cubans on the team, Rodolfo Fernández, would hear them and swear that nothing of the kind ever happened. And not even Satch, the raconteur extraordinaire, told of any unfriendly gunfire, though his later descriptions of the title series made it seem as if he had expected it at any moment.

• • •

Ciudad Trujillo versus San Pedro de Macorís was, of course, Rafael Trujillo against the rival whom he wanted crushed. As this was sure to be another coronation for *el jefe*, the city was festooned with flags the day before the opening game, and a huge parade was held downtown that night in which jeeploads of sloshed soldiers danced in the street and accosted young women while shooting off rounds of ordnance into the sky.

Satch, who had been to more pleasant parties in his time, never got to see this one. As night fell on the revelers, the militia came to the Hotel Inglata and took the American Dragones to a new location. Chet Brewer, who at the end of his team's season had come to Ciudad Trujillo to watch the series, would never forget what he heard that night.

"We went by where the ballplayers liked to socialize," Brewer once recalled. "We were lookin' for Satchel and them and we couldn't find them. So a little kid on the street—they knew all the business—he said, '*Está en la cárcel*'—that they was in *jail!* Trujillo had put them in jail the night before they played, so they wouldn't 'rouse around."

Again, Trujillo had been overly concerned with his players' safety; but the next day, at Estadio Quisqueya, was when they felt most unsafe. The usual detachment of soldiers grew to a large column stationed elbow to elbow along the third base stands—uncomfortably eyeing the uniformed "security" guards of Trujillo's rival, who lined up menacingly along the first base stands. With the two people's armies staring daggers at each other the whole game, Satch squeezed between the soldiers and took the mound, his stomach in open revolt.

"I knew then," he said later, "that whichever way the series went, I lost."

Inhaling antacid between innings, he never got into his rhythm and was beaten. Just as jittery, Leroy Matlock lost the next game, and then a Dominican pitcher dropped the third. Now the panic was genuine, and later accounts of the situation have the sinister undertones of a Graham Greene novel. As reported by *Collier's* Richard Donovan in his profile of Satch, "When Paige met Dr. Aybar, the doctor explained that the situation was very serious and that Trujillo's team must win . . . at whatever cost. . . . All Dr. Aybar could do was wring his hands when Paige asked how his chances were for getting back to the States."

Los Dragones roared back with three straight wins. But in the final championship game, with the soldiers taking their places along the baselines, Satch took the ball and again fell behind. Trailing 5–4 in the seventh, his imagination seeing himself caught in a crossfire between fanatical soldiers, he would say later that "you could see Trujillo lining up his army. They began to look like a firing squad."

But again his team rallied, going up 6–5 when Satch singled and Sam Bankhead hit one over the wall. "You never saw Ol' Satch throw harder after that," he said of the final two shutout innings, in which he struck out five of six men to bring victory to Los Dragones.

Now Rafael Trujillo prepared another parade through the streets, but none of the Americans would be around to party. Rushing back to the Hotel Inglata after the game, they packed their suitcases and may have broken a land speed record clearing out of Ciudad Trujillo. "It was twenty-five minutes for us to get together and be on the dock waiting to get out," Satch would say.

That, however, was merely Satchel Paige's rewrite of history, adopted years on, when the notion of sharing time in hell with other legendary men obviously appealed to the bard in him. In truth, he may have been the only American *not* to scramble for the dock that day in Ciudad Trujillo. While the others ran, Satch was more than content to stick around in the Dominican Republic until his job status back home could be cleared up to his satisfaction.

In fact, on July 31, several days after Los Dragones won the title, the *Baltimore Afro-American*'s Ollie Stewart, who was visiting Ciudad Trujillo, got Satch to do a first-person bylined story for the paper—and Satch used the forum to explain why he stayed behind while the other Americans were, he said, "running away like the world was on fire." Accusing not Rafael Trujillo's regime but rather Gus Greenlee's of being the biggest threat to his freedom, he wrote:

> I would be willing to go to South America and live in the jungles rather than go back to the league and play ball like I did for ten years. . . . The opportunities of a colored baseball player on these islands are the same or almost the same as those enjoyed by the white major league players in the States. That's something you think about, you know.

But there was also an artful plea for understanding and exoneration:

> I am pretty sure when I get back to America I will not be a stranger to the NNL. Likewise I find it hard to believe that the people back home would turn their backs on me, simply because I wanted to earn more money. If I was such a bad fellow, why did such men as Josh Gibson, Matlock, Bankhead and Cool Papa Bell and others follow me?

For the time being, Satch hung around in the tropics, pocketing a few bucks here and there pitching exhibitions around the country. But it soon became clear that Rafael Trujillo was not pleased by the return on his American investment, not when $30,000 couldn't keep his team from flirting with defeat. Moreover, all of the clubowners' mad spending spree bankrupted the Dominican League; forced to disband the very next year, there would be no organized ball in the country for twelve years, sacrificing an entire generation of talented players.

They were not the only ones to suffer. Doing away with elections shortly thereafter, Trujillo began the systematic genocide of the country's 18,000 Haitians, whom he loathed for their *dark skin*. Trujillo himself was removed from office in 1938, but when he returned to power in 1942 he was able to elude the usual fate of the mad dog, until an assassin's bullets finally took him down on May 30, 1961.

But Rafael Trujillo did provide a context, albeit a subversive one, for the repatriated Americans to keep on playing—and as such, a perfect path back home for Satch. Still suspended by the Negro leagues, about twenty of those who had gone south decided to form their own rebel team. Banking on their notoriety as fugitives and international champions, they went under the names of "Trujillo's All-Stars" or the "Santo Domingo Negro Stars." But when Satch finally came home and agreed to join them, the *Chicago Defender*'s coverage of one of their games called them "Satchel Paige's Negro All Stars."

This had to delight Satch, who used to make these rebel excursions alone. Now it seemed that he had been on to something all along. Undeniably, the Trujillo/Paige cachet carried great leverage in the overall baseball market, the Negro leagues notwithstanding. Making that point with emphasis, Satch had written in his bylined *Afro-American* piece, "If you ask me what was the big event for colored baseball in 1937, I'd say winning the pennant of the Dominican Republic by the best players in the league."

Now he warmed to his desperado status. In late August, when the *Chicago Defender* ran the headline SATCH SAYS HE'LL BE SATISFIED TO BE AN OUTLAW, he had for all purposes renounced his loyalty to any team, any league, and any color. He was, first and last, Satch. And Satch belonged only to the ages.

11

Go Down, Moses

My name is Might-have-been.
I am also called No-more, too-late,
Farewell.

—Dante Gabriel Rosetti,
Sonnets from the House of Life

Like most makeshift operations in the American heartland, the Trujillo All-Stars had a J. L. Wilkinson connection. Smelling box office with all those outlaw superstars, Wilkie circumnavigated around the NNL-NAL prohibition against all contact with them by having promoter Ray Dean schedule House of David games with the All-Stars—and, in a coup de main that rankled Gus Greenlee and Tom Wilson, used his influence to get Paige's All-Stars into the *Denver Post* tournament just one year after the Wilson touring aggregation was told not to return.

But Denver, the site of Satch's most acclaimed victories, would this time become a touchstone of blackball disunity—and specifically the ongoing breach between Satch and nearly everyone else in the black game. While these men had made a load of money through his lead, many were worried that they might be blacklisted in the Negro leagues for it, and none had the feeling that Satch would go out of his way to find them work. While they could accept his making the team seem like his footmen because he boosted them all at the gate, their mutual interests ended once he stepped off the mound.

During the late summer and early fall of 1937, Satch was giving the Trujillo crew a day or two a week of his time; the rest of the time he was doing solo gigs again, booked by Abe Saperstein, who was now practically his personal agent-manager. But Abe himself was having *shpulkis* about Paige. More than a few times, he would wire money for an appearance to Satch, who would then not show up for the game. Saperstein would have to repay the money from his own pocket. Satch's explanation for such incidents was flippant: "When you're on top and you got so many jobs going," he once said, "you just might forget one or two."

Recalling years later how he treated people he deemed small and grubby—and he *always* avoided guys he'd run across who had known him on the streets in Mobile—he admitted to pangs of guilt in his conscience as he rode to fame.

"You forget how you grew up," he wrote in his autobiography. "You think you always were high society, always knew all the actors and singers and boxers and politicians. You don't remember you once never knew anybody and nobody knew you.

"You change, nobody else does. And when you change, what you do and who you know changes. Before you know it you get sort of uptown. I know. . . .

"I ducked out [on people] and never thought anymore about it. It took me a lot of years before I found out it was a mighty little man who did things that way."

At the *Denver Post* tournament, his character had indeed made him seem petty in his teammates' eyes. Since Satch hadn't bothered to travel there with the team, the pitching rotation of Chet Brewer, Leroy Matlock, and the St. Louis Stars's Robert Griffin was set without him, and in his absence each man won two games to get the Trujillos to the edge of the title. Only *now* did Satch make his entrance in Denver. With a $1,000 bonus at stake for the title-winning pitcher, he demanded the ball—and promptly lost to a semi-pro team from Oklahoma 6–4, though he struck out his usual (or so it seemed) fourteen.

Because Denver was a double-elimination tournament, and this was the Trujillos' first loss—necessitating another game between the same two teams—suspicion persisted that Satch's teammates did what they could to lose that first game to spite him. Satch, not deigning to recognize the loss, never mentioned it in his memoirs—which may have been a tacit admission that he indeed hadn't earned dibs on that bonus money simply by his presence.

COUNTY HEALTH DEPARTMENT
VERIFICATION OF BIRTH RECORD

This is to certify that there is in the ___ **MOBILE** County
Health Department a record of the birth of

Leroy Page

Sex _m_ Race or Color ___ c ___ born in ___ **MOBILE** ___ County, Ala.

Date of birth *July 7, 1906* Date of filing. ———

Verification issued *Feb. 5, 1954*

J. L. Chason, M. D.

COUNTY HEALTH OFFICER.

Note: If no erasures or alterations are made in above entries this card will be accepted as proof of age for enrollment in school and similar purposes. A legal copy of the birth certificate may be obtained in the Bureau of Vital Statistics, Montgomery 4, Alabama. In accordance with that agency state your parents' full names and the date and place of your birth.

Alabama State Department of Health—50M—11-52   Birth Verification Card CVS3

1

Mystery solved? In 1954, the Mobile, Alabama, Health Department confirmed Satchel Paige's birth-date. Note the spelling of the last name.

TWIRLS NO HIT GAME

★

SATCHEL PAIGE

Sensational right hander who holds three shutout wins over Cole's American Giants entered the hall of fame July 4, when he twirled a no-hit no-run game against Posey's Homestead Grays. Paige shut out the Grays, 4-0, allowing only two men to reach first, one on an error by Mornay and the other on a base on balls.

★

By the early thirties, Satch's exploits were dominating the black press, as in this *Chicago Defender* notice of his July 4, 1934, no-hitter for the Pittsburgh Crawfords against the Homestead Grays.

The Crawfords fielded four future Hall of Famers: (left to right, in uniform) Judy Johnson, manager Oscar Charleston, Satch, and Josh Gibson. The dapper man in the middle is light heavyweight champion John Henry Lewis.

Gus Greenlee, boss of the Pittsburgh numbers racket and owner of the Crawfords.

5

Paige jumped from the Crawfords in mid-1935 to join this integrated semipro team in Bismarck, North Dakota. With Satch (top row, middle) are other blackball greats Quincy Trouppe and Ted Radcliffe (top row, last two on right).

Paige with teammates Josh Gibson (middle) and Bill Perkins, on the Ciudad Trujillo team in the Dominican Republic in 1937.

6

Though Satch commanded rave notices in the white press, some of the coverage took racial stereotyping to great depths—as in this cartoon from the *Bismarck Tribune*.

The black press had its own slant, though it was similar in some ways. From the *Chicago Defender*, circa 1940.

Effa Manley, owner of the Newark Eagles. When she wouldn't play ball with Satch off the field, he refused to play for her on it.

10

Satch with Kansas City Monarchs patriarch J. L. Wilkinson, who rescued Satch from the scrapheap after his 1939 arm injury.

Satch comes to Harlem, as seen through the lens of
Life magazine in 1941.

12

Satch shows off his "wife," Lucy
Figueroa, in 1941—ignoring
the wife he already had in
Pittsburgh.

Always on the move, Satch
lived out of a huge steamer
trunk that held his natty suits,
his gun collection, and the
same size-11 baseball spikes he
wore for years.

14

At Satchel Paige Day, Wrigley Field, August 1942: Satch accepts an alp-sized bunch of flowers from model Edith Chamberlin before 18,000 fans and a military honor guard.

To some big leaguers, Paige was an equal. He won this status in exhibitions against white stars like Dizzy Dean (center) and Cecil Travis, shown here before a 1942 charity game in Chicago.

16

Often embroiled in controversy, Satch halted the 1942 East-West Game to tell 48,000 fans he was misquoted by the press when he appeared to caution against big-league integration.

The quintessential Satchel Paige pose: left leg high, right arm cocked.

17

For a 1946 barnstorming series against a big-league group headed by
Bob Feller, the Satchel Paige All-Stars were given an airplane,
salaries, and Satch had a personal valet (standing next to him in
doorway).

Satch with his Kansas City Monarchs teammate Jackie Robinson.

Satch with Bill Veeck, the Barnum-like owner of the Cleveland Indians, who brought the 42-year-old Paige to the majors in 1948.

The "rookie" with Indians teammate Larry Doby, the first black to play in the American League. They roomed together—until Doby became terrified of Satch's guns.

The first Satchel Paige book, published in 1948.

Other big-league spoils included Satch's likeness on a bubblegum card, like this 1949 Bowman version.

The world champion Indians appeared in the movie *The Kid from Cleveland*. As in this scene, Bob Feller and fellow Indian pitcher Steve Gromek kept their distance from Satch in real life. (Rusty Tamblyn is at left.)

Although Bill Veeck seated Paige in a canopied easy chair when he brought him to the St. Louis Browns in 1952, Old Satch pitched some pretty fair country hardball for the Browns.

Satch inspects a piece
of finery from his
impressive collection of
antiques.

Satch, an American
League All-Star in
1953, regales fellow
Stars Mickey Mantle,
Allie Reynolds, and
Dom DiMaggio before
the game in Cincinnati.

28

Satch with Robert Mitchum in the 1959 movie *The Wonderful Country*.

29

Old soldier Satch, in his *Wonderful Country* costume, found a commanding officer in his second wife, Lahoma, who bore him a platoon of eight children. Here he holds daughter Lula in 1959. Lahoma's daughter from a previous marriage, Shirley, is at left.

30

First-class immortal Satch accepts congratulations from Commissioner Bowie Kuhn on his induction into the Hall of Fame in Cooperstown, August 2, 1971.

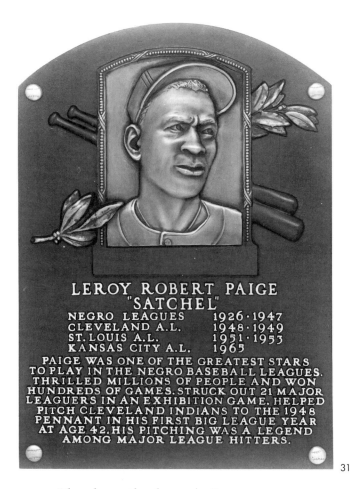

LEROY ROBERT PAIGE
"SATCHEL"
NEGRO LEAGUES   1926·1947
CLEVELAND A.L.   1948·1949
ST. LOUIS A.L.   1951·1953
KANSAS CITY A.L.   1965
PAIGE WAS ONE OF THE GREATEST STARS
TO PLAY IN THE NEGRO BASEBALL LEAGUES.
THRILLED MILLIONS OF PEOPLE AND WON
HUNDREDS OF GAMES. STRUCK OUT 21 MAJOR
LEAGUERS IN AN EXHIBITION GAME. HELPED
PITCH CLEVELAND INDIANS TO THE 1948
PENNANT IN HIS FIRST BIG LEAGUE YEAR
AT AGE 42. HIS PITCHING WAS A LEGEND
AMONG MAJOR LEAGUE HITTERS.

31

The plaque that hangs in Cooperstown.

A showman to the end, Satchel Paige went to his grave in 1982 milking the gag that fostered his legend through so many seasons in the sun.

32

PAIGE ISLAND
DEDICATED IN HONOR OF
SATCHEL PAIGE
"?"   X   1982

On the other hand, Leroy Matlock had—and banked it with his 11–1 victory the next day.

If Satch wasn't openly aroused that his team may have taken a dive behind him, he may have wondered if perhaps his karma was catching up to him after his next start for the Trujillos. This came on September 20 and was the latest installment of the "greatest game ever" in Negro ball. Matching the Trujillos with Tom Wilson's latest Negro league all-stars, on its surface the contest pitted the establishment guys against the outlaws. This was a first in black-ball, and its enormous gate appeal prompted Gus Greenlee to ease up on the ban on league players being on the same field with the jumpers.

Greenlee and Tom Wilson were nonetheless petrified that the rebels would blow the NNL's loyalists off the field. Wilson, whose Baltimore Elite Giants now made up the core of his newest all-star team, saw so little hope for victory against the Paige club that he included on his team the independent New York Cubans' twenty-one-year-old ace Johnny Taylor—who had played for the Aguilas Cibaeñas of Santiago that summer. Wilson also chose as his manager Martin Dihigo, who had managed the Aguilas team.

Paige and Taylor met at the Polo Grounds, drawing a Sunday crowd of 22,500, and Taylor upheld the NNL's tattered honor by pitching the game of his life against a masterful Satch. As it wore on, and one after another of the Trujillo batters went down without a hit, the drama grew. Satch, who had given up six innocuous hits through seven innings, kept wriggling out of jams with clutch strikeouts.

Tiring in the eighth, he yielded a two-out single to Henry Kimbro. He then got ahead of Jim West when, wrote the *Afro-American*'s Joe Bostic, "Satchel sent up his high hard one which was just what Mr. West was looking for and he promptly poled [it] high into the left field stands for a four-baser."

In the top of the ninth, Taylor—who'd given up three walks but whose hard, darting curves kept the hitters off stride—breezed past George Scales, Spoony Palm, and Cool Papa Bell to salt away a spellbinding no-hitter. Beating Satch did wonders for Taylor, who earned his first big headlines and this heavy-breathing lead paragraph in the *Afro-American:* "The select circle of baseball's immortals has a new member. His name is Johnny Taylor."

But fame could die a quick death when those who irritated Paige had to meet up with him again. As with the star-crossed Slim Jones,

Taylor had a short run in the spotlight. Taking this loss harder than most, Satch seemed to hold Taylor personally accountable. In recalling it years later, he got into a lather, referring to Taylor not by name but as "that young punk" who had caused him much self-doubt by outpitching him. Saying that he had felt like "an old man" after the game, he insisted that he "ran back to the hotel and locked myself in my room" in shame when it was over.

The effect of all that anguish was to fire up one more shot of redemption. One week later, before a huge house of 35,000 fans at Yankee Stadium, Taylor was blasted from the game after five innings. Satch, posted to a four-run lead after Bill Perkins's three-run homer in the first, had to do little to win 9–4, and though it was hardly one of his polished gems, Satch still could find allegorical use for doing in poor Johnny Taylor.

"Fact is," he burbled, "I was still pitching long after everybody'd forgotten what that . . . boy'd done against me."

•   •   •

Gus Greenlee, clinging to a thin reed of power, tried to contact Satch on his stops in the boonies. But Satch, who was never big on returning messages, was more than willing to let Greenlee twist in the wind and contemplate how much he needed to have Paige back in Greenlee Field. And Gus surely did. The bottom dropped out on his team in 1937, and he was mortified when Cum Posey's resurrected Grays ran away with both halves of the season and were named NNL champions.

Posey, of course, was luxuriating in Greenlee's agony. Not easily forgotten was the way Gus had held all the cards in the early days of the NNL, how cavalierly Posey was kicked out of the league, and how he was treated like a poor relation when reinstated in 1935. Posey endured all that, and kept a conspiratorial eye on Gus's jugular all the while.

Playing Gus's game, when Posey returned to the league he went against all of his longtime principles and hired a Gus Greenlee of his own—Rufus "Sonnyman" Jackson, the numbers king of Homestead, whose bankroll saved the Grays from bankruptcy and whose dark image gave the rather square Grays a dose of badman cool. Younger and tougher-looking than Gus Greenlee, with at least as many bodies (imagined or otherwise) in his closet, Sonnyman could also boast a legitimate business—he supplied jukeboxes to most nightclubs in Pittsburgh—and his own club, the Skyrocket Cafe, was as jumpin' a place as the Crawford Grille. Assuming greater power when Posey was named league secretary in 1937, Sonnyman was elected to the league's board of trustees.

While Jackson could talk Gus Greenlee's language, Posey remained a baseball purist. Gus had built his teams on glittering names, but Posey's teams were molded as intertwined parts of a whole, with an almost organic fit of man to position. While the Crawfords never endured as a winner and were destroyed by attitude and avarice, the Grays supplanted them and went on winning without end. Indeed, Gus Greenlee had few quibbles with his clone Sonnyman Jackson, but he simply could not stand Cum Posey for being everything Gus wasn't.

Now, as the ground was parting beneath Gus's feet, he could not help but notice that Cum was doing little to keep him upright. While Posey had supported the one-year ban Gus imposed on the Dominican Republic jumpers—not unmindful that most of them were from the Crawfords—he allowed Josh Gibson to get right back into a Grays uniform upon his return, claiming with a straight face that he had given Gibson permission to leave.

More insidious still to Gus was Posey's newest ally—not Sonnyman Jackson but Philadelphia promoter Eddie Gottlieb. Years earlier, echoing Rube Foster, Posey had railed against white booking agents, blaming their onerous fees for breaking Posey's East-West League. Negro league club owners, he said, had to "shake off the sinister influence of the great booking agents of the East." But as Greenlee escalated the war against Gottlieb and Nat Strong, Posey, along with other Eastern teams, brazenly dealt with Gottlieb, which helped the agent gain official ownership of the Philadelphia Stars in 1936.

Though Posey knew all along that he was personally weakening Greenlee, the Grays were hardly thriving. Financially, 1937 had been a disastrous year for all of the league's teams; and even in getting close to toppling Greenlee, Posey was about to move his Grays part-time to Washington. With the league needing a stimulant, Gus Greenlee made his last stand in vowing to provide it. "There will be a reorganization and the NNL will be placed on a solid foundation in 1938," he declared.

But even though he could do nothing without the repatriation of the Dominican jumpers—who had outdrawn the league teams on their brief tour—Greenlee tried to have it both ways with the players. Having dropped all of its lawsuits, the league assessed a nominal fine amounting to a week's salary for each player, an act that was more an overture than a punishment. But Gus still urged owners to teach the players a good lesson by holding the salary line. For this, Greenlee intended the biggest object lesson to be Satchel Paige.

Satch, who could see right through Gus's now feeble tough guy routine, would have none of it. Negotiating long distance through the press in March and April of 1938, he scorned both the fine and Greenlee's offer of $350 per month—a pay cut of almost fifty percent off Satch's last Crawford salary—with the memorable quotation that "I wouldn't throw ice cubes for that kind of money."

Given that Satch had a gift for using the press for bargaining leverage—witness his Ciudad Trujillo column—the NNL burghers moved to combat him in kind, by pressuring the black papers not to give Satch a public platform. Citing "errors made in reporting league activities," Cum Posey, going along with Greenlee, sent out a directive to the black press's sports editors, instructing them "not to print unfavorable league publicity unless assured of the facts," presumably by the league office.

Shortly thereafter, the *Courier*'s Wendell Smith seemed to fire the first shot in a campaign to de-mythologize Satchel Paige. In his April 16 column, Smith wrote that he'd heard from "inside dopesters" that Satch had been made a $500 a month offer by another team—but that Paige turned it down because the contract had stipulated that he'd be docked fifteen dollars for every game he missed. This "news"—no doubt the kind that NNL censors had at once cleared—prefaced Smith's own cutting remarks that Satch "is not the pitcher he once was. He is getting older and his famous fastball has slowed up to the point where batters can distinguish it between a pea and a bullet. There was a time when they couldn't see it."

Smith concluded: "Considering the number of games he would be required to pitch, $450 a month [sic] is more than a fair offer. It is even better than some of the major league pitchers. . . . His stubborn attitude is getting him nowhere."

But the NNL and its mouthpieces could not have chosen a worse time to play hardball—nor a worse candidate for a press blackout. For one thing, the league was now facing raids from all over the hemisphere, from summer leagues in Mexico, Argentina, Panama, and Venezuela; rather than succumb to Greenlee's sanctions, Cool Papa Bell had already fled to the Mexican League, where he'd stay for four profitable years.

For another, Satch surged ahead in the battle of newsprint in no time. Only days after Wendell Smith's castigation, he sat for an interview with another *Courier* reporter while hanging out in Harlem's Woodside Hotel with the Mills Brothers. Satch, the paper dutifully noted, "wore a brand new gray tailor-made Easter suit and light hat and said he was having a fine time learning to dance the Boogie-Woogie under the tutelage of [professional dancer] 'Reds' Graham of West 145th Street. Graham said Paige was an apt pupil."

Clearly doing a boogie-woogie on the press, Satch grabbed an immense *Courier* headline on April 23 with a name-dropping first for a black athlete—swearing that Joe DiMaggio himself, who was concurrently involved in a contract holdout with the Yankees, had "advised" him to "keep holding out until I get results." This was in exchange, he said, for showing DiMaggio "how to put something on the ball" in that 1935 game in Oakland. Satch also went on record by naming his price to pitch—$3,000 a month.

Oddly enough, such posturing allowed Gus Greenlee—whom Satch again said he would quit rather than play for—to finally exorcise the demon of Satchel Paige, gracefully and at a nice price if it could be worked out. As things now stood in Negro ball, the only club owners who could even consider money like that were Abraham and Effa Manley. After forming the Newark Eagles by merging their old Brooklyn Eagles with the Newark Dodgers in 1936, the Manleys had taken to spending hand over fist, stocking the Eagles with blackball oldies but goodies such as Willie Wells and Mule Suttles.

Having once offered $5,000 for Paige, they were prepared to make the same deal with Gus Greenlee now—and this was an idea that intrigued Satch, for reasons that had nothing to do with money or baseball and everything to do with the Manleys, or at least one of them.

Abe Manley, an affable, aging black numbers man and gambler in Newark, had no trouble gaining entrance into Greenlee's fraternity of scoundrels in 1935. But while Abe was the juice man of the club—playing to his fantasies by managing them while wearing sharp suits instead of a uniform in the dugout—it was really his young wife who ran the operation. Effa Manley made the personnel moves, scheduled games, and represented the Eagles at league meetings; for her to carry this kind of power in a black man's world was the fruition of *her* fantasies.

The "white sheep" of an interracial Philadelphia family—born illegitimate, the product of her white mother's dalliance with a white man—Effa's entire life was aimed at brushing away the guilt of white bastardy by fitting herself into the black culture. Dying her hair black, she lived in Harlem, described herself as a light-skinned black, and worked for the NAACP. After marrying Abe Manley in 1932, her biggest charge was using their ball team to heighten the cause—and her own fondness for lithe, young black men.

Strong-willed and PR savvy, Effa draped her ushers with sashes that read "Stop Lynching" and sent them through the stands to pass the hat for the NAACP. Committed to higher player salaries and better playing conditions, her self-promotion—a newspaper photo of her with one foot on the top dugout step and wearing an Eagles jacket and cap made her as identifiable as her players— would win crucial attention for Negro ball. But to the players around the league, her prime cause seemed to be choosing from among them for her bed partners. When one Eagles pitcher, Terris McDuffie, became the ace of the staff and began walking around the clubhouse like he owned it, the word on the club was that Mc-Duffie had earned his sway on a different ball field.

Satch, of course, had heard all the gossip, and he would get a chance to test its veracity. Gus Greenlee had had enough of the ludicrous, no-win war of words in the press with Satch and now accepted the $5,000 offer for the rights to sign Paige.

In considering whether to go to Newark and press his salary demands there, Satch was tempted not by the money but by bagging the woman who was supposedly hot to trot with the best Negro ball had to offer. Given the attentions of Bertha Wilson, he had no doubt that he qualified on that count. What's more, if he had few qualms about encroaching on Abe and Effa Manley's marriage— and his amorality about such things was made obvious by his fling with Bertha Wilson—he had less about flouting his own marriage.

He had not seen Janet for months. Having no contact whatsoever with her estranged husband, she could still get a rise out of attending parties at the Crawford Grille and signing checks as Mrs. Satchel Paige. But if she was determined to wait him out, when Satch heard from friends that she was a Grille regular, he irrationally regarded it as a betrayal. As far as he was concerned, Janet was yesterday's news and the marriage simply did not exist anymore.

When the deal with the Eagles was proposed, he was amenable about reporting to Newark—on the condition that Effa Manley play ball with him. This he laid out in another of his letters, the kind that could make Bertha Wilson weep. But when Effa received it, she did not weep, except maybe in pity for Satch. Effa didn't much care for pushy men. For all of her "black like me" activities, she retained an imperial air when it came to her carnal desires. *She* chose her partners, not vice versa.

When she read his missive, she could not imagine that she would actually have to *discuss* it with him. Instead, she thought and said nothing more about it until she related the tale shortly before her death, more as a nutty memoir of those delirious years than anything else. Of Satch wanting her to become his "sideline girl-friend," she said with a sad laugh, "I didn't know what to say, so I just threw it [the letter] away."

Just how far Satch pressed his case with Effa is not clear, but in the taillight of history one can erect an entire scenario of Satch's intentions between the lines of some of his mundane statements at the time. The *Courier* dispatch from the Woodside Hotel, for example, included a few paragraphs that in retrospect can seem positively salacious:

> Asked about the Newark Eagles offer he said: "I am going over to Mrs. Manley in Newark Sunday afternoon."
> Paige missed Abe Manley by one day, the latter having left for Jacksonville early Saturday. Mrs. Manley, told in Newark Sunday that Paige planned to visit her, said:
> "I don't know about seeing him. . . . However, if he comes over in time I will talk to him on general matters."

Whether or not Abe Manley ever knew of Satch's proposition to his wife, he was now obsessed with getting Paige into an Eagles uniform. While Satch sat out while awaiting the high sign that never came from Effa, Abe obtained a court injunction forbidding Paige from playing for any other team in New York or New Jersey. Abe even asked a sheriff to serve the injunction on him.

By then, the sheriff would have needed a very long arm to serve it. Having learned of the injunction, Satch was mailing his letters from across the border—the *Mexican* border.

•   •   •

The newest benefactor in Satchel Paige's near-lifelong litany of baseball sugar daddies was a moneyed Mexican beer distributor, Jorge Pasquel, who with his four brothers was beginning to play a dangerous game of chicken with American baseball. This happened after the Pasquels had assumed control of Club Azules de Vera Cruz in the Mexican League; what they had in mind went miles further than Rafael Trujillo's baseball politics.

Their sights were not nationalistic but global; by elevating the Mexican League—at the expense of American ball—the brothers hoped to make their circuit a competing major league. The first stroke would be to use the great black resource ignored by the big leagues. They then would raid the big league teams themselves and field integrated clubs in the name of international baseball.

It was a cockeyed dream, but because the Pasquels took it so far they probably did provide a kind of backdoor entrance to the big leagues—for the blacks, who would soon play alongside big leaguers in a natural symbiosis. That, however, was still a good distance down the road in the spring of 1938. In the incubancy of the Pasquels' dreams, it was more than enough for men like Cool Papa Bell and Satchel Paige to put some teeth into the Mexican League for the first time in its history.

This was why Satch—a hired gun paid the stunning fee of $2,000 a month—was placed not on the Pasquels' Vera Cruz team but on the moribund Agrario club of Mexico City, to create a rivalry for Club Azules, a powerhouse bunch led by the peripatetic Martin Dihigo.

Satch took receipt of his two G-notes at a propitious moment. Back home, not only were the sheriffs after him, but Gus Greenlee—again left high and dry, and now out $5,000—had declared Satchel Paige "banned forever from baseball."

That was nearly a prophecy. In the thin alkaline air of Mexico City, Paige's career seemed to be suddenly drying up. Almost from the start, he could not loosen the knots in his overworked arm and shoulder, nor could he shake the runs he had from the food and water that left his whole body bone-weak.

He had always gone on the assumption that because he pitched so much, his arm was a vessel immune to harm. As indifferent as he was to hard exertion, running, or much rest between starts, he still kept a careful checklist before activating that precious arm.

"I always took care of my weight and back muscles," he once said. "Those muscles gave me balance. That kept my arm from getting strained, ever. . . . I never threw until every muscle, every single one, was all loosed up. . . .

"I never threw them cold. No day. I took a bath, hot as I could stand it, when I got up in the morning and then I took one hotter than that after a game, so hot nobody else could stand it. Near boiling, that's how hot I took it. And it kept my arm from ever getting sore, and it kept my arm alive."

And so he went out and threw, trying to bust each pitch harder, as though that arm could unleash a magic bullet. But he was thirty-two now, and all he found was more pain and fatigue. He went through three games of this, all downers. Suffering with every delivery, he won one, lost one, gave up runs by the sheaf, and could not finish any. After the last, his arm was almost shucked, the veins screaming with each pulse beat.

"It kinda burns in there, feels like somebody pinched off the blood," he told his manager.

"Take a few days off," he was told.

Repairing to his room, he crawled not into the bathtub this time but into as familiar a sanctuary—the bottle. "I went to my hotel and had a little of that tequila," Paige would recall. " 'That ought to burn what I got in my right arm out,' I muttered. Man, but that stuff put a kick in you."

And laid you right out. Never seeing the night come and pass, he awoke the next morning, sat up in bed, and fell to the floor in agony—"My stomach got sick with the pain that shot up my arm. Sweat popped out all over. The pain wouldn't quit. . . . I just sat there, sweating, hurting enough to cry, getting sicker in the stomach and getting scared—real scared.

"My arm," Satchel Paige remembered. "I couldn't lift it."

But even now, he was petrified to surrender to the terrible meaning of the pain. Instead of resting, he pitched in relief over the next several weeks. But now the fans were openly questioning his dedication to the Mexican League, and with a climactic game between Agrario and Martin Dihigo's soon-to-be-champion Club Azules upcoming, he lied to his manager that his arm was healed. This meant that he would face Dihigo *mano a mano*, with an arm cut off at the shoulder. Amazingly, he made a real game of it.

Considering that each inning was a dip in hellfire, this was possibly one of the best games Satchel Paige ever pitched. Played on September 5 in Mexico City, the game—inexplicably ignored by Paige in his autobiography—was a curious study in contrast: Dihigo throwing white-hot fastballs, Satch getting by on an assortment of junkballs. Indeed, the crowd thought Paige was fooling around until it became clear that he simply could not cut loose.

Through six excruciating innings, Satch threw from every angle, from overhead to crossfire, even underhand. The one thing he did constantly was to tickle the corners of the plate. This he could do in his sleep by now, and if the brush moved slower, it dabbed only the extreme edges of the strike zone. The hitters—who could not chance to stop looking fastball and could not set their feet properly for the slow stuff—were flailing one-handed at, then taking for strikes, those pitches as they went by.

But in the seventh, the arm gave out and the game was up. With the game still scoreless, Satch gave up a hit and two walks. Trying now to uncork the long-delayed heat, he screeched in pain as the ball sailed two feet wide of the plate and skipped to the backstop, a very wild pitch that scored a run. And still he toughed it out, retiring the side with no further damage by going with the junk.

But for his incredible resolve, that might have been Satchel Paige's farewell to baseball. He was removed—mercifully—for a pinch-hitter in the bottom of the inning, and Agrario tied it up against Dihigo, taking Satch off the hook, though Dihigo broke up the game with a two-run homer in the ninth.

This game electrified all of Latin America, but for Satch it had the tone of an elegy. Largely because of him, the Pasquel brothers could now turn up their feeding frenzy. Beginning in 1939, and stretching into the mid-1940s, they paid big money for dozens of high-profile Negro leaguers, headed by Josh Gibson, to again forsake their teams and play the summer season in Mexico.

Satch would not be among them. Devastated by the betrayal of his near-ecclesiastical throwing arm, when doctors in Mexico City told him he would likely never be able to pitch again, they might as well have told him he was going to be destroyed like a broken-down horse. While the other Negro leaguers were streaming in, Satch was milking a heavy grudge against Mexico, which he cursed for apparently ruining him and for reminding him of his mortality, as well as of the cruel deceits of fame. He could also never forget the racial slurs from the *fanáticos* that greeted his hard times. Once he was told not to pitch anymore, he tartly recalled years later, the Mexican honchos couldn't wait to get him out of the country.

"Once you couldn't make them any money," he said, "they didn't care about you."

That lesson learned hard, he came back to Pittsburgh—the closest thing he had to a hometown—and wallowed in a bitter malaise while he kept secret from everyone the awful truth, at least until he could be convinced of it himself. While the Manleys—who were more than ready to break Greenlee's lifetime ban if he would sign with the Eagles—and the rest of Negro ball assumed he was playing his usual game of hard-to-get, he shunned even gripping a baseball. He paid rent in a rooming house by pawning his shotguns, fishing rods, and snazzy suits.

"I just sat then," he said in his autobiography. "I didn't want to go nowhere. I didn't want to see nobody. I could see the end. Ten years of gravy and then nothing but an aching arm and aching stomach."

Going back to Janet was out, too—though his reasoning was swathed in self-pity. "I knew if I couldn't keep her when I was a big man," he averred, "I sure wasn't going to be able to keep her when I was a broken bum just wandering around looking for a piece of bread."

This would be only so much more Paige melodrama but for the severe payback dealt him when he returned stateside that fall of 1939. The whole unpleasant decade of dealing with Satchel Paige and his shifting demands and allegiances turned most of blackball to the sport of goring his legend. Having learned to live without him, and having taken back all the others who had defected with him to the Dominican Republic, when rumors got around about his arm the league fathers now wanted to enjoy the sight of the king of terrors with no teeth.

Making cursory feelers around the NNL about possibly coaching or managing, he recalled later that the indifferent response convinced him that "Negro baseball was closing in on me tight. They wouldn't even take me for my name. . . . They all seemed to be saying something like, 'Well, Satch, you treated me pretty rough back in '35,' or, 'If you'd joined my club like you were supposed to in '36, if you'd taken care of me then, maybe I could take care of you now. But things are pretty tough right now. You know how it is?' "

Since he knew what a jerk he had often been, he could almost see all this as a requisite outcome, and a necessary tribulation to purge his sins. Thus, in remembering the slow suffocation of the "dead arm" phase of his career, he could be allowed a little melodrama. Said Paige, "I was beat. I knew it. There was no place to turn. I was a big man who was just falling into that old land where nobody knows you."

Or so he had thought.

12

He Is Risen

When you been at the top and hit the bottom, it's a mighty
long fall. I know.

—Satchel Paige,
Maybe I'll Pitch Forever

This is the noble truth of the arising of sorrow. It arises from craving, which leads to rebirth, which brings delight and passion.

—the Buddha

Although Satch at first feared he might have broken his arm in
Mexico, what felled him was likely a slight shoulder separation.
But slight or not, in this antediluvian age the only diagnosis that
mattered was that he could not throw a ball sixty feet six inches.
For Satchel Paige, that was tantamount to a death sentence.

At a time when sports injury rehabilitation meant a massage and
an ace bandage, and Satchel Paige's rotator cuffs were what he
changed to match his spats, he was no different than the white
jocks in one sense: all of them were routinely sent to their doom
far more quickly by perforations to tendons and ligaments than to
muscle and bone. Medical eons later, these injuries would be
among the easiest to repair, but with a term like arthroscopy as
alien as, say, television, ignorance was a condemnation: Satch, at
thirty-two and with his shoulder tissue shredded by years of abuse,
was now disabled. Next case.

The rub, the fear, for Satch was that he knew no other life, and
with so little money put away and so little ability to do something

else of substance, he could not make peace with a retirement that could only have led him back to the cavity of Mobile.

"It'd been a long time since I'd thought about having nothing, about how it was to grow up in Mobile," he reflected later about this stage of his life. "Ten years can make for a lot of forgetting. Now I started remembering. I didn't want to go back, but baseball was the only thing that'd keep me away."

Even if he had to be a second-class Satch, he would avoid being a second-class citizen of Mobile. For this, he knew of only one man who might accept Satchel Paige as damaged goods. That was J. L. Wilkinson.

When Satch called on J.L. for a job in the spring of 1939, he leveled with Wilkie, telling him, "My arm won't do any throwin'." But Wilkie still had use for Paige, if not for his arm, then for his name. *Assets* was the operative word. Though Satch's ego was turned off at first by it, Wilkie made it clear that the best he could do for him was to put Satch on one of the Monarchs' satellite teams—not as a pitcher but as a front man to draw a crowd.

If the spirit of charity helped Wilkinson toward this decision— and Wilkie, maybe alone among Negro league owners, looked beyond Paige's comic book character to find the troubled human within—so too did the spirit of commercialism. J.L. was not above using almost anything living and breathing to put people in the stands. And if a large audience came to see Satch Paige pitch— whatever team Paige would be with, Wilkie was going to bill it as "Satchel Paige's All-Stars"—only to see him playing first base or standing in the coach's box, well, they had at least seen a living legend standing there.

Best of all, to perpetrate this charade, Wilkinson had only to make a small accommodation with the NNL, most of whose owners wanted nothing more than to scrub from their hands the stain of Satchel Paige as part of their general housecleaning after the fall of Gus Greenlee.

Finished as a power broker in 1938, Greenlee had spent that season selling off the remnants of the Crawfords' glory years to other teams. His biggest gate attraction was to have Olympic hero Jesse Owens run against racehorses on the field before games. The end of his reign came in a two-stage razing.

First came the shuttering of his castle of dreams, Greenlee Field. When Greenlee closed the ballpark after the season, leaving the Crawfords without a home, he was besieged with criticism from the black press. Even his old lackey, John Clark, scolded him in the *Courier* for a lack of "foresight and courage" and—in the unkindest cut of all—for not taking a "purer racial interest" in the operation of the park. The lesson of that failure, wrote Clark with undue harshness, was that "Pittsburgh is no place to attempt big things for Negroes."

Then, in February of 1939, Greenlee resigned as NNL president and was replaced by Tom Wilson. He then sold off the Crawfords to Clark and Greenlee's own younger brother Charles—who could find a new home for the team in 1939 no closer than in Toledo, Ohio.

Defending his abdication of the power he had fought so hard for, Greenlee slung a last handful of mud at the same owners who, as a sop, had named him "honorary president" of the league he quit on. Writing in the *Courier* on April 8 that his resignation "will serve the best interests of all concerned," he again dumped on the other owners for violating "their pledges to respect" player contracts. Greenlee wrote, "It is safe to say that 95 percent of my roster has been approached with offers from different owners." He did not note that they had learned that game from Gus Greenlee himself.

Gus's farewell address followed by two months the end of his other sports conceit. Having upped the ante for his prizefighters, Greenlee got John Henry Lewis a title shot against heavyweight champion Joe Louis. For Louis, a friend of Greenlee's who once thought of buying into the NNL as an owner, the bout was more a favor to Gus than a genuine title defense, and it was nearly homicidal for John Henry. Outweighed by twenty pounds, he was knocked down three times and counted out at 2:29 of round one.

It was an apocalyptic defeat for Gus. The day before the fight, his other younger brother, Jack, was killed in a car crash. The day after, John Henry Lewis was forced to retire with an eye injury, leaving Gus with no sports chattel of any kind. In a matter of months, the original vehicle of his fantasies—the Crawfords— would fail to make a go of it in Toledo and become a discarded piece of NNL flotsam. As Greenlee withdrew to the Crawford Grille and pondered his next move, the league that he had kept alive went on without him, trying to purge his memory—and that of his collaborator in chaos, Satchel Paige.

That became evident at an NNL owners' meeting in Philadelphia in early May. Discussing J. L. Wilkinson's request to sign Satch—J.L. having decided not to step on the league's toes this time—the black *Newark Herald News* vouched that "hardly an owner

was willing to be troubled with the eccentric hurler." Reflecting league-think, the *News*'s story went on with admirable candor:

"Two things stood as obstacles to signing Paige—high salary demands and his temperament. . . . In the major leagues it has been the policy to cleverly ease troublesome players out of baseball and it looks as if the colored owners are going to do the same thing with Paige. Many express regrets that such an outstanding star should prove so hard to handle but point out that both sides probably feel they are right and that it would be dangerous to compromise."

The now inviolate Cum Posey, doing his part, bade a public farewell to Paige in his *Courier* column. Likening Satch to a "child who has been brought up wrong," Posey virtually eulogized him as a "phenomenal well-publicized pitching ability [that] could not be expressed in terms of finance. No colored club drew enough . . . to pay him a salary commensurate with his ability."

Then, getting with the program, Posey seemed to drop his objectivity for what was more like a stoning, insisting that "Negro baseball has been very good to Paige," and that "his unreliability . . . kept him from being really a valuable asset to any team. Personally, we never considered Paige as good a player as Joe Williams, Dick Redding, or Jesse Hubbard in their prime." In the end, Posey admitted that even though Satch "would have drawn many customers to the league parks this season, some owners are genuinely glad to have Paige leave."

That went for Abe and Effa Manley as well, though their willingness to kiss off Satch had more to do with the state of his arm than with his character. Indeed, J. L. Wilkinson had found it useful to leak word about Paige's injury as a way of scaring off anyone who had ideas of signing him. On March 11, the black *Kansas City Call*—which J.L. could manipulate the way Greenlee and Posey could the *Courier*—went heavy on this angle, not to mention alliteration, in reporting Paige's imminent signing by Wilkinson as exclusively an act of charity.

"The great one owned a wing that was as dead as a new bride's biscuit," the story read. "Satch's great flipper just wouldn't work any more. It was at that time that [Wilkinson] toyed with the idea of employing Satch, who was nursing the once-poisonous paw in pathetic pity."

Wilkinson's control of the press would be a regular and major component in the remaking of Satchel Paige. Releasing information sparingly, and as censorially sneaky as Greenlee and Posey ever dreamed of being, J.L. quickly put the clamps on any further details about Paige's "paw" once Satch was safely squirreled away. A long *Chicago Defender* piece on June 10, touting a local appearance by the "Paige All Stars"—its facts fed to the paper by Wilkie's people—included a detailed bio right down to a rough Paige birthdate (August 1907), but nothing about any arm trouble; the article declared that "Paige is credited with having a faster ball than Bob Feller or any of the white major leaguers."

And yet—just in case Satch would not be able to throw even a slow ball—Wilkie's flacks manufactured the weird claim that "Paige is a good hitter. He can play first base. . . . His total batting average is .343 for all games he was worked in"—which surely qualified as the best fiction of 1939. Though rumors would abound about the arm over the coming months, only much later, when he could make his recovery into an appropriately heroic tale, would Satch himself go public with the story.

For now, J. L. Wilkinson wanted the news splashed across the sports pages that Satch was his. As early as April 21, the *Call* ran a headline reading SATCHEL PAIGE JOINS KANSAS CITY MONARCHS, though Wilkie had no intention of putting a crippled Satch on the big team. But with the Monarchs' imprint established, Wilkie could send him out, to be paid according to a percentage of the gate, with the "All Stars"—the actual name of which was the Travelers, a loose, ever-shifting squad of Monarchs wannabes and has-beens, as well as sundry current Monarchs playing for a few bucks before the big team began its season.

Managed by the former longtime Monarchs third baseman Newt Joseph, the Travelers' big-name Monarchs refugees included first baseman George Giles and pitchers Big Train Jackson and John Marcum. Specially selected by Wilkinson to be Paige's traveling companion was infielder Byron "Mex" Johnson, an NAL all-star in 1938. Johnson bridged several worlds of Negro ball; born in Little Rock, Arkansas, he had earned a degree in English at Wiley College. Wilkie figured Mex could furnish down-home comfort for Satch while having the smarts to keep him out of trouble.

What Johnson remembered most about the interlude was that, out there in the sticks, he never saw as many people in his life as the masses who came out to catch a glimpse of Satchel Paige. "We played all through Kansas and Missouri and Illinois and, boy, the people really turned out to see him," Johnson said.

Most significant of Johnson's recollections of that season, however, is that—even though he rarely left Satch's side—he had no idea that Paige was less than whole as a pitcher. For Mex, as for many other players who only heard of it later, there would always be a trace of doubt about Paige's arm injury, partly because Satch kept to himself about it. To a man, the Negro leaguers neither knew when he lost his pitching arm, nor when he found it again.

What is known is that, in accordance with J. L. Wilkinson's plans, the black press began right away to hype the erstwhile Travelers' appearances by using the Paige imprimatur. Even thousands of miles away back in Pittsburgh, an upcoming game in Milwaukee between this team of factory seconds and the lamentable Ethiopian Clowns of Indianapolis was hyped with the two-column headline "SATCH" PAIGE AND HIS ALL STAR 9 TO PLAY CLOWNS.

These low-level games were often covered in royal prose. After another distant meeting between those teams, the *Courier* spared no detail in reporting that "Satchel Paige, the gangling pitching whiz, and his Kansas City All-Stars had to be content with an even break when they faced the flashy Ethiopian Clowns . . . before 4,698 baseball-minded fans at Woodruff Field [in] Peoria."

Absent in these Wilkie-provided game summaries was any word that Satch was crimped; even if this was by J.L.'s design, the fact was that early in the season he was throwing two or three innings a game, just as in the old barnstorming days—though Satch years later pleaded guilty to hosing the customers in order to cash in his percentage.

"I started doing some throwing . . . but it was just a lot of fooling," he wrote in his autobiography. "I had to pitch . . . because all those people expected to see Ol' Satch. . . . But what they saw was something else.

" 'How'd he ever get anybody out?' I heard one kid ask his dad. . . .

"Talk like that hurt you, deep inside. Everybody'd heard I was a fastballer and here I was throwing Alley Oops and bloopers and underhand and sidearm and any way I could to get the ball up to the plate and get it over, maybe even for a strike.

"But even that made my arm ache like a tooth was busting every time I threw. And the balls I was throwing never would fool anybody in the Negro leagues, not without a fastball to go with them. And those major leaguers I'd used to flatten would feast real good on that stuff."

And, with more emotive self-pity: "I'd lived high, way up, but when I'd come to the end of the road I didn't have a quarter. . . . Now I didn't have that arm to bring in the real stuff. I didn't have the arm to make a killing so I'd have enough to get something going for me when I was through with baseball.

"All I had was . . . a job wandering around the bushes. All I could do was hang on, hang on until they wouldn't pay to see me anymore. After that, I didn't know."

When Paige retroactively went public about the injury, for a 1953 profile in *Collier's*, this supposed ebbing of his life came out bathed in tears and schmaltz:

> The only job he could get was a coach for the Kansas City Monarchs. For the next year, he traveled with the Monarchs' second team, growing more and more obscure and irascible. "Man," Paige says, "it was a long year."
>
> It was an interminable year, hard on the young players trying to expand under the brooding shadow of the former "greatest pitcher in the world," and impossible for Paige, who seemed to grow taller, thinner and grimmer-looking every day. By 1940, when he was thirty-four, or thereabouts, and hadn't pitched for fourteen months, Paige was ready to quit.

The only problem with this sob-story scenario was that, way before the dawning of 1940, Mex Johnson and a good many others were seeing Satch vaporize hitters once again. One of these witnesses was a seventeen-year-old pitcher, Connie Johnson, who played that '39 season with the Toledo Crawfords.

"I was in Toledo and my season was over, but I heard Satchel was coming to town so I stayed over a week to see him," Johnson said. "I'd never seen him before, but my uncle used to talk about him like in 1926, how great he was and all that. So I had to go see him.

"They was playing the Toledo Mudhens, which was a white team, a Triple-A farm team, and the ballpark was jes' packed, and mostly with white people, 'cause *everybody* heard of him. And so I'm up there in the grandstand and I'm watchin' Satchel warm up and it's like . . . there was a team back then called the Clowns and they had a little show they would put before the games called 'shadowball,' they'd make like they were throwin' the ball but they didn't. So the first man Satchel pitched to, I thought he was playin' shadowball. 'Cuz I didn't see the ball.

"I said, now wait a minute, somethin's wrong here. He wouldn't be playin' no shadowball out here during the game, but I can't see it. So I know what I'm gonna do. I'm goin' down there closer and see, was he throwin' it or not. And I went down there behind the catcher, and he was throwin' it but you just couldn't see it, that's how fast it was.

"I think he was comin' off an arm injury, he was comin' out of it. And as hard as he was throwin', they said he used to throw harder before. Man, how hard could he throw it if he threw it harder than he did that day?"

Late that season, the Paige team—so wildly popular an attraction that it was now outdrawing the league teams—pulled into Chicago for a September 22 doubleheader against the venerable American Giants. With his ragtag team sweeping both games, Satch was anything but a manikin. Facing Sug Cornelius in the second game, he got a 1–0 lead in the first inning and was lethal in holding it. Scattering five hits, he struck out ten "big league" hitters and walked not a man before darkness halted the game in the seventh with the score still 1–0.

The *Defender*'s game story described not a brooding shell of a man but rather a pistol. It read:

> The fans came to see Satchel Paige and they saw the elongated, carefree, happy pitcher whose name has been skyrocketed to fame and to the very door of the major leagues. The great majority believed Paige would go but three or four innings. Many had heard that Satchel had "lost" his fast ball. Instead Mr. Paige went the entire seven innings and could have gone seven more.
>
> What did Satchel have that balked the Giants? He had everything. . . . He waved to the crowd at the start and went to work like a big leaguer. . . . Satchel purposely took a long slow windup and . . . [the Giants] blinked as they missed Paige's fast ones.

Not that Satch hadn't by necessity learned to use more finesse, or even trickery. Mex Johnson remembers that Paige had begun to use his devious Hesitation Pitch to set up hitters for his fastball, which he never before needed to do. "See, he was using it as a change of pace, 'cause he didn't have a curveball. I don't ever remember him throwin' no curve," Johnson said.

"And when he did this with men on, he'd be lookin' around while he did that hesitatin', and it was really a balk. He balked a lot of times only they didn't call it. Mebbe they was told not to call it, or else they was lettin' him get away with it 'cause of who he was. But them runners had to hold up, and they couldn't score when they should have."

But, on the whole, it seems plausible that Satch's rebirth wasn't

really the stuff of miracles as much as simple enforced rest—and
the irrational pluck to believe that the doctors were full of it. For
the first time in over a decade of seasons without end, Paige had
gone an appreciable time without punishing that fabulous arm.
When he went out with the Travelers, it had been seven months
since that terrible day in Mexico City. In spite of the doctors' prog-
noses, the idleness had at least convinced him that his shoulder was
healing and regenerating strength in his pitching arm.

But if the "Miracle on the Mound" may have been nothing more
than the course of common biology, Satch would pinpoint with
dramatic embellishment the precise moment of the resurrection.
As the story was told in *Collier's* by writer Richard Donovan, it happened this way:

> Just before a Monarchs game . . . someone overthrew first in a
> pre-game warmup and Paige ambled over, picked up the ball and
> threw it back to the pitcher. It was the most unobtrusive of acts, but
> just about every player on the field seemed to see it and to stop
> stock-still.
>
> Walking thoughtfully toward the dugout, Paige picked up a glove
> and called for a ball. Without a word, the Monarchs' catcher left the
> plate and stationed himself about pitching distance from Paige.
> Then Paige began to throw, easily at first, then harder and harder.
> Nobody moved, the stands were silent, the game waiting. Then,
> abruptly, he stopped, and gazed around at all the eyes upon him.
>
> "Well," he said, "I'm back."

Mex Johnson scratches his head and smiles. Then he says, "Well,
let me tell you something 'bout Satchel. He wasn't educated, but
he had a whole lotta common sense. He was a born entertainer. He
didn't know too many verbs, but he could sure tell a good story."

•   •   •

Rather than Purgatory, it seems that this year of avowed depression was more like a highly paid rollick in the country. While
Paige's All-Stars meandered through the Midwest in two blighted
Lincoln Mercurys, Satch would take Mex Johnson into his long
Chrysler Airflow and tell Newt Joseph they'd be seeing him at the
next game. As it turned out, in fact, the only trouble that Mex had
to contend with in the company of Paige was his demented driving.

"I don't know what it was with that boy," Johnson said with a
shudder, "but when he got to drivin' it was hell on wheels. He got

that big old Chrysler up on them mountain roads and he just loved
to go fast. I'd tell him, 'Man, I don't wanna ride with you, Satchel.'
'Cause he'd . . . and he was crazy enough to do this. He would see a
deer cut across the highway and *follow* it. I mean, that boy would
turn around on the highway, or cut 'cross the divider and go after
that deer on foot with his rifle. Aw, man, I'd be sittin' there in a big
jam-up waitin' for him to come on back."

As Jimmie Crutchfield had before him, Mex Johnson learned little about the man behind these hair-trigger impulses. Even though
he was in Satch's favor, Mex could be displaced at a moment's notice if a more diverting companion came along. "The women always wanted to be with him, especially the white women. There
was this one lady he took up and down the West Coast and up into
Canada. That's when he really isolated himself from us."

As isolated as he was from the Negro leagues now, his name was
hotter than ever. If the NNL people had hoped to embargo his visibility—and were no doubt pleased that he all but vanished from
the newspapers while he was in Mexico—they were treated to that
obeisant *Chicago Tribune* column by Dizzy Dean being picked up by
nearly every black paper in the land. Even as Satch wondered if
he'd ever be able to throw again, the *Defender*'s September 24,
1938, issue came with the headline DIZ SAYS PAIGE IS BEST
PITCHER IN BASEBALL.

And out there in the hinterlands, in the oddest of places, the
name had a powerful ring to it. When the Paige All-Stars visited
Cheyenne, Wyoming, a hassle developed when they pulled into a
roadside gas station–diner. "That was the first time I ever heard the
word 'nigger,' " Mex Johnson recalled, "and it shocked me because
I thought that was a Western city, not like the South. What happened was, I got out of the car and asked about food and the guy
said niggers couldn't get any food there. And then Newt and Satch
came in and there was a heated conversation and then we left.

"Well, we stopped at that same fillin' station on the way back and
they said, 'Yeah, bring 'em in, they can eat here.' See, I think it had
gotten around that the guy had refused to serve Satchel Paige and
that you just didn't do that to a star like him."

•   •   •

After five profitable months along the back trails, the Paige All-
Stars ended their season by rubbing off *their* popularity on the
showcase Negro teams of the Midwest, in games first with the American Giants and then the Kansas City Monarchs themselves. How-

ever, the juice that was turned on in Satch's arm by the Chicago game drained off in his last outing of the season, an October 5 game in Kansas City.

Matched against the Monarchs' ace, the stocky Hilton Smith, Satch was undressed. He gave up four runs and five hits in the first inning, two on a Turkey Stearns homer in the third, and three more in the fourth before removing himself as the emphatic loser in the eventual 11–0 Monarchs rout.

Still, from what the Monarchs' superb first baseman Buck O'Neil saw of Paige that day, there was nothing to pity. O'Neil, who had first batted against Satch in 1935 as a member of the Shreveport Acme Giants—and then again in the '36 *Denver Post* tournament when his Mineola (Texas) Black Spiders were crushed by Paige's legendary Bismarck club—could notice only a marginal dropoff in the old heat.

"I know I didn't do nothin' against him that day," O'Neil laughed. "If we beat him big, you gotta understand that we had the big ballclub and those guys were the kids we were gonna bring up, it was like a farm team. They had a pretty good ballclub, but we couldn't let them beat us. You know, we were the Monarchs.

"But Satch. Oh, man. He could still throw hard. Not as hard as he had thrown, but you're talkin' about somebody throwin' ninety-eight, a hundred miles an hour. But now he's throwin' maybe ninety—which is still more than the average guy.

"I know when I first saw him, we didn't have a chance against him with that little old ballclub I was with. He was the best and, actually, he was so deceptive! You'd look at that big ol' slow arm movin' and—*chooo*—that ball's just right by you. And then he'd come up and throw you a change of pace and, oh, man.

"He had a curveball, too. It wasn't a Hilton Smith curveball and he wouldn't throw it that much. But when he did, he'd spot that sucker right out there on that outside corner, and a lotta times the guys would take that pitch, they couldn't do nothin' with it."

Given that unstrained, smoothly consonant pitching style—the slow buildup to the launch of a guided missile—O'Neil doubted that *anything* could take a toll on that famous arm.

"Satchel had the greatest right wrist I've ever seen on any man," he said. "Satchel actually didn't use his shoulder or elbow. He was more of a wrist guy and, oh, could he thunk that ball. He'd snap that wrist and that ball would be up there at ninety miles an hour before you'd know it.

"With the way he threw, he couldn't hurt hisself from throwing. He coulda just caught a cold in the shoulder, but it wasn't anything like you had to cut on the shoulder, even though at that time you didn't even think surgery; when a guy's arm got bad, he was through. But, see, a lotta times I don't think they need to cut on 'em like they do all the time now. Satchel proved that.

" 'Cause he didn't go to no doctor for it. What happened was, Jewbaby went out on the road with Satchel," O'Neil said, referring to the elderly Frank "Jewbaby" Floyd, longtime trainer of the Monarchs. "Wilkinson sent Jewbaby out with that ballclub and Jewbaby worked on that arm, just rubbin' it with different things. It couldn't have been too serious, 'cause Satchel went out there and pitched and the arm came around and he came right back.

"The doctors said it was serious, and for most guys that woulda been it. But the doctors didn't know Satchel."

•   •   •

Encouraged by his resurrection, Satch went back to the tropics to pitch over the winter. He did not go with the in crowd to Mexico, instead going all the way to the Venezuelan League. But he was out of there after one game, terrified because the gamblers were as well armed as the military. In Paige's only game, he once recalled, when he lost "a bunch of soldiers had to march me out of the park to keep away about a hundred guys with machetes who wanted to carve me up because an error cost me a ball game."

He then hopped to Puerto Rico, where the gamblers were virulent but not bloodthirsty. But in his first game, he was right back in the frying pan. Pitching for the Guayama Brujos against Los Indios de Mayagüez, which had Buck Leonard and the Crawfords shortstop Bus Clarkson, he loaded the bases with two outs. Now, with Clarkson coming to bat, Satch decided to walk home a run and pitch to a local nobody rather than see Clarkson do more damage—while also setting up another of his renowned high-risk confrontations, the kind that Satch always knew to be low-risk.

Unfamiliar with Satch's wacko riffs, the Guayama manager flipped out. Buck Leonard, who was very familiar with the riffs, could only giggle, then and now. "The manager, he came running out screaming, '*No, no,* don't walk him!' Satchel said, 'I know what I'm doin'.' So the catcher stepped out to the side and Satchel threw four balls and the run scored and the people were goin' crazy. And Satchel said, 'Now that's all you fellas are gonna get today.' "

Quickly blowing out the next hitter, Satch did only give up that one run in winning 8–1. Buck Leonard, though, would not soon allow him to forget that he had taken the easy way out. Spreading around the story, even years later, he said, "We were still kidding Satch about how he walked that run home."

The rest of his season on the island was stirring. He went 19-and-3 with a 1.93 ERA, a league-high 208 strikeouts in 206 innings, and had six shutouts. While his fastball had lost a few inches on its rise, and did not slam into the catcher's mitt with the crack of a Molotov cocktail, his control of it was still impeccable. And because he now had a serviceable curve, what was left of his fastball was plenty.

Josh Gibson was in Puerto Rico as well that winter, playing for the Santurce Cangrejeros, and Satch's recovery could also be gauged by their first head-to-head confrontations—which were a wipeout by Paige. Satch held the big man to three hits in sixteen at-bats, *outhitting* Gibson in those games, though Josh was mainly in the country to party and was frequently seen stinking drunk or dragging on reefers of the island's best bud. One morning, the *policía* found him butt-naked and wandering through the streets. When they tried to put him in the wagon, Josh ripped a tire right off its axle before he was subdued. It was not a good omen.

But for Satch, the signs were all a go, and the best was the burn that he laid on the San Juan Senadores in the playoff final. The Senadores's big guns were Negro leaguers Gene Benson, Spoony Palm, and Roy Partlow. It fell to Homestead's Partlow to stop him, but Satch beat him in the first game, then again three games later to sew up the Guayama title sweep and win the league's most valuable player award.

•   •   •

When word got around that Satch was not a scrap-heap rind after all, Abe and Effa Manley thought they had been had. With the end of the Puerto Rican League season in May 1940, Satch could sense not just that the Manleys were going to reenter his life, but that the Negro National League was no longer so eager to see him go.

Even before he left the island, the Manleys were trying hard to build a case that despite their part in the NNL kiss-off of Paige they still owned priority rights to him. They even sent him two contracts, both ignored by Satch. While it was mainly a pipedream, Effa Manley insisted that a contrite Satch was "about to arrive" in Newark—a claim that the *Afro-American*'s Fred C. Clark shot down in the May 11 edition of the paper.

"Again the Manleys are spreading their same old propaganda," Clark wrote. "We know that Paige is not even thinking about the Manleys because he knows that they will not pay him his price for pitching."

Actually, once he heard of the renewed interest by the Eagles, Satch did think about what he could get out of such a deal. On June 15—after Satch returned and picked up again with the Paige All-Stars—the *Afro* reported that although Paige denied he had an agreement to play for Newark, he had "corresponded with the ownership of the team." Once again, that meant contact with Effa Manley. Judging from another quite intriguing takeout in the *Afro*, this may have been to revive his very personal quid pro quo: "Mrs. Effa Manley came [to see him] recently to talk over the matter, but they failed to reach any agreement, Paige said. He stated that Mrs. Manley was very insistent about what she would have and not have before they could reach even the basis for an agreement."

Evidently, what Effa would not have led Satch to spurn the Eagles yet again—and now a crisis developed around Negro ball, centered solely on who owned Satchel Paige.

That the NNL cared so much about him only put Satch in a foul mood. Although it had been his and J. L. Wilkinson's duplicity that helped gain his release from the NNL, it had not been lost on him that the league couldn't wait to get him out. Thus, with self-exonerating overkill, he explained during this war-nervous period that he had fled the league in the first place because it smacked of "Hitlerism." And, with accurate cynicism, he noted that when his arm was gone, no one in the league had offered him any work—but now that he was in form again, they insisted that he work for them.

Not that Satch had to be reminded that he had created this paroxysm within the game—that he had been the role model for its current problems. With the league's season under way, nearly two dozen players had defected to play in the Pasquel brothers' Mexican money fields—and the Eagles had been hit hard in these raids, losing pitcher Leon Day and third baseman Ray Dandridge. Now, with the external threat to the black game greater than it had ever been, the exquisite irony was that all of Negro ball needed, and badly, the all-time league-jumper himself to lend stability and decorum to the situation—to play the good guy in a world he helped to make bad.

Obviously—and this was not lost on Satch, either—blackball was surely close to its last act if he was going to have to save it from mercenary men. Mulling this over, he did not object to playing Messiah to a league he loathed; but, again, it would have to be on his terms. And one of these now was that he would not toddle to Newark to be ignored by Effa Manley.

This decision, however, precipitated the crisis. In late June, the NNL and NAL called a joint meeting to discuss the Paige road-block. As the owners gathered in Harlem's Woodside Hotel—coincidentally, one of Satch's favorite haunts—not a few of them approached each other warily, as if this was the last stop before the shooting started. As the *Afro*'s sports editor, Art Carter, described the tense scene, "War clouds which threaten to disrupt the [NNL] schedule . . . and probably lead to a split in the loop hovered" over the meeting, and that because of "the stormy issue over the ownership of Satchel Paige, recalcitrant pitcher . . . fireworks are slated to boom."

As much as by Paige's refusal to report, the Manleys were offended by J. L. Wilkinson, openly charging that Wilkie had orchestrated the crisis. J.L., they said, was bearding for Satch, and by shunting him to the Monarchs' traveling club—which was technically owned by Wilkinson's brother Lee—he could keep Satch for himself without conflicting with league rights. This of course ignored the NNL's virtual eviction of Paige only the year before, but the livid Manleys were seeking conflict-of-interest conspiracies all over the place, further pointing out that Wilkie had used an NNL booking agent to schedule games for the Paige All-Stars with the league's own Brooklyn Giants.

Demanding satisfaction, the Manleys' bite was indeed menacing. Having gotten promissory votes from the league's Cuban Stars and New York Black Yankees, if the Eagles withdrew from the NNL those two teams would go with them. As Art Carter noted in the *Afro*, "If justice is not done [as the Manleys saw it] by the league moguls . . . and if this triumverate is maintained it may throw the league into complete discord."

It took two days of rumors and wrangling for a solution to be worked out, and then only after the owners reached the brink of anarchy. That happened when an exasperated Abe Manley tried to hold the talks hostage by raiding the Toledo Crawfords—which had become an NAL club in its short life—and signing Bus Clarkson and Spoon Carter; if Wilkinson was going to flaunt interleague agreements on contract sanctity, so would Abe.

The moment of high crisis came when both Tom Wilson and J.B. Martin, the two league presidents, ruled that the NNL could not compel Paige to go to Newark so long as he remained out of the league, and that Clarkson and Carter were NAL property and had to be returned to Toledo. This, said the *Afro*, precipitated a "bitter fight" that eased only when the leagues knuckled under to Manley's threats and allowed him to keep Clarkson and Carter as an equalizer and a way to keep the peace.

Satch cared nothing about these arcane matters, but it must have given him a warm feeling to know that he had brought the shadow of Armageddon across the Negro leagues. Now, maybe they'd leave him alone already.

• • •

For J. L. Wilkinson, the battle was irrelevant all along. He had too much invested in Satch—and was, with Paige, making too much on their percentages of the gate to turn him over to Abe Manley. He would have separated from the NAL on the spot had the ruling gone down that way.

As it was, Wilkie had already planned a massive PR offensive with Satch. Working through his flacks, he lined up some of the most important breakthrough coverage of black sports in the white press. Thus, on the eve of the owners' meeting a two-column profile of Paige ran in the June 3 issue of *Time* magazine—identifying him for all of white America as a member of "the Travelers, a roving division of the Kansas City Monarchs."

The piece strained to introduce a brand-new idiom of socially aware sports reporting—which, given the fact that white opinion-makers knew next to nothing about Negro ball, came out as hybrid of self-conscious wonderment and crudeness. Having little else to go by but the rabid testimonials of a Marvin McCarthy or a Dizzy Dean and the cartoon journalism of the black press, *Time*—Henry Luce's salutation to the American ruling class—could not keep from drafting a fresco of "large, dark Leroy (Satchelfoots) Paige."

Not able to grasp the concept of his actual sobriquet—or how the name could describe something other than the mutation of a black man's anatomy—*Time*, in rechristening him, insisted that "Satchelfoots owes his nickname (optionally shortened to 'Satchel' or 'Foots') to his size 12 shoes. . . . Apparently, Satchel got strong by shouldering 200-lb. blocks of ice. Last week his old ice-wagon employer recalled his prodigious appetite: 'That boy et mo' than the hosses.' "

What separated this odd salvo from the florid sycophancy of a

Dizzy Dean was *Time*'s earnestness in laying out the case for big league integration—and in one paragraph advanced the case more than anything had in half a century of baseball:

> Columnists Westbrook Pegler, the late Heywood Broun [both onetime baseball writers] and many a sportswriter have protested against color discrimination in big-league baseball. The owners and managers say that their Southern players and their visits to Southern training camps would make trouble if Negroes were on the team. But many a shepherd of a limping major league club has made no secret of his yearning to trade more than a couple of buttsprung outfielders for colored players of the calibre of Satchelfoots Paige.

Much less valuable to the cause, however, was the next penetration into whitebread journalism. This was the July 27 issue of the *Saturday Evening Post*, a huge-circulation magazine that hired the great writers of the day to portray the middle class as the ideal American condition. While this obliging rendition of the Paige style was certainly useful to him, it took a pickaxe to the intellectuality of blackball.

In this long article, Satchel Paige was no longer "Black Matty" but—after the turn-of-the-century Hall of Fame pitcher and noted goofball Rube Waddell—a "Chocolate Rube," an incorrigible colored sideshow. Only now was it possible to see how innocuous Marvin McCarthy's tribute had been seven years before—and as deleterious, as writers bade to top that kind of hyperbole. Thus, where Satch had been a "gigantic African" for McCarthy, he was now a tribal lord among morons. Antithetical to the solicitous tones of *Time*, writer Ted Shane's piece read:

> Their baseball is to white baseball as the Harlem stomp is to the sedate ballroom waltz. They whip the ball around without looking where it lands, and woe to the receiver if he isn't there instinctively. They play faster, seem to enjoy it more than white players. . . . [They] play way back on the grass and rush up on a ball like tumblers. They think it a weakness to catch a ball with two hands, and enjoy amazing dives into the bag to outfoot runners. Players clown a lot, go into dance steps, argue noisily and funnily. . . .
> Some are positive magicians at bunting. . . . "We plays for home-run bunts," Oscar Charleston, a great player and now manager of the Crawfords, says. Charleston could also hit, I'm told. "Once Charleston, he start to bunt, decided to cross up the infield in-

stead—hit the ball so hard he bus' the ball to pieces—the covah flyin' one way—the pieces the other," a licorice enthusiast thrills.

Paige, always the showman . . . would crank his apelike arms a half dozen times, uncrank them, lean back till he almost lay on the ground, bring that huge left foot up till it almost kicked out a cloud, then would suddenly shoot the ball from somewhere out of this one-man melee.

"You cain't see nothin' but dat foot," complained his league victims. "It hides the ball park and Satch, too! Sometimes you don' know the ball's been pitched till it plunks behind you!" . . .

Unfortunately, adulation, white and black, made a problem child out of Paige. On his way to the ball park on an afternoon, Satchel could never resist . . . anything from a fishing pond to a crap game or a stomp palace filled with admiring belles. . . . When he did show, his excuses were marvels of Stepinfetchit disingenuousness. . . . Usually [his] car was the villain. "Ah hit a dawg," Satch admitted one day. "Jes' bad enough to need to go to the hospital. Ah rushed him there and that poor dawg looked like he was fixin' to die. It had me worried, so I stayed all afternoon and I pulled that little dawg through!"

Charleston tore his kinky hair and took it. For with Paige in there, the Crawfords were unbeatable on the field and at the box office. The problem was to get him in there. . . .

Of Paige's personal life, records are as hazy as those of his no-hit games. . . . It is known that he has been married, that the gals are fond of him, and that he spends his money "faster than he makes it." He never has had a home—other than his car. . . . He is rarely out of condition, despite his queer hours and nocturnal habits. He is an expert dancer and singer. He usually carries a huge guitar around with him, and plays it beautifully during the rare interviews he grants, strumming background chords to fit his mood—like in a movie.

[Paige] affects a Stepinfetchit accent in his speech, but behind his sleepy eyes his brain works shrewdly. . . . He loves to call Mule Suttles "Donkeyhorse" and "Horsehead." He gets spells of nicknaming everyone Tub. A bonehead player he terms a Hawgcutter. . . . Harlem calls him a freak man because he does everything well. . . . He is one of the best-dressed men in Negro baseball. While he goes for spats and cane, his suits are quiet and well-cut.

Satch mingles very little with his fellow players except around the ball park. After barnstorming games he will put on a show for his white pals, and they in turn treat him genuinely. But colored ballplayers know him as a "loner." They don't, however, resent him.

As for his eccentricities, the feeling is that "Satch had a tough time as a kid, and is making up for it in his way."

For Satch, this was advertising that money couldn't buy; for all else in blackball, though, it was glory's smallest change. But, now, with Satch's name recognition on a par with any other sportsman in America, the man who had been close to breaking up the Negro leagues—and was damn proud of it—was being counted on to keep alive the very existence of organized black baseball.

13

I'm Not Selling Out, I'm Buying In

The sports writers loved . . . me acting the big shot and living it up like that. They started talking about me like I wasn't even a real guy, like I was something out of a book.

—Satchel Paige,
Maybe I'll Pitch Forever

Barred from organized professional baseball because he is a Negro, Paige has played against many of the major-league stars in exhibition games. According to them he has more than proved his ability to play in the big leagues. He won four out of six games from Dizzy Dean in a series and Joe DiMaggio says Paige is the greatest pitcher he has ever batted against.

—*Life* magazine, June 2, 1941

Satchel Paige is the Joe Louis of baseball. Perhaps it is more proper to say Joe Louis is the Satchel Paige of boxing, for old Satch was tossing 'em plateward long before Joe cut his first wisdom tooth.

—*Baltimore Afro-American*,
June 13, 1942

Fittingly, the same printed page that represented the height of his fame also told of Satch's long-avoided return to the nadir of his youth. *Time*'s lead paragraph unwittingly hit it on the head in reporting that Paige "went home to his native Mobile last week for a day of triumph."

Only through twelve years of inordinate success could he forget the foul stench of the Mobile county jail that had greeted him on his last visit. During the interim he had thought often of Lula Paige, and had eased his separation anxiety from her by sending her money even when he was down to near nothing. Now, in scheduling a tour stop for the All-Stars in Mobile to play the local semi-pros, he felt that it was high time to remove his guilt once and for all.

Before he went to see Lula, he looked around the good neighborhoods and put a down payment on a large house on South Cedar Street, which sat on a birch-lined block where the sky wasn't quite as dust gray and where blacks could live as though they didn't have those "c" designations appended to their names in the city directory.

Lula herself had moved from the old hovels down by the river as the Paige family had spread out across the South Bay. Still working as a domestic, Lula now lived a mile or so up on South Franklin Street. But neither Lula's nor any of the other children's lives were any different than they had been two decades ago; as Satch had feared for himself, none of his siblings had made it even to the good side of Government Street, much less out of Mobile.

Even Wilson "Paddlefoot" Paige, who had shown him the way through baseball, was now a middle-aged laborer; and John Paige, Jr., the son who had challenged John Page's servility and in so doing given the family a new surname, was no more than eking out an existence with his wife, Viola. The baby boy of the brood, Clarence, for whom Satch wanted to set an example of self-respect, was working as a porter at the old L&N train depot, the scene of Satch's youthful crimes of poverty; only two years later, trying to make a niche, Clarence would migrate to Ohio to work on an oil rig in Lake Erie, only to fall in the water and drown.

Lula Paige, however, would not stand for the notion that her family need be pitied—and she certainly was not about to see Leroy through starry eyes when he walked into her home after all those years. This stoic, self-possessed woman, unthawed by time, bridled when Satch told her of the surprise he had for her on South Cedar Street, angry at his presumption that she would need him to set the options in her life.

Putting him in his place, she asked him sardonically if he was a big star. The biggest, he said. Lula thought for a moment, bit into her cheek, and told him that when he was so big that she would know it, *then* she'd think about bending to him as the head of the family.

Reluctantly recovering his down payment, Satch had to once again marvel at how Mobile could defeat him every time. But at least he left on better terms with himself, satisfied that he had done his part to reestablish his lacerated family ties. Still, he was no less eager to get out of the place than he had been twelve years before.

•   •   •

While Abe Manley would continue to press his claim to Satch's services, the two leagues' practical decision to leave Satch be reflected their desire not to alienate him again. The Mexican raids were fraying nerves all around blackball, and the last thing anybody needed was another dumb show of force against Paige at a time when he was so comfortable back on the edges of Negro ball.

J. L. Wilkinson sensed, correctly, that he now had carte blanche to do as he wished with Satch. Though the NNL had not officially waived Paige at the Woodside Hotel peace conference, taking the out that the Paige All-Stars were not any league's property, Wilkie had seen enough of Satch's recovery to try to promote him late in the 1940 season to the Monarchs, where the PR values of team and man could combine into a mountain of profit.

Wilkie knew he could not use Satch on the Monarchs the way he'd been used on the All-Stars. If Satch went only a few innings for the benefit of the big crowds he drew, it might disturb the chemistry and image of his revered Monarchs, a team that never shorted its fans and as a league team had to go for wins. Thus, in Satch's first round of starts in a Monarchs uniform, he was to extend himself. Drawing 10,000 people in Chicago on September 12, he went all five innings, and was ready to go nine, in a game against the American Giants that was called by darkness; the Monarchs won 9–3, and Satch struck out ten. This outing earned him a gigantic photo next to the *Defender*'s game story, under the heading SATCH SAYS IT'S IN THE BAG, THEN WINS.

Unfailingly, in the big cities that had been bypassed by the Paige All-Stars, he proved to be blackball's biggest drawing card. When Satch went up against the Detroit Stars in the Motor City, the local black paper reported that "more than 12,000 fans stormed through the gates of the park, while several thousand were unable to get in. Thousands more were kept away because of threatening weather." That mob scene, which necessitated a hastily scheduled return to the city, was typical of the air of expectancy that accompanied Satch's arrival wherever he went.

Still pitching on percentage, sometimes as high as twenty-five percent, Satchel Paige would never again have to hock a rifle in order to afford a meal.

•   •   •

Back in everyone's graces, Satch went again to the Puerto Rican League for the winter—only to make himself a pariah there. Having owned the island the year before, he now took the Josh Gibson approach and lazed around between half-hearted pitching appearances for the Santurce Cangrejeros, and paid the price for it.

Characteristic of his indifferent outings was a relief stint against the San Juan Senadores. Called on to protect a one-run lead with two runners on base, he faced Homestead's nineteen-year-old third baseman Wilmer Fields, who was scared to death.

"I got the lightest bat I could find so I could get around on him," Fields recalled, "but he threw one right by me, and he yelled at me, 'Aw, you can't hit.' "

Satch expected to finish off his man, but Fields, looking fastball again, tore into the next pitch and tacked it over the center field fence for a game-winning homer. For Fields, the trip around the bases was a taste of ambrosia.

"As I went around, I hollered to him, 'Go back home, old man!' " Fields said with a joyous blather. "I mean, you didn't do that to Satchel Paige, and you had to enjoy it. The Puerto Ricans loved it. They passed me money through the chicken wire in front of the stands. One guy gave me a hundred dollar bill for it."

That was likely a sign of how much the locals could clean up by hitting a bet against Satch, who was considered such a lock to win. But for Satch there were no dollar bills passed through chicken wire when he won, only escalating catcalls when he didn't. When that happened, an infuriated Paige went to the Santurce owners and demanded more money. When he was refused, he forgot to show up for several games, whereupon the league's commissioner told him he was being suspended for a week.

Satch had a different idea. "Forget 'bout the week," he said. "Go ahead an' make it for life." He then cleared off the island, and crossed one more Pan-American country off his travel list.

He did not come away empty-handed, however. During his many off hours in Puerto Rico he spent more and more *siesta* time with a young native woman named Lucy Figueroa; when he returned stateside, she came through customs and then moved in with him in Kansas City. Satch, who was always circumspect in describing his carnal interests—normally neglecting to describe them at all—would later try to pass off his time with Lucy quickly, cleanly, and euphemistically.

"Lucy had a hankering to get into the United States," he wrote in his autobiography, "and after we got friendly I gave her a hand.

"Lots of folks tried to spread around the word that we were married and later on when they'd see her at the park when I was pitching, they wrote she was my wife . . . but there wasn't any truth to it. Lucy was a fine woman and we were good friends for a while in the States and that was it. Then I went my own way."

The problem with that story was, for all of his uneasy tiptoeing on the subject, Satch was taking Lucy—"Lucy Baby," as he called her—on his rounds with him and was himself introducing her as his wife. In fact, when Satch attracted yet another choice notice in the white press, he was anything but reluctant to show her off as such.

The third piece of the Satchel Paige mass-magazine trilogy of 1940 and 1941 ran in *Life*, the outsized, then-three-year-old photojournalism stablemate of *Time*. The issue that hit the nation's newsstands the week of June 2, 1941, carried in big, evocative black-and-white glossies what Satch had probably seen in Technicolor in his dreams for years. Here was Satchel Paige, the onetime urchin from Mobile, spread across three pages and posed for eternity as the sharpest, coolest hepcat in Harlem—opportune timing having put him in a New York Black Yankees uniform in time for the *Life* shoot.

The sharp irony here was that—at a time when Paige was rescuing the identity of the Negro leagues—no mention was made in the *Life* text of those leagues beyond his fleeting affiliation with the Black Yankees. Not even J. L. Wilkinson—whose Monarchs were among the unmentioned—could deny now that his reclamation project was bigger than any existing team, albeit still not big enough for big league people to take him seriously.

In the early spring of 1941, with the Monarchs' league season not slated to begin until July, Paige was—with Wilkie's forbearance, and at a price for both—bouncing back and forth from the Paige All-Stars to league teams that needed him to sell out a house or make a payroll. The Black Yankees were the first, at the time of the *Life* pictoral, and Satch brought in 20,000 people including Mayor Fiorello La Guardia to Yankee Stadium for a May 14 game with the Philadelphia Stars—a game he won 5–3, going the route.

For all these selected outside gigs, according to a story in the *Afro-American*, Satch's contract called for $500 for a minimum of five innings. "He works more if the opposition is tough," said the paper, "but usually when the fifth comes, Satchel saunters to the seclusion of the dressing room to duck the mob of autograph seekers who demand his John Hancock."

But, for Satch, the real reward in New York was to have his picture taken by *Life*. This photo essay—with the sapless title SATCHEL PAIGE, NEGRO BALLPLAYER, IS ONE OF THE BEST PITCHERS IN GAME—was Paige's rhapsody in white. Probably never before could any black man boast of being profiled on a page graced by nobility (Sir Alfred Lunt, the great British actor, who appeared in an ad for Williams Shaving Cream). And yet, for once Satch's blackness seemed natural in the context of a well-paid athlete. In an array of day-in-the-life pictures, he was the beau ideal of the black leisure class, not the Watusi tribe.

There was Satch in the definitive Paige pose: front leg raised almost perpendicular to the ground, kicking skyward.

Satch in the barber's chair, spatted shoes visible under the sheet, "getting shaved, clipped and maincured on three sides at once."

Satch firing up a butt while perched on the front grille of his car ("Satchel likes to drive big fast automobiles. His cars are usually bright red.").

Satch mugging with Fiorello La Guardia.

Satch, cigarette dangling Bogie-style, bent over a pool table in the dandiest of double-breasted suits and "narrow, two-toned, pointed shoes."

Satch at the piano, in Fats Waller style, noodling "some boogie woogie for [other members of] the Black Yankees. His playing shows more gusto than polish and considerably less talent than his baseball playing."

One other photo would be of particular interest to at least one reader: the picture of Satch, a sprightly carnation in his lapel, beaming at a beautiful Latin woman with a polka-dot scarf about her neck. This appeared over a caption reading: "Satchel's wife, Lucy, is from Puerto Rico. They met while he was playing ball down there. She can't speak English and Satchel doesn't know many words in Spanish."

Back in Pittsburgh, Mrs. Janet Howard Paige—who was also rather interested in the text block stating that her still-husband "gets as much as $500 for a single game"—was taking notes.

•   •   •

While Satch could draw a crowd anywhere under the sun, the fact that the Monarchs were rooted in the Midwest posed a dilemma for J. L. Wilkinson. The really big houses, he knew, were generated in the big-city, big league ballparks of the East, especially Yankee Stadium and Forbes Field.

The Monarchs rarely spent more than a few weeks a year east of the Mississippi. J.L. could take some solace from the fact that Satch had the power to open for the club the large stadiums in the heartland that had been closed to black teams. One of these was St. Louis's Sportsman's Park; black teams hadn't played in the place for twenty years when the Monarchs met the American Giants there on July 4, 1941.

Still, J.L. longed for the gate-busting potential of the East. During the '41 season, he cut back on his small-town barnstorming dates to schedule a number of glamour games in New York, Philadelphia, and Pittsburgh. Those games would line Paige's and Wilkinson's pockets and turn the Monarchs further away from their Everyman traditions. All but a one-man carnival show now, when Satch was with them the Monarchs were nearly an updated Satchel Paige All-Stars.

Evidently, the Monarchs players had no beef with this. For while it had to be a jolt to the other pitchers that Satch would start nearly every game and stay in as long as his whims dictated, they bowed to an irresistible imperative. "With Satchel," said Buck O'Neil, "*all* of us made more money than we would have made without him. Satchel really was the cause of black baseball bein' publicized in the first place."

One of the pitchers directly affected was Connie Johnson, who came to the Monarchs in 1941 after the Toledo Crawfords disbanded and found himself on the same staff as the legend he'd heard of as a kid. "We understood that Satchel was a drawin' card," he agreed. "I pitched behind him and I never worried 'bout it. 'Cause I knew he was Satchel, and he had established how great he was."

Still, while no one lacked reverence for Paige's walk-on-water perquisites—they could do nothing but look on in awe later when Wilkie purchased a DC-3 airplane just to ferry Satch around to his outside gigs—there were those who surely suffered in silence. Prime among them was Hilton Smith, who became a displaced ace in the new Monarchs pecking order. Money aside, Smith's reputation atrophied as Paige's soared in 1941. Not yet thirty and just hitting his prime, Smith would go 21-and-3 that season—10-and-0 in league games—but his role was mainly as a supporting actor.

Over the next two years, until Smith hurt his arm and laid off for two seasons, his problem was manifest: it was Hilton who had to come in cold to pitch after Satch's billboard innings. But while he often outpitched Paige in these games, he was normally boxed out of getting wins—and certainly could get no big-time ink for himself, since the games Smith did start were generally the ones in Kansas City, where Wilkie thought Satch would be wasted since the club drew well there anyway. Out on the big-city stops, in the big ball yards and in front of the national black press, Smith was an afterthought.

"I won 161 games and lost twenty-two, but most people never heard of me. They've only heard of Satchel," Smith lamented in the 1980s, after many years of holding his tongue. Pointedly, he went on, "I took my baseball serious. I just went out there to do a job. But Satch was an 'attraction,' he could produce and so he'd clown a lot." Of his being snubbed, he admitted, "I guess it really hurt me . . . but there wasn't anything I could do about it."

Not with the way Satch's Monarchs career became cause for celebration all around Negro ball. The same league barons who had sought to expunge his name from the public record only months before now signaled to their conduits in the black press that the hero was to be hailed. Consequently, among the big-gun sportswriters, Paige could do no wrong now. As the *Afro*'s Ric Roberts pointed out in the July 2, 1941, issue of the paper, the Paige benediction was materially a group effort:

> The finest box office attraction ever developed by colored major league baseball, thanks to a cordial colored and white press, is pitcher Satchel Paige of J. L. Wilkerson's [sic] Kansas City Monarchs. . . . Wilkerson has been kind enough to struggling owners to allow his costliest property to jaunt around the country attracting unprecedented thousands and filling up coffers with good old American legal tender. . . .

Baseball owners should be thankful that Paige is too big for Mexico. He can earn more dough in the good old U.S.A., skipping about the cities. He is the story-piece of the finest season our baseball has ever known from the standpoint of box-office; this, despite the fact that our finest stars are below the Rio Grande.

For the Monarchs who saw him as a museum piece, getting to know Satch's quirks for the first time was a trip in itself. And if there was a certain caste system to his existence, few considered themselves to be on the same plane—literally—with him anyway, even those with some Negro league mileage on them. Buck O'Neil, for one, recalled that while Satch had arrived in style for the *Denver Post* tournament back in 1936, O'Neil had come from Wichita Falls to Colorado as a stowaway in a boxcar.

"He probably didn't remember me from then when he came to the Monarchs, but I sure remembered him," O'Neil said. "After the [Denver] ballgames, the players used to eat at the same place and guys would get together and talk and I would more or less be listening, because they had a lotta all-timers there: Quincy Trouppe, Double Duty Radcliffe, Red Haley. God, all I could do was listen. That's all I wanted to do."

The overriding impressions of Satch now were blurred ones, as that's what Satch was—a blur that was pinned to the earth only by the pitching rubber. Assuming he got to the pitching rubber. Whenever Satch got into his car, the anxiety began.

"Sometimes he'd get with us in the bus," Connie Johnson recalled, "but mostly he went alone. The guys who went in his car with him were mostly [pitchers] Booker McDaniels and Lefty LaMarque—they had to go with him, too, 'cause if they didn't, he'd get on the road and take that Highway 71 and he'd go straight. No turns, he'd just go. So he got to have somebody with him, or he'd just be lost. You had to be lookin' all the time, 'cause he'd be talkin' and take a wrong turn and he might end up anywhere.

"One time we was in Michigan and it was game time and we were waitin' for him. Frank Duncan, our manager, said, 'Where's Satchel? Ain't somebody with him?' And [second baseman] Newt Allen said, 'There's McDaniels and there's LaMarque. There ain't nobody with him—he's by hisself! Uh, oh. We might never see him again.'

"An' after a while, about the second inning, something went by.

In this ballpark you could see the highway behind the fence an', boy, a car came by, *yeee-ooom*, and we said, 'That must be Satchel—an' he don't even know this is where he's supposed to be!' So Newt tells me, 'Go get him. Go catch him.' An' I said, 'Catch him? With *what?*'

"So what we do is, we go an' call the police and they caught up to him. And Satchel come in and said, 'Man, I'm gonna kill everybody in here. Who in the hell sent the police for me?' And we said, 'Man, that's the only way we could get you!' "

Another who sometimes took the perilous ride with Satch was Chet Brewer, the grand old Monarchs scuffballer who himself had been one of those Bismarck players of renown, and had thrown that no-hitter against Paige in Trujillo City. In 1941, Brewer came back from pitching around Latin America for the past year, but was shunted into a backup role and won only three games, losing seven. As if that wasn't hard enough on Brewer, Wilkie wanted him to try to keep Paige in line. He had no chance. Once, out on the road, they were running late because Satch was occupied by a crap game. In the car, Satch shrugged at the time and said, "If the red lights are gonna make us too late, I won't stop at 'em no more."

As Brewer related, "He's blowin' his horn, goin' right through the red lights. He was goin' so fast that we went about a block past the ballpark and had to turn around. We walk in in the fifth inning and people are goin' home, demanding their money back because Satchel didn't pitch."

Another time, Satch took a shortcut—by going the wrong way on a one-way street. When he was pulled over by police, the cop asked him if he knew it was a one-way street.

"I'm only goin' one way," Satch replied pleasantly. That cost him a fifty dollar conviction—one of so many such violations in his life that Satch himself would wonder in time whether he had made as many appearances on the nation's ball fields as he did in its traffic courts.

Brewer, a baritone-voiced man with a very slow fuse, could put up with a lot, but Satch brought him dangerously close to his breaking point. Clearly chafing years later, Brewer told author John Holway in *Black Diamonds* of Satch's weekly routine: "In New York, Satchel would pitch on Sunday when they had the big doubleheaders in Yankee Stadium. You wouldn't see him until the next Sunday. He was off in his big Cadillac, just having all his fun.

"Naturally, he showed up the next Sunday and pitched one heck of a game, gets all the publicity, gets in his car and [he's] gone again. The Monarchs put up with it, because they were making money off him. J.L. got rich on him."

Soon, prodded by Paige, Chet Brewer would go boom.

But to most Monarchs, Satchel Paige—an inestimable relic of their sport's golden age—was a wondrous commotion to behold. "He'd get into Detroit and he'd have all his boys with him at the hotel, like Cab Calloway and all like that," said Connie Johnson, "and he'd be tellin' all his lies and everything, grabbin' all the attention.

"You gotta understand. He was like a Babe Ruth to us, but he was *our* Babe Ruth. I think it's hard for people nowadays to understand how big he was. He was like the biggest guy we knew. It didn't make no difference what kinda stuff he did, 'cause that only made him *more* bigger than life. An' don't you believe Satchel didn't know he was, too.

"I mean, all this talk about him not goin' nine innings—what everybody misses is that he was pitchin', literally, *every day*. A man who pitched as much as he did couldn't pitch nine—I don't know how he pitched three! But in any of those games, he could have pitched nine and pitched a great game. That's what you gotta think about. Nobody else coulda done that."

• • •

The hot summer months of 1941 were a cool salve for Satch. The black papers were charting his comings and goings on a near daily basis, and these passages dominated news about Negro ball—with cause. On the Monarchs' Eastern tours, attendance figures for their games at the big league palaces ran consistently around 30,000 according to game reports; if so, this was often more than any big league game played on those big Sundays. Such numbers could not be ignored by baseball men of any color.

Within blackball, he was the whole show. Paige made a shambles of the fan voting in the '41 East-West Game, garnering 305,311 ballots, over 40,000 more than runner-up Buck Leonard.

Because he had sustained a minor injury to his left arm when hit by a pitched ball on July 23, Satch did not start the game—appropriately; Hilton Smith got the nod—but Satch's presence at the East-West Game after a five-year absence broke the bank for the leagues' fathers and their most favored promoter, Abe Saperstein. In blackball's most profound statement yet, 50,256 people jammed into Comiskey Park on August 1, and 5,000 more were turned away; this, rather than the feat of any player, became the *Afro*'s banner headline the next day: 50,000 FANS SEE EAST BEAT WEST 2–1; LARGEST CROWD IN HISTORY OF CLASSIC.

Satch, sitting in the merciful shade of the bullpen in the hundred-degree heat, did not stir for seven innings. Then, with the East having put the game on ice—they led 8–1, with the New York Cubans' Dave Barnhill turning in the day's most important pitching work—he came in to begin the eighth. With the sold-out house not leaving until Paige got in, he diligently went to work. He struck out Lenny Pearson and Bill Hoskins, then got Buck Leonard on a pop-up. In the ninth, Monte Irvin flied out. The Baltimore Elite Giants' Roy Campanella—the NNL's new star catcher, with Josh Gibson still in Mexico—beat out a slow roller but was caught stealing. Satch then walked a man and terminated Dick Seay on a fly ball.

For this mop-up stint the black press went delirious. "Satchell Gives Crowd Greatest Thrill!" was the subhead on the *Defender*'s account, which read:

> [The] stars of the day were Buck Leonard and [Roy] Campanella. But the man whom the vast multitude came out to see [was] canny Satchell [who] pitching against the advice of his physician actually stole the show. . . . There's a certain grace, a deliberate calm, an uncanny relaxation, plus a great pitching head and a whip-cracking arm which still knows how to get his "fast one" up there with the speed of lightning. . . .
>
> The man who is today the most colorful figure in baseball, may be in the afternoon of his . . . dazzling career, but today he's as great a pitcher as there is in the country . . . and that takes 'em all in!

In the *Afro*, Art Carter's take on the two trivial innings merited the title OLD SATCH BASEBALL'S MOST COLORFUL and swooned about Paige's "sterling display . . . when the West's cause was hopelessly gone. . . . Satch's double wind up, slow motion delivery and lanky arms in action are easily worth the box seat admission price."

White baseball, of course, did not need to read about two-inning gigs and Negro all-star games to know what Satchel Paige was worth to *them*. And, now, with Paige practically commandeering Yankee Stadium every other Sunday, J. L. Wilkinson's agents and Bob Feller had incentive to renew the postseason barnstorming contests that Satch had skipped since his duel with a young Feller melted the Iowa corn fields in 1936.

Following up on that hugely successful July 4 blackball game in St. Louis's Sportsman's Park, Wilkie booked an October 5 game there between the Monarchs and a reconstituted squad of big leaguers under the name of the Bob Feller All-Stars. Once again, the raw power that Satchel Paige invested in black baseball overwhelmed old habits.

Sportsman's Park had segregated seating for everything but all-black events, and while the park's managers knew that the crowd for the game would be mostly black, they would not change policy. As noted by the *Kansas City Call*, the stadium had an "unsavory reputation [as] the only major league park in the country where Negroes are relegated to the bleachers and pavilion and denied grandstand seats." As the game approached, though, the *Call* happily reported that "several Negroes have managed to obtain grandstand seats" and by game day the management bowed to the demand and threw open the grandstand to blacks. Then, without incident, over 20,000 black and white fans commingled and watched a minor classic with major historical implications.

With Satch not in top form, the game's defining moment came when the hometown Cardinals' Stan Musial—fresh off his rookie season—clocked a Paige fastball over the right field pavilion roof. However, even though Hilton Smith turned in a spotless five-inning relief stint in the Fellers' 4–3 win, the marquee yoking of Paige and Feller was what would linger in the baseball culture—and lay down the blueprint for the glories that would soon come out of it.

•　　•　　•

There was another reunion for Satch after the season, when he went back to Joe Pirrone's California Winter League with yet another edition of Tom Wilson's Negro All-Stars. There, he pitched against a team that had Jimmie Foxx and, coming off his .406 season, Ted Williams. But this time Satch did not come to play until the early spring, having decided not to repeat with his new love interest the same conscious act of separation he had made from Janet Howard.

Although as recently as July 24 of the year before a photo of Satch and Lucy Figueroa arriving for a game in Philadelphia had appeared in the *Philadelphia Tribune*—with Lucy identified as "Mrs.

Satchel"—Satch had by now fallen for a gorgeous drugstore sales-woman in Kansas City, Lahoma Brown. Satch knew there was some-thing different about her because, as cool as he was, he could not keep from stammering and acting goofy when she was around.

Satch generally liked his women pliant, obsequious, and inclin-able. That he and Lucy Baby could not share a meaningful conver-sation—*any* conversation—was not necessarily a debit to that relationship. Having opened his heart and his inner being to Bertha Wilson, without requital, Satch now preferred his intima-cies to extend no further than the bedroom door.

Lahoma Brown changed that, but only gradually. At nineteen, she was a divorcée with a young daughter; a Southern girl, from Stillwater, Oklahoma, her warmth reminded him of Bertha Wilson. It was the wicked city women who had hardened him—just as Lula Paige had warned him they would so long ago—but Lahoma was as judicious as she was beautiful; she could make demands of the sort that Janet had made, but Satch never felt cowed. In no time, his dalliance with Lucy Baby was tapering away (no record could be found that she and Satch had in fact been married) and Lahoma had him craving her to fill his empty soul.

Though by habit he would speak of Lahoma in his memoirs as another wide-eyed girl gifted by him, his reverence for her was as a kind of matron saint for a wayward ballplayer.

"I'd never met anybody like her," he said in his autobiography, "and that slowed me down like no gal'd ever slowed me down be-fore." And: "She gave me that settled-down life I never had before."

Perhaps even Satchel Paige had to admit to himself now that as he had gotten further and further away from Mobile, he had needed another mother all along.

14

Night into Morning

Paige allegedly told reporters that he would not exchange his position in Negro baseball for a berth in the major leagues, expressing the doubt that any of the clubs would meet his present free-lance salary. "They'd have to offer me what I made last year—$37,000," he said.

—*Pittsburgh Courier,*
August 15, 1942

We were playing against a bunch of major leaguers headed up by my old buddy, Bobby Feller [and] I began hearing all these rumors flying around about getting some colored boys into the major leagues. I'd been hearing talk like that all through the 1945 season. But if there was anything to it, I didn't know about it. None of those white owners were coming to me about getting in the big time.

But with all of them reporters coming around to ask me about it, I got that old bug real bad again. I knew I was old, the way baseball men figured it, but I didn't think I was too old.

"I'm just prayin' I get into the big show before my speed ball loosens," I told those reporters.

—*Satchel Paige,*
Maybe I'll Pitch Forever

J. L. Wilkinson needn't have worried about the team chemistry of winning being altered by Satch. He was so dependable that the

Monarchs could reasonably expect that with Paige on the mound at the start, they would get an early lead; and if it was a critical game that broadened the appeal of blackball, Satch could be relied on to go nine, as he did late in the '41 season when he beat the American Giants with a seven-hit shutout in Detroit's cavernous big league park, Briggs Stadium, before a mixed crowd of 32,000. That win helped to preserve the Monarchs' hold on the NAL pennant for the third straight year.

As it turned out, this would be the last Negro league season played in the era of compliance that gave no urgency to big league integration. That era was ended—or at least was goaded toward an end—by the terrible events of Sunday, December 7, 1941. By the end of that long and vulnerable morning, men of intolerance everywhere had to know that the world was not going to be the same—not if the American war machine was going to be a window of the American soul. In the microcosm that was American sport, the center of gravity was already shifting.

Actually, it was the big leagues that shifted, in an ironic hoisting of privilege and class. Practically compelled by white public opinion to enlist in the armed services, the biggest big leaguers were swept onto military bases around the world over the next four years.

In 1942, the majors lost a twenty-five-game winner—Bob Feller—and a .359 hitter, the Senators' Cecil Travis. The next year, they lost Joe DiMaggio, Ted Williams, Bob Lemon, Big Cat Mize, and Country Slaughter, all future Hall of Famers, and all gone for the next three seasons—and Red Ruffing for the next two. Luke Appling would go for 1944 and Billy Herman for 1944 and 1945; Duke Snider, Stan Musial, and Bobby Doerr missed the 1945 season.

The black game was also disturbed. Although Satch was too old and his feet were too flat for service, great numbers of blacks served with distinction in segregated units. Some great black players were used as a kind of barter; Quincy Trouppe was playing in Mexico when he was drafted, but was given an exemption in an agreement between the government and Jorge Pasquel to transfer 80,000 Mexican workers to U.S. defense plants.

But while Satch didn't come near the flames of war, he considered himself a good soldier. Man of the world that he was, he even took to counseling other players on filling out their draft forms—which, of course, almost put them directly on the battlefront. The New York Cubans' Armando Vásquez, who was 4-F, was unable to read and write English and had Satch complete his form—whereupon he received notice of his reclassification to 1-A. It took the Cuban embassy to straighten the situation out for Vásquez.

When the '42 Negro league season began, Satch committed himself to pitching in frequent exhibitions to sell war bonds and raise money for war-related charities. One of these was a May 24 game in Chicago's Wrigley Field for the Navy Relief Fund. Pitting the Monarchs against a team billed as the Dizzy Dean All-Stars, the only "star" of this collection of army base–bound current and ex–big leaguers was Cecil Travis, who came in from Camp Wheeler in Georgia to play. Although Bob Feller had been billed to play, he was ordered back to his post in the Providence navy yard. That left the black press and the integrated crowd of near 30,000 feeling cheated, since this was another milestone for blackball—the first time a colored team played in the hallowed, ivy-draped Wrigley Field.

Where in the past blacks did not dare to deride the reputed big league "all-stars" they faced, playing this diluted bunch led by the sore-armed Dizzy Dean—who could barely retire the side in just one inning of work in the Monarchs' 3–1 win—made many in blackball fume that this had been the only way to get into Wrigley. The big turnout for the game, wrote Frank A. Young in the *Defender,* "proved once and for all that America's baseball fandom wants to see a ball game regardless of race, color or creed of the performers. And while the White Sox were taking a 14 to 0 licking [at] Comiskey Park, here was Satchel Paige, Hilton Smith and the Monarchs performing in big league style but denied the right to play in the big leagues because of their color."

Young continued: "Maybe the front office at Wrigley Field will sit up and take notice. The best part of the crowd . . . was not white. These brown American fans are baseball-hungry but they are sick and tired of paying their hard-earned money to see second rate performers because the performers must necessarily be white according to Judge Landis, high mogul of organized baseball and the various prejudiced club owners. . . .

"White and black fans were out to see Satchel Paige—and don't you think they didn't . . . they wanted to see Paige win because of the color prejudice in organized baseball."

When the Homestead Grays—with Satch on loan—played the Deans in Forbes Field on June 5, the largest crowd to see a game at that park all season saw an 8–1 laugher that gave the *Courier* the chance to sneer at the "big league" entry. Sticking in the harpoon, its headline read "THE GREAT SATCHEL" PROVES HE'S A BIG LEAGUER BEFORE 22,000 WITNESSES. Its game story noted, with barbed effulgence, "The 22,000 wild-eyed fans saw sepia baseball's greatest battery, Josh Gibson [who had returned from Mexico under threat of court order from Cum Posey] and Satchel Paige, supported by one of the greatest all-around clubs in baseball, out play and out class the All-Stars from the first through the ninth. As usual, Satchel lived up to expectations."

•   •   •

Satch was becoming a palpable symbol of continuity on the home front for millions of blacks who felt left out of the nation's war-fed community. It was almost a chauvinist duty now to lionize him, and the black press went with the roll, the *Defender* driving home the point with maximum impact on July 4, when it ran a large caricature of Paige next to a scroll of twelve "Other Great Negro Athletes." That list included such sociopolitical hallmarks of the struggle as Joe Louis, Jesse Owens, and Paul Robeson, with a little stick figure in the corner of the frame saying, "An for Mah Money Satchel Is Tops!"

Blackball was certainly aware that such adulation now crossed racial boundaries, since, with Bob Feller gone, the ironic twist was that there were no *white* Satchel Paiges in the big leagues. And, for this, Satch reaped huge rewards. In a time of food and gasoline rationing and fixed incomes, his income was nearly $40,000 a year—which, when DiMaggio and Williams did their hitches in the service, made him easily the highest-paid athlete in the world.

The wartime boom in blackball probably marked the first time an existing *group* of ballplayers would demand greater compensation as a matter of rights. This happened when Negro league stars threatened to boycott the East-West Games unless the owners spread more of the wealth for their participation in the games.

And wealth was what these owners had. J. L. Wilkinson took in over $100,000 in 1942, and he was willing to provide at least Satch with the kind of workman's compensation benefits few others had. When Satch suffered constant pain from his long-neglected teeth early in 1942, to the detriment of his pitching, Wilkie paid for eight extractions and a set of dentures for him.

Wilkie's windfall came despite wartime travel restrictions that returned the Monarchs to their Midwest turf. Deprived of those showcase games in Yankee Stadium during the regular season, Wilkie fine-tuned his marketing and turned Chicago into his quasi–home base after the tremendous success of the Wrigley Field exhibition. It was there, on July 26, that J.L. arranged with Abe Saperstein a major spectacle: Satchel Paige Appreciation Day.

Hyping this one for all it was worth, Wilkie's men scheduled as their opponent that day the Memphis Red Sox and their young ace Verdell Mathis—who had, like Connie Johnson, heard and read about Paige as a kid and had bested him in two earlier meetings that season. Beating the drums of the latest game and pitching clash for eternity, the *Defender*—which had come to adopt Satch as a favorite son and sponsored the day in his honor— primed a running "grudge battle" between the two men.

"Bring me Mathis," it quoted Satch. "I've beaten better pitchers than he is."

"I beat him before and I'll beat him again," was Mathis's printed retort.

Once again, Satch could have written the script. As these grudge matches almost always seemed to go, he came out on top, this time by a score of 4–2, scattering seven hits and striking out six in seven innings before darkness halted play. But on this day, he got more than satisfaction and ink. He was, said the *Defender*, "showered with gifts"—the best that the black community could give in 1942.

After being presented with a solid gold watch from Abe Saperstein, and a three-foot-high basket of flowers from the *Defender*, he was given a twenty-five dollar "slack suit" from Chicago Credit Clothiers, a portable radio from Henderson's Chicken Shack (which was shut down during the game in homage), a traveling bag from the Savoy Ballroom, and a bathrobe from Albert's men's shop.

What was important about such rituals was the implicit belief by black fans that black ballplayers were being deprived of a national stage as much because they were good as because they were black. More than ever, celebrating the identity of the race, and not just the players, was a moral crusade, since victory now seemed to be a real possibility.

As Joe Louis had shown with one frightful punch against Max Schmeling, black American symbols could stand in the first tier of patriotic heroes. Accordingly, black Americans drew closer to men like Satchel Paige; with millions of blacks working in defense plants for good wages, they came out to the parks by the hundreds of thousands during the war—a movement that in retrospect can be seen as the last great heave that took baseball across the Rubicon of integration.

Undeniably, the caretakers of whiteball knew they had a problem. The old prevarication about the ability gap was now certifiably specious, and the very basis of segregation was taking a serious beating now that black men were in combat from North Africa to Guadalcanal. Absolutely skewering the hypocrisy of America's fighting for the rights of non-Aryans while American baseball remained the province of two seemingly Aryan leagues, the black press poked and prodded Judge Landis's kingdom. "Are colored servicemen fighting for a separate democracy?" wondered the *Kansas City Call* in noting the ongoing big league obstinacy.

The *Defender* made the point like a fastball between the eyebrows—"Remember Pearl Harbor and Sikeston too," was its rallying cry, the latter a reference to a ghastly lynching in that Missouri town in 1941. The *Afro*, meanwhile, took a more assured line of attack, printing under its masthead the motto "Colored America's share in the war effort will determine its share in the peace that follows."

What is more, as the war and separate-but-equal baseball proceeded apace, it was suddenly difficult to make the case that whiteball could play even with blackball. In the wasteland of the big league world, centerpiece stars were replaced by, among others, a one-armed pitcher and an outfielder whose right leg had been amputated below the knee.

Feeling the heat of the new reality, Judge Landis insisted in 1942 that "there is no rule, formal or informal, no understanding, subterranean or otherwise, against hiring Negro players." But this had to be a lie if big league owners could look at their withering game and then look at the crowds at Negro league games and still resist signing black players.

Rather, the big league owners—hopeful that the black game's solid footing would make *it* want to avoid a rush to integrate—opted to hold out long enough to survive the duration before growing fat again. But their delusions were on borrowed time.

•   •   •

The new common spirit of challenge in the Negro leagues led J. L. Wilkinson and Cum Posey—the rudders of each league—to finally stage the Negro World Series for the first time since 1927. This was done to further extend and contrast their product with that of the big leagues, right up through the climactic crowning of the champs. Not incidentally, with the Monarchs and Grays running off with their leagues' pennants in 1942, the two teams' highly publicized meetings during the season were proving to be a font of profit for Wilkie and Posey. A World Series between blackball's most kingly teams, it was reasoned, would bring a crown of gold.

When the Monarchs and Grays met in a June 24 game at Washington's Griffith Stadium—where the Grays had taken to playing most of their games—it was the first blackball game ever played at night in a big league park. Before a record Grays crowd of over 28,000 fans, Satch started against Roy Partlow. Paige left after five innings, and with the game scoreless after nine, Hilton Smith drove in a run to make it 1–0, but then the Grays notched two in the bottom of the tenth—Partlow driving in the winner, whereupon the fans streamed onto the field and carried him to the dugout.

With this bacchanal of excitement as their cue, Wilkie and Posey made two other matches between the teams, to occur after the August 16 East-West Game—although the events of that game, centered once again around Satchel Paige, threatened to overshadow all else about this season.

This time, it was what Satch did *before* the game that caused seizures around blackball—by becoming involved in a hornets' nest of debate regarding the Negro leagues' impending role in possible big league integration. The politically frothy *Afro* started the tempest on August 8 when Ric Roberts quoted Grays manager Vic Harris's remarks opposing a too-sudden integration, on the grounds that the big league owners had hoped the blackball people would invoke: that the Negro leagues would be ruined after just now gaining altitude.

"If they take our best boys," Harris said, "we will be but a hollow shell of what we are today. No, let us build up our own league and . . . then challenge the best white team in the majors and play them."

This came fast on the heels of a similar plan advanced by the Washington Senators' owner, Clark Griffith, who had a real motive in delaying integration—the rental and concession fees he was taking in at his stadium from Grays games. With Cum Posey playing to D.C.'s huge black population, Griffith could have his black money and his major league pie, too. As Ric Roberts pointed out in the *Afro*, "Griffith has never made it known how the best colored team would challenge the best white team, or where, when and for what they would play."

Roberts also reminded blackball that, for all its optimism, the big leagues were still a world or two apart from them—and would remain so regardless of how well the Negro leagues "built up." He wrote: "Regular big-league baseball requires an economy that the colored people and their resources simply cannot match. The NNL and NAL are largely week-end and night ball groups that freelance during week days. As long as they must depend, for the most part, on colored pocketbooks [they] will remain horse and buggy leagues."

Cum Posey took up the middle ground in his August 1 *Courier* column, as he had to as a prospering Negro league owner and an advocate of integration. "Negro baseball owners have had a very hard time building up Negro baseball into a paying business," he wrote. "We are going to continue to build [it] up. . . . If we get our clubs so that they can play for a real world's championship, we will play it. If some clubs of the white major leagues wish our players we will sell them. We have a business and we are going to attempt to protect it the same as any other Negro or white businessman.

"In the meantime, we would advise all Negro players to do all in their power to improve their playing, so if the chance ever does come to join a major league club, they will be ready."

He even put forward a few names whom he deemed ready right now—most prominently Josh Gibson, Roy Campanella, Ray Dandridge, Monte Irvin, Sam Bankhead, and Satchel Paige.

Even if Posey was a tad deluded himself about the proprietary rights he believed the Negro leagues had, J. L. Wilkinson joined him in trying to gas up a bandwagon for immediate big league entry by blacks. He "nominated" twenty-five Negro leaguers who, he said, "could make any major league team." Inclusion of these men—headed by Paige and Gibson—"would be a fine thing for the game, even though we would lose our stars."

The central figure of all this overheated speculation, meanwhile, was having none of it, having lived through too many broken promises already. The last time Satch's hopes were raised was only a year before when a Western League promoter, Lee Keyser, made a deal with him to play for a team in that high minor league, one step from the big leagues. But when white newspapers carried news of the deal, it fell through, reportedly once the news reached Judge Landis.

Having given up on the direct route, Satch turned away from the notion of individual advancement in favor of routinely challenging big league teams to ignore the old Landis prohibition and play his Negro teams as a way of forging an alliance. Now, hearing more poop about token promotion, he slammed the idea in comments attributed to him by the Associated Press just days before the East-West Game.

While maintaining that he would reject big league offers on principle—or princip*al*, the capital kind, which he doubted any big league team would deliver to him—the real weight of the quotes was that, money aside, the time wasn't right for integration. Citing "unharmonious other problems" that might arise, he was uneasy about playing "not only in the South, where the colored boys wouldn't be able to stay and travel with the teams in spring training, but in the North, where they couldn't stay or eat with them in many places."

His own solution, he said, would be to put an entire black team in one or both major leagues. But, soured as he was by years of betrayal from the Man, his final analysis was bitter fruit.

"All the nice statements in the world from both sides aren't going to knock out Jim Crow," said Satchel Paige.

Although he had raised legitimate concerns, it drove Negro league people up the wall that he would utter the same exact rationalizations as big league obstructionists. By his comments, if not his intent, Satch was playing into the hands of the devil. Some even saw the supposed tirade as sheer sedition, especially since the story originated in the white press and received major play by white papers with access to the AP teletype.

Just as vexing, Satch was posited in the white press as the spokesman for blackball. As much as blackball was indebted to him and could deal with his spasmodic urges within their world, he was the *last* guy the Negro leagues wanted to be their proxy. As far as the black game had come, it was bad enough that Negro ball was still being defined for large numbers of whites by such teams as Abe Saperstein's odious Ethiopian Clowns, for which—just a few years before Jackie Robinson—superb black athletes were made to play under names like Tarzan, Monkee, and Wahoo. Indeed, Satch had recently used the Clowns for burlesque value, with contrived "feuds" between him and certain of their players.

The controversy came to a head at the East-West Game. Although the fans had given Paige almost 80,000 more votes than anyone else, he came to Comiskey Park not as the "elongated hurler" but as the black man who seemed to endorse segregation in baseball. That is, *when* he got to the park. Though slated to start for the West, either because he was stewing about the flak he was taking or just late for the usual reasons, he got to Comiskey in the second inning and was spared hearing the fan reaction that would have greeted his introduction.

Instead, he sat in the cool sanctuary of the bullpen. But if he was hoping that he might stay there for the whole game in reproof for his tardiness, his absence only heightened and focused the tense vibes in the park. When the seventh inning began with the score tied 2–2, Paige was beckoned into the tinderbox by West manager W. S. Welch.

Walking toward the mound, he was escorted by a wall of sound spilling from three tiers of grandstand and an ambivalent crowd of 45,179 people—some cheering, some booing, all at the top of their lungs. For Satch, the old showman, the vibe was a splendid one to clear the air, call off the dogs, and unveil a new riff. In fact, he may have anticipated such a moment all along, because when he did not go to the mound and instead walked to the dugout, there was a microphone there waiting for him as if by plan.

This was Satchel Paige in his most mesmerizing virtuoso performance. Taking in hand the microphone, which someone in the press box knew to turn on, he stretched its cord to home plate, and with every other player standing in place, he began to speak.

"Ladies and gentlemen," he said forcefully and calmly, "I would like to take this opportunity to deny a statement which the daily papers credited to me.

"I want you to know that I did not say anything against the use of Negro players in the big leagues. A reporter came to me and asked me what I thought about playing on major league teams. I told him I thought it was all right. He said, 'Satchel, do you think the white players would play with the colored?'

"I told him I thought they would, but that if they wouldn't it might be a good idea to put a complete team in the majors."

His piece said, he went to the rubber to the sound of great cathartic cheers—and proceeded to let the game get away. Though the three runs he surrendered in his three innings were unearned due to errors and a fly ball lost in the sun, Satch still couldn't get the big out when he needed it; with the bases loaded in the ninth, Wild Bill Wright knocked in two key runs with a clutch hit.

More than the score—the East won 5–2—or Satch's first East-West loss, it was his home plate oration that underlined the game, and the black press was certainly eager to side with Satch and against the white press it blamed for provoking an exercise in Negro dissension. "I WAS MISQUOTED," SAYS SATCHEL the *Courier* bannered, its game story calling the recital an "epochal defense speech" and "the most dramatic contribution" of the game—"probably the first time in baseball history that a player gave his side of a newspaper story credited to him."

Curiously, about the only observer not overly taken with Satch's demurral was *Afro* sports editor Art Carter, whose game piece didn't even mention Paige until the third paragraph—and in a sidebar groused that Satch had "gummed up the program with a three-minute pointless statement over the public address system about how he was misquoted in the press anent the subject of colored players entering the major leagues—a speech few people heard and fewer were interested in at the time."

But if the *Afro* wasn't about to cut Satch any slack for his original remarks, Paige himself seemed not to dwell on the entire matter. For the next several years he said little more about the convulsive issue of integration. And while many years later he would imply that he had been all for it, as if to wipe out of his mind the tumult he had caused with his lip, he expunged that East-West Game and its sideshow drama altogether in his autobiography.

What he did do in the countdown to integration was to hold himself up as the ultimate reason why—"unharmonious other problems" aside—baseball segregation was folly. While in Philadelphia for a game in the mid-1940s, he told the *Tribune* that even if the New York Yankees were to come to town and play the Phillies, and it was announced that he was to pitch for the Monarchs, the *big* crowd would come to see him pitch.

This simple statement of fact needed no clarification.

•   •   •

The last great performance of Satchel Paige's blackball life came at the end of that '42 season in the Negro World Series. This was a matter of vindication for Satch, who had pitched against the stately Homestead Grays four times during the season—including once in Forbes Field before 11,500 fans, which marked his first Pittsburgh appearance in six years—and saw the Monarchs drop all four. Paige pitched brilliantly and went the route in each game save for that wild affair in D.C. against Roy Partlow, but three of the defeats, all by one run, were pinned on Satch.

The Negro World Series, which opened on Tuesday, September 8, under the arc lights of Griffith Stadium, began with the Monarchs as clear underdogs. But Satch mowed down the Grays from the start, retiring the first ten hitters and giving up two hits in five shutout innings before coming out with a 1–0 lead—this after he had pitched only two days earlier in a Yankee Stadium game against the New York Cubans. In relief, Jack Matchett pitched no-hit ball the rest of the way to assure Satch of the win in the 8–0 laugher.

The second game, two days later in Forbes Field, was a true role reversal—Hilton Smith started, threw five scoreless frames, led 2–0, and then was relieved by Satch, who, while shaky, held on to the lead to give Smith the decision in the eventual 8–4 win. Smith would remember that game fondly, recalling that Satch had told him beforehand, "You're always saving games for me. Tonight, I'll save one for you."

But, even here, poor Hilton Smith was shorted, because this game happened to feature the Negro World Series' all-time climactic rush: one single at-bat between the icons of blackball, Satchel Paige and Josh Gibson.

It came during the seventh inning, with two on and two out and the Monarchs still up 2–0. Satch, having just given up a base hit to Jerry Benjamin, got that crazy look in his eye. Buck O'Neil, recognizing that look, knew right away that this was going to be one for the books—though more suited to burlesque than *The Baseball Record Book*—when Satch called him over from first base and asked him with a crooked grin, "You know what I'm thinkin'a doing?"

Buck, fearing the worst, told him sternly, "I know what you *betta* do—get the next guy out!"

Alas, it wasn't going to be that simple. Rather, Satch said that he was going to intentionally walk the next *two* hitters, Howard Easterling and Buck Leonard, and pitch to Josh with the bases loaded, *mano a mano*, winner take all. A freeze-frame of challenge issued and met, a moment for eternity and for the gallantry of blackball, where Olympus-like personal confrontations and triumphs trivialized team standings and World Series victories.

Buck O'Neil could dig that, but, Lord have mercy, did it have to go down *right now?*

"Aw, man," Buck told Satch. "You gotta be crazy!"

As he found out, it was the *best* time. O'Neil recalled, "I'm the captain of the team and so I called out Frank Duncan and I said,

'Skipper, listen to what this fool's talkin' 'bout.' And when Satch told him, I said, 'You know he's crazy, don't you?' And Frank said, 'Now listen, Buck. You know all these people we got in this ball-park? They came out to see Satchel and Josh. So whatever he wanna do, let him do it.' "

Actually, there were some subtle baseball factors involved in this decision. Satch always seemed to have Josh's number, and Josh always seemed to *know* he did. Josh could never relax or concentrate against Satch. Not that Satch wasn't wary of Gibson—only a masochist wouldn't be, and in a similar situation in Game One Josh had sent one screaming to the base of the center field wall, a 420-foot out. While a cautious Satch had intentionally walked Josh *twice* in the East-West Game, Gibson was 0-for-7 in the Series and not hitting well of late.

In pitching to him now, Satch sought the edge, to get inside Josh's head by trashmouthing him as he came to the plate. Said O'Neil: "He was talkin' to him, 'Hey, Josh, you remember back when we were playin' wid the Crawfords and you said you was the best hitter in the world and I said I was the best pitcher? I told you then, I said one day we were gonna be on diff'rent teams and we gonna meet and we'll see what's what.' And Josh said, 'Yeah, Satchel, I remember that.'

"Now everybody knows just what's happenin',' O'Neil went on. "They're *all* standin' up." And now, even Satch was getting himself worked up. Before the first pitch, O'Neil said, "Satch calls for Jew-baby Floyd to come out and Jewbaby come out to the mound with a cup, probably Alka-Seltzer or something. See, Satchel always suffered with his stomach, he'd get that gas. So he drank it down and Jewbaby went back. And, with people standin' up and screamin', Satchel let out a hell of a belch."

O'Neil, who has sung the Ballad of Satch and Josh over and over at blackball reunions through the decades, delivers it with the practiced cadence and rhythm of an old salt's sea chanty. Telling what occurred when Satch got back on the hill, he went on:

"First Satch says, 'All right, Josh, I'm gonna throw you some fast-balls'—and Josh says, 'Show me what you got.' But now right before he winds up he says, 'Now listen, I'm gonna throw you a fastball letter high'—and, *boom*, it's strike one. Josh didn't move the bat. Satch gets the ball back and says, 'And now I'm gonna throw you one a little faster and belt high'—and, *boom*, strike two. Josh didn't move the bat.

"Now everybody's standin' and goin' crazy. And Satch looks in at Josh and says, 'Okay, now I got you oh-and-two, and in this league I'm supposed to knock you down. But I'm not gonna throw smoke at yo' yolk—I'm gonna throw a pea at yo' knee'—and, *boom*, strike three. Josh didn't move the bat. And Satch walks off the mound and the crowd is yellin' and screamin' and he walks by me and he says real slow, 'You know what, Buck? Nobody hits Satchel's fastball.'

"Josh wasn't just psyched out. He didn't know if Satch was jivin' or was gonna do what he say. Josh never did make up his mind so he just stood there."

When Satch told of the showdown in his memoirs, he was not as expansive. The butt of it, he said, was a fin bet he'd made with Josh before the game that he could strike him out. Then, "Going into the last couple of innings, I guess it was the last inning, I was ahead by one run but I still hadn't struck big Josh out. . . .

"I got the first two batters out [but] there were three guys up before Josh was due to bat again. There weren't three guys anywhere that could get on base against me one after another when I had my stuff working and I had it working that day. So I walked all of those guys. . . .

" 'Don't worry about Josh,' I said [to Frank Duncan]. 'He's not gonna do anything. I'm telling you so.' . . .

"I wound up and stuck my foot way up in the air. It hid the ball and almost hid me, too. Then I fired.

" 'Strike one,' the umpire yelled and you should have seen Josh. The way he was looking you could tell that ball must have looked like a white line to him.

"I fired again and I had two strikes on Josh.

"One more to go. I knew it. Josh knew it. The crowd knew it. It was so tense you could feel everything jingling.

"I took one look around the infield and then threw fast. It was strike three.

"Josh threw that bat of his four hundred feet and stomped off the field. I don't think he ever paid me that five dollars, but that didn't matter. It was just something to strike out Josh like that after I'd told him I would."

In truth, neither Satch nor Buck O'Neil got it quite right. Aside from Satch's memory lapses about the inning and the number of men he walked, according to the *Afro*'s game story Gibson did in fact swing, fouling the first two pitches off and "whiffing on the third." But the headline—SATCH FANS JOSH GIBSON WITH

THREE ON BASES—was the ultimate blackball consecration.

Not surprisingly, Satch now wanted to *own* this series, and he demanded the ball at the start of the remaining games, commencing with Game Three at Yankee Stadium—the site a reminder that while this may have been the World Series, big crowds such as the 30,000 at this game were still the priority. But now Satch was off form. Down 2–0 after Howard Easterling clubbed him for a homer in the first inning, he came out after the third, though with a 4–2 lead after the Monarchs' big right fielder Ted Strong hit a three-run shot in the top of the inning. That made him a winner when the Monarchs put the game away later by a 9–3 score.

Now, mortified that the Grays were a game from being swept, a desperate Cum Posey—who had lost five players to injury—did a new variation on the old Negro league shuffle. When Game Four began in Kansas City's Ruppert Park, the Grays took the field with *four* fresh players—Posey having signed, on a per-game basis, three Newark Eagles including starting pitcher Leon Day, as well as the Philadelphia Stars' Bus Clarkson.

Although the game went on without delay, when Day defeated Satch 4–1, J. L. Wilkinson filed a protest with both leagues' commissioners on grounds that the Grays had used "ringers." Defending his move, Posey insisted that Tom Baird, the Monarchs' general manager, had agreed beforehand to the signings—and that Baird had suggested them in exchange for unspecified "demands."

But when Baird denied any such arrangement, the game was voided—along with much of the working relationship between Wilkie and Posey. Indeed, it was an obliging coincidence that these two transcendent teams would never meet for the championship after this defining moment; while the Grays would go on winning, the Monarchs would decline, and then when the Monarchs revived, the Grays ebbed.

The teams did replay the fourth game, and on a bone-chilling October night in Philadelphia, Satchel Paige won his World Series—though his warmup came at a Lancaster, Pennsylvania, traffic court. Caught speeding on the way to the game, he was in court paying a twenty dollar fine when the game began.

When Satch arrived at Shibe Park, Jack Matchett was dying on the vine. The Grays, having taken a 5–4 lead in the bottom of the third, had two on with two out. As soon as Satch had changed into his uniform, Frank Duncan had him on the mound—just in time to face what should have been Josh Gibson. But this confrontation was not to be. Josh, mired in a Series-long slump and his body aching, had taken himself out in the top of the inning. His replacement was Robert Gaston, and Satch blew him down with a hard-sinking fastball.

Then, reported the *Defender*, "Paige went to town." Only two Grays reached base the rest of the game, both on walks. This was the middle-aged Satch at his peak as a complete pitcher. In striking out seven on a smorgasbord of deadeye pitches, the paper noted, he "had plenty of speed and his fast breaking curve added to the misery of the Gray batters. He mixed these with a baffling slow ball." When the Monarchs put five runs on the board over the seventh and eighth innings to win 9–5 and go home champs, Satch—who saw to it that he had pitched in every game, and won three of them—would recall it with understandable hubris.

"Sometimes it seems to me like that was the best day I ever had pitching," he said. "Maybe it was, but when a fellow has pitched two thousand games there's a lot of best games."

•   •   •

If Satch's pitching was still a blur, Lahoma Brown did indeed slow him down at home. Once, he had not wanted to even consider owning his own house, so as to avoid the permanence that frightened him. But by 1943, he had purchased a spacious A-frame on Twelfth Street in the integrated east side of Kansas City. Although wealthy whites had begun to leave the neighborhood, fearing its infusion of blue-collar ethnic whites, a black man who could afford these surroundings could boast of hardy "upper-class" status.

Satch moved quickly to fill the two levels and twelve rooms of his home with the trimmings of wealth and hearth—though, given his old tastes and newfound longings for refinement, the decor was rather eclectic. The living and dining rooms testified to his pursuit of culture. Almost daily, furniture pieces were delivered from antique stores and auction houses, chosen by Lahoma, who, having moved in with her daughter, Shirley, brought her passion for fine collectibles into Satch's life.

In the first year alone, she committed some $20,000 of his earnings to Renaissance, Victorian, and Ming bric-a-brac—including an eighteenth-century Tudor Chippendale breakfront, full sets of Wedgewood and Sevres china, a Queen Anne dining table, Fischer Hungarian plates, and Ming vases. One Meissen drinking stein cost $300.

Not that Satch could have distinguished a Duncan Phyfe from a

Satchmo Armstrong trumpet, but he sure knew he'd never seen these things on his long-traveled road—the origin of which was now pushed further away. "It was a sign that poor little colored boy in Mobile had grown up to be a big money-maker," he recalled later. "It proved how high I'd climbed—how I'd gone from a place where sometimes we didn't have money even to buy a little piece of meat to go with the greens to a place where I could buy the best stuff or the oldest and most expensive stuff if I just took a liking to it. . . . People always think antique and real good china come high. And the man who got them is sitting 'way uptown."

Still, if he opened the door to his den, he was as good as in the woods. Hunting rifles and fishing rods lay in thickets of wood and wire and bullets and bait. And if he opened the rear door, he was in Ma and Pa Kettle's backyard—at one point, over a hundred chickens mingled with his twenty hunting dogs. "And," he once remembered warmly, "just to make things real easy when I got hungry, I bought me a cow and put it out there." He insisted that "nobody around my house said anything, even though I was living right in downtown Kansas City. They'd just come around for eggs."

That went on only until the city found him in violation of zoning laws and closed down Paige Farms, allowing him to keep only his beloved dogs—though some of the wildest creatures may have been Satch's buddies, who turned the dwelling on Twelfth Street into a frat house. Never a man who could say no to moochers, he'd put them up for a night and not think anything amiss when they were still there months later.

His life now a godsend, every day was another excuse for him to forget his lean years of struggle and the wife who seemed to vanish in the mist somewhere back then. But just when the summer heat was intensifying the Monarchs' 1943 season, the ghost of his past dealt him a Trouble Ball under the chin. Satch learned how foolish he had been to try and wish away Janet Howard Paige instead of making a clean and legal break when his financial condition was very different.

Janet's sense of timing was sublime. Satch had just come onto the field for a game at Wrigley Field when a man handed him a piece of paper. Thinking that the fellow wanted an autograph, he looked down and saw it was a summons to appear in divorce court in Chicago—where Janet had moved—on August 4.

Janet Paige brought her divorce suit on grounds of desertion and bigamy, pursuant to Satch's alleged marriage to Lucy Figueroa. Clearly, Janet had done more research about her husband's life than just reading *Life* magazine; her suit placed his income at $40,000, his property value at $25,000, and his antique and china collections at $30,000. Her request for relief was alimony of $100 per week over a fifteen-week baseball season and $50 per week over the remaining thirty-seven weeks—a bite of $3,350 yearly, not small change in 1943.

Considering that Satch had to answer the charges on August 4, it was scant wonder that he suddenly saw the August 1 East-West Game in a new light. Again the top vote-getter by far and having received a percentage of the gate from the '42 game—this while all the other players were receiving $50, and that only after threatening to boycott the game if the owners persisted in stiffing them—Satch now demanded, and got, from J. L. Wilkinson an astounding $800 up front.

While that stickup imperiled Satch's sainted image in Negro ball—the *Defender*, reflecting the latest league-think, hectored him for "stuffing his pockets [while] other players have been scuffling along"—the '43 East-West Game in Chicago became another milestone for him. Starting before a Negro league record crowd of 51,723 in Comiskey Park, he pitched three faultless innings, striking out four and walking one. Ahead 1–0 when he left, the West won 2–1 to give him his second East-West victory.

He wasn't so fortunate on August 4. Appearing before Circuit Court Judge Benjamin P. Epstein, he denied that he had legally married Lucy Figueroa, but not that he had abandoned Janet Paige. Days later, Judge Epstein announced the terms of the divorce settlement: in lieu of weekly alimony, Satch had to cough up a flat payment of $1,500 plus attorney's fees of $300.

"When it was all over, I didn't feel anything," he recalled of the courtroom dress-down years later. "I'd won a lot of decisions in the past, but this was one I lost bad."

•   •   •

Satch turned up his nerve when it came to playing his East-West Game trump card the following year—though the '44 game changed the luck of the draw for him. Fully anticipating that Paige might try and hold them up again, the owners had cut into his and all of the players' bargaining power by taking the player selection away from the fans. As arrogant and as risky as it was to disenfranchise black citizens at a time like this, the issue of economic self-preservation was more convincing.

In the name of *fairness*, Commissioners J. B. Martin and Tom

Wilson—not to avoid the "sentiment of fans," they said, but to re-ward lesser-known but deserving players—took the selection process in their own hands, beginning with the '44 game. Heading off individual deals, they also came to an agreement with the play-ers on game pay: $200 per player, $300 for managers, and a pool of $300 per club to be split by players not chosen for the game.

Of course, this was still lower-case money next to the owners' take; after Abe Saperstein's cut, they made around $3,500 each. More important, they succeeded in fencing in some of Satch's most profitable turf. Unequal as he was, no longer could his avarice be bonded to the will of the fans. The leagues took back the power to reproach him, and would use it.

Thus, a week before the game, when Satch demanded a percent-age of the gate, as he had extracted in 1942, J. B. Martin was well prepared. Rejecting any favoritism as an affront to the new agree-ments, he made a point of telling the press that he could not meet Paige's demand because it not only would be unfair to the other players, but that—in forking over so much to them—the NAL might go bankrupt as it was.

Satch knew he'd been co-opted and made to look like a malcon-tent and league-breaker. Coming so soon after his infamous re-marks about integration, he now had to scramble to save face. On the eve of the game he called together reporters and, in a patriotic clatter, said that unless all the proceeds from the game went to the Army-Navy Relief Fund, "I'm gonna lead a walkout and they won't have any East-West Game."

Martin wasn't about to knuckle under. Knowing that Paige was whistling through his hat, that the other players were secure, and that the fans weren't going to stay away from the game, the com-missioner deflected the war-charity question as a red herring, a dodge, and declared Satch insubordinate and ineligible for the game.

The immediate reaction by the black press was to sympathize with Satch. The *Defender*—Satch's latest effort to "stuff his pockets" notwithstanding—called his proposal "commendable" and the league response "inexcusable." And Satch, warming to the positive reception that this emotion-charged issue could bring him, contin-ued to wrap himself in the flag. "I'd like to pitch in this all-star game thinkin' it was for white and Negro boys in the South Pa-cific," he said. But, in letting his mouth run on, he may have unwit-tingly identified the real issue.

"With all I've done," he added, "I figure I got the right to tell the owners how they should toss around that money from the East-West Game."

In the end, J. B. Martin nailed Satch by pointing out that the war-charity proposition hadn't been made until after Martin had rebuffed his percentage demand—an assertion Satch was still trying to deny decades later. "[Martin] knew better. I didn't want any money for playing that game," he tried to explain in his autobiography. "I'd gotten the idea for playing for the soldiers that winter [when he had visited wounded soldiers in army hospitals]. I told some of the managers and owners that we ought to give them soldiers ten thousand dollars from the game." When nothing happened, he said, "I just let it ride for the time being."

Or until the East-West Game, which went on without him—then and thereafter, as Satch expediently found himself unavailable for all future games, which spared J. B. Martin from having to take the same unpopular stand against him. For a few of the games, his absence was conspicuous, then a mild distraction, then hardly news at all—a practical barometer of his ensuing Negro league years.

Increasingly, Satch wanted less to do with organized blackball. Not by coincidence, after his East-West obloquy the idea of splitting fees with J. L. Wilkinson in the name of saving league teams now seemed a criminal waste of his time, what with his honor besmirched by those very leagues. Satch decided he was bored with the structured grind; he craved his independence again.

While remaining affiliated with and on call to the Monarchs, as the team declined he went back to barnstorming as a solo act most of the year, appearing for a profusion of semipro teams looking to scare up a crowd—a drift that coincided with the grudging realization that he was pushing forty.

"I could tell I was slowing down a little," he allowed later of those crossroads years of the mid-1940s. "My arm never bothered me, but I was weak in the knees. I could feel it. . . .

"I still had my trouble ball, though. And I could do the same old thing with that ball that I could do five years before. Only . . . I couldn't do it as long. But that's still something for a guy who [had] been pitching for more than eighteen years, ain't it?"

When he pitched in league games, he was still news. But the black press no longer rolled and tumbled every time he sneezed. With his presence shrunk to human size, it was even safe to attack him. Once, when Satch was billed to pitch against the Grays in Forbes Field but instead rested a sore arm, a bilious *Courier* man tore at his making "suckers of the fans. . . . He made 'em turn out, stand in line, and then crane their necks like a flock of kangaroos looking for him after they had paid out their hard-earned dough to see him pitch."

To some, he was more a pariah now, an ingrate, a leech hanging on for his marquee value. Only sarcastically did the *Courier* reporter aggrandize him. "He's the 'Great Satchel,' " the story read, "the man who has received more than any other player in the history of Negro ball for doing less."

This, the second professional death of Satchel Paige, seemed sure to be his permanent requiem, and it was not all due to Satchel Paige alone. By V-J Day, there was a new story line—and a new main attraction among black ballplayers—occupying everyone's attention.

●   ●   ●

Purely by happenstance, the integration of American baseball was hastened by another rounder from the Negro leagues—none other than Gus Greenlee himself. After a few years in exile, Gus had made a move to reenter blackball in 1940. But if Gus hadn't realized before that his honorary league chairmanship was an opulent sham, he did when he sought to reconstitute the Crawfords.

Hoping to reinvent himself as a man of benign and warmhearted interests, his idea was to peel back time and stock the new club not with anymore raided players but local sandlot stars—just as it had been when he first took over the team. But Cum Posey had not worked so hard to chase Greenlee out of the NNL only to welcome him back in the guise of an honest man—and Posey looked perceptive when, after getting the league to reject Gus's applications in 1940 and again over the next three years, Greenlee went on choleric rampage in 1944. The same men he had wanted to be at one with, Gus now vowed to "wipe out" for "ruining" his grand old league.

With that pledge, Greenlee declared civil war on the Negro leagues. Working as a provocateur, he was a backstage presence at that year's already stormy East-West Game, lobbying players to join Satch in driving up the pay scale—his mission being to break the two leagues right then and there. Then, in early 1945, he created a new Negro ball circuit—the United States League—and went about raiding the NNL and NAL teams all over again, though few star players were willing to jump their now stable leagues and join

Greenlee's new Crawfords and the seven other USL teams.

In trying to get the new league off the ground, Greenlee did find what he believed to be a helpful partner—Branch Wesley Rickey, a man who soon would be dominating blackball news.

Rickey, the flinty quarter-owner, chief executive, and general manager of the Brooklyn Dodgers, had plans for black players, though even he may not have known exactly what they were and how far they went. But by the end of 1945, he had done two profoundly important things: First, just months after the death of Kenesaw Mountain Landis, he committed the Dodgers organization to the USL, offering its teams the use of Ebbets Field and all other stadiums in the Dodgers' minor league chain.

And then, making the first move among a legion of timorous men, on October 29, 1945, he signed a bulky Kansas City Monarchs infielder named Jackie Robinson to a Dodgers contract and assigned him to their Montreal farm team for the '46 season—with barely a nod and not a cent in compensation to J. L. Wilkinson.

In due time, all these acts would sort out to everybody's understanding, if not everybody's satisfaction.

15

Deliverance

[Bill] Veeck has gone too far in his quest for publicity [by signing Paige to the Cleveland Indians], and . . . has done his
league's position no good insofar as public reaction is concerned. Paige said he was 39 years of age. There are reports
that he is somewhat in the neighborhood of 50 [and it] would
have done Cleveland and the American League no good in the
court of public opinion if, at 50, Paige were as Caucasian as,
let us say, Bob Feller. To bring in a pitching "rookie" of Paige's
age casts a reflection on the entire scheme of operation in the
major leagues [and is] to demean the standards of baseball in
the big circuits. Further complicating the situation is the suspicion that if Satch were white, he would not have drawn a second thought from Veeck.

—J. G. Taylor Spink,
The Sporting News, July 14, 1948

As far as I'm concerned, the signing of Satchel Paige to a
Cleveland contract is far more interesting than was the news
when Branch Rickey broke baseball's color line by signing
Jackie Robinson to a Montreal contract. It was inevitable that
the bigotry which kept Negroes out of Organized Ball would
be beaten back, but I'd never heard of Robinson at that time.
With Paige, it's different. The Satchmo has been a baseball
legend for a long time, a Paul Bunyan in technicolor. More
fabulous tales have been told of Satchel's pitching ability than
of any pitcher in Organized Ball.

—Tom Meany, *New York Star,*
July 21, 1948

While Branch Rickey had money and his personal influence invested in Gus Greenlee's United States League—as well as his own colored team, the Brooklyn Brown Dodgers—it did not concern him at all that his signing of Jackie Robinson became almost the *only* story pertinent to the blackball world.

Under the skyrockets that followed Robinson to Montreal, it went all but unnoticed that Rickey had quietly signed three other Negro leaguers, again with no compensation to their clubs, just before the 1946 season. These were Baltimore's Roy Campanella, Homestead's Roy Partlow, and Newark pitcher Don Newcombe; Rickey sent them to other outposts in the Dodgers' chain, to excel or fail in relative peace.

There would, of course, be no such tranquillity for Robinson, and that Jackie handled himself so well under the glare in the International League pleased Rickey—but only slightly more than the fact that the black press was practically reducing Negro league business into a filler item while its big writers traveled with and covered Robinson game by game.

Moreover, though the USL was a financial stiff from day one, its coverage for a time in the *white* press, because of Rickey's association, was strangling the NNL and NAL from the other end. This slow death of old-line blackball was at the heart of Rickey's plans. If Robinson made good in Montreal, leading to a shakeout in the Negro leagues, Rickey's intention was to get league stars not by dealing but by stealing.

This was the shame of Branch Rickey, who in all other ways was as visionary and courageous a man as any ever found in sports. It was no great crime that Rickey, as head of a flourishing business concern, was more Machiavelli than Lincoln; that he waited to see which way the integration pendulum swung before saying "I cannot face my God much longer knowing that His black creatures are held separate from His white creatures in the game that has given me my own"; that he was prepared at first to profit from either integration or continued segregation.

Rickey would have been foolish to do otherwise, when Clark Griffith was living off of black gate proceeds in Washington and the New York Yankees' management was culling $100,000 a year in rental fees from Negro league games played in Yankee Stadium. Indeed, the presumption that Rickey was trying to organize a black league so as to *retard* integration and exploit blackball for himself united black and white baseball in contempt for him. Clark Griffith was particularly incensed that a "carpetbagger" like Rickey would dare set himself up as the "czar" of Negro ball, since this would have undercut Griffith's own blackball exploitation.

Rickey's real sin was that, in opting for integration, he was prepared to quash not just the Negro league owners but those players who were too strongly identified with their teams and might create sympathy for them. Players like Satchel Paige, for instance. Even though the leagues were ready-made minor leagues, composed of long-betrayed "creatures of God," Rickey pronounced them unfit, countenancing them only as "a booking agent's paradise" and for being "in the zone of a racket" for past links with people like his USL partner, Gus Greenlee.

If Greenlee believed that he had been elevated by that association, he learned otherwise. Though the USL lasted two wheezing seasons, Rickey pulled out during the first, leaving Greenlee to fend for himself while Rickey took a scalpel to what was left of blackball as a whole. Out of the shambles of this sorry episode came a vengeant pride for Gus—that the Negro leagues would now pay the piper big-time for disdaining him.

This was made evident by the death of Cum Posey on March 28, 1946. Coming right in the middle of this last suicidal war between brothers, it left blackball without its single strongest force, and naked to the barricuda-like instincts of Branch Rickey.

If Gus Greenlee ever felt any guilt or regret that his final legacy was not quite serendipitous to other black men, it probably happened at Posey's burial. Posey, the onetime robust athlete, had been ravaged by cancer the last year of his life and died without being able to fight at age fifty-three. His funeral was attended by hundreds of the Pittsburgh upper crust—the pallbearers included Art Rooney and Josh Gibson—who grieved at the sour irony that as Jackie Robinson was about to play his first game in whiteball, the wisest of Negro league men left the field with too much game left to be played. Gus Greenlee knew that there would be no such mass grieving at his own funeral.

Though they couldn't know it then, those at the gravesite heard the last rites of blackball that day. But even if Gus Greenlee realized that, he may have comforted himself with another thought: after all, Gasoline Gus didn't only get to *see* Jackie Robinson get to the big leagues; in being sold out by Branch Rickey, he had helped to make Jackie Robinson's route easier.

• • •

When Satch heard about the Robinson signing, he—like almost everyone else in the Negro leagues—was stunned. Though teammates for the last year, Satch had hardly spoken with Jackie, not having much reason to believe that the muscular twenty-five-year-old was much more than a good hitter, an unspectacular fielder, and a rather hard guy to be with.

In fact, most of the Monarchs kept at a distance from Robinson, who seemed to want little to do with them. While Hilton Smith had gotten Jackie on the team after Robinson came out of the army and was looking for a job, Jackie hung with no cliques and constantly complained about the peonic conditions in the black game, as if they were far beneath the level he deserved. Rickey certainly had to admire Robinson's lack of respect for blackball, and it may have paved his way, since little else justified his historical elevation over men who were superb all-around baseball players.

If anything, baseball was Robinson's weakest sport. Having been a truly outstanding athlete at UCLA, he was primarily known as an all-American halfback and the leading scorer on the basketball team, though he won letters in baseball and track as well. While he could excel in any sport he tried, on the baseball diamond he appeared to be a football player without a gridiron—especially when he tried to play shortstop for the Monarchs, a club decision that caused flak among the players, since Jackie had moved out the popular Jesse Williams, who'd been an all-star at the position.

To Satch, the verdict on Robinson was open and shut—"I wouldn't put him on my all-time great team," he said many years on. Few Negro leaguers disagreed, and there was some speculation that Robinson was chosen in order to fail and end all this talk of integration. But while Satch's own ambivalence about integration had always kept his expectations low to nonexistent about the big leagues, when word broke about Jackie it kicked him hard in the gut.

"Almost twenty years after I fired my first trouble ball as a full-time professional, Jim Crow'd gotten busted on the nose," he would write in his autobiography. "I hadn't thought it'd ever happen, but it had. . . . Somehow I'd always figured it'd be me. But it hadn't."

Satch knew this to be irrational (though not false) pride. By his age, his reputation, and his habit of taking nothing in stride, he actually was much like Robinson in temperament and nothing like him in comprehending the price of this fateful role. While Jackie too was on the hotheaded side, he had endured racism on white terms; as a morale officer for black troops at Fort Riley, he had succeeded in desegregating the PX, but clashed with a white officer who said he didn't want his wife "sitting next to a nigger." Robinson was court-martialed but defended himself with such grace and reason that he won an honorable discharge.

Jackie was well prepped to go through hell and hold his tongue, even just to get out of the minors. Satch, on the other hand, knew he'd be a disaster on those terms. As he later admitted, with a prickly bravado that would have been a foreign language for Jackie Robinson, "They'd have had to put me right in the majors and that might have caused a revolution because the high-priced white boys up there wouldn't have had a chance to get used to the idea that way. Some of them weren't taking too good to the idea even though Jackie was going to the minors."

That attitude held fast for all Negro leaguers with a past, from Josh Gibson to the two Bucks, Leonard and O'Neil, to Hilton Smith. But, again, that was only rational. In Satch's gut, in his pride, there was pain: "Signing Jackie like they did still hurt me deep down. I'd been the guy who'd started all that big talk about letting us in the big time. I'd been the one who'd opened up the major league parks to the colored teams. I'd been the one who the white boys wanted to go barnstorming against."

To be sure, it was of some solace that in the middle of the Robinson media stampede, Satch was sustained in his opinion by whites who seemed taken aback by the Robinson breakthrough and wanted to use Paige as the Anti-Robinson—though not quite to the point of actually petitioning for *his* signing by the big leagues in Jackie's stead.

This happened almost immediately after Robinson's signing. *The Sporting News*, the presumed baseball "Bible" and champion of the game's classical traditions, truculently declared in a November 1, 1945, editorial that "there is not a single Negro player with major league possibilities." On November 10, Bob Feller, tapped by the *Los Angeles Times* as an expert blackball witness—though he had only played against Robinson briefly after Jackie's season with the Monarchs, when the Feller All-Stars had played a black all-star squad in the California Winter League—nonetheless asserted that he "could not foresee any future in the majors" for Jackie. Feller said that Robinson had "football shoulders" and that he "couldn't hit an inside pitch to save his neck. If he were a white man, I doubt they would consider him big league material." (Possibly clouding

Feller's judgment was the fact that Robinson had threatened not to play unless Feller's promoters gave him more money, a demand he flatly rejected.)

Of all the black players he had seen, there were only two that Feller considered big league material: Josh Gibson and Satchel Paige. The president of Feller's Cleveland Indians in 1945, Alva Bradley, later recalled a more specific mode of thought around baseball. "In 1945," Bradley said, "there was only one [black] player mentioned as being of major league caliber. That was Satchel Paige."

To his great credit, Satch—who had no myopia that Jackie Robinson, as the first in, had a larger meaning than any individual on earth—did not publicly endorse the hasty slights of Robinson, possibly because he believed—as did Jackie—that they came from the mouths of racist men. At the very least, as a black man, he would not, nor would any other black man, wittingly divide the cause by quibbling with the choice—as none would openly quibble with Satch's later promotion in spite of their personal feelings about *him*.

Of Jackie, he told reporters at the time, "They didn't make a mistake in signing Robinson. He's a No. 1 professional player. They couldn't have picked a better man." Against his inner feelings, he also called Jackie "the greatest colored player I've ever seen."

But, good company man that he could be, Satch was powerless to keep from being used as a tool to blunt the impact of Jackie Robinson. As baseball-playing GIs swarmed home to reclaim their jobs in the postwar blush, Jackie Robinson was mainly a novelty act to everyone but those in the black press. With whiteball still years behind Branch Rickey's perceptions and no one following his lead, the big leagues' use for colored players had not changed: Jackie Robinson aside, the white game simply went on cashing in on the spectacle of black *versus* white.

Accordingly, Bob Feller and Satchel Paige now built the biggest stash of lucre that baseball—all of baseball—had yet seen. At Feller's urging, they arranged to reprise their celebrated rivalry after the '46 season. As Feller couldn't wait to get on with this huge attraction, he asked for permission from the new big league commissioner, A. E. "Happy" Chandler, to begin barnstorming with his Feller All-Stars even as the World Series was being played. Chandler, who had signaled his amenability to integration when he took over after Judge Landis's death, readily agreed, and also waived the limit of ten barnstorming days that had been stipulated by Landis when Feller agreed to conduct an instructional school for returning veterans prior to the next spring training.

The Feller-Paige tour of 1946 was staged on the scale of Barnum & Bailey. With Feller footing the tab, two DC-3 airplanes were leased—at the time a means of travel unused by any athlete but Satch—to ferry the Feller and Paige teams on a month-long jag across the nation. With the help of hired publicity and advance men, the tour nearly trivialized the World Series in some parts of the country.

The pay arrangements for the players on this tour were a true indicator of the times. Feller, who with Paige was to work on a gate percentage, paid his players—a solid crew led by American League batting champ Mickey Vernon, Johnny Sain, Spud Chandler, Phil Rizzuto, Kenny Keltner, and Bob Lemon, with Stan Musial jumping aboard after the World Series—salaries ranging from $1,700 to $6,000.

The black players, meanwhile, were to get what the promoters deigned to give them, and Satch had a trying time finding guys who would accept these conditions—especially since Jackie Robinson, plying his sudden fame, had formed his own colored traveling team, boasting the likes of Roy Campanella and Buck Leonard. Other players Satch was dickering with went to the Puerto Rican League instead after the Negro league season.

The core of this edition of the Paige All-Stars turned out to be Satch, Hilton Smith, Buck O'Neil, the Monarchs' outfielder Hank Thompson, the Cleveland Buckeyes' heavy-hitting outfielder Sam Jethroe, and graybeard Quincy Trouppe, and the Philadelphia Stars' outfielder Gene Benson. Making calls to players around the clock, Satch was so preoccupied with the planning that when the Monarchs won the NAL pennant and went east to play Abe and Effa Manley's Newark Eagles in the 1946 Negro World Series, he seemed to brush aside that series as a distraction—as did much of the black press, which was so obsessed with Robinson that his exhibition games far outweighed the threadbare coverage now of league title games.

The most interested observers of the series were big league scouts; within four years, the Eagles' Larry Doby and Monte Irvin and the Monarchs' Hank Thompson would be major leaguers. So would Satch, though any scout or owner at the time would have been scared away from him off this series alone. With magnificent disregard, he showed up late for most of the games and was highly erratic in three relief stints as the series became a seven-game trench war.

After winning Game One out of the bullpen with an eight-strike-out, four-inning job, he came into Game Two with the score tied and was rocked for the three runs that lost it. Down 4–1 when he entered Game Four, he gave up a three-run homer to Irvin. But he saved his biggest crime for next—not showing up at all for the final three games, the last two of which the Monarchs lost in his absence.

Amazingly, he wasn't the only Monarch who ducked out on those games. Ted Strong, the slugging outfielder, also split. And while some accounts had it that Strong—whose impeccable credentials would later earn him a managing job in the Negro leagues—had caught a freighter for the Puerto Rican League to fulfill a contract and that Satch had been tending to Paige All-Star business, Monarchs outfielder Willard Brown decades later provided a whole 'nother explanation. Interviewed by journalist Jim Riley, Brown said that Satch and Strong had in fact met up with two wild women after Game Four in Chicago, and were still there partying as the club went off to three other cities to finish the series.

The timing of this harebrained escapade may also have been Satch's way of giving the finger to the Negro leagues that he had again grown to despise after his East-West Game facedown. Indeed, bouncing right from the series to the Feller tour, he managed to make every game in that series with no problem at a time when his standing was really on the line with the whiteball people.

As it stood even before the tour, everyone in the big leagues was aware of, and trembled at, how big-time this Feller-Paige thing was. As a result, Feller had problems himself getting players—not because guys wouldn't want to play, but because so many did. For this month of work, players could earn as much as half their yearly salaries; Stan Musial, playing only part of the month, made more than his $3,000 winning World Series share. Looking cheap by comparison, the big leagues would have to raise the Series shares thereafter. Because some owners feared that their star players might go down in one of those tin-can planes, they paid them not to go out; Ted Williams, for one, got $10,000 from Tom Yawkey to stay home in Boston.

Convinced that this sideshow was subversive, those owners watched in horror as overflow multiracial crowds crammed into big league and other ballparks from coast to coast to see the highly pub-

licized games. On another level, they were uneasy that the Paige
team—a middling black squad at best—was winning about as many
games as it lost against top-shelf big leaguers. For Bob Feller, coming off a twenty-six-win season, Hank Thompson alone was a night-
mare. Hank hit several moon shots off Feller, one into the center
field bleachers at Yankee Stadium in a 4–0 win by the Paige team.

But even Feller, whose dismissal of Jackie Robinson was on the
record, countenanced the competition only by its effect on the
cash register, which rang often as around 400,000 people paid
their way into those stadiums during the twenty-seven-game tour.
In his 1990 autobiography, *Now Pitching, Bob Feller*, Feller deliberated on the tour in detail while mentioning none of the black men
who made October of 1946 spurt dollar bills for him—with the
sole exception of Satch, whom Feller managed to describe with all
the warmth of an accountant checking an asset sheet.

"Satch and I were friends, teammates, and business associates,"
he wrote. "We were a successful partnership, always aboveboard
with each other. We worked hard for each other in our mutual en-
deavors and at the end of our projects, we were still friends."

Still, Feller was correct in taking a bow, pointing out that "those
barnstorming games we pitched against each other . . . helped to
get Satch into the Hall of Fame." For Paige, in fact, this tour was a
personal revival show. Seeing his popularity decline during the past
season, he had sought to reestablish his relevance in Negro ball by
occasionally going the full route in games—as many as fourteen innings twice. Now, needing to go no more than the first three innings against Feller—who found this to be harder than it looked on
a daily basis and came up with a sore arm, forcing him to cut back
on his starts—Satch was again relevant in the *white* world.

Thus did Satchel Paige become something of an agent in the as-
cent of Jackie Robinson. Jackie opened the door, but Satch was the
lightning rod on the roof, collecting and distributing the fury
around it. Although Happy Chandler reacted to the huge success
of the Feller-Paige series by doing an abrupt about-face and rein-
stating limits on any future series, these games spun heads in the
big leagues. Chandler himself knew that, having gone on record
for integration when he became commissioner, it was about time to
start getting used to a new ballgame.

• • •

For blacks whose lives would not be changed for the better in the
coming years, however, Satch's philanthropic effect had a limited

reach. The men of the Paige All-Stars came home with oddly mixed feelings about the tour; the inconsistent pay they made was not enough to mask the incivilities dealt against them in the name of privilege. Gene Benson, for example, recalled that he bought his first house with the proceeds of those games. But Benson, who had played in the Negro leagues since 1934, came to regard the tour as a journey into an open mine shaft.

"I remember the first night that we played was in Pittsburgh and the crowd was pretty good and we made $400 a man," he said. "We'd never made that kinda money before. After that, though, the money started goin' down and we were goin' to places where there were *more* people in the park. So somebody was gettin' into the money.

"So we went and talked to Satchel about the unfairness of the thing, 'cause we knew that there was more money made than they were showin'. And Satchel, he agreed with us, he was on our side. But the only thing about that, the ballplayers from the West were so happy to make whatever they got, they didn't put up any complaints. We guys from the East, we were used to better conditions but we couldn't do anything by ourselves so we just had to go along.

"Then, too, Satchel was separate from everybody else. He didn't get what we got. He had his own contract. And even though he knew we were bein' robbed, there was nothin' he could do about it and I don't even know if he tried.

"I find about people that when they're doin' all right, they don't worry 'bout the other guy. And he wasn't too concerned about us. He thought about himself. He wanted what he wanted and if he couldn't get it, he didn't care 'bout the rest of the fellas, and we really didn't pay much attention to him.

"Now, if the black owners had gotten together and set up a league and drawn up a schedule for that tour, we wouldn't have needed Satchel. Because we had a lotta good ballplayers outside a Satchel. And he would've been one of the players, just like the rest of us."

But blackball had run out of such ideas now and—even as it grossed $2 million at the gate for the first time in 1946—its owners were absorbed with how to survive big league integration. Even a strong man like Cum Posey had been disconcerted about it. Before he died, Posey had sent a melancholy letter to Tom Wilson, whom promoter Eddie Gottlieb was trying to replace in a power play with a white co-promoter named Frank Forbes. As Branch Rickey had said, these promoters were part of the Negro leagues' "racket"; Posey felt this move would be suicidal and begged Wilson to fight the takeover.

But Posey knew that his and Wilson's day was over. "We are get-ting so much hell, which we don't deserve, as we have built the league and did not hurt anybody while we were building it," he lamented, adding sadly that "we both took office together and we will go out together." Posey was right; the league president's job would soon be taken from Wilson and made purely titular, leaving the owners' rights as a whole left unattended.

In dire need of positive signs after Posey's death, the game suf-fered again early in 1947, with the horrible demise of Josh Gibson.

Lost in the maelstrom of headlines about Jackie Robinson and the Bob Feller–Satchel Paige flying circus was the alarming decline of the most useful metaphor of blackball strength. Although Gib-son's hard drinking and drug habits were an open secret in the blackball scene, most players assumed that Josh's corrugated body made him resistant to dissipation that might destroy lesser men. Many a time he had come to the plate in a haze only to hit one nine miles.

What was not generally known was that Gibson's body was termi-nally ill. Suffering terrible headaches that he believed to be from hangovers, when he blacked out and was hospitalized in 1943 he was diagnosed with a brain tumor. But he would not consent to an operation, fearing he would live out his life as a potted plant—and instead he went on bigger and bigger binges, trying to forget that he was a dying man. Meeting up with a self-destructive woman whose husband was away in the service, he began fooling with a new high: heroin.

Incredibly, he continued killing the ball, and even when Cum Posey suspended him from the '45 East-West Game for violating training rules, his reputation was that of blackball's solid citizen. Two years after commemorating Satch, *Time* turned its attention to Gibson in 1943, and, knowing nothing of his wild side, contrasted him favorably with Satch, maintaining that Josh "is no gaudy ec-centric. He drives no cerise roadster, makes no startling statements about a strict diet of fried food, and receives no $40,000 a year salary."

And yet it was during these years that Gibson was frequently be-ing treated in hospitals for alcohol and drug dependency and for mental illness—though neither sedation nor straitjackets could keep him confined to his bed for very long.

By 1946, Josh Gibson was no longer a hard pumice of a man; he was soft pulp, a fat man whose knees were so maimed that he could not squat behind the plate and caught in a stoop, and often a stupor. Still, he hit .361 and led the league in homers, but on January 20, 1947, a month after his thirty-fifth birthday, he had his final blackout. Collapsing at his mother's home, he was dead of a stroke by the time doctors arrived.

Josh Gibson did not die, as has been made his coda, of a heart broken by being snubbed by the big leagues; the timing only made it possible to gild his legacy with a deep shade of bathos. But it was nonetheless a uniquely American anomaly that in the year forever to be synonymous with Jackie Robinson, a large piece of the Negro leagues went into the grave with Josh Gibson.

● ● ●

The way was long and the wind was cold, but on April 15, 1947, Jack Roosevelt Robinson was in the Opening Day lineup as the Brooklyn Dodgers played the Boston Braves at Ebbets Field. But even by then, the big leagues had in no way responded to the inevitable by finally getting with the Branch Rickey modus operandi. Rickey himself signed another Negro leaguer, Memphis Red Sox pitcher Dan Bankhead (brother of Sam Bankhead), in August of 1947 and brought him right to Brooklyn in the heat of a pennant race—too soon, as Bankhead pitched poorly and was soon sent to the minors.

In the meantime, only two other teams made similar moves. On July 5, Bill Veeck, who had assumed ownership of the Cleveland Indians in 1946, signed twenty-one-year-old Larry Doby—considerately making a token $10,000 payment to Abe and Effa Manley to acquire Doby's Newark contract—and made him the American League's first Negro player. Eleven days later, the St. Louis Browns' new owner, Richard Muckerman, signed, also at a small purchase price, the Monarchs' Hank Thompson and Willard Brown and brought them to the cellar-dwelling Browns.

But unlike the spasms of excitement that awaited Jackie Robinson, these lesser-known players even in the Negro leagues generated barely a twitch—though many of the players themselves were near paralyzed by the pressure on them. Unimpressive on the field, after an initial bustle they settled into the background of their teams, or in the case of Thompson and Brown, back in the Negro leagues (though Thompson would make good on another big league call later). By the end of 1947, the cause seemed to be stuck in neutral.

To be certain, there had been no fundamental change in segregation, and the same long-held objections still applied among most big league owners. Protecting their investments, their vanity, and for some their Negro league rental fees, the owners kneaded baseball "tradition" into a pretzel of canards about economic survival. And, always, whichever shibboleth they grabbed on to, the owners portrayed themselves as the innocent parties: it was Jim Crow laws or the distinct "crowd psychologies" of black and white fans that stood in the way of integration, and it was "social and political drum-beaters" who were pushing for it.

All the status quo rationalizations, of course, ignored the pervasive influence that the owners' ballclubs had in spring training and minor league towns in the South, which presented them the opportunity to create social change. They also ignored that black and white fans had mixed quite well when allowed to.

Change, not really the "Race Question," was the real enemy of the big league establishment. As in any other white neighborhood, there were quails about "property values" plummeting should blacks—i.e., black *fans*—begin displacing the white bedrock. Small wonder that, as a last refuge, big league people professed solidarity with those Negro league people who sought to protect *their* investments.

In one of his last acts as NNL president, Tom Wilson, along with the NAL's J. B. Martin, met with Happy Chandler in 1946 to propose that the two Negro circuits be given official status as minor leagues—and came out endorsing Chandler's less-than-charitable assessment that "Organized Ball cannot afford to tie up with any ally with less than rigid standards." Livid that the two chieftains of blackball could play into the hands of big league Pharisees, Wendell Smith—once the NNL's most reliable conduit for Cum Posey's ordinances—savaged Wilson and Martin in the *Courier* for "whimpering" before Chandler and for trying to salvage "the perpetuation of the slave trade," by extending the life of blackball.

Wrote Smith: "[They will] shout to the high heavens that racial progress comes first and baseball next. But actually the preservation of their shaky, littered, infested, segregated baseball domicile comes first, last and always."

The black press could indeed deal harshly with those who seemed to be holding back from full and unconditional support of the integration movement; recriminations such as Smith's influenced Tom Baird to withdraw a lawsuit he had filed against Branch

Rickey for taking Jackie Robinson without compensating the Monarchs. When Bill Veeck paid the Newark club $10,000 for Larry Doby, Effa Manley was insulted and at first balked. "You know, if Larry Doby were white and a free agent," she told Veeck, "you'd give him $100,000 to sign as a bonus." She took the money, she said, partly because Veeck promised to pay the Eagles another $5,000 if Doby remained with the Indians for thirty days, and partly "to get the Negro papers off of me."

The greater good now was integration at any cost. But if blackball became united under that banner, Happy Chandler—as demonstrated by his meeting with Tom Wilson and J. B. Martin—was not as ready to march with them as he had implied when he was chosen as commissioner. Then, he had loudly pledged himself to the "Four Freedoms," the chief objectives of American and United Nations policy, as proposed by FDR in 1941: freedom of speech and expression; freedom of worship; freedom from want; freedom from fear. Years after, he just as grandly claimed to have steered the way to integration. In truth, as a Southerner and a former Southern politician—a man who, as governor of Kentucky, had sanctioned a separate school system for blacks—his role was more that of a back-seat passenger.

Chandler was far more decisive when he threatened to ban for five years the several dozen players who, in keeping with the Pasquel brothers' Phase Two plans, had accepted huge offers to jump to the Mexican League after the war. As the Pasquels' next move was to go after the big-name big leaguers, many owners only now found integration to be a useful concept—if only as a skiver to sharpen players' anxieties about job security should they even consider jumping across the Rio Grande. By the end of the decade, when the expatriates had been granted amnesty by Happy Chandler and returned to their teams, the number of black players who had been employed in the interim could all have fit into the corner of one dugout.

Beyond factors such as these, then, the grudging concessions of 1947 seemed to be most owners' notion of desegregation—which made it all the more nutty that now, at the best and the worst of times for baseball integration, the time was getting close for Satchel Paige.

•   •   •

Satch himself was about the last man expecting a call from the big leagues in 1948. Having received not one during the year of

Jackie Robinson, he seemed to have come to a reluctant peace with himself about it. Not that he hurt any less; indeed, when Jackie broke the seal by getting to the Dodgers, the sudden reality of integration melted away his old cynicism. Now his rationalizations about big league pay and social "complications" could not gauze his wounded pride. With the door open, he wanted in. By rights!

Years later, he wrote with great feeling in his autobiography that the wound of not being first in the bigs was a "hurting like you do when somebody you love dies or something dies inside you. . . .

"That was my right," laid down Satchel Paige. "I should have been there. I got those boys thinking about having Negroes in the majors, but when they got one, it wasn't me."

But back in 1947, before it was clear what not being first would cost him in the long lens of history, Satch—with the same class he had demonstrated in 1945—continued to maintain that "Jackie was the right guy." Insinuating but not really believing that the pressures and abuses Robinson would encounter were not for him, he said, "I'm glad it wasn't me, 'cause I sure couldn't take it."

In his soul, he still burned, though like all seasoned Negro leaguers he more than understood the narrow context of this grudging phase of integration: the granting of recognition to blacks would come not with a proclamation but a mortgage. As with any other prospects, the colored players would have to go through the big league process, meaning as much as a half decade in the minor leagues. This was a condition plainly unacceptable to those like Satchel Paige. Gene Benson, for instance, had played in the Negro leagues since 1934. "I certainly wouldn't have gone to nobody's minor league," he said, " 'cause I figured I was as much major league as anybody."

Satch, of course, was just as stubborn, and once recalled that if the big leagues had called him in those formative years, his feeling then was that "they'll have to come real pretty-like. They've been puttin' me off too long to just wiggle their fingers at me now." But when they didn't come, wiggling or otherwise, he gradually turned away from his past conceits and found he could be contented as a forty-year-old living a facsimile of the suburban American Dream.

On October 12, 1947, right after his least active season thus far—pitching in only two league games for the Monarchs all year—Satch felt secure enough to finally marry Lahoma Brown in a civil ceremony in Hays, Kansas. A month later, when they were in Los Angeles for a now truncated series against the Bob Feller All-Stars, Lahoma became pregnant with their daughter, Pamela.

That was Satch's first achievement in L.A. The second would come against Feller, whose team was even stronger with the addition of the Reds' lanky no-hit pitcher Ewell "The Whip" Blackwell and the Pirates' musclebound slugger Ralph Kiner. But, again, while the going was good on the field in these well-attended games, the Negro league players were the real losers—including, for a time, Satch.

The black team this time was Chet Brewer's Kansas City Royals, which had been Chet's entry in the California Winter League for the last few years and had been Jackie Robinson's entrée to the Monarchs. But with the big business of the Feller games, Brewer now found himself cut into lots more money—and cut out of any administrative role. With Feller's cabal of people running the entire show, Brewer recalled that "they didn't even let me come up to their office. I didn't have the privilege, even though it was my team out there."

Chet made enough of a fuss that they gave him some ledger sheets, possibly figuring that he wouldn't be able to read them and would just drop the subject. Brewer, though, knew well how to read them, and saw a major discrepancy in Satch's allowance: contracted to receive fifteen percent of the gross receipts, he had been getting paid fifteen percent of the *net* receipts. Going to Satch with the information, he told him, "Satchel, Feller owes you $2,400."

A startled Satch went to see Feller about it—"They didn't stop *him* from going up there in that office," Brewer mused—and came away with his money but apparently no hard feelings against Feller—who, in turn, held the embarrassing incident against Brewer. "Boy, Bob Feller hated me for a long time," he said. "I saw him once in an airport in Phoenix and he didn't even speak to me. He hated to pay Satchel that $2,400."

Brewer wondered if perhaps Feller's bookkeepers did not like the idea of paying all of the black players a deserved wage, and if Satch shared his outrage. Later, when Chet visited Satch's hotel room, he got the answer when Satch reached into his pocket and threw three ten dollar bills Brewer's way. Blanching at the thought that this measly "reward" evidently was supposed to make him drop the matter—and knowing now that even if he didn't, the pay scale would not change anyway—Chet Brewer reached his breaking point with Satchel Paige. When Satch put the money in his hand, Chet let it drop at Satch's feet.

"I'm not hungry—you keep it," he said, jaw clenched, as he walked toward the door.

As it turned out, that series of games was the last Brewer would see of Satch for many long years, by Chet's choice. Refusing to go back to the Monarchs for as long as Satch was around, he hopped from team to team for the rest of his career. And while Satch could only shake his head at Chet's indignation, somewhere inside he may have understood it—and may have even blamed Chet for exposing his moral indifference toward other blacks. Even back then, Chet could feel Satch's eyes burning a hole right through him.

"Satchel didn't like me," Brewer said without hesitation a few years before his death in 1991. "As a matter of fact, all his wives threw me up to him; they'd say, 'Satchel, why don't you act like Chet?' . . . Boy, he hated [to be told] that." Certain that Satch loathed him for being everything Satch was not, Chet felt that Satch always had it in for him.

"All Satchel had to do was say a word and I'd be in the Hall of Fame," he said. "But he didn't. He wrote a book and mentioned all the pitchers in there that couldn't even carry my glove, and he didn't even give me a mention."

Still, if this round of games against the Feller All-Stars saw Satchel Paige at his pettiest, it also saw his pitching virtuosity reach its dramatic crest. Having struck out twenty-nine in eighteen innings over four games, he agreed to a dream promotion—a November 2 "challenge" contest between him and Feller at L.A.'s Wrigley Field, a game in which both were contracted to pitch nine innings. Satch and "Bob Rapid," as he called Feller, did their part, selling out the game by playfully ragging on each other for the press.

But even though Satch candidly recalled the promotion as "just a way for Feller and me to get a few more out for one last game," and Feller's barbs about his opponent's age—a gag that Satch was now milking, not denying that he could even be *fifty*, for all he knew—provided an effective new riff for his self-promotion, it struck him that this was not quite the wisest thing to do if he still had hopes of getting to the majors.

Giving no special thought to the game when it was made, he approached it with his gut burbling, and that hadn't happened since the duel in the sun with Josh Gibson in 1942. Satch now wanted the game, needed it, lest he be minted now and hereafter as a baseball joke, a three-inning freak show. He still had to be a *pitcher*.

"I'd really worked myself up over it," he wrote in his memoirs. "I drove out to the ball park and smoked about five cigarettes getting there."

Satch's prescription for the care and feeding of his arm had not changed in two decades: hot water, hot as he could stand it, and plenty of it, that was still the great restorative of those weary muscles and tendons. Six years after joining Satch on the Monarchs pitching staff, Connie Johnson was still astounded by him.

"That's all he'd do, let hot water run on his arm," Johnson said. "I used to ask him, 'How come you don't get more exercise, man?' But you know what I found out from him? The older you get, the less exercise you need. I used to get up, my legs would be weak, and I'd say, 'What's wrong? I ran all day yesterday.'

"So one day I said, I'm gonna do like Satchel. I go out and shag flies and run one lap, that's it—and I pitched a one-hitter that day, my legs were *driving*. And from that day on I didn't do no hard work, even in the big leagues. But you know who run himself out of baseball? Bob Feller. He run every day, he run too much.

"Satch, though, he'd go down to third base, take a few grounders, and that'd be his workout. Plus, he'd just sling that ball. Overhand, underhand, sidearm, all kinda ways—he just had a whip with his arm. I tell him one day, I says, 'Man, you ain't got no muscle!' And he'd laugh. He knew it. He knew he was born to throw. And he always swore his brother could throw harder than him!"

As Satch once said, "When that arm was loose, it could swing forever." And at Wrigley Field against Bob Feller, he was more than loose. It mattered not who the hitter was—Satch always found out later who he had cut down. Ahead 2–0 after two innings, when the Cubs' Bob Sturgeon doubled, Paige mowed down Roy Partee, Feller, and Peanuts Lowrey, with not so much as a foul tip. His old arm spitting fire, he whiffed fifteen competent big leaguers on that day, and gave up but four hits as the Royals pounded Feller in the 8–0 win.

Although Satch couldn't have known it, that was his ticket out of the shadows of baseball. It had been many years since anyone had asked if Satchel Paige was ready for the big leagues. And now, one big league owner was busy making up his mind about whether he was ready for Satchel Paige.

•   •   •

Unbeknownst to Satch, his big league employment had been under consideration for a year and a half, or ever since Bill Veeck purchased the Cleveland Indians in June of 1946. And, the truth was, only Bill Veeck could have put this discussion on the table.

Veeck, whose father, Bill Veeck, Sr., had been one of the most sober of baseball men in the Roaring Twenties, as president of the Chicago Cubs, had made *his* bones skewering all forms of sobriety in the game. In Veeck's big-top world of baseball, everything from door prizes to fireworks displays to midget races were on the score-card. Even losing a leg in 1946 to a degenerative disease could not slow Veeck; bounding around on crutches, he called only more attention to himself as the game's peg-legged Barnum.

Not incidentally, Veeck was also a knowledgeable baseball man, with an eye for pieces that could fit together on a team. For the thirty-four-year-old Veeck, the seed was planted as far back as 1934, when Satch beat the Dizzy Dean All-Stars in Los Angeles with his 1–0, thirteen-strikeout masterpiece and became a white attraction for the first time. One of those in attendance at Wrigley Field was Bill Veeck, who even decades later would recall that game as "the greatest pitcher's battle I have ever seen."

Almost alone among big league owners, Veeck was a regular at Negro league games and had a firsthand grasp of their level of talent. In fact, pre–Branch Rickey, he had planned to mount a bold frontal attack on baseball's intolerance in 1944, when Veeck had apparently consummated a deal to buy the bankrupt Philadelphia Phillies. Veeck made it perfectly clear to Judge Landis that he would sign at least some Negro league players to the new Phillies—all but challenging the old man to step into the modern world, since the commissioner, by his own disclaimers, could not legally forbid these signings without an overt admission of racism.

"Judge Landis wasn't exactly shocked but he wasn't exactly over-joyed either," Veeck recalled in his autobiography *Veeck . . . As in Wreck.* "His first reaction, in fact, was that I was kidding him."

Only Landis never laughed. Veeck was a kidder, but not about building teams. Shortly thereafter he was informed that the Phillies had already been sold—for half of what Veeck had agreed to pay.

Veeck's next chance came with the signing of Larry Doby. His third would be with Satchel Paige—whom Veeck would have just as soon brought in first had the circumstances been right. From day one in Cleveland, Veeck had asked his Negro league contacts—primarily Abe Saperstein—if Paige could throw anything like he did against Dizzy Dean. Assured that he could, Veeck still held off.

The Indians hadn't won a pennant in twenty-six years when Veeck arrived, then the longest drought by any American League team, and they finished in sixth place in 1947. In rebuilding from top to bottom, a fortysomething Satchel Paige—whom Veeck projected as a spot starter and reliever—was not the answer. Veeck knew exactly what he'd be in for if he had made Satch the first Negro in the AL. That, he later said, "would be giving the Old Guard a chance to muddy up the waters by charging that my interest in Negro players was entirely promotional and mercenary."

This, of course, was not much of an explanation for Satch; from where he sat, he was owed, and when Veeck signed Larry Doby, Satch—aware of the feelers made to Saperstein—impatiently sent Veeck a Western Union telegram reading: IS IT TIME FOR ME TO COME?

Veeck immediately wired him back, with the philosophical words ALL THINGS IN DUE TIME.

The problem was, Satch didn't know if he had any time left to wait. Again, the realist in him understood the situation. "When 1948 come around," he told *Collier's* a few years later, "and I still got my nose to the window, I realized what the club owners was thinkin'. They was thinkin' that when I was with Chattanooga, Larry Doby wasn't bawn."

Worse, neither did the Negro leagues have much more quality time left. Nineteen forty-eight would write an end for good to the Negro National League—another event that Gus Greenlee would get to see, outliving by three years the house of matchsticks he built and then helped to torch. When, on July 12, 1953, Big Red followed Cum Posey and the NNL down the last dugout step, it was with not half the fanfare of Posey's grand finale; still, Greenlee would have his homage, albeit by accident, when the Crawford Grille that he left behind was later torn away and replaced by Pittsburgh's largest indoor sports arena. Gus would have wanted it that way.

As for the man who had rescued more Negro leagues than he cared to remember, Satchel Paige was still loosely tied to the Kansas City Monarchs—a team now suffering the distemper that would eventually strangulate the remaining life out of blackball. Playing now in a re-formed, ten-team Negro American League, the Monarchs could hardly get a game even in Kansas City. If allegiance to Jackie Robinson had made the Dodgers the "home team" for the fans back east, seeing Jackie on the road became the clear priority of fans anywhere near a National League city—and it was to St. Louis, to buy tickets at Sportsman's Park, that J. L. Wilkinson's nest of fans made their way.

Faced with dwindling houses, the aging Wilkie would only be

able to hold out through the '48 season, and only by slashing his payroll in half. He was not alone; that summer would pass with time marked by carillon bells, as these would be the last months not only for the NNL but for the presence of Wilkinson, Abe and Effa Manley, and Sonnyman Jackson on the blackball scene.

Despite the decline of the Negro leagues, barnstorming in the sticks was still a profitable gig for Satch. But he now sensed how tenuous a line he was walking. With big league integration a fact, the context of segregated ball was now chipped off of the big league block. Being an outcast had no heroic sheen anymore; it was now only a mark of failure. More than ever, it was imperative that he do the majors.

As it happened, his luck was as charmed as ever. At this very moment in history, he was getting the cooperation of the only possible vehicle for his advancement: Bill Veeck's Cleveland Indians. After the first three months of the '48 season, the Tribe was in a battle for first place, they had already pulled over a million in attendance, and they needed another arm in preparation for the coming stretch run. In Veeck's mind's eye, now that he didn't need Satchel Paige to sell tickets, it was all right to sell tickets with him.

But first, Veeck had to sell the idea to his team's strong-willed player-manager, Lou Boudreau. When Veeck approached him about signing Paige, Boudreau was unequivocally against it. At thirty-one, baseball's "Boy Wonder"—who was leading the league hitting close to .400 at the time—simply could not buy the premise that an old goat who'd never faced big league hitters for real, or even knew who they were, would be able to get them out now. Even if he could, risking a pennant in order to find out seemed like rubber-room thinking to Boudreau.

Veeck was not about to overrule his manager. Only the year before, he had ordered Boudreau to overwork Bob Feller so that Feller could break the strikeout record, a move that resulted in more arm problems for Feller. So Veeck didn't pull rank; he pulled a Bill Veeck. On July 7, he brought Satch to Cleveland in secret and then told Boudreau he had a "young pitcher" for him to see.

When Boudreau got to Municipal Stadium, he knew he'd been had. Entering the clubhouse, he saw Veeck, Indians vice president Hank Greenberg, Abe Saperstein, and the *Cleveland Plain Dealer's* baseball writer Gordon Cobbledick standing around an ectomorphic black man sitting naked on a stool. Boudreau knew of only one man who could be that skinny and still be a Bill Veeck prospect.

"I looked at this guy, who was built like a pencil, sitting there,"

Boudreau remembered, "and I recognized him right away—there's only one ballplayer in the world who looked like that. And I knew right away that Bill wasn't gonna let him get away until I had a look at him."

Satch, who was a little stiff from the plane ride in from Kansas City that morning, needed to get loose. After he dressed and came onto the field, he took a few jogging strides, then stopped.

"Mistah Lou," he said, his deadpan in place, "this here park is too big to run around. I pitch with my arm, not my feet."

Boudreau, who was experiencing one of the strangest moments in his Hall of Fame career, still wasn't sure that this wasn't some kind of a joke being played on him. When Veeck told him to catch Paige, he shrugged, slid on a catcher's mitt, and squatted behind the plate. For fifteen minutes, Satch threw baseballs easily and at medium speed, and Boudreau barely had to move his glove to get the pocket around all of them.

For Veeck, watching this scene was more than strange; it was damn near *unthinkable* that Satch, one day after his forty-second birthday—and Veeck thought he was at least six years older—had to audition, and almost demeaning that he had to do so for a white man so much younger. "As ridiculous as it was for Satchel Paige to be on trial," Veeck said later, "that was precisely the situation."

Satch may have been amused by the irony, but even his Confucius-like outer layer was buckling a bit under the pressure that Veeck—who obviously was making this tryout a test of his own acumen—was laying on him. Just before he began to throw, Veeck impressed upon Satch that it was "important to me" that he do well, given that "I've been telling everybody for years that you're the greatest pitcher in baseball." Satch loved to hear that kind of talk, but didn't need to hear it just now.

Momentarily, Satch owned up to feeling the heat. "Man," he told Veeck, "I ain't ready for this." But, as always, gripping a baseball by its seams was his tonic. With his pitches popping straight and true into Boudreau's mitt, it became just another home plate he had to cover. Climbing into the role of Satch now, his brain culling old riffs, he could have been back in Chattanooga again, looking for bottles to knock down. Telling Boudreau to wait, he stopped throwing and pulled a handkerchief from his back pocket. Then he walked his stooped, old man walk and laid it over the middle six inches of the plate.

This was Satchel Paige's plate within the plate, and when he got back on the hill, he had *it* covered as well. "He put nine of the next ten pitches over that handkerchief," Boudreau recalled. "Then he asked me to move it to the outside of the plate and threw sliders and a change-up right over the thing. It was amazing."

It was also routine Satchel Paige in clover. But what clinched it for him was when Boudreau grabbed a bat and stood in against him. Satch, sizing up the league's best hitter by his knees, and by his stance, gave him the full treatment: fast, slow, and in between, for twenty pitches. As Veeck once related, "Nineteen of them were strikes and [Lou] had nothing that looked like a base hit."

Now Lou Boudreau had seen enough. Walking off the field with Veeck, he said, "Don't let him get away, Will. We can use him."

On that July 7, Satch put his marker on his first major league contract, thus becoming the first Negro pitcher in the American League and the seventh Negro big leaguer overall, just months behind Roy Campanella's debut with the Dodgers.

Veeck could not have been more generous with Satch, paying him his accustomed $40,000 salary now for just three months' work; Abe Saperstein made out like a bandit by collecting a $25,000 finder's fee—a $10,000 bonus on signing and $5,000 for each of Satch's three months. But there was a doleful postscript: for relinquishing a man who was reputed to be the greatest pitcher in all the world's history, the Negro leagues again got the shaft.

Years later, when Bill Veeck took a slap at Branch Rickey by noting in *Veeck . . . As in Wreck* that "for anyone to take advantage of [Negro league club owners], particularly while talking about equal rights, was terribly unfair," Tom Baird would have agreed, and noted Veeck as an example. For Paige, Baird received less from Veeck than the Manleys had for the obscure Larry Doby—just $5,000, and that only after Satch had implored Veeck to do right by the Monarchs.

Far more concerned with his own world, Veeck felt he was on safe ground in signing Satch. But even in his own city, one with a large black population, the white press whose support Veeck needed was divided. While Gordon Cobbledick and Ed McAuley of the *Plain Dealer* gave Paige vivid, affirmative coverage, sports editor Franklin Lewis of the larger *Cleveland News*—which owed its allegiance and page count to a huge amount of advertising from white businesses in the city—held his reporters in check, downplaying the story. As Veeck geared up a PR offensive, dispensing a flood of Satchel Paige data to newspapers and wire services around the nation—cementing this as one of the biggest sports stories of the year—the July 8 *News* carried a Lewis column calling the flaunting of Paige "crude," befitting two men who were vulgarians rather than sportsmen.

But it was an editorial in the July 14 *Sporting News* that stunned and sickened Veeck. Without waiting to see if Satch was big league stuff, the weekly's hoary editor J. G. Taylor Spink was adamant that Veeck had surely sullied the dignity of the game. Spink, perhaps professing too much his paper's alleged commitment to baseball's integration—most readers could easily recall its protracted support of segregation in the game—began the editorial in a stew.

"Many well-wishers of baseball emphatically fail to see eye to eye with . . . the signing of Satchel Paige, superannuated Negro pitcher, by Bill Veeck, publicity minded head of the Cleveland Indians, to 'save the pennant' for the Tribe," he wrote. While Spink allowed that "no man should set himself up against the achievement of another man's chances for life, be that other man Negro or white, Chinese or Indian," he asserted that "any criticism by this publication of the addition of Paige to the pennant-seeking forces of the Cleveland club obviously is not based on Paige's color."

All the same, Spink's censure of Veeck for applying reverse racism in "demeaning the standards of baseball in the big circuits" was a decidedly ugly "criticism," as was his indictment of American League president Will Harridge, who, he sniffed, "would have been well within his rights if he had refused to approve the Paige contract."

For Veeck, this was most puzzling in view of Spink's past support for his ringmaster tendencies as being good for the game. But Veeck had not invited a black act into the ring before, and he was disturbed by Spink's flawed racial dialectic: "If Satch were white, of course," Veeck later rejoined, "he would have been in the majors twenty-five years earlier and the question would not have been before the house."

Nor was Spink moved by the jubilation of the black press, which more than understood the big picture. In response to the editorial, Wendell Smith directed an open letter to Spink in his July 24 *Courier* column. Describing the Paige signing as "a beautiful gesture," Smith—who in leading the Cum Posey–inspired press uprising against Paige in 1938 had taken him to task for hanging on at age thirty-two—now drew parallel lines around Paige, Ty Cobb, and Cy Young, all of whom played well into their forties.

"A venerable halo adorned their persons as, heroically, they approached the golden sunsets of glorious voyages," Smith emoted. "Unlike you or I or the common run of humans, they are immortals."

For J. G. Taylor Spink and others, though, one rub was that if Satch wore such a halo, Bill Veeck must have bought it for him in a five-and-dime store. Indeed, much of Paige's life from here on in would be refracted through the filter of Veeck's plebeian-centered tastes. Lost now to many would be Satchel Paige's own luminescence, the one that extended over decades, continents, and epochs.

This context—that Satch, all by himself, had earned his big league reward—was the crux of Tom Meany's *New York Star* column reminding baseball fans that Satch's signing was in many ways more significant and certainly more gratifying than was Jackie Robinson's. Meany's remarks were picked up and run in *The Sporting News* itself, as if in the interests of equal time, one week after Spink had his say. But by then, Satch's heroism was already being compromised at the expense of his dignity.

The carnivalizing of Satchel Paige had begun.

16

This Fabulous Character

One of my own unfulfilled ambitions is to start a game with an entire team of midgets and let them go a couple of times around the batting order, walking endlessly. Another of my unfulfilled ambitions is to pitch Satchel Paige against that same team of midgets. Satch, I think, is the only pitcher alive who could get the ball consistently into that tiny strike zone.

—Bill Veeck,
Veeck . . . As in Wreck

I couldn't afford to lose money pitchin' for nobody but Bill Veeck. With Burrhead, I didn't feel it so much.

—Satchel Paige,
in *Collier's*, June 13, 1953

When the Indians players got word that Satch was now a teammate, they, like the white press in the matter of Jackie Robinson, turned to Bob Feller for clues about another enigmatic black man. What they were told did not overly impress them, and for reasons that had nothing to do with race or even ability.

Feller apparently spoke in a very different way about his relationship with Satch out on the barnstorming circuit than he did in those succinct but sanguine terms years on. It appeared that, under the facade of mutual gain and respect, there had been some bad feelings between the two great pitchers that came close to cracking the union at times. Indeed, they may have come to swords' ends after Chet Brewer combed through the Feller All-Stars' allegedly juggled account books.

If Feller held a grudge against Brewer over the issue of money, he might have abided a larger one against Satch over the same issue. Even as Feller and Paige were posing for smiling pictures together in Indians uniforms, Steve Gromek, one of the Tribe's pitchers, thought he could see a tensing of Feller's cheek muscle.

"I knew they weren't close, and that it went back to when they went out on tour in forty-six," Gromek said. "The story I heard was that Satch signed a contract with Feller, then he realized how many people they were drawin' and he wanted to get more money.

"'Cause they were packin' 'em in. Oh my God, Feller made a lotta money and bought a ranch in Texas with that money. And Satch, he may have been getting a piece of the gate, but he knew he wasn't getting enough to buy a ranch. So he told Feller, 'Well, I'm not gonna show up.' And Feller said, 'If you don't, you'll never play another game of baseball, I'll see to it. 'Cause you signed a contract.' "

If Feller's version of events was to be believed—and this rendering for his Indians teammates seems at least contrived to make Satch's well-known avarice and lack of responsibility the issue, not those account books—then it is possible Satch was close to ducking out on the tour just as he had the Negro World Series. In the Feller version, as retold by Gromek, "Bob thought he was bluffing" and refused to cater to Satch's extortion; in the end, it was Satch who caved in and the tour went forward without turbulence.

Whoever had the details right, it was clear that the whole incident was not forgotten, though Feller and the other Indians kept any bad blood far beneath the surface so that the club could enter the age of integration painlessly. This whitewashing was priority one for Bill Veeck, who knew that Satch was no saint but intended to turn him into one now that he had gone out on a limb to liberate him from the plantation.

In Veeck's heavily managed press campaign, friendly sportswriters would look the other way if Satch showed vulgar tastes and vile habits. There were two ways to go with Satchel Paige: one, laugh; two, laugh harder.

To obey had rewards. When the *News*'s Hal Lebovitz began to broaden that paper's coverage of Paige, it won him the rights to co-author Satch's first "book," which was really a first-person expansion of Lebovitz's folksy newspaper articles patched into a pamphlet-sized soft cover titled *Pitchin' Man.*

In coveting Satch, and riding him hard now, Veeck could not have been accused of simple and tasteful emancipation. While shunning the grandstanding liberalism of Branch Rickey, Veeck did own up to exploiting the race card in ways that were commercially crass. Once recalling his plan to unilaterally integrate the Phillies, he noted the suspicions that "it was only because, showman that I am—promoter, con man, knave—I was grabbing for the quick and easy publicity." Said Veeck: "I am not going to suggest that I was innocent on [that] count."

Satch hardly needed help from Veeck in drumming up interest. With the Indians on a homestand at the time, for the first few games in which Paige wore his new uniform a palpable sense of anticipation ran through the crowds inside Municipal Stadium. Lou Boudreau, who had wanted to avoid just that kind of distraction, knew he had to get Paige in at the first feasible opportunity.

That opening came on the afternoon of July 9. With the Tribe down 4–1 to the St. Louis Browns, Boudreau pinch-hit for starter Bob Lemon in the bottom of the fourth inning and needed some long relief. After the last out of the inning, 37,840 heads turned to the Indians bullpen behind the center field wall.

For the last ten minutes, Satch had been warming up out there, and when the fans became aware of it, more and more noise began to build. Now, when the bullpen gate swung open, out came Satch, attired in a baggy flannel uniform.

In the bright sunlight of that Friday afternoon, Satchel Paige at long last stepped out of the shadows for all of baseball to behold. As it had taken him a while to get here, he did not let the moment pass fleetingly. Once on the field, each stride of those skinny legs and massive feet taunted the world he had now entered for its gross stupidity—now *they* were going to wait for *him*, and think about the shame of all those years when he could have been there.

Walking across the manicured outfield grass, his gait was slow . . . excruciatingly . . . s-l-o-w, and in this water torture of an entry, the noise in that gaping concrete basin of a stadium became a concussion of sound. As cool a hepcat as Satch was, the electric current in the air and the ear-splitting din still churned the contents of his high-strung stomach.

"I wasn't nervous exactly, but I was as close to that feelin' as I could be," he acknowledged in *Pitchin' Man.* "I never had a feelin' like it before." But beyond the obvious elements of white guilt and catharsis inherent in this outpouring of emotion, Satch could identify another element that he also had not felt before.

"I knew all those folks in the stands were studying me. I don't mind that. Folks been eyeing me all my life," he said. "But these folks were different. I could feel it. They were sort of like people at a circus. They were asking themselves, 'Can that old man really pitch?' "

Right away, then, Satch recognized that the nature of his big league existence was going to be a far piece from the august and sanctified tone of Jackie Robinson's. This *was* a circus, which was okay by him; pitchin' was pitchin'. Only, as he figured it, Jackie was gettin' a break over on the serious side. Jackie need only be good, not a hoot. This was why Satch described his debut in the big top as "a kind of a heavy pressure. I had been in many serious spots before, but this was most serious. Those flash bulbs popping all about me told me that."

As Satch began to take his warmup pitches on the mound, home plate umpire Bill McGowan broke convention and allowed not just the usual one or two photographers to come onto the field but a mob of them to capture the moment. With the incredible noise swimming in his ears and the flashbulbs stabbing his eyes, Satch never did hear the historic if slightly confused announcement that came over the public address system: "Now pitching for the Indians . . . *Satchel Leroy Paige!*"

When he met Satch on the mound and handed him the ball, Boudreau told him to "pitch loose like you always do." But with so many things going on in his head, that was impossible. As it was, the first pitch was almost impossible. The first time he tried, Satch looked in for the sign from catcher Jim Hegan while standing behind the rubber, just as he always had. Immediately, McGowan called time and instructed him to take the sign *on* the rubber, in big league fashion.

But the signs, too, were a problem. Although Satch hadn't told Boudreau, he wasn't fully schooled on the Indians' signals yet. Still, even though he didn't know what Hegan was calling, he knew he couldn't shake off signals in his first game lest he look arrogant. And so, facing his first few hitters, he didn't cut loose for fear that he'd cross up Hegan and hammer a fastball into his face mask.

The first hitter was Chuck Stevens, and Satch came out of his double windup and huge leg-kick delivery with no zip on the ball.

Stevens lined a clean hit to left field. But then, after Gerry Priddy bunted Stevens to second, he did the Satch thing against Whitey Platt: one overhanded serve for a strike, one sidearm for another strike.

Now came the hoot, as the major leagues met the Hesitation Pitch. Holding back his right arm even as his front leg brought his body forward, when he released the ball he had the crowd in a frenzy and Whitey Platt in a funk. Trying to hold back *his* body, Platt couldn't keep from lunging at the illusion of a pitch. When Platt swung and missed the actual pitch, his bat flew forty feet up the third base line. It was still rolling when Browns manager Zack Taylor bolted from the dugout to talk to Bill McGowan about this screwy pitch, which Taylor said had to be a balk.

McGowan, who was probably a little stunned himself, found himself in much the same position as the umpire who had to rule on Paige's pitch that cut through the strands of a House of David hitter's beard. Not really knowing what to call, McGowan let the strikeout stand, leaving Will Harridge to deal with it later.

His calling card—the joker—on the table, Satch then put away Al Zarilla on a fly ball and came off the field to a rousing ovation. In the top of the sixth, he gave up another leadoff hit, but with Hegan having switched to using basic signals that Satch could read, he erased the side on a double play and a pop fly.

Then he was gone, pinch-hit for, with a certain symmetry, by Larry Doby. His two impressive innings became the subject of the headlines and the buzz of the town the next day; for Satch and Bill Veeck, it was the real opening whistle of the Paige circus.

"I used my single windup, my double windup, my triple windup, my hesitation windup and my no windup," an elated Satch discoursed with gusto for reporters after the game. "I used my step-n-pitch-it"—a take-off on Stepin Fetchit, even now—"my sidearm throw and my bat dodger."

The white press was about to swoon before this daffy romance language of Satchel Paige. Though the game's traditionalists were none too pleased about it, the major establishment press organs were already crackling with upcoming pieces about him. Indeed, with even more symmetry, *Time* and *Life*—the same periodicals that had broken Paige to the white world back in 1941—came out with happy-ending reporting on his big league entrance; *Time*'s SATCHEL THE GREAT take ran on July 19, *Life*'s pictorial "SATCH" MAKES THE MAJORS (subtitle: "The Middle-aged and

Fabulous Leroy Paige Starts Work for Cleveland") one week later.

While *Life* persisted in calling him "Satchelfoots," this was far more restrained coverage after seven years of man's progress—and yet *Life*'s choice of a lead photo may have been a regression of sorts; no more the icon of Harlem's smart set, he was shown sitting on his stool, covered only by a towel, a large gold medallion around his neck and a straw hat pushed back on his head, and strumming a huge guitar—a more generic, middle-American clown.

What's more, by the time these new huzzahs of legitimacy ran in Henry Luce's dynastic magazines, Satch had appeared in several more games, pitching extraordinarily well in relief. The first, a charity exhibition against the Dodgers on July 14, brought together half of the big leagues' quota of blacks—Paige, Doby, Robinson, and Campanella. With a raucous crowd of near 65,000 in Municipal Stadium, it was estimated that one out of every six blacks in Cleveland came to see that benchmark game, in which Satch set down the side in the seventh and eighth innings, striking out all three hitters in the seventh on just twelve pitches.

He showed his old resilience the very next night in Philadelphia's Shibe Park, which was sold out on the chance that he might pitch at some time during a twi-night doubleheader with the Athletics. When he did, it was merely with the bases loaded and a 5–3 lead on the line in the sixth inning of the nightcap. Stoking the same torturously slow buildup of emotions when he ambled in, he quickly got Eddie Joost to fly out. However, after retiring the first two Athletics in the seventh, he was given a big league lashing when Ferris Fain doubled high off the right field wall and Hank Majeski crashed a not-very fastball over the left field grandstand to tie the game.

These kinds of lightning-bolt setbacks always woke him up in the Negro leagues and did so now. From that point on, Satch's dumbfounding array of windups, deliveries, and speeds kept the hitters swinging under his rising pitches. Giving up just one hit, he got five of the last six outs on fly balls; the other was a strikeout. When Larry Doby and Ken Keltner hit homers in the ninth to post an 8–5 lead, Satchel Paige walked off as a major league winner for the first time and the Tribe had a two-and-a-half-game lead in the American League standings.

That he was in fact a real pitcher with a distinctly surreal bent was underscored by his July 19 outing against Clark Griffith's Senators at the Washington ballpark Satch knew so well. He was again called in at pressure time, with the game deadlocked 6–6 in the top of the eighth.

In trouble right away, he gave up a hit to Bud Stewart, who was sacrificed to second and, an out later, went to third on a wild pitch. Now controversy erupted as it only could have with Satch on the mound. Going to the still unresolved Hesitation Pitch while facing Al Evans, he did a doublewhammy hesitation, first bringing his hands together over his head for several seconds and then stopping in mid-delivery. Evans managed to get just enough bat on the ball to loft a fly ball for the third out.

Although Satch pitched superbly into the tenth, the Indians pushed over the winning run an inning too late for him to get the decision. Even so, he was the cause célèbre once it ended. The Senators filed a protest with the league over that befuddling Hesitation Pitch—which, had it been ruled a balk, would have brought the winner home for the Senators in that eighth inning.

The problem for Will Harridge was that the umpires were still as perplexed by the pitch as the hitters. According to the July 28 *Sporting News*, Cal Hubbard, the third base ump that night in Washington, had made the "tacit admission" that Paige had balked, but had deferred to home plate ump Al Papparella, who made no call. When Harridge pored over the rule books, he could find nothing close to covering it. But still Harridge—no doubt repelled by the thought of the national pastime gone to the clowns if other pitchers began copycatting Paige—ruled that any future use of the pitch with men on base would be considered a balk.

This seemed like a logical ruling, and while Veeck and Paige believed it to be patently unfair, for Satch it was flattering in a way, and it allowed him to indulge in some big league preening. "I guess Mr. Harridge didn't want me to show up those boys who were young enough to be my sons," was his one-liner.

That, of course, had become the overall theme of Paige's newest saga, and even shorn of the Hesitation Pitch it ascended to ever higher levels. Making his first big league appearance in Yankee Stadium on July 21, he came on in the sixth inning and promptly struck out Tommy Henrich, threw out Yogi Berra on a grounder to the mound, and got old "pal" Joe DiMaggio on a fly out. The next day, brought in after DiMaggio drove out Feller with a grand slam, he threw two more shutout innings, highlighted by his strikeout of Joe D.

He did run into trouble his next two games, in Boston against a

Red Sox club that had won eighteen of its last twenty games, when he was tormented by a different DiMaggio, Joe's younger brother, Dominic. The lower-case DiMaggio had a homer to break open the first game, and a double and a walk to help turn a 7–6 Tribe lead in the second game into an 8–7 Bosox win. Still, two misplays in the outfield in the latter game were really what hung Paige with his first defeat. And even with three runs he yielded in those seven innings of work, his six other stints out of the pen up until then yielded one run in eleven innings.

By the end of July, Lou Boudreau had come full circle. On the night of August 3, with the Indians sitting a game behind the Athletics in the standings, Boudreau finally started Satch against the Senators in Cleveland.

All during that afternoon, fans stood in long lines outside Municipal Stadium buying tickets, and when Satch strolled to the mound there were 72,562 people in the place—a new attendance record for a major league night game. Not wholly at ease, he walked two of the first three hitters, then gave up a triple to Bud Stewart to fall behind 2–0. But, finding his groove, he got eight men in a row, and by the time he came out after seven innings, he led 4–3. The Indians held it for him, delivering his second victory.

Alternating now as the number five starter with Steve Gromek, Satch was slated to go against the last-place White Sox on August 13 at another lair he knew like a glove, Comiskey Park. For this game, it seemed that all of Chicago wanted in. While the crowd was announced as 51,013, a night attendance record there, many thousands more stormed the turnstiles and crashed into the park, overwhelming the few dozen ticket-takers.

Recalling this scene years later, Bill Veeck said that he was "nearly torn apart in the swirling mob" when he entered the stadium. "There was not a place in the park that was not covered by human, sweating flesh. People were jammed there, shoulder to shoulder, with nothing to look at except hot dog stands and each other."

Satch, who was familiar with Comiskey Park mob scenes from his East-West Game appearances, was wired up from the first pitch. Though he struck out only one man all day, his pitches spluttered out of every conceivable kind of delivery—and seemingly out of the heavens, as four times he threw a Rip Sewell–type, "Ephus Pitch" blooper—and ended their flight on the fringe corners of the plate. Using what the *Plain Dealer*'s Ed McAuley described as an "arm-cranking style that went out with the electric automobile,"

Satch may have had the White Sox counting the revolutions of his windup instead of concentrating on the pitch. Walking not one man, he would later say the ball on that day "was flowing out of my hand just like it was some water." Scattering five singles in a tidy 5–0 shutout, he rousted the assumption that nine innings of pitching were now beyond his capabilities.

As these last two victories had moved the Tribe into a first-place tie each time, Satch had become more than a reliable pitcher; he was arguably the best pitcher on a staff that would count two twenty-game winners and a nineteen-game winner by season's end. And if this seemed unfathomable, for Satch it was, too—unfathomable that these big league hitters were making it so easy for him.

After the sheer carnality of the Negro leagues, the big league game seemed almost genteel to him. Whereas for all his years in blackball they had exploited his inability to field a bunt, these guys were too obsessed with the long ball to try it. "That was like cool water to me," Paige once said.

Despite Satch's success during his first weeks in Cleveland, many of the Indians players could not understand where all of those shutout innings came from.

"I mean, I didn't think he was that great a pitcher," said Steve Gromek. "I knew he *was* great, but when we got him he wasn't the guy he used to be. He had good control and he used a lot of deception and he could trick people with his windups and his hesitations and all like that. But he never ran to stay in shape and he was skinny as a rail. Old as he was, I was just amazed they didn't bunt on him more."

Satch harbored no illusions that the level of talent in the Negro leagues had been all that terrific. Still, the style of play in the leagues had undeniably prepared him to face any circumstance.

"Y'see, the way we had to learn to play, the things we had to go through, made us all better ballplayers," Gene Benson said. "Like in those games we played against the big leaguers. We didn't have to worry about gettin' thrown at and knocked on our asses. We could stand up and face the pitcher and not have to worry 'bout duckin' and divin'.

"And Satchel, he didn't have to worry about them guys up there runnin' all 'round the basepaths. He could just go through all the motions he wanted, throw whatever pitch he wanted to, not lay in the fastball. Couldn't have been easier."

Satch would later say this to author Donn Rogosin: "The thing I don't understand is, if one of my players [in the Negro leagues] made a mistake, the manager would tell him how he got beat. But when I got to the majors, it wasn't nothing like that."

As the *noble laureate* of the Negro leagues as well, Satch had now become the divining rod by which to compare the black and white baseball worlds. As more black players got their call, it had to be comforting to them that Satchel Paige had already bridged the gap between those worlds. What made it all the more comforting was that, for a time, he was on top of the white world.

His peak altitude was reached on August 20, 1948. Starting against the White Sox again, in Cleveland this time, on that night he was surrounded by a confluence of swelling tides. There was, first of all, the sizzling-hot pennant race. But there was also the Indians' pitching staff, which was a rolling fireball in itself—coming into this game, Bob Lemon, Gene Bearden, and Sam Zoldak had thrown shutouts to run up a thirty-inning scoreless streak, eleven shy of the big league record.

And, of course, there was Satch, who had drawn—by a conservative count—201,829 people in his last three starts. With this game a quick sellout-plus, Veeck could only imagine what the numbers would be now. When Satch walked to the mound, they were still streaming in, and would continue to until the count stopped at 78,382, a full 6,000 more than when Satch last broke the night game attendance record.

If the diamond head of this crest of fateful forces was to be Satch, if there was a karmic debt left up there on a pedestal for him to cash in, he was more than ready. This night game was Satchel Paige's twinkling in the sun. Locked with the Chisox's Bill Wight for four scoreless innings, fate indeed had much to say when, in the bottom of the fifth, Larry Doby—who always seemed to play particularly well when Paige was on the hill—lined a hit to drive home Lou Boudreau with the game's first run and then preserved that lead by making two game-saving catches in center field.

The league's first black player having literally gone to the wall for the league's first *commemorated* black player, the last five innings raced by as though nothing else needed to be said. Fanning five, walking just one, permitting two singles and a double, Satch was in and out in an hour and fifty minutes of tightly controlled brilliance. When he walked off with his second straight three-hit shutout, a good deal more than one overstuffed ballpark in Cleveland stood and applauded for Satchel Paige.

"That was the game I thought was the biggest in my career. And that covers a lot of ground," he would write in his memoirs.

•   •   •

A week before this magnum opus, the *News*'s Ed Bang had written in his column that, given Satch's other great outings, it had become clear that J. G. Taylor Spink "went off the deep end" in his objections to the Paige signing, and called for Spink to offer a public apology. Now, with the whole country abuzz with Satchel Paige talk—his record was 5-and-1, his ERA a remarkable 1.33—Bill Veeck went Ed Bang one better. He giddily sent a harpoon on its way to the St. Louis offices of Spink's *Sporting News*, in the form of a cheeky telegram that read:

PAIGE PITCHING—NO RUNS, THREE HITS. DEFINITELY IN LINE FOR
THE SPORTING NEWS ROOKIE OF THE YEAR AWARD. REGARDS, BILL
VEECK.

By the time Spink could respond to this snickering attack on his credibility, he had the benefit of seeing the results of Paige's next start against the Red Sox, in the opener of a three-game series at Fenway Park on August 24. Lou Boudreau—possibly believing too much in Satch—elected to move him up ahead of Steve Gromek in the rotation and pitch him on three days' rest against the best hitting team in the league in a battle for first place.

Clearly, this was asking for an awful lot, and Boudreau needn't have. His staff, its rotation unaltered, had set the shutout-inning record after Bob Lemon had notched eight more the night after Paige's three-hitter, bringing its total to forty-seven. But this time, fate couldn't compensate for raw and tired body tissue.

Although lines of people had formed outside Fenway at daybreak hoping to buy tickets to see Satch, and several thousand more were turned away, he was not around for long, as he was yet again snakebit by his new nemesis, Dom DiMaggio. Up 3–1 beginning the third inning, an errant fastball hit pitcher Joe Dobson on the arm. DiMaggio then lined a triple into the right-center-field gap and scored on Johnny Pesky's sacrifice fly.

Satch's keen wits were no match for sharp batting eyes, and when Ted Williams and Vern Stephens cracked hard base hits, Boudreau had to come over and yank him—replacing him with Gromek, who got out of the inning, though the Bosox eventually won the game 9–8 in the ninth on Stephens's two-run homer off reliever Russ Christopher.

Paige's failure in this big game seemed to be manna for J. G. Taylor Spink. In his humorless editorial reply to Veeck's snarky wire in the September 1 *Sporting News*, Spink wrote that his paper "would make no change in its original editorial except to express its admiration for any pitcher—white or colored—who at Paige's age can gain credit for five victories over . . . six weeks in any league, major or minor. But it cannot express any admiration for the present-day standard of major league ball that makes such a showing possible."

Spink could now point out that Paige had excelled primarily against the White Sox—"and even Chicago sportswriters have occasionally expressed doubt as to whether the Hose merits the rating of a big league club"—and not against the "hard hitting" Red Sox. Saying nothing of Paige's fine work against the contending Yankees and Browns, Spink wondered whether Satch's "early successes" were due to "his sterling pitching abilities or to the fact that some major league clubs still have a considerable distance to go before they attain prewar standards."

Just so no one missed the point, the editorial was bordered by two sidebar items. One was headlined "Three of Five Paige Wins Over 2nd Division Teams." The other carried the head: "Red Sockers Send Satchel Packing," under which it was snidely reported that Satch had not seen the end of the game because "he had gone to the hotel to get some much needed sleep."

By coincidence, it was also on September 1 that the AP moved a story quoting two American League umpires on the topic of Paige's skills, and their unusually effusive praise seemed to effectively rebut Spink's latest putdown. One, Bill Summers, said, "There are few better pitchers in baseball today" than Paige, that from what he'd seen, Satch's slider "cracked like a whip," his curve "exploded," and that "he was plenty fast."

The other ump, Art Pasarella, said, "There's a rocking chair if ever there was one. The old boy's around the plate all the time. . . . I was behind the plate for that shutout he worked in Chicago and I never had an easier game in my life."

And, once again, Bill Veeck would be able to poke a drafty hole in Spink's key argument, since Spink had originally invoked the criteria of major league "standards" to *enjoin* Paige. Using them now to diminish Paige's success meant, Veeck later wrote, "that Satch wasn't demeaning the standards of baseball as much as the standards of baseball were demeaning Satch."

To the national baseball audience, however, such debates were immaterial, as the major element of the Satchel Paige craze wasn't his pitching as much as the persona that *The Sporting News* had identified in another item about that Boston game. Because the crowd at Fenway Park had included few blacks, the piece reported that "the white folks had come out to see this fabulous character— and they cheered him as loudly when he was knocked from the box as when he was introduced."

This was what Veeck wanted him to be: a "fabulous character," adored by his new white audience. It was apparent that the influx of black players would only marginally alter the overall racial com- position of the crowds—*both* races came out in higher numbers— in this white man's game. And Veeck could breathe easy that in no way would Satchel Paige, a man who was naming pitches after Stepin Fetchit in 1948, be made to serve his time as a political icon—or even one concerned much at all with the changing role of black people.

Veeck may have believed he was being complimentary when he wrote in his autobiography that Paige "never appeared to be inter- ested in fighting battles, changing social patterns or winning ac- ceptance beyond what seems to come to him naturally as a legendary American folk hero." But it was because this was true that the coming age of black players ignored and even resented him, for what he represented.

What's more, even Satch had a little trouble digesting the way he was being marketed. For instance, the ongoing "Satchelfoots" ref- erences, with its connotation of elephantine physical deformity, moved him to complain at length to the *News*'s Hal Lebovitz:

"I don't like it, I don't want it, and I don't care who knows it. . . . My feet have nothing to do with my [nickname]. The sports writers claim my feet are anywhere from size 13s to size 16s. They ain't. My feet are size 11s. Triple A. Maybe 'cause they're so shal- low they seem so long. It's funny. When folks get the impression a fellow's got big feet, soon the feet begin to look big.

"If I had big feet the kids woulda called me 'Gunboats' or 'Canalboats' but they didn't. They just labeled me 'Satchel.' Not 'Satchelfoot' either."

As well, Satch needed no instructions in blackness from anyone. Having once gotten off on being able to choose the lodging of his choice in Jim Crow America, he didn't care whom it offended that he exercised the same option in reverse now to live in a hotel on the black side of Cleveland. The thought simply never occurred to Satch that he should have to step away from his blackball lifestyle. On the road, avoiding his new team between games, he would in- stead meet up with old buddies—whom he had in every town—and keep to the old haunts.

"We used to get into a town and have a bus waiting to take us to the hotel," recalled Lou Boudreau. "Satch always had somebody there in a big shining Cadillac. You'd see those white teeth in the back seat as the Cadillac whizzed by us."

Furthermore, unlike Jackie Robinson, he had an easy humor about racial matters, which acted to deflate the uptight defenses of others. On one team train ride, Satch approached a claque of card-playing teammates and waited around to be invited into the game. Finally, after a long, uncomfortable silence, he said in a loud and self-mocking screech, "Did sumbudy ring fo' da portah?" And only Satch could in good humor turn around a pejorative in order to snuff it—such as nicknaming Veeck "Burrhead" for his sprigs of kinky blond hair.

Seeing how cheerfully diffident Satch was about race etiquette, Veeck was struck by the universe of difference between his two Negro players. To accommodate the young and insecure Larry Doby, Veeck had moved the Indians' spring training site from Florida to Tucson, Arizona, that season. But while Doby went out of his way to avoid provoking incidents—if the man ahead of him hit a home run, he would wait to shake hands until both were out of sight in the dugout—he encountered so much verbal abuse on a swing through Texas that he retreated into an uptight aloofness.

Doby, too, stayed in the company of other blacks, but only because Veeck feared he might crack up otherwise. But if Doby was withdrawn, his isolation only caused his competitive fire to burn crimson hot. When racism was thrown into the burner, or when his abilities were questioned, his bat turned molten. Seeming to terminate every budding slump with a hot streak, Doby hit just .156 in a cup-of-coffee rookie year in 1947, but with his big league career at stake, rebounded big to hit .301 in 1948 and went on to a productive thirteen-year major league career with the Indians and White Sox; he also managed the Chisox for Veeck in 1978, though he would also run a foul of the law when he left the game.

It was truly absurd that according to the conventional wisdom of 1948, Doby owed his maturation to the presence of Paige. It was true that Satch did run interference for him on the racial battlefront, diverting attention away from him and allowing Doby to carry on in his quiet fury without incident. But all Doby really needed was time—and, as far as their relationship went, Larry would have wished Satch to be as far away from him as possible.

"Larry roomed with Satch for a while," Steve Gromek recalled, "but Satch used to carry a gun with him. He said he needed it for protection, and Doby didn't wanna be in there with him. Larry said, 'Christ, one day maybe he'll come in and he's had a few too many and the first thing you know he'll pull out the gun and I'm gonna wind up dead!' "

For the masses, Paige and Doby maintained a congenial politically correct union, but it was never warm and it was sometimes strained. One day, they were on the field engaged in a running by-play of brackish humor that included some unmistakably sharp edges.

"You gotta act big league up here," Doby told him at one point. "None of that show-off crap you got away with on the exhibition circuit. You're in the majors now."

At another point, Satch was telling Doby about the early night games he'd played with the Monarchs. Doby speculated that the lights must have been pretty bad back then.

"No, they was pretty good," Satch insisted.

"Good for you," Doby said. "You're a pitcher. Man, I'm glad I never had to bat against you under those lights."

Satch squirted some tobacco juice through his teeth. "Wouldn't make no diff'rence, son. Day or night, good lights or bad lights, I strike you out every time."

As for the other Indians, most agreed that, as Gromek said, "You couldn't get close to Satch; he'd go his own way. Even on planes and trains, I don't think I was ever in his company. I mean, everyone liked him and appreciated him. But he just kept at a distance."

Although under the surface this alienation was causing some internal problems, by mid-August Paigeism in all its Veeckian glory was reaching a crescendo level. Typical was a *Boston Globe* column by Harold Kaese, which read:

Satchel Paige was around long enough to prove that the big leagues missed a great character as well as a great pitcher when they clung to the color line. . . . Asked what he thought of [teammate] Gene Bearden . . . Paige replied, "You mean that lefthanded white boy? That boy believes in hisself, and when you believes, man, you doos." . . .

One day he was dozing on Fenway Park's bullpen grass when Lou Boudreau summoned. Another day he was under the right field stands getting a brew. What was in the towel-covered pail he carried so carefully from the visiting dugout to the bullpen? Two bottles of beer. "Man, it gets hot out there." . . .

"Whatever his age, wherever his fast ball, Old Satch never lost control [of] himself. When he last pitched at Fenway Park, he said, "Ah may not be the bestest pitcher in the world, but ah sho' out-cutes 'em."

There were reams of newsprint mounting in this patronizing vein, fixated on such trivialities as Satch's huge steamer trunk, which by habit he continued to carry around for a time on road trips. "You've got to see it to believe it," wrote Hal Lebovitz in sheer wonderment. "It's three times larger than any other ballplayer's traveling bag. . . . We got a peek inside [it]. Satch carries seven (count 'em) natty summer suits . . . two dozen of the loudest ties ever created . . . an abundance of toiletries, silk underwear and sport shirts. In addition, he carries his own training equipment, a collapsible heat lamp and an electric massage machine. And he also collects guns [one] about a foot and a half long."

There was also, of course, the constant angle of his age, out of which he and Veeck were wringing every last drop. Sought out by the press in order to solve this growing riddle, Lula Paige would only add to the confusion. "I know forty-four is correct," Lula insisted, knowing no such thing. His holding the interest of so many big-time city folk told Lula eloquently how many worlds from the Mobile South Bay her son had come.

"It looks like he's realized his ambition, doesn't it?" she said to *The Sporting News*.

Not by happenstance, it was after this baseball season that Lula finally allowed herself to be moved to that new home on the other side of Government Street.

• • •

By late September, the baseball public was inured to the caricature of Paige drawn by *The Sporting News* when the paper worked up a lengthy two-part profile. SOLEMN, SKINNY, ANCIENT—BUT GAME'S TOP ATTRACTION was the headline of part one, with the subhead: "Cuts 'Cute' Stuff in Majors but Still a Showman; Chronic Stomach Trouble Produces Gigantic Burps."

And yet, as these wry articles ran, Satchel Paige was all but a nonperson with the Cleveland Indians.

His descent came so abruptly that there was an almost audible grinding of gears. But the truth was that certain events had presaged it almost all along. Only days after he was knocked out of the box by the Red Sox, he did beat the Senators 10–1 on August 20 with a complete-game seven-hitter. But in this game there was an air of foreboding.

First, umpire Bill Summers—who had lauded Satch in the press—called a balk on him, not for a Hesitation Pitch but for "wiggling the fingers of his glove hand just before he pitched." Then, in the eighth inning, he doubled over and had to repair to the dugout for a triple bicarbonate of soda.

His indigestion was only just beginning, though, the result of his season-long diet of self-indulgence. Mere weeks after Satch's arrival, Lou Boudreau had reason to fear that the most incorrigible of Paige's old habits could not be broken and were clearly corrosive to the team. On July 23, Boudreau fined Satch fifty dollars for missing the team train from New York to Boston—that after failing to show up at Yankee Stadium for a scheduled game that was eventually rained out.

When Satch caught a plane and arrived in Boston, Boudreau demanded an explanation, first about Satch not getting to the ballpark. Boudreau must have thought he was the straight man in a comedy routine.

"I knew there wouldn't be any game," Satch told him.

"How'd you know that?" asked Boudreau.

"Just looked out the window."

As much as the deed, Satch's blasé attitude offended Boudreau, who was like a maiden aunt in his finicky sense of discipline. As often as Satch missed or delayed other trains, broke curfew while out on his own, and showed up just in time at the park—and as many times as he was quietly fined—not once did he seem contrite.

Worse, at a time when anything negative was apt to be used to smear the new citizenry of black players, Satch's near total lack of discretion about his alley-cat habits and hours threatened to mock the cause and undermine the team. Bluenosed as Boudreau was, at least the pretense of morality, the only kind practiced by many other ballplayers, would have palliated the general unease about Paige on the club that began with Bob Feller's bitter tales from the barnstorming trails.

Incredibly, not even the fact that Lahoma delivered Satch's first-born child shortly after he joined the Indians could crimp his nocturnal prowling; rather, he seemed eager to find out how many more bedroom doors could be opened by his being on the bigger stage. Still a newlywed when he blew into Cleveland, the first AP interview with him—which ran in major papers including the *New*

York Times—carried this thumbnail sketch: "The newest Indian stands 6 foor 3 inches and weighs 180. He is unmarried."

Fourteen years later, in fact, Bill Veeck told a story about Paige, which occurred to him only as an example of a good Paige bon mot. "All of our players were given personal questionnaires to fill out," Veeck said. "Sometimes Satch would write that he was married, other times that he wasn't. Every day, though, he was leaving a ticket at the box office for Mrs. Paige, and every day a different woman was picking it up. At length, we cited this phenomenon to him to try to get his marital status straightened out for our records.

" 'Well,' he said, 'it's like this. I'm not married, but I'm in great demand.' "

If Veeck treated Satch's casual adultery as part of the Paige catalogue of one-liner fodder, it was no wonder that he also treated Lou Boudreau's penalties as a private joke between him and Satch. Whenever Paige would incur a fine, it was understood by both, the laugh would be on Boudreau.

"I remember after he missed the train to Boston," Steve Gromek recalled, "and we were sitting in the bullpen the next day, I hear him say real loud, 'He fined me but I's got mah money back.' And that's what happened. If he got fined Bill Veeck would give him back his money. And if he had any bills or expenses, he'd turn 'em in to Bill. Bill Veeck was his bobo."

Gromek went on: "Satchel had his own rules, and it got so that Lou was disgusted many times by the stuff he pulled off. And it was a lot of stuff. Everything didn't come out in the papers."

Actually, very little of it did—and, certainly, Satch would not go beyond that in his later writings. If the local press was aware of many incidents, they went unreported. Then, in late August, Frank Gibbon of the *Cleveland Press*—a paper that had remained unenthusiastic about the Paige story—created a minor stir when he alleged in print that some of Satch's teammates were "unfriendly" to him. At once, the beat reporters of the *Plain Dealer* and the latecoming *News* leaped to Satch's defense. The former's Ed McAuley used his column to respond that "it was an exclusive opinion, apparently based on . . . mysterious information. Reporters traveling regularly with the club have gained just the opposite impression."

"The story was completely untrue," agreed Paige's coauthor Hal Lebovitz. "His teammates were the first to deny [it]. They enjoy his humor and have a deep respect at his ability. But Satch was irked.

'Now why would somebody want to write something like that?' he kept asking."

Satch probably didn't even realize the anxieties he was causing. As ever, he was blissfully lost in the world of his own head. "Down in the bullpen," related Steve Gromek, "he'd talk to people in the stands during games. He didn't pay attention to the game until they called him in to pitch."

Even then, reported Lebovitz in the foreword to *Pitchin' Man*, "He rarely knows the name of the batter he's facing. Neither excitement nor worry seems to be part of his personality. From his walk to his windups, he appears to be a picture of relaxation."

By the stretch run, Lou Boudreau didn't care at all for the artwork. Although Bill Veeck had surely undercut his manager's authority to deal with Satch, Veeck never encroached on Boudreau's managerial authority. And in the chill of September, after Satch was driven out early in two games against the Browns, Boudreau went to a four-man rotation, with Satch the odd man out and reduced to mop-up work, as Boudreau used Sad Sam Zoldak as his closer out of the pen.

As the Tribe went down to the wire with the Red Sox, Satchel Paige appeared not once after September 20.

Boudreau's public explanation for the move had only to do with baseball, and remained so after rumors spread that Paige was somehow in the manager's doghouse. That assumption, said Boudreau, "was completely untrue. The simple fact was that every game during September was the big one and I had to use a pitcher who was familiar with the batters. Satchel knew the weaknesses of only a few hitters [and] each pitch was important in the final stretch, so we couldn't afford to throw a batter his best pitch, by mistake, even once."

Boudreau could not easily forget a game in Washington when, with the tying run on second and one out, Satch had come in. He got the second out, then called Boudreau over from his shortstop position and asked if he should intentionally walk the next batter—apparently having no idea it was the opposing pitcher.

That Boudreau had ample justification in writing off Satch was shown by the fact that there was no great outcry—or even a small one—about it in the city. In a sense, this proved Bill Veeck's point, made before he brought in Satch, that he wasn't making the move as a sideshow act to pump up attendance. Indeed, the gut-wrenching pennant race—which Veeck knew was the world's best promotion—was the main factor sending the Tribe to a record for season attendance. It was the only story in town now. Paige and his novelty having burned out, his pitching solvable the second and third time around the league, he was a warm summer memory in the cold business of autumn.

To his credit, Satch kept his displeasure to himself and played the good team man all the way. "Mistah Lou's the manager," he would tell the reporters who queried him about his exile.

What he *could* do, however, with a little stretching of the truth, was quantify his contribution in the context of a winning pennant run. The Tribe and the Red Sox tied for first after that September—and when Gene Bearden won a one-game playoff in Boston, the Tribe were in the World Series and Satch had earned a license to upgrade his overall role, with technical truth overshadowing the whole truth.

"It was Cleveland's first pennant in twenty-eight years," wrote Satchel Paige proudly in his autobiography, "and they hadn't done it until Ol' Satch came around and won them six while losing only one down the stretch drive."

•   •   •

The '48 World Series, for which the Indians remained in Boston to play the Braves of Warren Spahn and Johnny Sain, emerged as a pitcher's series. This meant that Satch had almost no chance to see any meaningful action.

Bob Feller set the tone for the Tribe in Game One, giving up only two hits, though he lost 1–0 to Sain. Bob Lemon then won the second game 4–1. Gene Bearden, his knuckleball flickering, faced just thirty hitters in taking Game Three 2–0. Steve Gromek took Game Four. All four performances were complete games.

On October 5, Feller tried to close it out in the final Series game at Municipal Stadium. But before 88,288 screaming fans, the most people to ever see a big league game up until then, Feller faltered early. He gave up two homers to Bob Elliott and fell behind 4–1 in the third inning. Feller got to stay in the game when the Indians rallied and went ahead 5–4 in the fourth, but the Braves tied it in the sixth, and when Feller gave up a hit to start the seventh, Boudreau used his bullpen for the first time.

Three guys were warming in the pen when Boudreau walked to the mound to get Feller: Eddie Klieman, Russ Christopher, and Satchel Paige. Getting Satch up may have been more the crowd's call than Boudreau's. All Series long, both in Boston and Cleveland, fans had taken to chanting for Satch to get in. Getting him up, as he had late in Game Two, may have been Boudreau's way to pacify the crowd, since he seemed to have no intention of using Paige with the game on the line—even though Satch certainly knew no less about the Braves hitters than anyone else in the pen.

But Boudreau was almost forced to get Satch in now, because after Klieman and then Christopher failed to stem the Braves—who murdered them for six more runs in the inning—the game receded into a background setting for a massive, resonating "We want Satch" chant. Only now, down 11–5 and the game lost, did Boudreau accede; it was almost insulting that this was the moment designated for the appearance of the first black man to pitch in a World Series.

Still, Satch would make two thirds of an inning memorable stuff—but only because the National League umpires were completely unprepared for him. Instead, seeing him as an oddity, as soon as he went about his business, home plate umpire George Barr went into a dither. With runners at the corners and one out, Satch stood on the hill licking the tips of his fingers. But even though he wiped them off on his shirt, Barr dramatically called time and asked for the ball—a preemptive inspection he needn't have bothered with since Satch never threw a spitter in his life.

Returned the dry ball, Satch got in a pitch for a ball to the hitter, Warren Spahn. Then, in *mid-pitch*, Barr again called time. He made no call but rather, with extraordinary condescension, lectured Satch on how to pitch out of the stretch, telling him he could not hold his arms still above his head before bringing his hands to his chest for a final stop. This weird tutelage had Boudreau racing over to the mound to complain that Barr was picking nits just to give Satch a hard time.

Satch, obeying Barr's Law, got the good-hitting Spahn on a sacrifice fly. But, in facing Tommy Holmes, his arms descended to his chest for a one-second pause and he was about to push off the rubber when now the third base ump, National Leaguer Bill Grieve, halted play and motioned the runner, Eddie Stanky, to second—the balk caused once again by Paige, and almost imperceptibly, "wiggling" the fingers that were hidden by his glove.

With the enormous crowd roiling in crosscurrents of booing, Satch kept cool. And before they could call anything else on him, he retired Holmes on a groundout and walked off to the accompaniment of a deafening ovation—and into the shower, as Boudreau pinch-hit for him in the last of the inning.

Thus began and ended Satchel Paige's one World Series gig. Like so many other Satchel Paige gigs in the great expanse of history, it was a small and precious bagatelle—superfluous, unprecedented, and over much too soon. It was enough for him to save historical face and not nearly enough for him to forgive Lou Boudreau.

A day after, Bob Lemon—with Gene Bearden nailing the last four batters in relief—clinched the long-overdue championship for the Tribe with a 4–3 win. Because Satch was warmed to no end by the championship cloak—and by the not inconsiderable sop of being named AL Rookie of the Year by J. G. Taylor Spink's *Sporting News* (which may have been a conspicuous, self-conscious makegood by Spink, since the official award went not to Paige but, properly, to twenty-game winner Gene Bearden)—he said nothing untoward about Lou Boudreau.

In future years, though, it occurred to Satch more and more that he had a good deal to be crotchety about regarding his abbreviated share of personal World Series glory. Or at least he played up that angle for the public. On being bypassed for a start, he gnashed his teeth in more self-pity in his autobiography: "I felt sick. . . . I felt low as anybody felt. . . . I just sat in the bullpen hoping and hoping. Why? All I could ask myself, 'Why?' It was the same why I used to ask myself when I couldn't get into the major leagues and there wasn't never an answer."

Actually, the answer had been clear enough: the Indians didn't need him, and while he obviously felt he was due a start, it was also obvious that by October he wasn't only an extraneous pitcher but a rusty pitcher—a rusty forty-two-year-old pitcher. Perhaps this is why Satch waited until 1962 to file his complaint publicly; by then, the details of 1948 were as faded as the Indians' winning legacy. To those who *did* remember the details, the plaint was either fanciful or pitiful.

Still, Satch had his first big league summer on his long résumé, and it was nothing if not the improbable success story of the year—and that implausibility, more than his 6-1 record, 2.48 ERA, forty-five strikeouts, two shutouts, and even two base hits, made for a born-again Satchel Paige. Now, his one-liners were *major league* one-liners.

Of J. G. Taylor Spink's Rookie of the Year bauble, said Satch, "I declined the position. I wasn't sure what year the gentleman had in mind."

The black press, however, wasn't overly enamored with Paige's year at the summit. Many of his old courtiers, who had always put their personal dislike for him on hold, were affronted by the gossip of his roundering sloughed off by Bill Veeck and most of the Cleveland press but which the black press had reason to believe. In the past, Satch's lechery was an open secret, but that he continued these ways at the peril of big league ostracism only a year into the Great Experiment was seen as intolerable, or even treacherous by black sportswriters, and some of them would no longer cover for him.

Only days after the last out was made in Boston, amid rumors that Satch might not be asked back to Cleveland, Fay Young addressed the issue head on in a forthright and scathing *Defender* column.

"It has been reported that Paige hasn't the willpower to give up his playboy antics," Young wrote, adding that Satch "should not be allowed to jeopardize men like Larry Doby, Jackie Robinson and Roy Campanella, all of whom have acquitted themselves as gentlemen on and off the field."

For Wendell Smith, Satch had turned a "beautiful gesture" to an obscene one that, as Smith fretted in the October 16 *Courier*, "may have major repercussions and fatal effects on the future of the Negro players in the majors." Rhetorically, Smith asked, "If you were Satchel Paige would you represent your people admirably or would you remain Satchel Paige?"

To Satch, of course, the answer to that question was a cinch. Indeed, Fay Young indirectly answered his colleague's question in that same *Defender* column. "No one changes a leopard's spots," he wrote, "and no one is going to change Satchel Paige."

17

Those Who Must Remain Are Still the Same

The acceptance of black athletes by white fans was more spectacular and noble than all the [civil rights] laws ever devised.

—Cleveland *Plain Dealer*,
August 22, 1948

The livelihoods, the careers, the families of 400 Negro ballplayers are in jeopardy because four players were successful in getting into the major leagues.

—Effa Manley, in *The Sporting News*, October 20, 1948

A more pertinent question to men like Fay Young was this: were the Negro leagues going to change after the tremors in the baseball landscape over the last two seasons?

At first, blackball people kept up the brave front that big league integration was good for both sides of that landscape; with a new baseball order in its infancy, the agents of change could be seen now at a stadium near you. Expecting to get all the attention that a cultural outrider would deserve, the blackball leaders instead were stunned that just as whites did not care about their game, neither did most blacks anymore.

Almost from Jackie Robinson's first pigeon-toed steps in Brooklyn, a near-communal attitude arose within black America that change itself was the main message, not appreciation for what had been done to achieve it. In 1946, Abe and Effa Manley's Newark Eagles drew over 140,000 fans en route to the Negro National League title and a seven-game Negro World Series victory over Satch's Kansas City Monarchs. The following season, with Robinson a Dodger, attendance fell to 57,000; in 1948, it was 35,000.

By contrast, Robinson's Dodgers set National League records in both home and road attendance in 1947—and, critically, black attendance at Ebbets Field shot up by 400 percent, at once destroying the old sophistries about blacks driving away whites and the races not being able to mix at games.

This process drained the fans and the plasma out of blackball all across the land. Editorializing in sorrow about this instant bandwagon trend away from the colored game, the *Pittsburgh Courier* called blackball's fan desertion "like a Joe Louis right cross to the jaw—and today Negro baseball finds itself flat on its back, attempting to rise after suffering a knockout blow."

In reality, the black press was in no position to do any handwringing, since it was partly responsible for the terminal stage blackball was in now. It had been only a couple of years since the *Courier*'s Wendell Smith lit into the two blackball commissioners for "perpetuating the slave trade," describing the black game as "shaky, littered and infested." In the early 1950s, with the last blackball teams going underwater one by one, the same Wendell Smith pounced on the blackball powers once more—for not holding on. "The only thing wrong with black baseball," Smith wrote, "is that the men who made money out of the leagues in the past threw in the sponge the first time things got tough."

By applying this weathervane approach, its perspectives sent spinning in the Jackie Robinson wind squall, the black press had all but abandoned colored baseball; the very appellation made younger reporters cringe. Suddenly, as though by a giant fillip, all was centered on Robinson, who had received scant attention with the Monarchs.

JACKIE'S NIMBLE, JACKIE'S QUICK, JACKIE MAKES THE TURNSTILES CLICK, headlined the *Courier* on December 29, 1945, well before Jackie had made one big league turnstile click. But this craving, that Robinson would pay immediate economic dividends—and thus make palatable the entire integration movement—was a self-fulfilling prophecy among black opinion leaders, and black fans fell in line behind it. In 1947, the *Courier*, which was fairly ignoring blackball, ran a story about a black Pittsburgh businessman named Sam Jackson who had organized a group of 500 fans to attend Robinson's first game against the Pirates at Forbes Field. "Anyone with the least bit of racial pride should join us and show Mr. Rickey we are grateful," the paper quoted Jackson, expressing the new reality: real black pride *excluded* blackball. Added Jackson, directing blacks on how to use their economic power, "When [the Pirates' management] sees us out at the park, they may realize how much money [they] are missing by refusing to sign Negro players to the Pirates."

The energies of the black press and its readers went full-throttle into a white game that employed a handful of blacks—and where only one black seemed to matter. In 1947, Wendell Smith went out and spent weeks at a time with Robinson, and ghosted a column Jackie wrote for the *Courier* about his experiences. This continued into 1948.

Satchel Paige's entry in Cleveland was greeted with appropriate glee in the black papers—SATCH MAKES IT BIG, bannered the *Courier*—but the Paige coverage curiously faded away, as though his ascension was more symbolic than relevant to the cause of young black players, who, like Larry Doby, were followed more closely. This would seem to explain why the black press came down so hard on Satch's conduct after the season ended; a foot in the big league door, their columnists seemed to be saying, should not step on any toes.

While Satch's conduct had been attended by so much picturesque coverage in the black press in the past, it now bore a scarlet letter. Similarly, so did just about anything related to blackball's past. The lovable zaniness of those cracked Negro league World Series was no longer a legacy when the Homestead Grays met the Birmingham Black Barons in the '48 edition. This matchup brought together half a century of blackball tradition and lessons—and it was treated as a speck on the horizon in the black press. The *Courier* devoted exactly two paragraphs to the Grays' five-game victory, and only when it was over. Not surprisingly, with no pre-Series buildup in the papers and no ongoing coverage, the games were poorly attended; also not surprisingly, this would be the last Negro World Series ever played.

By the end of 1948, only two years since Jackie Robinson's inauguration, the Negro National League could not survive the death of two of its premier teams, the New York Black Yankees and the Newark Eagles. For Abe and Effa Manley, the last and cruelest cut may have been the opprobrious treatment they received from the black press near the end. When Effa had asked the black papers to publicize her plea to help raise attendance for Eagles games in the name of black cohesion, she was dissed amid the spiral of blackball devolution. One paper, the *Kansas City Call*, was brutally unkind, branding her plea a call for segregation in reverse.

"The day of loyalty to jim crow . . . is fast passing away," read a June 24, 1949, editorial. "Sister, haven't you heard the news? Democracy is a-coming, fast." Shortly thereafter, the Manleys, sick of fighting alone, sold out to a group of businessmen from Houston, who kept the team in Newark but changed its name to the Houston Eagles and joined the NAL.

The next to go down was the peerless Homestead Grays. Sonny-man Jackson, who had gone on running the club after Cum Posey's death, died in 1949. Posey's and Jackson's widows, Ethel Posey and Helen Jackson, tried to keep the team alive as an independent. They turned it over to Cum Posey's brother, Seward "See" Posey, who had once been Gus Greenlee's booking agent and then the Grays' business manager. But, with the club now consumed by bad luck, See Posey fell ill, and with the Grays having lost $30,000 in 1950, he folded the club just months before he died.

For a time before *he* died, Gus Greenlee considered taking the carcass of the Grays and re-forming the Crawfords. But while he was running the Crawford Grille—and running it well, receiving an award in 1948 as the outstanding local businessman of the year—the feds abruptly interrupted his dream of legitimacy and docked him for thousands of dollars in unpaid income taxes, ending any notion of a baseball investment. With no resurrection of blackball in Pittsburgh, the Black Babylon had met the Pale Horse.

The remaining survivors of the NNL—the New York Cubans, Philadelphia Stars, and Baltimore Elite Giants (now owned by Dick Powell)—had no choice but to join the ailing Negro American League in 1949, forming the league's fledgling Eastern Division with the Indianapolis Clowns, as the old Ethiopian Clowns were now called, and Louisville Buckeyes. Even so, the NAL was hanging tougher mainly on the strength of the Kansas City Monarchs' continuing muster among black fans.

Still, it was by mutual agreement that the league pretty much stuck it out merely to stoke blackball's sole surviving raison d'être, the East-West Game. This event, of course, was in headier days the cynosure for all attention on the black game, its "dream teams" gaining for the leagues and their players important crossover publicity. With integration, the game took on added importance as a big league tryout—or so the blackball panjandrums hoped.

Yet this dream too was dashed. Although a coterie of East-West all-stars were to win status as big league timber—six players from the '48 game (Newark's Monte Irvin, the Cubans' Minnie Minoso, Baltimore's Junior Gilliam, Homestead's Luke Easter, Chicago's Quincy Trouppe, and Kansas City's Willard Brown) eventually made it to the show, as did Baltimore's Joe Black, who played in the 1950 game—attendance at Comiskey Park dipped from a typical 48,000 to 24,600 in 1950 to 10,000 in the mid-1950s.

Now, with blackball in freefall, with the big cities moving out of its reach, the lessons of survival led back to the doorstep of one of the few teams to still turn a profit, the venerated Monarchs. Still an attraction out on the dusty prairie trails more than in burgeoning Kansas City, their driving image as rustic, state-fair, front-porch-America totems was borrowed by all NAL teams, including the Chicago American Giants, once the paradigm of urban tastes.

But the Monarchs themselves were far less sovereign; J. L. Wilkinson, seventy-four years old and with cataracts in both eyes, sold his interest in the club to his longtime partner and general manager, Tom Baird, in 1949. To keep up a profit, Baird had to slash player salaries in half, to about $200 a month. This forced some players to play out their careers in the Mexican League.

If there was a ruling power in blackball now, it was Abe Saperstein, who was still making a classical buck with the Harlem Globetrotters and slightly less with his abominable Indianapolis Clowns. The Clowns, still wearing clown white on occasion, had a new gimmick that went as far back as J. L. Wilkinson's All Nations: in the early 1950s, the Clowns employed not one but three women players, Tony Stone, Connie Morgan, and Mamie "Peanut" Johnson. Stone was so good, in fact, that Tom Baird purchased her to play for the Monarchs in 1954.

A slightly more important find for the Clowns was a young outfielder named Henry Aaron, the son of Herb Aaron, who had seen Babe Ruth put one into a railroad car back in Satchel Paige's Mobile. In Clowns tradition, Aaron had to bill himself under a nickname regarded as applicable to his race, so in 1952 Hank Aaron took the field under the name of "Pork Chops."

Saperstein, who had been taking a ten percent cut from the East-West Games from the start, was spreading himself out now as the chief counsel to the last remaining Negro league, the NAL. As a self-appointed "world scout," as he billed himself, he acted as go-between in securing contracts for several blackball players in another new market, Japan. Hoping to fill that same role for the big leagues, he urged J. B. Martin, who was still NAL commissioner, to once again petition the major league commissioner to sanction the NAL as an official minor league. Martin chose not to suffer the same indignity of rejection to which he had become accustomed.

Other owners had different ideas for their self-preservation. As early as 1947, the black press had begun to promulgate the idea of mutual integration in all baseball leagues. "We believe that it is inconsistent for Negroes to clamor for the right to participate in American sports without penalty for their color and yet maintain a color-locked policy as regards players of other races and colors," read an editorial in the *Kansas City Call* in February of 1949.

Responding to the notion as a means to survival, the Chicago American Giants—once the haughty cornerstone of Rube Foster's all-black empire—became the first Negro league team to field white players. Three of them—Louis Clarizio, Lou Chirban, and Ed Hammer—were in the lineup in 1951, but when they played in Birmingham that summer, the local police stopped the game and implemented the Jim Crow laws by forcing the white players to leave the field and go into the stands; the next day, the authorities prevented them from entering the ballpark at all.

This bizarre vignette provides an accurate reading of the desperation of blackball as it stood in the early 1950s. Worse, neither did the decline of blackball occur in direct ratio to big league integration.

As it turned out, neither Jackie Robinson nor Satchel Paige had much concrete effect on the immediate future of blacks in the bigs. After the first reluctant wave had established a Negro presence in the majors, the second wave was even more hesitant, as though the recalcitrant owners—who were still in the vast majority—had determined that a taste of integration was enough to put off the social critics. And, for years more, it did.

In the late 1940s, the balance of owners were not disturbed by the fact that Branch Rickey and Bill Veeck had free reign in loading up on promising young blackball talent. The Dodgers' newest plum, Don Newcombe, late of the Newark Eagles, won seventeen games as a rookie in 1949. Veeck had Luke Easter and Minnie Minoso in the Indians' farm chain.

Otherwise, only the New York Giants seemed to be making any strides to keep pace. In 1949, the Giants brought up Monte Irvin and the erstwhile St. Louis Browns' bust, Hank Thompson. In 1950, the Giants paid the Birmingham Black Barons $15,000 in exchange for another young blackball outfielder, Willie Mays. While the New York Yankees signed several blackballers in the early 1950s, no one in this early harvest was promoted to the big club just yet. And, significantly, no minor league team in the South had suited up a single black player, nor would any until 1952.

In all, there were thirty-six black players in organized baseball in 1949—fourteen with Cleveland, twelve with Brooklyn. In 1950, when Cleveland Buckeyes outfielder Sam Jethroe went to the Boston Braves, it brought the total of integrated big league teams to five. Three years later, twenty blacks were playing on seven teams; four years later, thirty-six on fourteen. It would take until 1959 before the last holdout, the Boston Red Sox, promoted its first black players (though the Sox did sign Birmingham's Piper Davis to its farm system as far back as 1949).

Effa Manley, with all her ambivalence about the net result integration would have on blackball, nonetheless couldn't help but notice the widespread big league temporizing. "Why are the major leagues so stupid with respect to the Negro player?" she wondered in 1948.

Given the unctuous passivity—or stupidity—of the big league powers, the abiding resistance to integration gave rise to the use of ridicule in covering the story. One New York columnist described the local teams' pursuit of blacks as a "carnival." And despite J. G. Taylor Spink's generous citation of Satchel Paige as *The Sporting News* 1948 Rookie of the Year, by the spring of 1949 the sports weekly saw fit to run a story about the Indians' black minor league contingent, using the headline TOILING ON THE TRIBE PLANTATION. The piece maintained that "Lincoln freed the slaves and Bill Veeck gives 'em baseball jobs."

The Indians had the last laugh for a time. No fewer than ten of the first twelve blacks signed up by Bill Veeck won promotion to the big club and helped keep the Tribe in contention for years, though neither Veeck nor Paige would be around the club much longer.

As for Satch, his viability had been only strengthened by "his" championship season. His stock on the still lucrative barnstorming circuit shot through the roof again. After the '48 World Series, he went right out there with an updated Paige All-Stars comprised mainly of Kansas City Monarchs scrubs. Cashing in on offers from a gaggle of promoters, the largest gig was a game against a team that his teammate Bob Lemon had formed to play in Joe Pirrone's California Winter League, which included seven Indians and featured Jackie Robinson.

For this game, Satch was given control of the old Kansas City Royals, Chet Brewer's erstwhile entry in the CWL, and—showing a rare sense of appreciation for where he had come from—he used the club to obtain for at least one grand old Negro Leaguer the requital that Josh Gibson and a thousand other worthy men never had: a chance to play a prestige gig in post-integration baseball.

Needing real players against the very competent big league Lemon squad, he first prevailed upon Jesse Williams, the man whom Robinson had displaced as the Monarchs' shortstop, and Lefty LaMarque to join him. But the man he really wanted was the idol of so many Negro leaguers through the years: Cool Papa Bell.

Now forty-five and mostly forgotten, Cool Papa had been kissed off right away when the big leagues considered blackball players for advancement. Satch, seeing so much blackball legend dying before his eyes, had kept Bell's alive, telling and retelling the tale that would become this magnificent player's epitaph: Cool Papa was so fast, Satch swore, he could turn out the lights and be under the covers before the room fell dark. Now Satch saw a more rewarding tribute, and it was logical because he knew that Cool Papa—who was knocking around on the barnstorming fields managing a Monarchs farm team—still had the wheels.

Played on October 24, 1948, at Wrigley Field in Los Angeles, the site of Satch's famous duels under the palms with Dizzy Dean and Bob Feller, this was blackball's final blow. Even though Satch was bombed all over the park, giving up eight runs in five innings, and even though the Royals took an 8–4 defeat, this was to be Cool Papa's moment in the sun.

Going 1-for-2 against Lemon, Cool Papa's leadoff at-bat was a page out of the blackball playbook. On first base and with Satch up in a bunting situation, Cool Papa took off with the pitch, setting into motion Rube Foster's vintage bunt-and-run play. Satch did his part, deadening a soft bunt up the third base line, making the third baseman field it and leaving third base uncovered. As the throw went to first, Cool Papa—as he had done two decades before—kept right on chuggin'. When catcher Roy Partee saw the open base, he left the plate and ran toward third, until he realized that Cool Papa had no intention of stopping there. Indeed, now seeing the plate left naked because Lemon forgot to cover, Cool Papa rounded the bag and headed for home. Partee braked, spun around, and followed him down the line trying somehow to catch him. He arrived at the plate about an hour and a half after Cool Papa.

Although the game was quickly forgotten, in certain circles it would long be cherished, for it was in this game that Cool Papa bettered Enos Slaughter's legendary World Series dash. Country Slaughter had scored from first on a single. But Cool Papa Bell had scored all the way from first on a *bunt*. Hah!

18

Tomorrow Is Not, Until Today Is Past

Satchel can throw a ball at least twelve different ways and has at least four ways of winding up. [And] he is the slowest pitcher in the major leagues. A man with a stopwatch timed him recently on one and it took him a minute and nineteen seconds to deliver it. The major league rule says all a pitcher is allowed is twenty seconds, but you can't hurry Satchel.

—Bill Durney, St. Louis Browns
road secretary, in *The New
Yorker*, September 13, 1952

I uses more psychiatry than I used to. I stares at them, slaps some rosin around and by the time I lets go those batters' legs starts to wobble. . . . I ain't never thrown an illegal pitch. The trouble is once in a while I tosses one that ain't been seen by this generation.

—Satchel Paige,
in *Newsweek*, July 14, 1958

Bill Veeck's presence ensured Satch's return to the Indians in 1949, though as a veteran and not a myth-come-to-life his salary was adjusted downward on the big league pay scale, to a more prudent $25,000. But even at this reduced price, Satch provided diminishing returns now. Plagued by more stomach miseries, he recalled in his autobiography that the cramps and the runs he habitually suffered "were sapping my strength. I was a sick man." And if Lou Boudreau had decided that Paige was bad medicine in a pennant race the year before, he was even less generous to him in a season that was D.O.A. from the start.

Following the exhilaration of 1948, the Indians fell to earth, and to third place, as important hitters like Dale Mitchell, Ken Keltner, and Joe Gordon slipped and key pitchers turned sieve-like. Gene Bearden, for one, slid from twenty wins to eight as hitters began to lay off the knuckler and wait for submissive fastballs. The holes in the pitching staff offered an opening not to an indisposed Satch but to rookie Mike Garcia and recently acquired Early Wynn.

For the first two months of the season, Satch was winless in sparse action, mostly in relief, and he, like Bearden, was finding that the league's hitters now had him figured out. "In forty-eight, he put on so much showboat stuff that we were over-eager to get up there and belt his brains out . . . and we usually struck out," Joe DiMaggio, not cutting his "pal" any slack, told *The Sporting News* after the season. "We resolved not to get over-anxious. We just waited calmly for the pitch to come up. As a result, we got those hits."

As usual, there were moments of Paige brilliance. On May 29, he beat the White Sox 2–1 with a complete game, eleven-inning effort. But, used irregularly, his record stood at 4-and-5 in early August. It was now possible to gauge him not by the laws of pitching but by the laws of physical attrition—and by the years that he had paid scant attention to the laws of nature. While Satch himself was baffled by his turgid belly, others saw no mystery to it.

"It [is] no surprise that the Satch [has] stomach miseries," wrote Herman Goldstein in the *Cleveland News*. "I understand Paige is no drinker, and it doesn't matter. I do know he [is] far from a normal eater. When the others, after a ballgame, are tying into steaks, he might settle for a sandwich and pop. [In his room] spread conveniently around him [is] a large assortment of candy bars."

In truth, at age forty-four and with the nutritional and training regimen of a Little Leaguer, this was a man falling apart tooth by jowl by joint, and most ravaged by age were those spindly legs. Though Satch's waistline had widened somewhat and his upper body padded with the addition of some thirty pounds through the years, not an ounce had settled in those interminable, knobby limbs.

After almost a quarter century of kicking his leg into the stratosphere and long strides off the rubber, the legs were splinted and scarred. Partly because he was embarrassed by how rickety they were and partly to soothe the burden of standing on them, he had taken to wearing two pairs of thick crew socks under his stirrups, which only made him look like a chicken wearing orthopedic pantyhose.

Amazingly, his right arm seemed immune to the ravages of age, at least to the degree that he was still a functional pitcher. But functional was a far cry from divine, and Paige's relegation to a bit player this season drew no loud chanting, no rumbling murmurs at the sight of him warming up, and little grumbling or open criticism about his rakish off-field behavior. Satch could still pull a good crowd, but with press coverage almost nil as the Indians fell far out of the race, an operative expression for Satchel Paige in 1949 could have been "ho-hum."

And now, not even Bill Veeck could save his job. This was because Veeck could not save his own, for reasons that Satch could appreciate. Having been sued for divorce by his wife in 1949, Veeck's bind was that he had placed half of the Indians stock in her name when he bought the club. The fact that the team was enormously profitable only meant that Veeck was liable for more alimony and community property in a settlement. A notorious spendthrift, Veeck had, like Satch, been living large and prodigally while separated. Now, with no real source of liquid assets other than his ball team, Veeck had no choice but to sell his majority interest to compensate his ex-wife and provide trust funds for his three children. This he did early in 1950.

On that day, the bell tolled for Satch. He had finished the '49 season with a 4-and-7 record, 1-and-3 as a starter, though some of his peripheral stats were actually quite good: in eighty-three innings he yielded only seventy hits, struck out fifty-four, and had a 3.04 ERA. Even before Veeck divested, however, general manager Hank Greenberg was playing nutcracker with Satch, forwarding him a contract for the '50 season that offered $19,000. If being cut $10,000 in 1949 was a realistic adjustment, docking him $6,000 more was clearly a nudge toward the down staircase; figuring that Satch would reject it on principle and ego, Greenberg may have designed it so that Satch would bow out without having to be pushed.

Offended he was. During the past season Satch had fathered his second daughter, Carolyn. Moving to a more commodious home, a fourteen-room manse on East 28th Street, an even more tony slice of the black Kansas City middle class, he parked three new cars and a motor boat in the garage. "I didn't save a penny of [my] money," Paige once confessed, and his standard of living again had him looking at the moonlighting possibilities after the '49 season.

But when Satch called Abe Saperstein to inquire about the barnstorming options, Abe told him the old trails were drying up as blackball was rapidly becoming an anachronism. Barnstorming itself was losing its impact, as the new medium of television began to create its wired global village. To go on even as a nostalgia act, Satch's stage had to remain viable, and visible, captured in that intimate looking glass shared by the masses.

And so Satch, swallowing hard and preparing to stretch every cent, decided to take the $19,000 from Hank Greenberg. For Greenberg and Lou Boudreau, though, all bets were off the table once Bill Veeck announced the sale of his stock. Shortly after, on January 29, Greenberg sent a "Dear Satch" telegram to Kansas City informing Paige that LOU FEELS HE CAN NO LONGER USE YOU.

That Satch was indeed oblivious to the crackly static around him in Cleveland was proven by his later contention that "I didn't hardly believe it" when he was summarily released. To everyone else around the Indians, it had just been a matter of time, and with the deed done the club's assistant GM Marsh Samuel felt free to retroactively rap Paige as a "special case," adding that Lou Boudreau "had two years of Paige and felt his constitution couldn't stand another."

From where Satch sat, he had reason to ignore both his age and big league reality and see only the painful irony of a dismissal that only merited a few sentences in the newspapers. "That was it," he wrote in his memoirs. "Just a few lines in the paper and I was out of the majors, out after only two years—two years it'd taken me twenty-two years to get."

But if Satch felt used in the white world, he now professed to realize how easily he had allowed himself to be used. Reflecting on this period, he admitted that his dignity had paid the real price in Cleveland. By example was his revelation now that photographers who came by "figured I ought to look funny in pictures and they did everything to make me look that way."

Said Satchel Paige, who'd never voiced objections of this sort before: "It'd gotten so I couldn't convince anybody I wasn't sort of a clown."

Not by coincidence, this dawned on him as his inactivity coincided with the first year of another decade, one that promised great change and great uncertainty. Still, in this modern Babel, when tranquillity came with doses of confusion and when old customs were a comforting insulation, he again would find a place in the culture—this time as an *alternative* to the temblors of change.

In the 1950s—the last complete decade of overt institutional racism and of resistance to integration in baseball—big league reality would again send in the clown.

•   •   •

It took a year for that to come to pass, and in that interim Satch, using his two-year-old big league éclat, squeezed some of the last drippings of profitable sap out of the barnstorming scene—squeezings that, as ever, were shared by Abe Saperstein and J. L. Wilkinson. Through arrangement with promoter Eddie Gottlieb, whose Philadelphia Stars were one of the three NNL orphans to enlist in the Eastern Division of the Negro American League, Satch was contracted to pitch for the Stars on a Northeastern tour. At $800 per game—even with the lion's share divided among the three white men—over several weeks in July he pulled in an average of around $2,000 per week.

Profitable as this remembrance of blackball past was, it was also a boon to Satch's security, and his ego. "I'd lose money by giving this up to go back to the big leagues," he was again chest thumping during the tour, masking his quiet desperation to get back to the majors. In fact, the July 19, 1950, *Sporting News* carried a report that he was dickering with two big league clubs and that "either could probably land him at the minimum of $6,000. He's that eager."

Those teams Satch later identified as the Giants and Braves—and he ultimately turned down their bargain-basement offers on the advice of Burrhead Bill Veeck, who had used his year out of the majors to map his own return and wanted Satch to remain available to him.

The only team Veeck could find for his readmission was the St. Louis Browns, arguably the biggest yutzes in the game. By July 3, 1951, Veeck had succeeded in buying enough of the club's stock to amass an eighty percent interest. But while the Browns had all of the problems that the Cleveland Indians had when Veeck bought that long-dormant team, he found that this team had none of the same means to prosper, either on or off the field.

Chronic losers that they were, the Browns had been dealt exactly one break in fifty years of existence. In 1944, the team was blessed with so many players with 4-F draft classifications that, in the wartime baseball wasteland, they actually made it into the World Series, and took the crosstown Cardinals to six games before expiring. But they rectified this situation by falling to the cellar within three years and they had finished no higher than sixth since then.

In their years of tedium, the Browns had become confirmed poor cousins to the town's real team, the Cardinals. Though both teams shared Sportsman's Park—and the Browns owned the stadium—the Cards owned the fans and names like Musial, Slaughter, and Schoendienst. Though subject to, and aided by, the same wartime deprivations, the Cards played in four World Series in the 1940s, winning it all in 1942, 1944, and 1946, and finishing lower than second only once in the last ten years.

When Veeck took command, it was to wage war with the Cardinals. In Veeckian fashion, his main weapon was to spend all of his money on his team. While he and his new wife lived in a makeshift apartment in the stadium (which had been a longtime dream of Veeck's anyway), Veeck brought to St. Louis his supply of fireworks, door prizes, and flying circuses. He brought in the Cardinals' most recognizable legend—Dizzy Dean—to broadcast the Browns' games on radio and television. He would soon raid the Cardinals of whatever popular players were let go. Less than a month after he arrived, Veeck, in a coup de main of his own, signed and sent a midget named Eddie Gaedel up to the plate with a bat, whereupon the little man walked on four pitches, came out for a runner, and vanished into the baseball sunset, and its *Decameron.*

But right at the top of Veeck's priority list was an old dog with false teeth and an ornery belly. According to Veeck's memoirs, "Satchel Paige was the first player I brought in," when he came to St. Louis. This was done even though Veeck and the Browns' holdover manager, Zack Taylor, had no real use for Paige beyond getting people interested enough in the team to buy Browns tickets—an act that few people in town were accustomed to, as only 247,000 of them had thought to attend Browns games the year before.

In fact, where the simple act of winning came to eclipse Veeck's theatrics in Cleveland, he had no illusions of same in St. Louis. Here, the concept of winning applied to a turf war rather than the outcome of ballgames. As Veeck would frankly define this mission, "I [came] into St. Louis to try to run the Cardinals out of town."

With the team in last place and already twenty-three games out when Veeck took over, his quick acquisition of a forty-five-year-old wraith of a legend signaled his battle plan. And yet Paige was quite more than an empty cannon. Over the next two and a half seasons, while the Browns would flirt only with seventh place, Satch huffed, puffed, limped, belched, clowned—and just happened to pitch some of the finest baseball of his life. The combination of all these elements helped Bill Veeck damn near scare the pants off the Cardinals.

Of much help to Veeck was the coverage of Paige by the St. Louis press, though the sportswriters traveled a familiar course. Having crossed the race threshold with Hank Thompson and Willard Brown, the city's papers now made an assuring regression and treated Paige as he had been in Cleveland, as the reliable, warmed-over cliché that he was. There was the usual palaver about his age—and even the Browns' yearbook would stray from the usual solemnities and list four different dates of birth for him, inviting fans to pick whichever one they wanted. Regurgitated treatments of his career filled the sports pages, with ever-changing details compliments of a fervid Satch.

He was likely at his most frothsome—and certainly his most art-fully conniving—during an interview with Ray Gillespie of the *St. Louis Post-Dispatch*. Picking material off the top of his head and off the wall, he discoursed:

"No, I ain't afraid of a sore arm; never had one in my life. Well, I'll take that back. I did have one once, but it was my left arm. Down at Caracas, Venezuela, where I was pitchin' two winters ago, I found my left arm, which I don't pitch with, went dead. 'Course, I could still pitch with my right. But it bothered me, this sore left arm. Finally, I went down to field a ball one day and my knee gave way on me and I couldn't come up. I saw a doctor and he told me that the cause of all my trouble was my teeth. I knew the teeth had given me stomach trouble while I was with Cleveland, but when I found out they were causing me all these other miseries, I had 'em yanked out. Now I'm fit as a fiddle. . . .

"Control? Why, mister, I ain't throwed a ball yet. Everything's strikes. . . . I gave up three runs and three hits in 78 innings [for the Philadelphia Stars]. Wait a minute. What did I say? Three runs? Say, they ain't scored off me yet. But they did get three lucky hits over in Washington a few weeks ago. You see, I was goin' right along, pitchin' my usual type of game, when a squall came up. Down came the rain and it got kinda cold. Well, I stood around and waited for the rain to stop, then went out and finished up my pitchin' assignment. That's when I gave up those three hits."

Rolling now, he found fertile territory for the old bunkum about his magic potion, a decade and a half removed from the Indian reservations of South Dakota: "I don't go in for those new-fangled lotions and liniments. I carries my own 'outfit' right with me. I mix up this concoction and use it on my arm whenever I pitch. Now, don't ask me to tell you what it is, it's a secret formula. Just a lot of nice mixtures. I had it in the clubhouse over at Cleveland and most of the Indians' pitchers used it and it helped us win the pennant, didn't it?"

Behind the twaddle, though, Satch approached this sojourn to the big leagues after giving serious reconsideration to certain aspects of his life. Only after reaching the bigs did he realize what major league visibility meant in terms of accountability. Before, he took his money and filled out his tax returns with equal indifference; some years there were no returns filed at all—which was fitting since he never kept receipts or pay stubs and most of his income was gleaned on the fly between one half-assed operation to another, and lost just as rapidly.

Because his only account books existed in long-faded memories, he knew what trouble he was courting if the tax man ever did come after him. And even though Lahoma had helped to transfer figures from his head to paper, his spinning wheel of a life made it impossible for her to keep up with him. Thus, it was with cold fright that he was told that he lived in the thirty-five percent tax bracket neighborhood.

His finances were under a magnifying glass now, he knew, and so he had J. L. Wilkinson fill out his tax returns, a role that Wilkie filled until his death a few years later. That simple delegation of power, Satch realized, may have saved him from the poorhouse, or at least a fate similar to another prototypical black hero whose travails were a lesson for all black men.

"If it wasn't for Mistah Wilkinson handlin' my finances," Paige noted in a 1952 interview, "ah'd come up like Joe Louis."

Guided by the Louis metaphor, Satch now was wise to the perils of open deceit. So when Veeck routinely had his public relations people fill out Paige's yearbook entry with the "unmarried" line in his bio, Satch immediately moved to correct it. And, just months after the birth of his third daughter, Linda, he pointedly drew attention to his now escalating fatherhood, with an eye toward the fact-checkers at the IRS.

"Ah has three children," he was quoted by Ray Gillespie at the time, "an' we might as well take out the exemptions so those tax people won't be askin' a lot of questions. . . . Ah knows [the children] wasn't listed befo' [in the yearbook] but you bettah get them down 'cuz ah thinks ah should get some refunds from the tax folk."

Not that he didn't continue his philandering, of course; he just felt he had to do it with his wedding ring on.

●   ●   ●

While there was again scoffing in pedigreed baseball circles when Veeck restaged the Paige show, conspicuous by his absence from that old-time chorus was J. G. Taylor Spink, whose *Sporting News* now went along with the Paige rap without comment and with deference to his esprit. "Leroy (Satchel) Paige, joining the Browns under his former Cleveland boss Bill Veeck," reported the paper in its July 25 issue, "was glad to get back into the American League because, he explained, he will have an opportunity to 'catch up on his rest.' In the Negro circuit and exhibition games the past two summers, Satch had been pitching three-inning stints six or seven times a week."

Spink's placid neutrality was possibly a mirror of the attitude about Satch nationwide, and even in St. Louis. Veeck himself seemed not in the mood for overstatement about Paige's pitching abilities when John Drebinger of the *New York Times* asked him why he brought Paige back. "Why not?" Veeck replied. "The Browns have been losing ball games with worse."

For Satch's first game, a July 18 start against the Senators at Sportsman's Park, a paid crowd of 7,848 attended, up a bit for this lame franchise but driblets by comparison with the sweaty rabble that swelled Municipal Stadium to the bursting point in 1948.

But Satch was still in '48 form. Pitching shutout ball for six innings, he weakened and gave up three runs in the seventh. Lifted for a pinch-hitter, unlike in Cleveland his team had no rallies in its bats; though the Browns lost 7–1 and Satch was raked for eleven hits, Ray Gillespie noted in his game story that "many of the hits he gave up were of the blooper or infield variety."

Astonishingly, he was, if anything, *faster* now. Ned Garver, who won twenty games that season for those sinkable Browns, spoke of a Paige who could "psych out or strike out" batters. Where most people believed his sundry pitching motions to be part of the Paige production number, to Satch this went to the heart of the matter of pitching, with every little move a response to a hitter's weakness.

Said Garver: "That fella knew more about attacking the hitter than any pitcher I ever saw. He didn't match his strength against theirs, he was too smart for that. He broke up their timing. He threw breaking balls from different angles. He never threw fastballs at the same speed, and when he needed to bust one he could throw it hard as Nolan Ryan and overpower guys."

In his next game, starting the opener of a July 22 doubleheader against the Yankees before 11,763 at Sportsman's Park, he was too strong at the start for his own good. The heat was oppressive in St. Louis that afternoon, melting the cricks out of Satch's arm and making him feel like a youngster of, oh, forty. Over five cyclonic innings he smashed the Bombers' dangerous lineup to bits, allowing but one ball to reach the outfield grass and nothing close to a hit.

But then, with Satch running low on gas under the high sun, Phil Rizzuto chopped a slow roller to the first baseman, and when Satch came over to take the throw, Rizzuto not only beat it, he stepped on Satch's left foot. In pain, he limped back to the hill and went on pitching, though with his long stride crimped, and walked Joe Collins. Trying now to power one past Bobby Brown, the fastball came in soft and Brown took it far over the center field roof for a 3–0 lead.

Flaccid now, he lost his edge, giving up six more hits until Zack Taylor removed him with two outs in the seventh, down by seven in an eventual 9–0 defeat.

Undaunted, he was back nine days later in the old lion's den of Fenway Park. Relieving Garver, who injured his leg in the fifth inning, Satch snuffed a bases-loaded uprising with a strikeout, threw three and a third flawless innings, and got credit for the late 8–6 Browns win.

Satch must have been good beyond all expectations because, even beset by his team, he was again causing a ruckus among opposing managers. In the Boston game, he had notched a crucial strikeout when he unveiled a new and improved version of the Hesitation Pitch—stopping his stride as usual, but now he kept his arm moving forward. This might have caused a less graceful pitcher to resemble a gooney bird, and certainly get very little on the pitch, but Satch was so smooth, the little deception so subtle, that the ever-confused umpires did not call a balk.

After the game, however, Red Sox manager Steve O'Neill—

egged on by his new shortstop, Lou Boudreau—filed a protest with Will Harridge, who probably thought he would never again be bothered with this matter. In his defense, Satch was canny.

"Lou used to tell me it was legal," he said, trenchantly.

Rather than deal with all this silliness again, Harridge just let the matter dangle, freeing Satch to go on flinging his signature pitch, possibly because he thought Paige wasn't long for the big league world. And while Will Harridge would be long out of baseball, having retired in 1958, by the time Satchel Paige would at last be done with the big leagues, his judgment was no different than that of most people around baseball. To them, it wasn't the pitcher but the persona that endured around Satchel Paige, who could now be seen as an elder of a dying idiom of man and could be cut his slack.

In Paige's first year in St. Louis, pitching sixty-two innings in twenty-three appearances, he went 3-and-4 with a 4.79 ERA, forty-eight strikeouts, twenty-nine walks. The numbers were adequate, what with the team behind him—and magnificently irrelevant. Just the fact that he was there at all won him the affectionate attentions that seemed to follow him wherever he went.

Still, as aloof as Satch generally was about matters of race, he could clearly see that the climate of post-integration baseball had still not warmed to men of color in the five years since Jackie Robinson.

"I found out one thing after I got back into the majors. Old man prejudice hadn't been killed," he wrote in his autobiography. "When I first joined Cleveland, it looked like it had been. But I guess that was because colored boys was so new in the big leagues that everybody treated them pretty good.

"But after that newness wore off, those mean folks started acting up again, started letting that meanness run out again."

Far more so than with the Indians players, he could feel cold eyes glaring behind his back now—though his skill in removing the glare was always effective. When catcher Clint Courtney came in a trade to the Browns in 1952 for his first full big league season, it was immediately apparent that this short, stocky man had one of the reddest necks in baseball. Born in Louisiana and bred in Alabama farm country, when Courtney arrived he refused to catch Paige, not even in the bullpen.

Having not come near blacks in his world, Courtney had never known a man like Satch, never known that there could be a man like him. Satch, on the other hand, had known men like Courtney, and had disarmed many of them simply by being Satch. Courtney was not to be spared that treatment. For every glare by the catcher, a nonthreatening verbal thorn was fired into Courtney's leathery hide.

"He'd needle Courtney in his sly way," Bill Veeck once said, "just sharply enough to let Clint know he was ready for him any time Clint wanted to make something of it."

But Satch didn't arise before Courtney with fists, only bonbons. "Say, d'you have a home plate in your pocket?" Satch casually asked him one day. Clint didn't know what he was talking about, so Satch picked up a gum wrapper and tamped it down into the grass in front of Courtney.

"He began using the gum wrapper as a home plate," Courtney later recalled. "I guess he threw forty or fifty balls without missin' that little piece of paper by more'n an inch. He's really got control!"

After a few weeks, Courtney began to catch Paige regularly in the pen. Then they were sitting side by side out there. Then—to the astonishment of everyone who knew both men—they were *socializing*, alternately running together at the white taverns patronized by Courtney and the black ones downtown where Satch made the scene. Veeck once ran into them at an interracial bar in Detroit called the Flame.

"You know," Courtney said, "it's a funny thing. My daddy is coming up when we get back to St. Louis. He's gonna see me sitting in the bullpen talking to this Paige and he's gonna jump right over the fence and try to give me a whupping. But Satch and I have it figured out that the two of us can whup him no matter what happens."

But Satch's powers of conciliation met their match in Zack Taylor's replacement as manager in 1952, Rogers Hornsby. This aging, chaw-cheeked crag of a man, who hit over .400 three times in his long career and was elected to the Hall of Fame in 1942, had been managing in the Pacific Coast League when Veeck heard that the Cardinals, for whom "Rajah" played for thirteen years in his prime, were about to make Hornsby their manager. Veeck rushed in to sign him to a three-year deal, making this Hornsby's second hitch as the Browns' manager.

A onetime member of the Ku Klux Klan, Hornsby—who had reluctantly agreed to barnstorm against black teams in the 1930s, only to be struck out by Satch five times in one game—had said of the Jackie Robinson precedent, "It won't work out." Still narrow, still nobody's idea of fun, when he was named as Browns manager, the *Courier*'s Wendell Smith wrote, in an inverted echo of J. G. Taylor Spink, "Now that the color bars have been dropped in the majors, we wonder if Hornsby is qualified to hold such a responsibility."

Paige treaded lightly on the subject of Hornsby and race. "Hornsby and me were from different schools, real different," he said a decade later. But if Hornsby's presumed racism was not an overt matter, it was because the man had a habit of treating everybody like dirt.

Intransigent as a donkey but far less congenial, Hornsby put his team through a Marine-style boot camp in spring training and never lightened up in his baleful, scowl-faced manner. For a nail-eating leader of men, though, Hornsby acted as though he cared nothing about the players he lived with day in and out and rarely argued with umpires to back them up. Actually, he seemed almost to loathe them, the coaches, the front office, and everyone on down to the Cracker Jack vendors.

Satch, trying to break down this hard-boiled egg of a man, made no headway. In training camp, Hornsby lined up his team and went around asking them their ages. When he got to Paige, he couldn't see the mirth of the situation, not even when Satch looked him in the eye and said straight-faced, "I'm sixty-one years old." Not finding it amusing, Hornsby sent Satch running laps around the field—*Satch,* taking *laps!* After another heavy workout, Satch had to ask him, "Are you trainin' Ol' Satch for relief pitchin' or the army?"

In the past, Hornsby had been fired for managing like the commandant of Stalag 17 and causing near-mutiny among the players. It was no different now. By the end of May, the players were cracking up and Satch was about ready to walk. "If it hadn't been for Mr. Veeck and the way I felt about him, I wouldn't have stayed," he later said.

As it was, he was touchy enough that when he was denied a room in a Charleston, West Virginia, hotel during a Browns exhibition swing, he remembered that "something exploded right in my head." Hailing a cab, he went to the airport, bought a ticket, and flew to Washington. There, he had to be coaxed to come back by one of Veeck's people.

At the same time, Satch recognized that, soft as he was in the gut, Rogers Hornsby succeeded in putting some needed muscle on him; and while this came almost totally against Satch's will, it would benefit him in 1952 since it became evident that Hornsby, despite his racial bile, was actually less hesitant to use Paige now than Lou Boudreau had been four years before. Satch was so effective that when Hornsby was inevitably axed by Veeck, his successor, ex-Cardinal great Marty Marion, seemed not to want to risk going as many as three games without using Paige in some form.

With no small thanks to Satch, in fact, the Browns actually hovered around first place in the early season. Not only was he a reliable closer; because he could still go nine as a spot starter, his role was broadened to longer relief as well. On June 3—when his record was 4-and-1—he came on in the twelfth inning of a 2–2 game in Washington. He pitched out of bases-loaded jams in the next two innings, pounced on a squeeze bunt and threw the runner out at the plate in the fourteenth, then—with the score still the same— got his *third* hit of the evening in the seventeenth inning to drive in the gamer.

The very next time he faced the Senators, he came on in the eighth inning of a 5–5 game. *Nine* innings later, when he came out for a pinch-hitter, he could have gone onward, as he did in a game against the Indians, pitching *eleven* innings of a nineteen-inning affair before finally retiring.

As these games grimly showed, the Browns' pitiful "attack" was taking no pity on Satch's old bones, but it was also making him a relevant pitchin' man all over again. By July 4, with Satch having worked in twenty-five games, Casey Stengel took the logical and popular step of naming him to the staff of the American League All-Star team.

Satch now entered history as the first black pitcher on an American League All-Star squad. "That," said Satch, "took care of the third one of my ambitions. . . . I'd played for a big league club, pitched in a World Series, and made the All-Star team. That did my stomach a lot of good."

This glorious precedent having been set, when a rainstorm cut short the July 8 game in Philadelphia after five innings and deprived Satch of a shot at the National League hitters, Stengel resolved to name him again the following season—and he carried through on his promise even though that season would be a more arduous one for Satch.

That '52 season, even more so than 1948, would be the last in which Satchel Paige made legend roughly equivalent with reality. With a team that lost ninety games on merit, he cranked out twelve wins, two more than he lost. In six starts, he won four and completed three. In 138 innings he allowed but 116 hits and struck out ninety-one. His ERA was 3.07. He had five hits. He made no errors in the field. As well, during the 1952 season he caught the fancy of two more major consumer magazines that specialized in stroking the conceits of the white establishment, entering for the first time the pages of *Newsweek* and that handbook of Manhattan's wine-and-cheese set, *The New Yorker*.

Both of these doting profiles cast Satch—much like Bill Veeck—as a serene and comforting fossil set in stone as the new decade bubbled restlessly around it. Midway through the '52 season, which was Satch's most productive one in the majors, John Lardner wrote in the July 7 *Newsweek:*

> If Paige had been born in modern times, like the rest of us, he would have received a bonus the size of the national debt [given] what children get for signing a baseball contract today. . . . Satchel is all that keeps the St. Louis Browns in business. And what do the Browns do for Satchel, aged meal ticket? . . . In lieu of a bonus, [they] give him a special chair to sit upon in the bull pen. It is a reclining chair with heavy padding. It has a canopy, to keep the fierce St. Louis sun off Satchel while he waits for the word to come in and save the franchise. It is said to be "contoured" [and] its creator, Hard Way Bill Veeck has embossed it with Satchel's name. . . .
>
> These small eddies in the timeless flow of human history mean little to Satchel Paige. After all, he got Hannibal over the Alps. He held Aaron Burr's coat when the latter fought Hamilton. . . . Maybe he thinks of such things, as he sits in the sun in his canopied chair. More likely, he thinks of the $200,000 bonus he'd get if he were modern.

The unsigned piece about Satch in the September 13 *New Yorker* was even more solacing about his place in the modern world. Headlined with the one-word title SLOW, the author wondered if Satch might offer some advice to his impatient descendants in the game. " 'Too many pitchers got the hurry-ups,' the old master counseled. 'When I talk to the young pitchers, I tell them to slow down. You last longer.' "

Further narrowing the ravine between old and new, his biggest problem seemed once again to be boredom. In tight games, with his juice running, he was a mortal lock; holding sizable leads, he was a flop—twice he gave up a grand slam to lose games that looked to be safe. Similarly, while he held Ted Williams and other superstars in check, the "humpties" could own him, since he cared not even to know their names much less their batting tendencies. In this new age of baseball, identification could be a problem anyway. As a rookie, Mickey Mantle jerked one out of the park batting right-handed the night before Satch faced him for the first time. Then, batting left-handed, the budding Yankee bruiser nearly decapitated him with a rocket of a line drive hit to center field. Satch was duly impressed.

"Geez," he marveled, "them Yankees sure get great kids. Last night a kid busts up the game and tonight this other kid hits one like that off the old man. Where they come up with two kids like that?"

•   •   •

Men like Rogers Hornsby and Casey Stengel helped lift the inhibiting pall that hung over the early years of integration. It was now time for the visionary madness of one Jimmy Piersall to take acceptance to Point B: equal opportunity ragging.

A rookie with the Red Sox in that '52 season, Piersall, a man well on his way to a nervous breakdown, took on Satch's prophylactic calm during a July 11 game in Boston. This was a game Satch would lose on a grand slam homer, but the match was struck when Piersall bunted his way on leading off the ninth inning—a bunt that was particularly irritating to Satch because Piersall came to the plate telling him that he would bunt and then went ahead and did it.

Once on base, Piersall took his lead while imitating Satch's deliberate progression of cockeyed moves and—for reasons known only to Piersall—oinking like a pig. But what distracted Paige the most was when Piersall screamed something that he swore later sounded like "black bastard." Although Satch had heard most every racial epithet under the sun in his time, he had not heard one so ringingly expressed in the bigs.

Rattled by the young tomfool's impertinence, he asked Piersall, "How'd you like this here ball where yo' mouth is, son?" Later Satch admitted that this had been the only time in his baseball life that he ever wanted to come to blows with a guy on the field. He also admitted that he lost it right there; unable to concentrate on the hitters while Piersall mimed and then defamed him, he allowed the Sox their rally. Ahead 9–6 at the time, he would lose 11–9 when Sammy White stung him with the game-ending grand slam.

The moral of this little scenario was not that racism lived in baseball; that was a given. It was that Piersall wasn't necessarily acting out a racist sideshow, only widening the parameters of the universal baseball language of bench-jockeying. Satch may have thought he knew the difference. But for all the racial bilge he had heard pollute ball fields in the last three decades, never before had he wanted to go to war over it. Now he did, and he would have his pay-back, also through universal baseball language—the next time he faced Piersall, he dusted him with a Trouble Ball, not in the mouth but close, under the chin.

What's more, Satch had no qualms using the same weapon without discrimination. The first time he pitched against the Indians, Larry Doby teed off on him—and teed him off—with two solid base hits. The next time the clubs met, Satch made his old roomie eat dirt the same way Piersall had. In its small way, that duster signaled that integration would not change baseball tradition one iota.

•   •   •

Before it got too late, Bill Veeck gave Satch a day in his honor, big league style. Held on July 28 before his first start of the '52 sea-son—a 6–3 win over the Senators—the spoils of this tribute was an-other measure of the distance between the Negro leagues and the majors.

Unlike the appreciative but meager alms laid before him at Wrigley Field in 1942, the merchants of St. Louis kicked in with a motorboat inscribed with the name "Ole Satch" on its hull, a televi-sion set, a camera, and a fishing rod and reel set. In keeping with the Veeckian marketing of Paige, a man with a long gray beard sat in a wheelchair and was introduced, facetiously, as Satch's first bat-terymate.

Perhaps these rites of final passage struck Satch as the last waltz, for he was to say some months later, "When the shootin' finally stopped [in 1952] I found out I was tired. I figured a few hot baths and a few days layin' around the house would take care of that, and it did, as far as my frame was concerned. But I had another kind of tired. I was kinda tired of baseball."

It was reported during that off-season that a crabby Satch, on his way to a luncheon in his honor in Kansas City, was asked what he intended to say from the dais.

"I'm gonna say that they got the wrong man for this speech," he said. "I'm gonna say I'm through with baseball! Worn out runnin' around! Sick and tired!"

In the past any such thoughts were crowded out of his head by winter ball in the tropics or the California League. But conserving his energies now in the tundra of the Midwest winter heightened his withdrawal pains. Now, it occurred to him that it was high time that a man of his age get on to doing other things with his life.

The first soothing breaths of spring, of course, thawed the growling in his bones. Unfortunately, in returning to St. Louis for the '53 season, he was pressing his luck. Walter Johnson would have been pressing his luck with this team. Consequently, as the Browns went from wire to wire in last place, negating the delectation of a seventh-place finish the year before, this long and forlorn season would become Satch's denouement—at least the latest one, the big league one, and only part one of that.

Ironically, it was just two months into the season that *Collier's* magazine, weighing in with *its* Satchel scroll, pronounced him fit for a hundred more seasons. In this essay, THE FABULOUS SATCHEL PAIGE, author Richard Donovan recognized something that the urchin children of Mobile had forty years before—that the face of Leroy Paige told no tales that his soul wished not to reveal. Not long before, as the piece pointed out, Satch had been stopped and questioned by St. Louis police who mistook him for a murder suspect. The suspect was a black man who happened to be all of twenty-two years old. Wrote Donovan:

> Lately . . . it has been noticed that Paige's delight at being mistaken for a youth by the officer has vied with uneasiness at not being recognized by the man. "He probably thought I was passed on," he has been heard to grumble. Even more aggravating are those who stubbornly accuse him of impersonating himself.
>
> Paige recently was asked to make a round of bars in Harlem with two reporters who introduced him to patrons and recorded their reactions. Twelve of the twenty-three people approached told him to his face that he was too young to be the original Satchel. . . .
>
> His face mystifies many fans who peer at it to discover the secrets of time. Head on, it seems to belong to a cheerful man about thirty. From another angle, it looks melancholy and old, as though Paige had walked too long in a world made up exclusively of pickpockets. From a third angle, it seems a frontispiece for the great book of experience, with expressions of wisdom, restrained violence, cunning and easy humor crossing it in slow succession.
>
> "We seen some sights, it and I," says Paige of his face.

History, and Satchel Paige, would become indebted to Donovan, if for no reason other than because the writer figured out a way to shoehorn some of Satch's more extraneous badinage into print. In a sidebar under the heading of "Paige's Rules for Staying Young," this classic spoof on the constantly rising phoenix of baseball took these words out of his mouth:

1. Avoid fried meats, which angry up the blood.
2. If your stomach disputes you, lie down and pacify it with cool thoughts.
3. Keep the juices flowing by jangling around gently as you move.
4. Go very light on the vices, such as carrying on in society—the social ramble ain't restful.
5. Avoid running at all times.
6. And don't look back. Something might be gaining on you.

In future years, Satch would come to see the universal merchandising power of these most wiling of nostrums about the human condition—particularly the last one. Appropriating them for himself, he had business cards printed up with a raised-letter rendition of the rules on the back. In 1953, however, when it was all he could do to walk off the mound and be in clear sight of a win, there were less cutesy reasons for his perpetuation. In a conversation he had with Marty Marion that season, he laid them out on the table.

"Why do you keep pitching?" the manager asked him.

" 'Cause of money and women," he said.

"Money and women?"

"That's right. They're the two strongest things in the world. The things you do for a woman you wouldn't do for anything else. Same with money."

Now that at least the second of those two spigots seemed on the verge of being turned off, Satch was cantankerous to the end. Marion, who had deferred to Paige's pitch selection—he had no choice, really, as Satch would never listen to anyone else on the subject—one day ordered him to throw a fastball, which Satch had been shaking off all day, in a crucial situation against the Red Sox. He relented and gave up a triple that scored two runs. Marion told the team afterward that he had erred and was taking responsibility for the game getting away.

"You gonna take the loss, too?" an unmollified Satch wanted to know.

That was one of nine losses accrued that season against three wins—though his ERA of 3.53 was in the same neighborhood as the year before—and in lieu of victories what remained for him was unfinished business. Primary was the '53 All-Star Game, when Satch finally got to check off the last of the three milestones in his catalogue with an inning of work in the July 14 game in Cincinnati's Crosley Field, though this was one chuckhole he could not crawl out of.

Entering the game in the bottom of the eighth with the American League down 3–0, he faced a chain-link of monster bats. He got Gil Hodges on a line out and then, after Roy Campanella singled up the middle, he popped up Eddie Mathews. But here he caved in. He walked Duke Snider, and then Country Slaughter lined a hit to center to score Campy. Then, relaxing against a supposed soft touch, he lobbed one in that pitcher Murry Dickson punched into left field for another hit and a 5–0 lead, though Dickson was thrown out trying to stretch the hit and Satch could walk off to his usual ovation with no further embarrassment.

The postmodern era of Satchel Paige rang down on September 22, 1953. Starting against the Tigers in Briggs Stadium, this angular man with the cracking bones and two pairs of sweat socks on his flat feet was twenty-one for one day again. After a first-inning homer by Fred Hatfield, there would not be another Tigers hit through seven innings. For once the Browns hitters cushioned him, and when he tired and yielded three hits and a run in the eighth, Don Larsen came in and hosed the fire to leave Satch with a 7–2 triumph.

Though his big league life was not yet dispensed with, his days of important games were. His twenty-eight major league victories against thirty-one losses over five seasons was a tease and a tragedy. Seeing him during those five roller-coaster years, it was impossible not to know that the toll of depriving Paige of twenty or so years in the sunlight had cost American baseball heavily.

Not that Satch was ready to admit he was through. At season's end, he opined that in 1954 he would ask to become a full-time starter. "If necessary," he insisted, "I could start with only three days' rest. And if the club got into a jam around third base, I could fill in over there on days I'm not pitching. . . . My hittin' might not be too good, but my fielding would trouble 'em good."

What's more, it might just have happened, had not history repeated. The end of the line in St. Louis came the same way it had in Cleveland—with the Bill Veeck big top pulling out of town after another short run. While Veeck had made a good go of it, the Cardinals did not go away, and when beer baron Gussie Busch purchased that club early in 1953, the war was over for Burrhead. In hock from day one, and $400,000 in the hole now, Veeck knew he could no longer lob mortars at the Cardinals and proposed moving the Browns in what would be the first franchise shift in baseball in half a century.

The problem was that the other owners in the league, seeing the chance to rid their ranks of him, shot down the proposal. There was already a conspiracy of sorts against Veeck; wrangling with him over television revenue owed the Browns when they played on the road, the big-market American League teams had refused to schedule any night games at home against them, costing Veeck many thousands. Further enraging the elite teams, Veeck had called for an equal division of *all* league television revenue.

With Veeck going down in St. Louis, few people in the baseball ruling class wished to resurrect him. Veeck's first choice of a possible new home was Milwaukee, but Commissioner Ford Frick held that city open so that the Boston Braves could move there that same year. Next Veeck eyed Baltimore, but that idea was nixed by the league—but only until Veeck, with no other option, sold the Browns for $2.47 million to a group from that very city; then, the vote to permit a shift of the club to Baltimore was unanimous.

"I had been kicked out of baseball, bleeding profusely," Veeck would say of his departure.

Along with him, with nary a scratch, went Satchel Paige. Dismissed by the owners of the new Baltimore Orioles, he could again only wait for Bill Veeck to get back on his feet. For the time being, he still wouldn't listen to his pleading body and give up the game. Money was still money, women still women, and so Satchel Paige was still gonna be a pitchin' man. But if he was going to do that now, he could go only one way, and to do that, he had to go back to the shadows.

19

Mine Eyes Have Seen the Glory

If I could make the majors just one last time, maybe that'd be enough to push me closer to the Hall of Fame. I didn't know many that should have been closer than me. I wasn't the only one thinking that way. David Condon of the *Chicago Tribune* wrote in his paper [in 1961], "If voting for the Hall of Fame was started all over again, Satchel Paige would be No. 5 on our ballot—behind Babe Ruth, Ty Cobb, Rogers Hornsby and Stan Musial. . . . " Babe, Ty, and Rogers played a long time back. Stan was still playing. But Ol' Satch played when Babe and Ty and Rogers was playing. And I was still playing when Stan was.

—Satchel Paige,
Maybe I'll Pitch Forever

In 1954, Satchel Paige came in search of Negro ball and found it in a graveyard. Where once dozens of teams abounded in numerous regional leagues, now there were only five.

All that remained of an American resource that existed for half a century were the surviving members of the Negro American League: the Kansas City Monarchs, the Indianapolis Clowns, the Birmingham Black Barons, the Memphis Red Sox, and the Detroit Stars. These teams existed not in any manner of mutual interest or out of any hometown fervor, but kept going on sheer wont.

The great old Monarchs—now one of the longest continuously

operated teams on the sports map—were not even playing their games in Kansas City anymore. Old Muehlenbach Stadium had been razed, and the high rental fees at the minor league park in town, Blues Stadium, chased the team out of town and out to the hinterlands, where their popularity was greater in any case. But where this traveling band once blew through the grottos of the Midwest like a nor'easter, now they were limp nomads lost in time, having to split their squad and play each other at times in order to get up a game.

As ungracious as Branch Rickey had been toward the Negro leagues, Rickey had correctly foreseen the coming racial crosscurrents: that giving blackball official minor league status would have undercut the dynamic effect of integration by keeping around something that would remind blacks of old subjugations, and whites of old sins.

For the lingering teams of the Negro American League, staying alive now meant turning themselves into individual ad hoc minor leagues, with players for sale at the ready (but not before all the players had been signed to legal and binding contracts, so as to avoid their being looted in the way Rickey had). In 1953, blackball made its most profound sale, when the Indianapolis Clowns sent Henry "Pork Chops" Aaron to the Milwaukee Braves.

There are grounds for the argument that this was always the role that blackball had intended for itself—an argument that in itself would undercut the enthusiasts' claims that the Negro leagues were equal to the majors—but now racial identity was clearly secondary to mere economic survival. Tom Baird had turned the Monarchs into a virtual lawn sale for big league browsers, selling off numerous players, including Ellie Howard to the Yankees and Connie Johnson to the Orioles. Baird made his biggest killing in 1953, when he sold shortstop Ernie Banks to the Cubs for $20,000.

In blackball's last mile, when its owners were like panhandlers in a black gold rush, it was no small irony that for some owners the final item sold would be themselves. In 1955, when the Athletics abandoned Philadelphia and moved to Kansas City, Baird cozied up to the big league club's owner, and after Baird sold the Monarchs that year, the Athletics hired him as a scout.

This happened at about the same time Alex Pompez gave up his longtime ownership in the New York Cuban Stars—and much of his racketeering interests in Harlem, after turning state's evidence against other mobsters in the late 1940s—to take a job with the

New York Giants as a scout; among Pompez's first signings was Orlando Cepeda, son of the great Puerto Rican slugger Petruchio, whom Satch knew so well from the Latin American baseball wars.

Satchel Paige was one of the few players in position to sell himself. And among others, he was bought by his old guardian angel, Abe Saperstein. Abe put him to work with his baseball version of the Harlem Globetrotters, which came no closer to playing in Harlem than Keokuk, Iowa. Satch swore that he pitched in 148 games for the hardball 'Trotters that year, but drew most of his attention after Saperstein also gave him a gig with the now internationally famous roundball unit. Not that Satch would get into short pants for Abe—or for anyone else outside a locker room or bedroom; instead, Saperstein developed what would become one of the Globetrotters' most popular "reams"—the "baseball routine." In this, Satch would be brought to midcourt in a natty suit to "pitch" the basketball to Goose Tatum, who would "bat" it down the floor with his arms, run around the "bases," and slide "home" safely. Satch's contribution was to stand around in his expensive suit, counting the house.

Making decent money on the 'Trotter beat, Satch still grew tired of the year-long travel grind. His family now enlarged by the birth of his first son, Robert Leroy, he preferred to stay closer to his Kansas City home. The Monarchs were still around and under new management, though the team had been turned upside down and shaken for loose change by Tom Baird before he left. Selling eight more players to the big leagues—the last two, George Altman and Lou Johnson, went to the Cubs, as did manager Buck O'Neil, as a scout—Baird went off to his job with the A's leaving the new owner, Ted Rasberry, with little more than the club's famous name.

Rasberry, a black businessman who also owned the Detroit Stars, was not caught up in the sell-off fever of blackball's desperate hours. Also assuming the role of NAL president, he plunged the Monarchs into an eight-game-a-week schedule, playing local semipros in the farm belt, just as in the salad years. For dressing, there was, again, Satchel Paige. Rasberry offered him just $300 a month and a gate percentage to rekindle the past, and Satch took it, though he later recalled that "playing for the Monarchs in 1955 wouldn't make any man rich."

Now, nearing half a century of birthdays, Satch really had to consider that the warm zephyrs of spring would no longer call him by name. Drawing his crowds in nowhereland, wearing his baggy uniforms, doing his riffs, all of it was just a temporary reprieve. As he recalled in his autobiography, "It seemed like everywhere I was going now I was hitting one of those slides downhill."

But again the slide was braked by a baseball bough, this time in 1955 when an offer came to pitch for the Greensboro Patriots of the Carolina League. This small ripple was part of a larger ripple in the secondary baseball world: the long-stayed integration of the minor leagues in the South. Although grandstand seating had remained segregated as a rule regionwide, half a dozen leagues had recently opened their doors to a smattering of blacks. Playing for Jacksonville in the Triple-A Sally League, nineteen-year-old Henry Aaron, fresh out of the Negro leagues, won that league's Most Valuable Player Award in 1953.

When the Hot Springs, Arkansas, team in the Cotton League signed the Clowns' pitching brothers Jim and Leander Tugerson that same year, the attorney general of Mississippi expressly forbade blacks from playing minor league ball in that state; the Cotton League, spurning a compromise by which the brothers could remain but would be held out of games played in Mississippi, expelled Hot Springs from the circuit. This sensitive issue fell into the lap of George Trautman, the president of the National Association of Professional Baseball Leagues, who overruled the league, reinstated the team and its two black players, and pledged that his office would support any team that chose to sign black players.

Now George Trautman was faced with the less emotional issue of Satchel Paige. On August 14, 1955, Paige signed a contract with Greensboro, becoming that team's first black player. He was scheduled to pitch at home three days later against Reidsville, North Carolina, a Phillies farm team. But before Satch could even put on a Patriots uniform, Eddie Collins, the Phillies' farm director, wired Trautman to protest the Paige appearance, calling it "a travesty of the game" and "a farce." Collins allowed that while baseball "needs promotions . . . if the minor leagues have to resort to this, they're in serious condition."

Trautman, his head no doubt spinning from the agonizing decisions demanded by integration against a Jim Crow backdrop, dropped the ball this time. At first he ruled the signing invalid, but only until the Greensboro team reminded him that the Carolina League had already approved the contract. Trautman then ruled that Greensboro could only use Paige in exhibition games.

That put Greensboro in a bind, since the game Paige was scheduled to pitch was a regular league game and it was sold out in advance; changing it to an exhibition now would have been to "defraud the public," wrote Greensboro general manager Rufus Blanchard in a letter to Trautman. "If you want to have a farce, that would be it."

In the end, though, the elements spared Trautman from having to make a further ruling. When Hurricane Diane deluged the Carolinas, washing away the game, the Patriots decided not to press the case and released him before he had thrown a pitch.

Satch now seemed to be truly at the bottom of the sliding board, but Bill Veeck was once again there to rescue him. By the purest of coincidences, Veeck had gotten back into organized ball in 1956 on the only level that offered Satch a realistic shot at steady employment—the same minor leagues from which he was just banished.

Veeck had agreed to take over the operation of the newborn Miami Marlins, a Triple-A International League team that had been moved from Syracuse after it was purchased by two of Veeck's business associates. Again, Veeck's first move was to send for Satch, and the irony was that Veeck had also arranged for the Marlins to be sponsored by the same Phillies organization that was so outraged on behalf of Reidsville. But with the team trying to build fan support in south Florida, Eddie Collins had an abrupt change of heart about Paige. Hearing no dissent from within the league, George Trautman rubber-stamped the contract.

While the Marlins were just a farm team, at least they weren't a rotting corpse drawing flies out on the farm belt like the Monarchs. This was the kind of obscurity Satch could live with; on a $15,000 salary and a percentage of the gate, he had a whole new regional audience and generation to draw from, and the gig was pressure-free. With no Dom DiMaggios or Mickey Mantles or even Jimmy Piersalls to have to face down here, his arm felt as loose as linguine.

In fact, this time he would even outlast Veeck, and become a cause célèbre for something like the hundredth time. At the outset, however, Veeck had to do the same hard selling he had done with Lou Boudreau to get Satch into the rotation. Don Osborn, the Marlins' manager, was firmly against it and conceded only that he might use Paige in exhibition games. To change that, Veeck and Satch needed merely to run an old game on Osborn.

Veeck made a deal with the manager, one he knew he'd win: Osborn could line up his best nine hitters, rotating them in from their positions on the field, and Veeck agreed to pay ten dollars to any of them who could get a clean hit off the old mongoose. The deal set, Satch got all nine. Don Osborn agreed to make Satchel Paige a roster player.

But Osborn was not yet ready to put the ball in Satch's hand, and his first appearance seemed to signify what he was really here for. On Opening Day, a chartered helicopter descended onto the playing field, and when the door opened, out popped Satch in his Marlins uniform. But after this raucous introduction, he did not take the mound; instead, he ambled to the bullpen, where Veeck had installed still another canopied contour chair for him.

And that was where he sat for four games, playing an Uncle Remus and doing nothing more physical than yawning. Only then did Osborn accede to Veeck's urging and use him—whereupon Satch gave him a 3–0 victory, throwing a complete-game four-hitter. Now, like Rogers Hornsby and Marty Marion before him, Don Osborn couldn't get enough of him. A former minor league pitcher, Osborn was soon tutoring this fifty-year-old prospect on how to throw a better curveball.

In retrospect, Satch was as amazed as Osborn that it took him half a century to learn how to throw the hook the right way, and he couldn't wait to step on the rubber to break some off. Loving every minute, he tore through the hitters of the International League. Starting and relieving, he hurled a one-hitter and in a matter of weeks had five wins against two defeats.

Bill Veeck, of course, did not watch his latest vindication pass idly. Satch always did get him to thinking big, and in the Veeckian fashion he took aim at another record: the single-game minor league attendance mark of 56,391, set in 1941. Angling to break it—no small pipe dream, given that Miamians had shown scant interest in welcoming the team—Veeck rented the massive Orange Bowl, the football stadium seating 70,000, for an August 7 charity game against the Yankees' Columbus team. Then he let the hype begin.

Billing the promotion as "The Baseball Party to End All Baseball Parties," Veeck encouraged maximum multiracial turnout by booking an eclectic lineup of performing artists before the game—Cab Calloway, Margaret Whiting, Ginny Simms, Al Hibbler, and other acts that turned the Orange Bowl into possibly the largest jazz café known to man. And with Satch billed as the evening's spotlight act, tickets moved quickly.

When Satch took the ball that night, Veeck had come closer to the record than any sane man could have expected he would. In fact, while the crowd of 51,713 was nothing special for Satch, it guaranteed that baseball would remain viable in Miami for quite some time.

As usual with occasions such as these, Satch tacked on the seemingly obligatory happy postscript. In the second inning, the Columbus pitcher intentionally walked the eighth-place hitter, loading the bases to get to Satch—who answered by belting a double to clear the bases. Up 4–0 now, he turned in a solid seven and two thirds innings in the 6–2 victory.

By then, his record was 9-and-3. At the end of yet another historic season, he was 11-and-4, with a beyond-belief ERA of 1.86, best in the league. In 111 Triple-A innings, this fifty-year-old antique collector had struck out seventy-nine hitters and walked but twenty-eight.

He had also earned a place in organized whiteball that was not dependent on Bill Veeck's good graces. Having made an enormous profit for the Marlins' owners, Veeck arranged to sell the club for them in 1956 and exited the game again. But Satch, who had been invaluable in taking the team to third place in the standings and second in league attendance, remained in Miami for two more seasons.

With Satch excelling once more against measurable competition, it took no time for the national press to locate and lionize him all over again. As an old and continually soothing caricature, even his roguish alienation from the norm, dependable as it was, was now a comfort at a time when the nation was watching Little Rock head toward a civil rights conflagration.

Twice within six months in 1958, *Newsweek* hailed him for enduring as a racial stereotype. John Lardner, hardly varying his puckish prose from the last time he observed him, wrote in the February 17 issue, "Leroy Paige, who relieved in the ninth inning of the first baseball game ever played, and struck out Doubleday with the bags full, served notice on the [Marlins] the other day that he would report for spring training shortly.

" 'But I won't train,' said Satchel quickly, to forestall misunderstanding. 'I'll just fish. The fishing is good around here. When a man gets to be 49, like I am, he don't need to train. All I have to do to get my arm in shape is walk up to the catcher and shake hands."

Then, in the July 14 issue, the magazine reiterated: "As he travels the baseball circuit for perhaps the thirty-fifth year, Satchel Paige still makes up his own rules. He misses planes, forgets curfews, and never bothers to run, but nobody around the Marlins complains. For Satch, who may be 50 or 55 or 60, is still unquestionably a magnificent pitcher. . . . Apparently, age cannot wither his right arm."

Apparently, as well, less than ten years before the Civil Rights Act and Martin Luther King's "We will not be satisfied" dictum, Satch was caught in the last draft of white wish-fulfillment. A hot media commodity, his appearances now included a guest shot on the popular and mawkish television reunion series *This Is Your Life*, which in 1958 rounded up and brought to Hollywood the now ninety-eight-year old Lula Paige and a number of others from the Mobile streets—although Wilbur Hines was about the only one of those whom Satch could clearly remember.

His stature within the mainstream now certified, it soon dawned on a good many people that, with the just-retired Jackie Robinson a lock to enter the Hall of Fame after the mandatory five-year waiting period, baseball owed Paige a place of honor at Cooperstown as well. By taking this step, it was reasoned, it would be the most meaningful reparation the game could give to him and to the ghost of blackball.

With monumental irony, this idea was first broached by the *Sporting News* of J. G. Taylor Spink. In its issue of September 26, 1956, the paper carried an editorial headlined PAIGE MERITS PLACE IN HALL OF FAME. While Spink took a lower profile now—he did not attach his byline to it, though he signed off on every word ever written on his pages—this editorial finally purged J.G.'s calumnies of 1948. The attitude that Spink endorsed was far more liberal this time around—and shockingly out of step with the baseball ruling class that Spink had served so well through the years. It read:

> Rules governing eligibility for the Hall of Fame require that the candidate must have spent at least parts of ten years in the majors. It's a sound regulation—but one to which a distinguished exception should be made.
>
> On the walls of the pantheon honoring the greatest players in the history of the game, there should be room for the likeness and the record of Leroy (Satchel) Paige. . . .
>
> There is no danger that the Negro race will not eventually be well represented at Cooperstown. Jackie Robinson is only the first of a long line of candidates bidding for attention.
>
> But Robinson and his contemporaries are eligible under the rules. Paige isn't. This is a situation that clamors for correction. The Hall of Fame is dedicated to the best players in the history of the

game. It would be an ironic comment on our sense of justice if one who meets that requirement . . . were barred on the technicality that he did not spend ten years in the majors.

He'd have spent ten or maybe 20 or 30—if baseball people hadn't discovered the true meaning of democracy belatedly.

In February of 1957, another eloquent plea came from Joe Williams of the *New York World-Telegram & Sun:*

> For as long as the game is played, the distinction of being the first Negro to break the color line must always belong to Robinson; this does not mean, however, that he was the best of all Negro players. . . .
>
> Robinson owes his enduring niche in history to factors that are so much more significant than his ability to field and hit a ball [but] there have been a number of Negro players, denied the calendar break that favored Robinson, who would have had the right to point to him and say: "There, but for the meanness and ignorance of man, go I."
>
> Leroy (Satchel) Paige would be one. For years we've been urging Commissioner Ford Frick to override the rules, red tape and legislative parsley that governs such actions, and personally install Old Satch in the Hall of Fame. . . . [One reason is] ability. Patently he was a very remarkable pitcher. [Another reason is] to right an old wrong. . . . To canonize Old Satch would be at least a symbolic gesture, a ritualistic confession that for far too many years the Great American Pastime was anything but American.

Oddly enough, one dissenter to this crusade was Jackie Robinson. Or maybe it wasn't so odd. At his career's end after the 1956 season, Robinson had come through his triumph and ordeal with a decidedly angry streak, and at times it almost seemed as if all the hard time he'd put in had led him to see other black players as lesser men.

Never overly solicitous of these fellow seafarers, Jackie had recently enraged his longtime teammate Roy Campanella by publicly condemning Campy as being "all washed up." When Campanella heard this, he let loose some things that had obviously been simmering on the burner for some time, labeling Robinson a "troublemaker" and "ungrateful," and maintaining that Jackie had "made a lot of enemies in baseball."

Jackie replied to that by saying, "Campanella's jealous because I am the first Negro to play in the big leagues."

Certainly, Robinson had never reconciled his distaste for Satch, both the man and the archetype; and that Satch had never cared for Jackie was telling in itself. Not by surprise, Robinson offered no ringing endorsement when Joe Williams queried him about Paige and a place for him at Cooperstown.

Wrote Williams: "[Robinson] lauded the pitcher's fast ball, okayed him as H.O.F. stuff, but pointed out that limited service in the majors made him ineligible."

It may not have occurred to Jackie that in nursing a pet grudge he was practicing the same catch-22 logic that had kept black men out of the big leagues for such an obscenely long time. But then, maybe only Satchel Paige could have made Jackie Robinson line up on the side of the baseball mossbacks.

•   •   •

For all of his new, new relevance, though, Satch found that he could stand on his own two feet only so long without Bill Veeck to hold him up. Despite the wonders of the 1956 season, the new owners cut his salary to a paltry $9,000 the following year. Satch said nothing, came back, and had nearly as remarkable a season in 1957, even though the Marlins slumped to sixth place and dragged him down to a 10-and-8 record. Even so, in 119 innings Paige struck out seventy-six and walked only *eleven* batters, and his ERA was an exemplary 2.42.

But Satch's relations with the new owners deteriorated badly the next year. That season, Don Osborn was replaced as manager by Kerby Farrell, erasing the last of Satch's patrons on the club. Osborn had never thought to discipline the living legend, but Farrell and general manager Joe Ryan did not tolerate this double standard.

Farrell and Ryan knew they couldn't make Satch obey curfews or attend workouts; indeed, there were as many sightings of him in the hotel nightclubs around Miami Beach as there were on the field, and many of his evenings were passed running until daybreak with Al Hibbler, with whom he often sang on stage.

But now, without Veeck around, they could apply some economic sanctions. Early in the 1958 season, Ryan agreed to Satch's usual request for a salary advance—but where Veeck treated these advances as handouts, never requiring him to pay them back, Ryan took escalating amounts of money out of Satch's paychecks. In late July, he took back one entire paycheck.

Since the club was on a two-week road trip at the time, Satch was left tapped out. He came to Ryan asking at least for his meal money.

"You didn't get any meal money for this trip," Ryan replied, "because you weren't present when it was handed out."

Pissed off by such insulting treatment at the hands of these bush leaguers, Satch picked up and left the club in Rochester. Days later, he agreed to return—only to be put on the inactive list by Ryan, meaning that he would have to go ten days without pay. Burned up again, he asked Ryan to release him from his contract. Ryan refused.

"I'm retired from them, but they ain't retired from me," he told the press. But he was contractually obligated to remain with the team and pitch when told to the rest of the season. Under such conditions, it was another wonder that in twenty-eight games he went 10-and-10 with a 2.98 ERA. But at the end of the season, he left no doubt where he stood. "I won't go back there next year," he said. "I'm through with Miami."

This development did not affect the Satchel Paige show biz promenade, which ran independently of his baseball meanderings. Immediately after the season, he went to Durango, Mexico, to appear in a United Artists movie, *The Wonderful Country*, which starred Robert Mitchum and Julie London. In this post–Civil War oatburner directed by Robert Parrish, Satch had the minor but vital part of a hard-bitten Union army cavalry sergeant of a segregated black unit—a breakthrough role given that Civil War movies had rarely presented blacks as anything but slaves.

He was paid $10,000 to be in it, and the movie became the pride of his life. He took acting and horseback riding lessons for the role, and even was able to cry on cue in one emotional scene when he had to bury two of his men. That in itself was a triumph for Method Acting, since he had long ago crusted over his inner wounds.

"It'd been a long time since anyone saw me cry," he admitted later, perhaps understanding that the rediscovery of his soft side was worth $10,000.

Over the next decade, pitching sporadically, he was never far from the media's eye—though his movie career ended after that one performance. His last chance at important pitching came and went in 1959, when Bill Veeck returned yet again to baseball after acquiring an eighty percent interest in the Chicago White Sox. Veeck insisted later that he wanted to bring in Satch for another big league run, but that with the "Go Go" Sox pitching-rich and gearing up to win their first pennant in forty years, the briny manager Al Lopez wouldn't hear of it.

"Al wants only the players who catch every plane and meet every roll call, and Satch [isn't] a particularly good bet to catch the next street car," Veeck said, though this wasn't something that had overly concerned Veeck in Cleveland and St. Louis.

Two years later, still only active on the ghostlike Monarchs' barnstorming routes, Paige thought the time appropriate to put his own spin and annotations on his incredible life now that his career seemed to be fully adjourned. Late in 1960 he began collaborating with writer David Lipman on his autobiography, which was to be published by Doubleday in April 1962. As Doubleday was owned by the Curtis Publishing Company, Lipman sold early excerpts of the tome to the *Saturday Evening Post*, which was also owned by Curtis.

These excerpts appeared in the March 11, 1961, issue of the *Post*, under the title *Maybe I'll Pitch Forever* and a blurb reading: "Some say he was the greatest pitcher—Negro or white—of all time. Even during his heyday Satch was a living legend. Here is his own story." That story, of course, was a light year or so from the whole truth; and if most of it was funny in the Satchel Paige, one-liner, fractured-syntax way, when the complete memoir hit the bookstores a year later to sell so well that Doubleday issued three printings, what came across to many reviewers was a tinge of self-pity bordering on seething.

"Satchel Paige's book . . . is touted on the front cover as 'the hilarious story behind the legend,'" wrote Arnold Hano in the April 15 *New York Times*. "More correctly, it is the bitter story behind the hilarious legend."

Hano went on:

> Born into a miserably impoverished life in Mobile, Ala., in 1906, a graduate of rock fights and reform school . . . Paige was very likely the finest pitcher in baseball in the early and middle Nineteen Thirties. He also was Negro, and by the time he got his chance, he was 42 years old, considered more a freak, a gate attraction, than a qualified big-league pitcher.
>
> He says at one point after getting to the majors: "It was pretty tough on those boys having to play against somebody like me. They hadn't had to get by like I'd had to. They'd had expensive coaches and guys like that to teach them how to throw. They didn't have to figure things out for themselves. They had those trainers to rub them down all the time. And they'd gotten plenty of rest between games. They hadn't had to come up with those trick pitches just to rest their arms and work out the tiredness. They never had to pitch

every day for a month at a time or play the whole year round."

Paige's story is gripping, but don't look to laugh at this man.

Actually, Satch put his own finger on the funny-ha-ha versus the funny-sad aspect of his more preposterous observations. "It seemed funny," he wrote near the end of the book, "that after better than thirty years of professional pitching, I was back to barnstorming. . . . I wasn't running out on baseball. It just looked like maybe baseball was running out on Ol' Satch, the way nobody seemed to be wanting me."

Indeed, readers could only have found it extremely funny and extremely sad that Paige, at around fifty-six, would be moaning about not being able to find a spot on a major league pitching staff. And yet, due to his continued viability, Satch had even before this found that he still had it as a public utility. The year before, he had picked up another minor league gig, finishing out the last month of the 1961 season with the Triple-A Portland Beavers of the Pacific Coast League. Pitching twenty-five innings, his arm still had it, too; he fanned nineteen hitters and gave up just eight earned runs. Maybe Satchel Paige was right. Maybe he would pitch forever.

•   •   •

Sadly, though, his constant regeneration and repeated visits to the Monarchs could not breathe any life into the Negro American League. Even so, J. B. Martin and Ted Rasberry kept punching, trying to stave off the inevitable before rigor mortis set in. During 1957, they took in new teams in New Orleans and Satchel Paige's Mobile, but both were gone inside of a year. Once, not long ago, Martin had rejected a National League team's offer to subsidize the NAL, on grounds that it would constitute a monopoly. Now, though, Martin made a last-ditch plea to Ford Frick to have baseball subsidize the last few blackball teams; Frick declined.

Finally, in 1960, as John F. Kennedy's "New Frontier" was about to ring in, the last Negro league rang off. All that was left now were two teams—the Monarchs and the Indianapolis Clowns—to plod along on the old, vanishing frontier of barnstorming, and one event, the East-West Game, to reconvene the days of heaven. Then, in 1963, East-West went south; playing to shrinking crowds for years now and shifted from an uninterested Chicago to Kansas City that year, the game generated only a few thousand dollars, less than its operating expenses.

Rasberry's Monarchs could still find games with sandlotters out on the range, and with Satch along for the ride in 1962, the team played 145 games, mostly one-nighters across the northern U.S. and Canada. Even with three-inning stints, Satch compiled over 200 innings by year's end while he awaited—and even pleaded for—a major league offer. "I'd make 'em a real deal," he told *Sports Illustrated* that year. "If I got back there and wasn't helping any, I'd pay my own fare around the league."

But he and blackball were now joined in mutual death throes. Together he and the Monarchs went on, until in 1965 Rasberry bowed to the long inevitable, and folded the team—leaving the legacy of Negro ball to Abe Saperstein's successor as owner of the team now called, simply, the Clowns. Of his team's place in this glorious legacy, the owner, Ed Hamman, said, "We are all show now. We clown, clown, clown. [We are] the Harlem Globetrotters of baseball." The Clowns would endure until the late 1960s before leaving the Globetrotters as the lone paradigm of black sports past.

That an important institution of black identity and self-reliance had perished in the same year that the Civil Rights Act was made into law was not lost on the black sportswriters who came of age covering the Negro leagues. Many of them felt terrible guilt that they themselves had trashed blackball when integration became a reality. Now, with the quiet death of that game and the legendary men who suffered in it, Wendell Smith regretted that "the big league doors suddenly opened one day and when Negro league players walked in, Negro baseball walked out."

Smith's sense of guilt was palpable, yet the collapse of this segment of black life was in fact essential to the changing culture and black people's place in it. But how does one honor men who had to be sacrificed? This was a dilemma that many would have to live with, and none too easily. This was where Satchel Paige entered into the modern racial equations. He was now the very symbol of that lowly pomp, the vessel through which to savor the fleeting delights of those old warriors' most beautiful days. Indeed, he was now their muse.

"You take some cash customer back there paying four bits to see us play and well, I'll tell you something—that scudder really got his money's worth and I want you to know it," Paige told *Holiday* magazine in August of 1965. "'Cause he ain't never going to see baseball like that again. No siree, not round here he ain't. Yeah, Bo, them were times, them were tall times."

As for Satchel Paige himself, he seemed useful only in terms of

parable. Now, alas, Black Matty and Chocolate Rube was Black
Yorick—a fellow of infinite jest and most excellent fancy. Writing
in *Holiday*, William Price Fox, Jr., observed: "Some people swear
that Leroy (Satchel) Paige is over eighty years old and a multimil-
lionaire. Others says he's just past fifty, stone broke and living in
South America. One 'knew' for a fact that he was still in Cuba and
pitching shut-out ball. They all had one thing in common: they
claimed to know him personally."

Still, as a parable, even a phantasm, his appeal was broad and
sharp enough to meet up with 1960s activism and feed a new drive
for inclusion—that of the Negro league greats in the Hall of Fame.

The notion put forward by J. G. Taylor Spink and Joe Williams
had gained a gradual momentum once Jackie Robinson was inducted into the Hall in 1962. And while the walls of Cooperstown
had become the Maginot Line of the old guard, stolidly deaf to the
voices that forced change in the world outside those pastoral walls,
the issue became a test not just of integration but of baseball's sincerity. Defining the issue under a margin-to-margin headline reading TOO BAD THEY CAN'T BEND RULES FOR SATCHEL, Bob
Sudyk wrote in the December 19, 1964, *Sporting News*:

> The grand old game's greatest pitcher can get into baseball's Hall
> of Fame only if he buys a ticket. Sure, he ranks among the all-time
> best, they admit. But he was born too soon. . . .
>
> Satchel . . . longs for a spot in the Hall of Fame. "Truly, I thinks I
> belongs. The world knows 'bout me. I don't want to do no braggin'
> on myself, you understand. But all the big wheels calls me the great-
> est that ever lived." . . .
>
> The Hall of Fame has a category for "meritorious service to base-
> ball." But Satchel, who gave the game the romance of a Babe Ruth,
> probably won't make it. Ken Smith, director of the Hall, said, "Sure,
> Satchel has done a lot for the game. But he just doesn't qualify for it
> on his major league record. We all love the guy. But it wouldn't be
> right to bend the rules."
>
> Commissioner Ford Frick added, "We can't alter the rules for old
> Satchel. In fact, I think we have been too lax in the past on admis-
> sion of players to the Hall. If you make one exception, you have to
> make many."

This new debate over integration, then, sounded a lot like the
old debate over integration. Ford Frick's stance was truly an omi-

nous reminder of the adage that the more things change, the more
they don't change at all.

As National League president in 1947, Frick had to rule on owners and players who were openly harassing Jackie Robinson. Giving
no ground, he warned that he would boot from the game any such
people, "even if there are so many of them that it would mean dis-
solution of the National League." Replacing Happy Chandler as
commissioner four years later, Frick prodded owners to employ
more blacks. But as he aged—he was now seventy-one—he fell
more and more into blind baseball parochialism, such as by his infamous intention, never put into effect, to place an asterisk in the
record book next to Roger Maris's name when Maris broke Babe
Ruth's home run record in 1961, because Maris had benefited by a
longer schedule than Ruth had.

When Frick announced his retirement late in December 1965,
he left with a farewell address warning against a too-modern brand
of commercialism that was crimping the purity of the game. Actually, the real problem in baseball was that the owners had, with
Frick's acquiescence, established more of a closed club than ever.
Just as Frick was a good company man for the club, so was his successor, William "Spike" Eckert. Spike, a courtly ex–air force
colonel, was kept grounded by the owners and seemingly hidden in
a wood pile.

And so, for the time being, Satch had to take his reparations in
small doses, from individual contractors. On September 1, 1965, he
came off the road during another junket with the Harlem Globetrotters to sign on for his third hitch in the majors; and though it
didn't even qualify as a sip of coffee, it was a goblet raised to his
greatness.

As with his last two stays in the show, this one would not have
arisen without the tender mercies of another baseball maverick.
With Bill Veeck out of the game again, not to return until he
bought the White Sox for a second time in 1975, his chalice as
baseball's most subversive man had been picked up by Charles O.
Finley.

By trade an insurance broker from Chicago, the silver-haired,
owl-faced Finley's alter ego came to life inside the ballpark. There,
he was "Charlie O," a rabid and clever promoter who created great
turbulence at every turn. After buying the Kansas City Athletics in
1965, he outfitted them in Kelly-green-and-gold uniforms and
white shoes, and brought in as team mascot a live donkey also
named Charlie O.

Later, Finley would be credited with such innovations as night World Series games, but some of his brainstorms—such as orange baseballs—and his impetuous firings of managers and other team personnel convinced many that Charlie O (the owner, not the donkey) was somewhat dotty. But, for Finley as for Veeck, the palette of baseball promotion was splashed with all colors. Finley didn't have Veeck's Negro league perspective, but he knew that Satch was a Kansas Citian, that this was his fortieth year of baseball, and that he might have just enough left in his arm and in his drawing power for one big promotion.

Signed without static from the outgoing commissioner, Ford Frick, Satch went straight to the bullpen, to sit in a rocking chair and be served coffee by a "nurse" between innings as Finley's public relations people hyped the September 25 night game against the Red Sox. That, the world came to know, would be Satchel Paige's last visit to a big league pitching mound.

When that night came, five days from the end of a dreary eighth-place season, the best that the Paige mystique could do was to put 9,000 people in the Kansas City park. Undaunted by the lagging ticket sales, Finley had graciously broadened the theme by inviting other Negro league veterans to the game for one last introduction, including Cool Papa Bell. And on that night, if not for a packed ball park but for yet another generation of baseball, Satchel Paige proved that while knowledge comes, wisdom lingers.

At fifty-nine, his legs were even more wand-like, his chest sinking to the point of excavation, his shoulders growing hunched. But even now, no moss had gathered on that anointed right arm. Sixty feet six inches from another big league leadoff man, he dispatched Jim Gosger on a pop foul. The next man, Dalton Jones, reached first and went to second on an infield error, but was thrown out trying for third on a pitch in the dirt.

Carl Yastrzemski then doubled, whereupon Satch got Tony Conigliaro on a fly ball to end the inning—and retired the next six Bosox hitters over the second and third innings; one, pitcher Bill Monbouquette, went down on strikes.

That was it, a near-pristine three innings to be remembered by. Before the next inning, Satch went out to the hill again, to be removed according to plan by manager Haywood Sullivan. He walked off with Sullivan to a boisterous ovation that belied the small crowd. He doffed his cap, disappeared into the dugout, and began to peel off his uniform in the clubhouse. Outside, the stadium lights were doused and the PA announcer instructed the fans

to light matches and cigarette lighters in the dark and sing along
to "The Old Gray Mare."

Satch, knowing none of this was to occur, was brought back onto
the field. He looked around at the smoky, flickering dapples of
light against the black night. Then, wearing the Satchel Paige veil
of impassivity, he took his leave. Saying not a word, he went back
inside and put on his clothes, never looking back at the big league
game he had to know he was leaving behind forever. But before he
left the stadium that night, he sought out Charlie Finley and held
Finley's hands tightly in his own.

"Thank you," he told Finley, "for bringing me here."

•   •   •

Finley, in the flush of the moment, had professed that Paige
would be retained by the A's as a pitching coach in 1966 so as to
qualify him for a big league pension. Just 158 days short of the five-
year pension requirement, he now stood close to pocketing $250 a
month. By the spring of 1966, however, no such offer was forth-
coming, and Satch had to make do yet once more with nickel-and-
dime baseball—enough of which could still make his pocket bulge.

He was even able to settle an old score that season by pitching
one game, without protest, for the Carolina League's Peninsula Pi-
lots of Hampton, Virginia—against the very same Greensboro Patriots who had been forced to release him before he could throw
one pitch back in 1955. Attracting over 3,000 fans to Hampton's
War Memorial Stadium, he gave up two runs in the first inning,
threw a scoreless second, and then left, exiting stage right on organized baseball, never to return as a player.

But the Satchel Paige show managed to go on. During 1966, he
barnstormed through Canada with the semipro Anchorage Earth-
quakers, a team that traveled and shared marquee space with a
troupe of Eskimo dancers. On a Globetrotters gig in Chicago, he
shared billing with the Bratislava Slovakian Folkloric Dancers. In
1967, lowering himself further, he consented to pitch for the Indianapolis Clowns. Being Satchel Paige meant never having to say
you were embarrassed, especially when the Clowns were paying
him a cool $1,000 a month.

About the only days he was not out performing his fossilized riffs
somewhere came after Lula Paige died of a stroke at age 104—or
so the records said—on February 5, 1966. Satch came back to pray
for his mother's soul, and to see her buried at Oaklawn Cemetery

in Mobile's South Bay. But even now he had no desire to remain in Mobile and effect a reunion with his two surviving brothers and two sisters.

His grieving done in private, after a few brief days in Mobile, he left that cursed city for the last time. Almost as though in reciprocity, while Mobile would name a highway after its favorite son, Henry Aaron, it would name nothing at all for its prodigal son, Leroy Page.

20
Eternity Is Now

Our sweetest songs are those that tell of saddest thought.

—Percy Bysshe Shelley,
"To a Skylark"

Baseball has turned Paige from a second-class citizen to a second-class immortal.

—Satchel Paige, upon induction
to the Hall of Fame,
August 9, 1971

Though withered, Satch had not yet left baseball for the last time as a peripheral figure, and 1968 brought two significant events that ensured his baseball afterlife.

Independently of baseball, he had discovered that his name was still a useful hood ornament for whites with an angle. He had recently assumed the position of deputy sheriff in Kansas City, apparently with the understanding that he need not bother to actually come to work in the sheriff's office. "That was like an honorary thing, he was a deputy sheriff on a piece of paper," said Larry Lester, a Negro league historian who that year was attending Central High School with Satch's son, Robert, and daughter Pamela.

The purpose of this charade apparently was to set up Satch—a man with a healthy disregard for politics—with political credentials. Soon after, he found himself talked into running for a Missouri state assembly seat by the local Democratic club. Candidate Paige never gave a speech, was never taken seriously—"Nobody knew what the hell Satchel Paige was doing running for office," said Lester—and was drubbed by his opponent on election day, possibly just as the political bosses had planned it.

"Satch was what they called a 'runner,'" his old Monarchs teammate Newt Allen said. "That's someone who gets in an election to keep somebody else from running and guarantee that the other guy'll win. They'll give him twenty-five dollars to run and then forget about him."

As Satch's political career began and ended with that kind of a handout, he preferred not to discuss it in his periodic forays with the press. Besides, even as the campaign raged on in Kansas City, more pressing business occupied his time out of state. That was in Atlanta, where he was again wearing a big league uniform.

In late August, the owner of the Atlanta Braves, William Bartholomay, signed him to a contract running through the 1969 season—supposedly as a pitching coach, but actually to raise some fan interest in the club's still new hometown at the same time that he was meeting Satch's pension requirements. Bartholomay, whose charitable gesture earned him the right to grandstand a wee bit, said at the signing, "Satchel is one of the greatest pitchers of all time and baseball would be guilty of negligence should it not assure this legendary figure a place in the pension plan."

But now while the big league stage made room for Satch again— even though he was not often seen around the Braves and spent most of the '69 season coaching them from his living room in Kansas City—a broader negligence issue began to flourish. *Sports Illustrated* touched on this when it reported Paige's signing.

"It is good, if incongruous, to see Satch get a chance to be a five-year man," *SI* editorialized. "But that gesture will hardly acquit major league baseball of neglecting him—or of cheating itself out of twenty years of great pitching."

The remedy to that, everybody now understood, was to be his ordination in the Hall of Fame.

• • •

Fortuitously, it was in that same year of 1968 that Colonel Spike Eckert decided—or it was decided for him—that three years of serving as the owners' footpage was enough for any good soldier. After resigning under pressure late in the year, he was replaced by corporate lawyer Bowie Kuhn. Kuhn was elected by the owners with the tacit compact that he would be as obsequious as Eckert was, so it seemed unlikely that any outside force would compel the old guard to let Paige through the door at Cooperstown. Excluded as he was from policy decisions and negotiations with the players' union, Kuhn was loath to cross the owners or the players, and seemed oafish on the rare occasions he tried to.

But Kuhn was prepared to do justice to Satchel Paige and the other great Negro leaguers—though, in true baseball fashion, justice moved in slow motion. The stimulus actually wasn't Kuhn at all; it was at the urging of the Baseball Writers Association of America that Kuhn decided to get moving. First he empowered a ten-man committee to sift through hundreds of names and nominate the first group of four blackballers to go into the Hall, not including the regular elections of Jackie Robinson and Roy Campanella, the latter of whom would be inducted in 1969.

The committee itself was a microcosm of Negro ball. Among the members were the stalwarts (Roy Campanella, Judy Johnson, Monte Irvin) and the heralds (Wendell Smith, *Afro* editor Sam Lacy), but also Eddie Gottlieb as a proctor of its Caucasian caretakers, and Alex Pompez of its racketeers-turned-solid-citizens.

One thing these diverse solons would easily agree upon was that Satchel Paige must be the first to go in. As it happened, Satch wouldn't be eligible until 1971, since he had played for Greensboro in the Carolina League in 1966 and a Famer had to be out of professional ball for at least five years. That left Kuhn with more than enough time to close the sale on some sort of Negro league Hall of Fame branch.

Having kept the whole process under wraps, it took Kuhn two years of behind-the-scenes arm-twisting in Cooperstown and along the ownership front before he could be reasonably certain he had the leverage to buck the hard-liners and make an accommodation with the private trust that operated the Hall.

The compromise subjected the blackballers to both approbation and exclusion. This was to be Bowie Kuhn's asterisk; while the Negro leaguers would get their plaques and their speeches at Cooperstown along with the regular inductees, those plaques would hang not in the main building of the National Baseball Museum but in a separate wing set up to serve that purpose.

Kuhn ultimately played it right. Satch was eligible in 1971, and Kuhn could take great pride in announcing that Paige was indeed going in as the first member of the Negro wing, with Josh Gibson and Buck Leonard to follow in 1972 and Monte Irvin in 1973. (In future years, the entrants would be Cool Papa Bell in 1974; Judy Johnson in 1975; Oscar Charleston in 1976; John Henry Lloyd and Martin Dihigo in 1977; Rube Foster in 1981; and Ray Dandridge in 1987.)

Bill Yancey, another venerable Negro leaguer on the committee, was chosen to make the call to Kansas City. "You're in the Hall of Fame, Satch," he said when Paige answered the phone.

"Stop messin' 'round with me, Yank," Satch told him, and almost hung up.

If Satch was surprised, such had been Kuhn's caution and concealment that when a press conference was held at Toots Shor's restaurant in New York on February 9, the very same writers who had begun the movement were stunned when Kuhn stepped to the microphone and divulged this "historic first" in the election of Satchel Paige to the Hall of Fame, or sort of to the Hall of Fame.

In explaining the "special" nature of this form of deification, Kuhn was direct. "Technically, you'd have to say he's not in the Hall of Fame," he said. Then, obfuscating somewhat self-consciously, he added, "But I've often said the Hall of Fame isn't a building but a state of mind. The important thing is how the public views Satchel Paige, and I know how I view him."

For Satch, a man supremely unconcerned with racial dogma or the writs of justice, the issue even now wasn't race or equity; as always, it was personal pride.

"I don't feel segregated. I'm proud they put me in the Hall of Fame," he declared for the reporters at Toots Shor's.

Indeed, even with the opening to air old peeves, he would not bite at the race bit when the boys in the press bore in on him.

"Quite a few people told me if I was white I would be playing in the big leagues," he allowed, "but I never did feel no bitterness. I was satisfied in my own world."

He thought a minute, groping for the right words even if they weren't the ones in his book. "I was satisfied to be playin' all over the world and bein' a keynote to black people," he said. "But I never did feel no bitterness about baseball. When Jackie went in, they asked me was I bitter and I wasn't. They said then they had to have a college boy as the first black player in the majors, and in my soul I believe Jackie should've been first."

However, both black and white sportswriters continued to take aim at the new separate-but-equal Hall of Fame. Even Wendell Smith admitted that while Satch was "a token, of course," the solution was justifiable as "baseball's acknowledgement of past sins." However, much of the black press regarded the compromise as an egregious sin in itself. In an editorial entitled A HOLLOW RING TO FAME, the April 7 *Ebony* magazine blasted it as "the biggest shortchange of them all [to Satchel Paige]. When it comes to baseball, the so-called all-American game, Satchel Paige and other black stars who were kept out of organized baseball for so many years do not belong in any anteroom. They belong in the Hall of Fame proper."

It concluded: "If state and national constitutions can be rewritten and amended to correct injustices, surely something can be done to the rules governing something so mundane as a sports Hall of Fame. . . . Black people will not in this day and age settle for just half a loaf."

As it turned out, by the time Satchel Paige traveled to Cooperstown for the August 9 induction ceremonies, he could enjoy the full loaf. Kuhn, again doing the right thing, finessed a final concession—there would be no "separate wing" after all. All who had been chosen, and would be chosen, for their service in the Negro leagues, would see their plaques stand side by side with the "regular" crowd of Caucasians. Now, those who were denied even citizenship in the baseball world would be recognized as part of its nobility.

Since some baseball adherents were still not happy about the Negro league inclusion in the first place, it fell to Satch to preserve the historical sense of tranquillity and tradition at the ceremonies. Introduced by an effusive Bowie Kuhn, who was also taking bows on this day, he slowly rose to his appointment with the gods.

He was sixty-five years old now. Thick horn-rimmed glasses sat atop his nose. His ears looked as large as cauliflower leaves, and his hair was a mottled pepper-and-salt. But still Satchel Paige stood tall and ramrod-straight, with the regality of a Namibian tribal liege.

Squinting out into the bright sun of Cooperstown, the calm that had risen through change and through storm now put his masters at ease.

"I am the proudest man on the earth today," he said at one point in his pastiche of prepared remarks and pure unadulterated Satch, " . . . and my wife and sister-in-law and my sons all feel the same. It's a wonderful day and one man who appreciates it is Leroy Paige."

He was, of course, the perfect tonic for a baseball world sick with guilt on this day. For them, or most of them, there was humility—

his sage line during his induction speech that "baseball has turned Paige from a second-class citizen to a second-class immortal" cut right down the middle between his pride and their unresolved bigotries. But for himself and his fellow victims, there was delicious irony and retribution to feast on.

"Since I've been here," he went on, "I've heard myself called some very nice names. And I can remember when some of the men in [the Hall of Fame] called me some ba-a-a-d names, when I used to pitch against them."

Meeting eyes now with Bill Veeck, who was sitting in the first row of the gallery, he proceeded: "Then there was that fellow who got my age mixed up when he called me to Cleveland. They told him to get anyone but Paige." A pause. "Well, Mr. Veeck, I got you off the hook today."

Said Satchel Paige: "They'd make fun about my not running, about being slow to get to the mound. But I never rushed myself. I knew that they couldn't start the game 'til I got out there."

And yet, before he left Cooperstown, this inscrutable man still felt something eating at him that tempered his sense of deference to the game that had denied him. His coyly pungent remarks hinted at some more things that he wanted to say. At a press luncheon after the ceremonies, Paige rose to speak again, but now in a different voice completely.

"I don't think the white is ready to listen to the colored yet," he said in response to a question about race and baseball. "That's why they're afraid to get a black manager. They're afraid everybody won't take orders from him. You know, there are plenty of qualified guys around."

He also made time for the men of the Negro leagues, stressing that many of these old warriors had been plenty good enough to "step right in and play in the majors," had they been given the chance. Knowing this, he surmised, the big league owners insisted that all the blackballers would have to detour to the minor leagues first. "That was how they kept 'em out of baseball," said Satchel Paige. " 'Cause they was too old to go to no minor leagues."

At the buffet table, some owners had trouble swallowing the remarks along with the pickled herring. A Hall of Fame press official motioned for him to leave the platform at once. Satch did, feeling much better now.

The repatriation of Satchel Paige complete, the 1970s moved on without paying much attention to him. And, in this, Paige's dark decade, he finally did settle down—though only to a restless repose. Now the father of six daughters and two sons, Satch did what he could to bond with them, but he was no less impatient in the area of human warmth than he was during the rakish years.

"I knew that when I would talk to Robert or Pamela, they would tell me, 'Larry, you know more about my father than we do,'" recalled Larry Lester, the Negro league historian. "And they were the ones who knew him best, because Pamela was the oldest and Robert was the oldest son. And Pamela loved her daddy very much, but she said they used to have a lot of arguments."

The waspish side of Satchel Paige would never really soften; even now he was pushing away people he loved, still uncomfortable having to peel away his defensive layers and reveal what was underneath. Accordingly, having not rubbed off on them, his children would inherit none of his materialistic urges and would not seek to escape their own roots.

"They're the kind of people who are just glad to have a job," Larry Lester said, "and they set their sights very low. You ask them about Satchel Paige, the Hall of Fame pitcher, and to them it's like that's the last thing they wanna talk about. It's just not relevant to their lives—*he* wasn't relevant to their lives. Robert later became a truck driver and he was very contented in that. Fame is something that doesn't matter to them."

Apparently, however, there is still some conflict about living with his name. Figuring that Satch's eldest stepdaughter, Shirley Long Miller, could discuss him with the most detachment—not being of his blood—this writer placed a call to her in Kansas City, soliciting her recollections of Satch for this book. At first, she was cooperative, inviting the author to call her back at any time, saying that she had Satch memorabilia in her possession that she would produce.

Unfortunately, this promise turned out to have the same ring as had those of Palestine Paige Caldwell in Mobile. She would produce none, and when a follow-up call was made, she acted as though she never took the previous telephone calls nor made any pledge of cooperation. "I'm not interested," said Shirley Long Miller brusquely, hanging up the telephone before the caller could say a word. Days later, her telephone number had been changed and was now unlisted. If the other Paige children have phones, they too had unlisted numbers.

Robert Paige, according to Larry Lester, did leave the door open to an interview for weeks, then slammed it shut. "It's been a long time since he's talked about him," said Lester, "and he's made too much of a break to go backward."

If the Paige siblings are not eager to relive the time of their lives that most children hold dear, it could be because the scars of a broken home life have still not healed. And it is possible the biggest scar was Satch's infidelity to Lahoma.

In the last decade of his life, that impulse was his rudder in the middle of a rummaging existence. Satch still spent his days on the run, though now only around his east Kansas City turf. His itinerary usually was the same: mornings and afternoons, he would meet his pals at the Twilight Zone Bowling Alley. Evenings he'd put on a jacket and tie and head for the Blue Room in the Street Hotel, where he would bend the ear of Jesse Fisher, the barkeep known to all in the neighborhood as "The Kingfish."

Nights would run into mornings in the dark and secluded lounges of the clubs where no cover charge was ever applied to Satchel Paige and where they kept sending over the drinks on the house. Satch and his cronies would sit in booths wearing yellow straw hats, waving to the crowd. And Satch would go about the room, working the crowd, goosing the women, warbling tunes from the bandstand, and insisting to people that when he was pitchin', he could thread a needle in the night with that baseball.

Lahoma was almost never along to share in his dimming spotlight. For years, their lives had been growing apart. She looked after the brood and took some of the load of clothing and feeding them by taking a job as pastry cook in a local bakery. Having made her lifetime covenant with him, she knew but said nothing about his well-known visits to various women's homes during these idle days. Down to a blue Ford station wagon now, he could be traced by the stops he made in those inviting driveways.

None of this carousing, though, could keep him young the way baseball had. And, but for an occasional baseball banquet or Old Timer's Day, the game was an avenue gone cold—and as far as baseball people were concerned, the icing apparently began right after his Hall of Fame outburst.

As far back as August of 1971, only weeks after the big event in Cooperstown, *Life* magazine reported, "Since his induction into the Hall of Fame . . . Paige, who had been surviving on a pension and personal appearances, is in greater demand than ever. He'll pitch an inning or two . . . tell a few stories at a dinner, dedicate a ballpark. Almost everybody, it seems, wants Satchel Paige—except major league baseball."

Gradually, the lower-case appearances dried up as well, and for this he held baseball responsible. What's more, time was taking a vengeful toll on him, catching up to his anatomy with a punishing lack of mercy. By the end of the decade, emphysema had clogged his lungs, cutting his breath and forcing him into a wheelchair to go even from bedroom to bathroom, and heart disease was corroding his arteries.

Still, some baseball men could not forget him, and the decade of the 1980s began with still another rediscovery of the Paige mystique.

First, a made-for-television movie purporting to tell his life story was shown on May 31, 1981. Titled *Don't Look Back*, it starred Louis Gossett, Jr., as Paige, Beverly Todd as Lahoma (there was no role or mention of Janet Howard), and Ossie Davis as a fictitious old-time Negro leaguer. But even with Satch as "technical advisor" to the project, the film took enough liberties with the truth to make many Negro league aficionados not want to look at all.

Satch, who was paid a trifling $10,000 for his participation—and spoke a few lines at the beginning and end of the vacuous and over-simplified movie—had also found bit parts in organized baseball again. His benefactor was A. Ray Smith, owner of the Triple-A Springfield (Illinois) Redbirds of the American Association. In the spring of 1981, Satch came aboard as a vice president, though again this was a paper job and a PR con and he almost never came to Springfield. Writing of him during this time, the *New York Times*'s Dave Anderson discerningly called him "vice-president of himself."

In August of that year, a benefit reunion of Negro league players held in Ashland, Kentucky, paid special tribute to Paige and Cool Papa Bell. Satch, with great difficulty, ventured out of Kansas City to attend the function, which attracted such blackball luminaries as Willie Mays, Buck O'Neil, Buck Leonard, Monte Irvin, Judy Johnson, Chet Brewer, and Gene Benson, as well as Bob Feller and an elderly Happy Chandler.

When Satch arrived, many at the gathering gasped at how he looked. Confined to his wheelchair and able to speak only a few words at a time, he was hooked up to a portable oxygen machine by two plastic tubes that ran into his nostrils. But, as ever, there was youth in those eyes, and despite his confinement he would not wither in silence as an object of pity. That morning, in fact, Craig Davidson, a film-maker who was producing a documentary on the reunion, was standing in the hotel parking lot and could hardly believe what he saw.

"All of a sudden," Davidson recalled, "a car comes roaring into the parking lot and spins around in a screeching, 360-degree circle, like something a teenager would do. And, lo and behold, there's Satchel Paige in the driver's seat, with his oxygen tank and Lahoma and his son next to him. That was his entrance, by roaring in and making a scene. There could be no mistaking: Satch had arrived. That's how he arrived his whole life."

Dressed in a light brown three-piece suit and bright yellow tie, he left tread marks with his wheelchair as well all around the Elks Lodge, where the main banquet was held. "He certainly was the center of attention," said Davidson, "and I think Willie Mays objected to not being the center, because he came in expecting to be. But he was overshadowed by Satchel Paige."

His own head turned by the mythic and near-divine corona around Paige's bodily form, Davidson was not particularly enamored with the man under the halo. "I didn't find him the most friendly person in the world; he was very standoffish and seemed bothered by a lot of things and a lot of people. I don't know, he was a hard drinker and that may have added to his frustrations.

"He just seemed to shrink before my eyes. He had agreed to sit for an interview for the film, then he didn't want to do it. So we talked to Lahoma, who seemed to be his centering influence. And she just turned to him and said, softly but firmly, 'Now Satchel, you sit down and do the interview.' And he sat down and did it. I'm telling you, it was like he was a child.

"And he wasn't the greatest interview. I expected the moon, but it was anticlimactic. He wasn't the storyteller or the provider of myths. That was done by others who knew him. His myth, which he had started, of course, was by now bigger than he was."

As Ashland was to be the future home of the Negro Baseball Hall of History, Satch felt no obligation here to assuage baseball's guilt. Having not forgotten the reaction in Cooperstown when he lodged his complaints, when it came time for him to speak he had no intention of taking the high road again. Instead, as with his buffet room blowup, his mind was set on condemnation.

Though every breath was a labor, his voice was hale and angry. "When I told them in Cooperstown that we had men who didn't have to go to their farm clubs to play in the majors, they told me to sit down," he recalled. "That's the reason I don't go back to Cooperstown."

His thoughts riding on mounts of insinuation and admonition, Cooperstown came out linked with the city of Cleveland. Rather than being appreciative for being given a big league life there, he growled at it: "I hadn't relieved in a game in fifteen years, and when I did I won six out of seven. And they pitched everybody in the World Series but me. I ain't been back to Cleveland either."

Actually, Satch had been back to both places—and when he went to Cleveland in 1965 for Satchel Paige Day at Municipal Stadium, he had said, "Cleveland has always been wonderful to me, when they signed me and now." But he was in no mood for details that did not reproach. Besides, he wanted it known that all the baubles, plaques, and awards of the white world were so much gilded garbage to him.

"I got trophies all over my house," he noted. "Anybody ever try to bite one of them things? I tried and I had to go back to the dentist."

Rather than shoo him off the podium, they cheered and laughed and cherished him at Ashland. In the bosom of his own, he may have been more comfortable now with these men than he had ever been when they were all young and strong. And yet, in his spirit of unforgiveness, even the small personal grievances were bricks and mortar in a large and unyielding wall. Much in the way Jackie Robinson couldn't abide him, Satch simply could not make up with Chet Brewer.

Chet, who was now seventy-four, thought enough was enough and tried to exchange pleasantries with him, but found that Satch was avoiding him, just as he had in the past life of 1946. At one point, Lahoma came over to Chet and asked if Satch had greeted him. Chet shook his head. Looking surprised, Lahoma said, "I told him to say hello to you." But apparently that was one order Satch would not obey.

•   •   •

Satchel Paige's last public appearance came ten months later. The occasion was the dedication of an old sandlot ballpark that had lain abandoned at the intersection of 51st Street and Swope Avenue in east Kansas City. On Saturday, June 6, 1982, that old ball yard, the center of a community-sponsored renovation of the area, was renamed Satchel Paige Stadium.

After the bitter taste of Cooperstown and his apparent big league extinction, this simple homage, far from the burning lights and blaring headlines, seemed to touch him more than anything had in nearly seventy-six years on earth. Propped before a microphone stand, his eyes welled with tears drawn from the soul and not from acting lessons. Grabbing the microphone, he had not a trace of bile in his brief speech; in its place was gallantry.

"Nobody on earth could feel as good as I do now," he said with bell-like clarity. "I thought that there was nothing left for me to do. I appreciate this from the bottom of my heart."

Satchel Paige then threw out the first ball to begin a Little League game.

Two days later, furious thunderstorms caused a power failure on the east side. When Satch awakened that morning, he was dripping with sweat and his breathing was arrhythmic. His oxygen machine useless, his humidifier and his electric fan lifeless, he needed his prescribed medication to get some relief, but his supply in the house was low and so Lahoma ran out to the drugstore for more. When she got back, he lay motionless, dying of a heart attack.

Frantic, she summoned an ambulance, and Satch was rushed to the hospital. When he arrived, he was already gone.

For most who heard the circumstances of his end, it was a death most foul, a tragedy made more terrible by how much of a simple, dumbfounding fluke it was; considering his knack for survival, it was easy to assume that this was the only way Satchel Paige could have lapsed without a fight, through an accident of nature.

Larry Lester isn't so sure. "The impression I got from the family was that Satch may have thought it was kinda the time for him to go," he conjectured. "When he sent Lahoma out, it was like he knew his time had come. They had dedicated this park to him, and for Satch that may have been the right note for him to call it quits."

If so, Satchel Paige had willingly found a time to die like King David, in a good old age, full of days, riches, and honor. As fleeting as those moments had been for him lately, death may indeed have been a relief.

•　　•　　•

The word came quickly, and the tributes were heavy. The *New York Times* ran a page one photo and caption recapitulating the now cosmic "Don't Look Back" proverb; *Sports Illustrated* lavishly praised him as a "hard worker who carefully cultivated his considerable gifts. . . . What he achieved in baseball, above and beyond the extravagances of his legend, was a career unparalleled in the long history of the game."

The funeral, held on June 12, was—as he would have wanted it to be—one of the great social events of the year in Kansas City. Among the 150 people who lined the Watkins Brothers Memorial Brush Creek Chapel were Senator Thomas Eagleton, Bowie Kuhn,

Buck O'Neil, Monte Irvin, and A. Ray Smith. But, apparently, someone who wasn't there had occupied Lahoma's attention in making the arrangements as much as those who were there. This was one of the women in whose driveway Satch often parked his station wagon.

"There were people who called her his girlfriend," related one close friend of Satch's who was privy to some lurid details. "She worked on Vine Street and Satch met her through [ex-Monarch teammate] Jack Matchett. She used to go with Matchett—and the story is that she once took a shot at Matchett.

"When things got a little troublesome between Satch and Lahoma, he came over and stayed the night. Lahoma knew of her but would not have her to the funeral. So the woman got someone to take a picture of him in the casket and hung it in her home."

Standing beside that open casket, the Paige family pastor, the Reverend Emmanuel Cleaver—later to be the first black mayor of the city—eulogized the Paige legacy as a work still and forever to be in progress. "The last page in the book of Satchel had not been written," he said. "Every black player whose foot has touched or will touch a baseball diamond in any major league park owes a debt to the giant named Satchel."

Buck O'Neil then arose and, speaking directly to America, poignantly asked that no one feel sorry for Satch or for the old men of the Negro leagues. "I feel sorry for your fathers and your mothers, because they didn't get to see us play. . . . I'm told we see the light of stars down here on earth long after they've burned out. And so we'll always see Satch, who lived with courage and died leaving an everlasting flame."

When the funeral party left the chapel, his body rode in a 1938 Packard hearse and then was buried, befittingly, on an island in the center of Forest Hill Cemetery, to be isolated by a moat forever from the world that filled him with so much hilarity and so much hurt. And when they unveiled his headstone, it was clear that Satchel Paige had precluded the possibility that anyone who came to visit him would leave his grave on a downer. On that shale marker were these words:

PAIGE ISLAND
DEDICATED IN HONOR OF SATCHEL PAIGE
"?"–1982

The man always knew how to milk a gag to death.

•   •   •

Satchel Paige's passing was pronounced the end of an era, and of course it was. But if Paige's long, long years of self-determination helped to usher change in the racial character of all sports, he knew better than most that in the end change can be a cosmetic front with few heroes. A decade after he breathed his last, hundreds of black men who could hardly recognize his name, and would have no idea what he had to endure to get where they were, ran in large numbers on those sanctified big league diamonds about which Buck O'Neil spoke so eloquently at Paige's funeral. And yet in many ways, baseball seemed to be very much immune to racial change.

A half century before, Judge Landis had said that baseball was in no big hurry to modify its basic structure and tradition, that such alterations were "awaiting societal changes." Given baseball's halting record of integration within front offices and among the ranks of managers, the same catchphrase might still be baseball's catchall pretext to circumscribe meaningful integration above and beyond the box scores. In this, their allies seemed to be the generation of black men portended by Satchel Paige.

In the prehensile 1990s, black players can be as wealthy as the white players, or even more so. Some of them can even forget there can be black-white problems in this sport.

Satchel Paige, who was once as wealthy as any white player, could never forget. He succeeded *in spite* of it. This surely qualifies him for hero's laurels, except that few young black players know even of Jackie Robinson, much less of Satchel Paige. This is a pity, yet it is somewhat understandable, as subsequent generations of blacks in baseball could attain levels of material and social prominence that most Negro leaguers could not imagine in even their private fantasies.

But history is best understood and the current world seen for what it is by the example of men who made their own luck. And Case Number One is Satchel Paige, who while he was collecting his bucks was an indentured servant of baseball's diehard white establishment, not to mention its lower-case black establishment as well. To Ol' Satch, the road to fruition led through the masses. The high muckamucks may have had the establishment, but he had his own political base: he had the people, and with them he managed to pull off one of the great iconizing—and conniving—jobs in sports history.

In the last analysis, Satchel Paige was the game's first free agent with an attitude, yet at the same time he never allowed the narrow eyes of other men to narrow his own—except when he believed those men were doing him dirty; then, as at Cooperstown or in the more strident passages of his memoirs, he lashed back. He had to. Even if it clashed with his carefree image, Paige couldn't blot out the vague unease he had that personal popularity and wealth were somehow not enough to make everything right.

Buck O'Neil, another of those hardy, self-sustaining men of the Negro leagues, is just as sentient. "We're still behind, we're so far behind, we can't ever stop paying dues," he said the day after Satchel Paige died.

O'Neil, eighty-one years old and infirm, had nothing of what the young men prospering under the cosmetic paint of the 1990s have as a matter of routine. Yet he still pities them for what they don't have—for what they never knew.

"If only they coulda seen Satchel," Buck O'Neil said with a genuine sadness in his voice. "If only they'd'a seen."

INDEX